The Brothers Grimm

The Brothers Grimm

A BIOGRAPHY

Ann Schmiesing

Yale UNIVERSITY PRESS

New Haven & London

Published with assistance from the Annie Burr Lewis Fund
and from the foundation established in memory of Amasa Stone
Mather of the Class of 1907, Yale College.

Yale University Press books may be purchased in quantity for educational,
business, or promotional use. For information, please email sales.press@yale.edu
(U.S. office) or sales@yaleup.co.uk (U.K. office).

Set in Adobe Garamond by Newgen.
Printed in the United States of America.

Library of Congress Control Number: 2024934528
ISBN 978-0-300-22175-6 (hardcover : alk. paper)

A catalogue record for this book is available from the British Library.

This paper meets the requirements of ANSI/NISO Z39.48-1992
(Permanence of Paper).

10 9 8 7 6 5 4 3 2 1

For my brother and sister

Contents

Introduction

Many years ago, an elderly woman approached me after a lecture I gave in Denver on the fairy tales of the Brothers Grimm. In describing the background to the Grimms' tales, I had spoken of the early death of Jacob and Wilhelm's father, the atrocities the brothers witnessed during the Napoleonic Wars, Wilhelm's precarious health, and the penury they and their siblings experienced as they shared meager food portions or sometimes skipped meals altogether. The woman standing before me in Denver told of similar hardship as she related how she had first come across the Grimms' fairy tales as a child in eastern Germany at the end of the Second World War. When food became scarce, her mother took up smoking to suppress her appetite and thus enable her young daughter to have as many of their rations as possible. The cigarette packages her mother bought contained coupons for collectible illustrations of "Hansel and Gretel," "Snow White," "Rapunzel," "Rumpelstiltskin," "The Bremen Town Musicians," and other Grimm fairy tales that could be glued into a book of tales printed by the cigarette manufacturer. Collecting these images and carefully pasting them onto the pages of the corresponding book constituted the woman's first remembered encounter with the legacy of Jacob Grimm (1785–1863) and Wilhelm Grimm (1786–1859).[1]

As she stood before me, the woman reflected on how her fascination with fairy tales arose from her mother's sacrificial act of forgoing food, and how this sacrifice and its wartime setting bore some similarity to the hardships the Brothers Grimm experienced in the late eighteenth and early nineteenth centuries. Although the Grimms had collected what became world-famous fairy tales and the woman who spoke to me mere cigarette-package illustrations thereof, she shared with the Grimms a desire to preserve before it might be lost something considered valuable. And like the individuals from whom the Brothers Grimm solicited tales, she was in her way a storyteller, standing before me at the podium recounting a highly evocative part of her past.

Personal stories such as hers highlight the enduring power of *Children's and Household Tales* (*Kinder- und Hausmärchen*), the collection that Jacob and Wilhelm Grimm first published in two volumes in 1812 and 1815 and which spanned seven complete and ten abridged editions during their lifetimes. It has been translated into more languages than any other German book and in 2005 was named a UNESCO Memory of the World heritage document. The continuing fascination with the Grimms' fairy tales was on full display in 2012, when the bicentennial of the first volume was celebrated in Germany and abroad. Grimm scholars gathered for academic conferences, Google greeted the anniversary with a Little Red Riding Hood doodle on its home page, and the *Deutsche Post* marked the occasion with a postage stamp that portrayed silhouettes of well-known characters from the Grimms' fairy tales superimposed onto the title page of the 1812 volume.[2]

A commemorative ten-euro silver coin was also issued, bearing the profiles of Jacob and Wilhelm Grimm and, on the coin's edge, a German inscription that translates as "And if they have not died . . ." Commonly regarded as the German fairy-tale equivalent of "And they lived happily ever after," these words typically read in full "And if they have not died, then they are still living today."[3] This matter-of-fact German ending is less saccharine than the "happily ever after" that Anglophone audiences have come to expect of fairy tales and Disney princess films, and as a commemorative catchphrase it pithily reminds us that the tales of the Brothers Grimm *have not died.* But while the Grimms' fairy tales have endured, the popular consciousness of Jacob and Wilhelm Grimm themselves has faded. As if the "Brothers Grimm" were a collective personage, even their first names are not generally known. From the nineteenth century to the present, the frequent usage of the singular "Grimm's" in the title of many English translations of their fairy-tale collection has only worsened this conceptual collapsing of the Grimms into a single entity. The many works beyond the fairy tales that the Grimms published together or individually are now also largely forgotten. Linguists are acquainted with Jacob Grimm from Grimm's Law, named after his detection and description of linguistic sound shift patterns, but few people today know of the brothers' vast work on mythology and medieval literature, their collection of legends, the German dictionary project on which they embarked, Jacob's extensive scholarship on grammar, or the cultural significance they attached to these various projects as the German-speaking lands sought an identity in the nineteenth century.

Although the Grimms' fairy-tale collection is still famous the world over, its origins, contents, and editorial history are largely misunderstood. Today, many Germans might assume that Grimm tales routinely end with the "And if they have not died . . ." phrase, but in fact these words appear in just one of more than two hundred tales in the seventh and standard edition of the Grimms' collection—and several Grimm tales actually do end with words akin to the English "And they lived happily ever after."[4] Accustomed to sanitized twentieth- and twenty-first-century retellings of fairy tales for children, some readers are shocked by the violence and darkness—including references to cannibalism and incest—that many Grimm tales portray en route to a happy ending; others, having heard of such references, wrongly assume that the Grimms' tales are saturated with bloodcurdling gruesomeness. As for the genesis of the tales, some readers erroneously believe that the Grimms authored their tales out of whole cloth. But the more prevalent misconception, widespread already in the nineteenth century, still abounds that the Grimms journeyed into the fields and spinning parlors to note down tales word-for-word from the mouths of peasants, even though scholars established decades ago that the majority of their tales came from educated young women and then often underwent significant editing at the Grimms' hands.

Dispelling such misconceptions opens a path to better understanding the Grimms' remarkable achievements and the social, cultural, and political context from which these achievements arose. Their lives and scholarly pursuits were substantially influenced by the many upheavals of the Napoleonic era, which included the end of the Holy Roman Empire in 1806 and the ensuing French occupation and temporary renaming of the Grimms' native Hessen and other German territories as the Kingdom of Westphalia.[5] The Wars of Liberation commenced in 1813 and, with the Congress of Vienna and the Treaties of Paris in 1814 and 1815, ended the Napoleonic Wars. Developments in the post-Napoleonic era included the 1819 Carlsbad Decrees and the revolutions of 1830 and 1848. Not mere abstractions for Jacob and Wilhelm Grimm, these various events palpably shaped their personal and professional circumstances.

Two of the Grimms' brothers were soldiers in the Wars of Liberation, and Jacob served not only as librarian to Napoleon's brother Jérôme, whom Napoleon had appointed King of Westphalia during the French occupation, but also later as part of Hessian delegations to France and the Congress of Vienna. In 1837, Jacob and Wilhelm were dismissed from professorial positions at the University of Göttingen when they and five other professors refused to take an oath of allegiance to the king of Hanover in protest over his annulment of the Hanoverian constitution. In 1848, Jacob served as a representative at the Frankfurt National Assembly, convened in the wake of the revolutionary fervor sweeping Europe.

The Grimms' scholarly work afforded them a sense of self-preservation amid personal losses and political and societal shifts. Concerned that forces including urbanization, industrialization, and war were imperiling the folk culture from which they believed fairy tales, legends, and related genres had emanated, they collected these and other types of folk texts and studied medieval and early modern literatures, mythologies, languages, and legal traditions.

So influential were they in these efforts that when, in 1846, the Englishman William John Thoms first suggested "a good Saxon compound, Folk-Lore" as a term suitable for capturing the "manners, customs, observances, superstitions, ballads, proverbs, etc., of the olden time," he did so with a call for a "James Grimm" to arise and do for the British Isles what Jacob Grimm had accomplished for the German-speaking lands. "Folklore," in other words, was an English neologism coined with direct connection to the Grimms. As a field of study, folklore was an invention of the nineteenth century (although inspired by late eighteenth-century intellectual currents), and it was created in great part in the image of the Grimms' scholarship.[6]

The Grimms saw their mountainous home of Hessen as relatively untouched by modernizing forces and thus a place that safeguarded German folklore from prior eras. However, the brothers' aim was not just to preserve these remaining stories and traditions, but also to uncover how they had descended (in their view) from a vast corpus of ancient epic literature produced by the collective voice of a people. The Grimms and other nineteenth-century intellectuals believed that reclaiming this "people's voice" was vital to the middle class's self-assertion and push for political reform. Additionally, since Germany did not exist as a united country during the Grimms' lifetimes, the Grimms and their contemporaries drew on Germanic heritage to articulate an overarching cultural identity for the patchwork of principalities in the German-speaking lands.

The Grimms thus explored the stories and languages of the Germanic past not merely to further scholarly understanding or to seek emotional refuge from the turmoil of their time, but also because they saw an understanding of this heritage, particularly as it existed before the advent of French cultural and political influence, as essential to a better future for German society. In studying the evolution, interrelationship, and manifestation of various kinds of folk literature, they frequently glorified the medieval past, idealized the fairy-tale storyteller as an older peasant woman, or expressed partiality to their native Hessen.

In any case, however, they considered their love of Hessen, like their respect for other regional traditions, as supporting, not supplanting, their articulation of a broader German identity. Furthermore, their focus on the German-speaking lands did not come at the expense of appreciation for other national traditions or transnational contexts. Not only did their study of German language and literature routinely involve tracing international story variations, for example, but Jacob and Wilhelm also together or separately published studies pertaining to the languages and literatures of Scandinavia, Spain, Ireland, and Eastern Europe, among other nations or regions. Their seminal contributions to medieval studies, folklore, and historical linguistics resulted from their work in philology—a term whose etymology captures the "love of the word" that this highly interdisciplinary field encompasses in its study of language, literature, and culture. Still today, the Grimms are regarded as among the foremost founders of this discipline.

The fragmentary literary, cultural, and linguistic vestiges of the past nevertheless presented interpretive challenges for the Grimms as philologists and folklorists. The Grimms were conscious of the way editing is always a form of mediation: in compiling their collection of fairy tales, they determined which tales or tale variants to include or exclude, what level of editorial intervention was appropriate in polishing tales, and what supplementary information to provide in their appendix. They used a variety of metaphors in conceiving of how to remain true to the text as they made these and other decisions. Jacob noted, for example, that storytelling is like cracking open an egg: while with each version of a tale some egg white will inevitably remain on the eggshell and thus not be transmitted, the trick is to tell the tale in a manner that keeps the yolk intact. Written principally by Wilhelm, the Grimms' preface to the second edition of their fairy tales compared the editor or author who engages in too much polishing of a tale to Midas, insofar as undue stylization will turn the tale into a gold that, unlike the green of nature, cannot nourish us. Jacob further compared older poetry taken out of its historical context to captured lions and tigers that can do nothing but pace hopelessly back and forth in their cages, or to the suffering that kangaroos might experience if transplanted from Australia to Europe. Although drawing on different images, these and related metaphors capture the Grimms' emphasis on editing as a gentle nurturing that preserves the organic nature of the text, instead of as a mechanistic process that yields only artificiality. Determining whether particular edits restored or adulterated the text was more subjective than the Grimms implied, however, a point often raised by their friends and critics.[7]

A biographer's endeavor presents challenges not unlike those the Grimms faced as editors: in addition to specific decisions about details and emphasis, the biographer must decide the degree to which events and outlooks should be viewed within the context of the subject's or one's own time. First and foremost, there is the realization that one can never fully understand either the subject's or one's own era, since the written record and other extant sources will present but a narrow account of a life lived so long ago, and one's ability to step outside one's own time and view a past life with objectivity is similarly constrained. Attempts to make life from an earlier era conform too strictly to modern norms might recall the Grimms' warning that radical textual modernization is tantamount to removing a wild animal from its environment and placing it in a cage. Similarly, undue smoothing over of events, personalities, and issues that are at odds with the narrative one is telling will result in the artificiality that the Grimms tried to avoid in editing their tales. No matter how it is told, every life story leaves some things behind, like egg white clinging to the shell. But akin to the tale variants the Grimms collected, each retelling can capture the essence, the yolk of the life, in its own unique way.

While writing this biography, I have often been asked for my "take" or "slant" on the Grimms. Understandably, the implied expectation is that one must have something novel to offer in approaching two figures known the world over. In truth, however, it has been decades since a full-length biography of the Grimms has appeared in English. Chapter-length biographical overviews of the Grimms have appeared in scholarly works such as Jack Zipes's *The Brothers Grimm: From Enchanted Forests to the Modern World*; in addition, in 2001 Donald R. Hettinga published *The Brothers Grimm: Two Lives, One Legacy*, written for adolescent readers. With respect to the Grimms' fairy tales more narrowly, a rich corpus of English-language scholarship exists, produced by researchers including Zipes, Maria Tatar, Donald Haase,

Ruth B. Bottigheimer, Marina Warner, and Vanessa Joosen. However, more than half a century has passed since the publication of Ruth Michaelis-Jena's biography *The Brothers Grimm* and Murray B. Peppard's *Paths through the Forest: A Biography of the Brothers Grimm*. In the intervening decades, significant discoveries have changed our understanding of the Grimms themselves along with their scholarly enterprise and cultural legacy. For example, in 1975 Grimm scholar Heinz Rölleke showed that several Grimm tales attributed by Wilhelm's son Herman Grimm and subsequent scholars to an "Old Marie" ("Alte Marie") were in fact collected not from an elderly housekeeper in the home of Wilhelm Grimm's future wife Dortchen Wild but from the young Marie Hassenpflug—a discovery that further dispelled the myth that the Grimms received their tales principally from older peasant women.[8] Since the appearance of the most recent German-language biography (Steffen Martus's *Die Brüder Grimm: Eine Biographie*), additional research has emerged on the editorial history of the Grimms' fairy-tale collection, their working methods, and the ideological functions of their scholarship.[9]

Any biography of the Brothers Grimm entails capturing the essences of two brothers and determining the degree of attention to give to each, but chronologically it begins and ends with Jacob alone. As the eldest of the six Grimm children who survived infancy, Jacob's recollections of the Grimm family's early years are more nuanced and numerous than those of his younger siblings, all of whom he also outlived. He was the more influential scholar, as exemplified by *Jacob Grimm und sein Bruder Wilhelm* (Jacob Grimm and his brother Wilhelm), a twentieth-century German study whose title casts Wilhelm merely in relation to Jacob.[10] Although the two brothers formed an exceptionally close bond, they were rather different in personality, appearance, and outlook. Whereas Jacob tended to be introverted, Wilhelm was more outgoing. Jacob was small in stature and curly-haired, while Wilhelm was taller and had a rounder face. Wilhelm married, but Jacob was a lifelong bachelor who lived with Wilhelm and his wife, Dortchen. Throughout their scholarly careers, Jacob exercised a more rigidly scientific approach to the editing of manuscripts and tales, whereas Wilhelm was more attuned to making texts appealing and accessible to a nineteenth-century audience. Their personalities complemented each other, and arguments between them were few. Their lives were so intertwined that their mentor and friend, Friedrich Carl von Savigny, found it impossible to think of one brother without the other, and the writer Clemens Brentano invoked the image of two conjoined prongs when he addressed them in one letter as "My dear double hooks!" Similarly,

Achim von Arnim, Brentano's collaborator and a close friend of the Grimms, opined that the Grimms' edition of the medieval *Lay of Hildebrand* was so learned that they should have submitted it as a doctoral dissertation, musing that then whenever they published works separately they could each use the title "1/2 Doctor" or "Dr./2."[11]

Whether they are viewed as double hooks or half doctors, the brothers' devotion to their work united them. The world knows them as storytellers, but they saw themselves as scholars and even scientists. Jacob equated the exciting and original discoveries he and others stood to make in their work on Germanic and European languages with findings then emerging from the comparative anatomical study of various organisms.[12] The tracing of complex patterns that evolved within and across a people's grammar, folklore, literature, and history involved painstaking research for which there was at the time little foundation. Their work on these myriad topics, of which fairy tales formed just one part, continues to underpin modern scholarship and popular culture. Today's depictions of the Middle Ages in popular media, for example, owe much to the fascination with medieval life and literature that the Grimms and their contemporaries ignited.

My own approach in writing this biography has been broad in scope, so that readers can better understand the "once upon a time" of the fairy tales in the fullest context of the Grimms' lives and their time. I seek to provide an overview that dispels misconceptions about their fairy-tale collection; that presents the development of their fairy tales over several decades while also featuring the brothers' many other groundbreaking but largely forgotten accomplishments; that probes nuances and inconsistencies in their work and worldview; and that examines the manner in which their work shaped and was shaped by the fascinating cultural, social, and political tenor of the time. Key themes and tensions that emerge concern how the Grimms' conception of authenticity and naturalness informed both their collecting of oral and written texts and their aim that such collecting would uncover and foster German cultural identity. That is, the Grimms' criteria for an "authentic" storyteller or folk text rested on dichotomies between rural and urban life, low and high culture, nature and art, and oral and written literature that were blurrier than they generally acknowledged. Consequently, their distinction between authentic and adulterated tales was itself artificial, or at least unstable. The Grimms' notion of authenticity informed their scholarly practice in numerous ways, including which passages to excerpt from written sources as they compiled notes, what instructions to give to collaborators,

which collected texts to include in their published works, whether to identify collaborators or storytellers by name and how to describe them, whether
and how to translate texts from one language or dialect into another, and
how to frame their editorial philosophy and practice. The preoccupations of
the Grimms and their contemporaries with attempting to define and discern
what constituted a genuine folk text versus a corrupted one resonate with
modern efforts to distinguish what is organic or unduly processed, real or
doctored, naturally or artificially generated.

More specifically, the act of collecting emerges in this book as a multilay-
ered and nuanced process. Not only did the Grimms collect tales and other
texts, but they also in effect collected collectors (albeit with varying success)
by enlisting collaborators in these efforts. Furthermore, the national cultural
aims of the Grimms' published collections and editions meant that, in an
overarching sense, they sought to collect the collective—to present and foster
through collections such as their fairy tales or legends a facet of a presup-
posed collective German identity. Although often effusively patriotic, their
articulations of this identity should not be conflated with later ethnonation-
alism; to the Grimms, a people (or *Volk*) was principally defined by shared
language, whereas later in the nineteenth century a more biological notion of
Volk took hold that defined a people in racialized terms of ancestry and blood.
Nevertheless, narrating the Grimms' lives entails navigating between too na-
ively or too judgmentally presenting the nineteenth-century constructions of
Germany and Germanness to which they contributed—constructions appropriated by late nineteenth-century ethnonationalists and twentieth-century
National Socialist ideology.

In exploring these and other issues, I have written not exclusively with
academia in mind, but in the hope that this book will interest a broader
readership. Scholars might thus be disappointed to find that certain figures,
concepts, or issues are given less specialized treatment than they would wish,
while nonspecialists familiar only with the Grimms' fairy tales will likely be
surprised to find attention paid not only to that collection but also to lexicography, mythology, grammar, law, and medieval literature. I have found
that both within and beyond academia numerous misconceptions of the
Grimms exist: while the general public might be unaware of the Grimms'
work beyond the fairy tales, I have encountered linguistic scholars who have
mistakenly purported that Jacob Grimm was interested in fairy tales only
insofar as they might inform his linguistic studies. While it is true that Jacob distinguished himself more in the field of language study and Wilhelm

more as a scholar of medieval literature and an editor of the fairy tales, the Grimms themselves regarded their various scholarly endeavors as inextricably interrelated. My take, then, is that the Grimms deserve a new look: one that probes the strengths and weaknesses of their prodigious scholarship while neither dismissing the Grimms as dowdy scholars nor mythologizing them as doughty fairy-tale icons.

The Brothers Grimm

CHAPTER I

Childhood Memories, 1785–1796

"As a mountainous land remote from the major roads and engaged principally in agriculture, Hessen has the advantage that it can better preserve old customs and heritage," the Brothers Grimm sanguinely asserted of their native country in *Children's and Household Tales.*[1] A midwestern region of the German-speaking lands, Hessen lies in the middle of the Central German Uplands, the mountain chain that runs across the country's midsection and surpasses rolling hills in elevation but lacks the commanding peaks of the Alps farther south. During the Grimms' lifetimes woodlands dominated Hessen, and even today it is one of the most heavily forested German states. It was settled in ancient times by the Chatti people, whom the first-century Roman historian Tacitus described as having greater mental vigor, fiercer countenances, and a tougher physique than other Germanic tribes. Jacob and Wilhelm Grimm used similar descriptors of the Chatti and their descendants as they extolled Hessian hardiness in the preface to their fairy tales: "A certain seriousness, a healthy, hardworking, and brave disposition [. . .], and even the large and handsome stature of the men in the regions that were the true home of the Chatti have in this manner been sustained, such that the lack of comfort and daintiness that one readily observes in comparison to other lands can be viewed more as a strength."[2]

In the very year that Jacob and Wilhelm Grimm penned these words, a traveling Englishman portrayed Hessen in topographically similar terms but did not share the Grimms' view of the region's rusticity. He was astonished by the narrowness of Hessian valleys, described the accommodations as "miserably bad," and noted that "the condition of the very few working cattle, and the dress and countenances of the peasantry, had the appearance of extreme poverty and depression."[3] Whereas the Grimms saw in Hessian rural culture an invigorating lack of unnecessary comfort that had safeguarded local customs through the ages, the traveler found a deprivation so endemic that it could not be attributed solely to the devastation wrought by the Napoleonic Wars.

Travel accounts from previous centuries lent credence to the view that Hessen was less prosperous and hospitable than other German regions. During a visit to Hessen in October 1764, James Boswell dubbed the primitive coach in which he traveled a "monstrous machine," and in doggerel verse complained of the desultory conditions at a village inn. With "a thousand flies" buzzing around his face, "cursed wine," a "lumpish Landlord," and "musty straw" on which to sleep, Boswell summarized his situation thus: "Here I am sitting in a German Inn / Where I may penance do for many a sin." The English traveler Fynes Moryson, who visited Hessen in the late sixteenth century, conveyed similar sentiments in his translation of a German verse: "High Mounts and Vallyes deepe, with grosse meates all annoide / Sowre wine, hard beds for sleepe: who would not Hessen land avoide?" Although foreigners invariably marveled at the beauty of the countryside, Hessen was a land whose meager commerce and lack of natural resources caused the many privations these visitors were so eager to escape.[4]

In contrast to such travelers, the Grimms longed for their native land during the periods of their lives when they resided elsewhere. They regarded themselves as quintessentially Hessian, though the hardiness they so confidently attributed to their countrymen showed itself not in the brothers' physical constitutions, but in the resilience with which they endured such hardships as the early death of their father, the destructiveness of the Napoleonic Wars, and Wilhelm's precarious health. Their upbringing inclined them to view constraints as beneficially formative and to search for opportunity in adversity. At times, this ability to find a silver lining was instinctive and winsome, if perhaps naive. At other times, compelled by personal, professional, or political circumstances beyond their control, it was tinged with acerbity and indignation. Regardless, this outlook informed the Grimms' conviction that Hessian deprivations had helped safeguard its heritage.[5]

At the time of Jacob Ludwig Carl Grimm's birth on January 4, 1785, and Wilhelm Carl Grimm's birth just over a year later, on February 24, 1786, Hessen had for more than two centuries been divided into the separate political entities of Hessen-Kassel and Hessen-Darmstadt. Each was designated a landgraviate and ruled by a landgrave, a German rank similar to a duke.[6] Hessen-Kassel and Hessen-Darmstadt were part of the Holy Roman Empire, that patchwork quilt of polities that had long been "neither holy, nor Roman, nor an empire," as Voltaire famously quipped.[7] Hessen-Kassel (where the Grimms resided) and the smaller Hessen-Darmstadt were wedged between several German states of varying political structure and power. Of the three hundred or so independent polities in the German-speaking lands on the eve of the French Revolution, Prussia and Austria were the most dominant. Brandenburg (along with its capital, Berlin) and Prussia were legally in personal union under the Hohenzollern dynasty, with Brandenburg within the Holy Roman Empire and Prussia outside it. In practice, however, Brandenburg was regarded as part of Prussia. Similarly, Austria as a designation was often used to refer not only to Austrian lands proper but more broadly to the Habsburg monarchy and the many territories over which it ruled. After Prussia and Austria, Hanover, Saxony, and Bavaria were among the more powerful states; Hessen-Kassel was no more than a middle power.

Hessen's fragmentation as a political entity had begun two centuries earlier, after the death of Philipp I. "Philipp the Magnanimous" was not only the last landgrave to reign over a united Hessen but also among the first territorial rulers to reform his church. In 1529 he sponsored the Marburg Colloquy, which brought together Luther, Melanchthon, Zwingli, and other leading theologians in his commanding hilltop palace overlooking the Hessian university town of Marburg. The colloquy unsuccessfully attempted to heal the rifts among these reformers and to advance Philipp's efforts to create a unified Protestant theology and political alliance of Protestant states. Whereas Hessen-Darmstadt emerged from the Reformation a Lutheran state, Hessen-Kassel was "Reformed," the term German Calvinists typically used to describe themselves.[8]

In 1508, just over two decades before the Marburg Colloquy, the Grimms' forebear Peter Grym obtained citizenship in nearby Frankfurt. His son Lotz

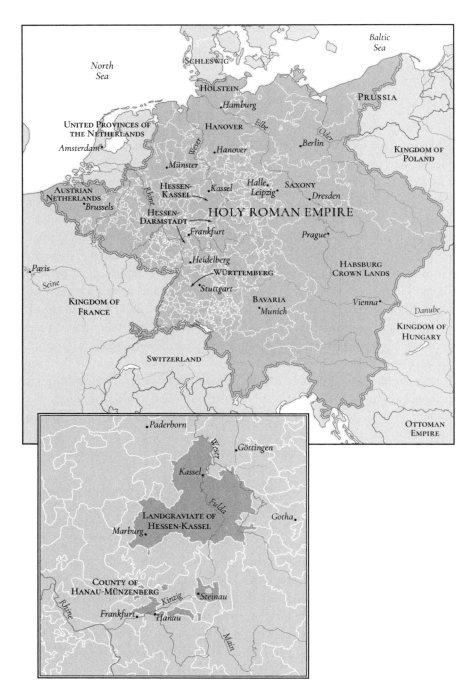

Central Europe on the eve of the French Revolution, 1789. White lines indicate borders of polities within the Holy Roman Empire. The inset shows the Landgraviate of Hessen-Kassel and the County of Hanau-Münzenberg, which Hessen-Kassel inherited in 1736.

became a guard in a Frankfurt watchtower one year later. Around this time, the spelling of the family name became normalized as *Grimm,* which in German means "wrathful" in its adjectival form and "wrath" or "fierceness" as a noun. The Brothers Grimm tired of the inevitable punning on their surname but also themselves engaged in it, as when Jacob wrote of his seminal *German Grammar* to a friend, "I do so appreciate that you have not chided my *Grammar* as a *Grimmer.*"[9]

Lotz's son moved from Frankfurt to Bergen (today a district in Frankfurt). In and around Bergen, descendent Thomas Grimm worked as a baker, miller, mayor, and representative to the regional court. His son Johannes moved in the seventeenth century to Hanau, just east of Frankfurt, where he became proprietor of the White Steed inn. Subsequent generations of Grimms rose to the clergy and civil servant classes. In the late seventeenth century, the Grimms' great-grandfather Friedrich Grimm served as clergyman in Hanau and inspector of churches for the Reformed congregation of the County of Hanau-Münzenberg. Also named Friedrich, the Grimms' grandfather later became pastor in Steinau, a town northeast of Hanau in the upper Kinzig River valley. It was there that the Grimms' father was born in 1751. Commonly referred to as Wilhelm by family members, Philipp Wilhelm Grimm was the tenth child of Friedrich Grimm and his wife, Christine (née Heilmann). At the time of the boy's birth, five of his nine older siblings had already died. The family's sorrows increased when, just three years later, his mother died giving birth to her eleventh child, a stillborn son, after four days of excruciating labor. Philipp Wilhelm's eldest sister, Charlotte, then almost twenty years old, assumed the role of caregiver to her younger siblings and later helped in the early education of the Brothers Grimm, her nephews.

Philipp Wilhelm studied law in the Hessian towns of Hanau, Herborn, and Marburg and in 1783 married Dorothea Zimmer, the daughter of Kassel councilman Johann Hermann Zimmer and his wife, Anna Elisabeth (née Boppo). Philipp Wilhelm and Dorothea's first child died within months of his birth. Jacob and Wilhelm were the second- and third-born, with siblings Carl (also "Karl"), Ferdinand, Ludwig (also "Louis"), and Charlotte (nicknamed "Lotte") following in 1787, 1788, 1790, and 1793. Two others did not survive infancy. In all, Dorothea gave birth to nine children within twelve years.

In the decades preceding Jacob's and Wilhelm's births, Hessen-Kassel was ruled by Landgrave Friedrich II, who aspired to be an enlightened absolutist like his idols Frederick the Great of Prussia and Joseph II, the Holy Roman

Philipp Wilhelm Grimm (1788). Painting by
Georg Carl Urlaub. Courtesy of Staatliche
Schlösser und Gärten Hessen.

Emperor and ruler of the Habsburg lands. Reigning from 1760 to 1785, Friedrich II reformed the judicial system, opened an academy of the arts, and attempted to revitalize the agricultural economy and spur commerce when bad harvests led to famine in the 1770s. In keeping with his adulation of French culture, he undertook several building projects modeled after French architectural styles. As a young man he had converted to Catholicism, whereupon his outraged father (Landgrave Wilhelm VIII) forced him to pledge that Hessen-Kassel would remain Reformed Protestant despite his personal conversion.

Friedrich II's conversion contributed to the breakup of his marriage to Mary, daughter of England's King George II. Friedrich's betrothal had been negotiated as part of a "subsidy treaty," in which Britain agreed to pay Hessen-Kassel to provide six thousand Hessian soldiers to fight for the British in the War of the Austrian Succession. Hessen-Kassel had long been known in the German-speaking lands for its proportionally large army. Subsidy treaties between Britain and Hessen-Kassel were common in the eighteenth century and a source of substantial income. The Hessian landgraviate provided soldiers to Britain, for instance, not only in 1776 during the American Revolutionary War but also as far back as 1677. Written while Hessen-Kassel was under French rule during a portion of the Napoleonic Wars, a French account derisively invoked the landgraves' practice of peddling soldiers to Britain as evidence of the alleged inferiority of Hessian peasants' character and intellect:

"The manners of these people, who live in a rude and mountainous country, partake of the rusticity of the primitive ages. The Hessian peasant, naturally a mere *machine*, is formed to a servile obedience, approaching to stupidity; he is told that nature designed him to be slaughtered in America, and he goes there to die without a murmur!" The commodification of the Hessian peasant as soldier is reflected in a letter written decades earlier by Landgrave Wilhelm VIII: alluding to legendary accounts of Inca gold, he described a Hessian corps in foreign service as "our Peru; if we lose it, we lose all of our resources."[10]

This assessment remained apt throughout the second half of the eighteenth century. Despite the reforms undertaken by Friedrich II, Hessen-Kassel's agricultural production was hampered by poor soil and mountainous terrain and its commerce constrained by the region's small number of towns and cities. The growth of Hessen-Kassel from around three hundred thousand inhabitants in 1770 to over a half million in 1800 occurred mostly among the lower classes, which only worsened existing economic challenges. Hessen-Kassel's soldiers remained its principal resource, enabling the landgraviate to participate on the European stage more extensively than its relatively small size and limited means would otherwise suggest. Stewarding the fortune amassed from subsidy treaties was Meyer Amschel Rothschild, founder of the Rothschild family dynasty. Indeed, it was the landgraves of Hessen-Kassel whose patronage first enabled Rothschild to establish his banking business. While the money Hessen-Kassel received from hiring out its soldiers enriched the landgrave's coffers and provided the financial means to further develop an absolutist state, the many foreign military campaigns took vital labor from agriculture and compounded the hardships of rural life.[11]

Hanau, the Grimms' birthplace, was the most important town in Hessen-Kassel after Kassel itself and a more prosperous place than typically encountered in Hessen. Nestled into a tuck of land where the Kinzig River bends sharply before flowing into the Main River and situated on roads that ran from Frankfurt to Nuremberg and Frankfurt to Leipzig, Hanau benefited from the commerce of river and land transport. The town's proximity to Frankfurt also enabled its inhabitants to buy and sell goods in that city's renowned trade fairs. In the countryside surrounding Hanau, agriculture proved relatively profitable: in contrast to the poor soil in most of Hessen-Kassel, the land around Hanau was rich and black, and whereas elsewhere in the landgraviate much of the planting was devoted to both potatoes—the foodstuff of the poor—and rye, in Hanau wheat was also cultivated.[12]

Founded in the Middle Ages, Hanau's Old Town abutted the Kinzig River, while south of the Old Town, toward the Main River, lay Hanau's New Town, built principally for Huguenot refugees who had fled the Netherlands and France in the late sixteenth century. Reflecting its medieval origins, the Old Town was a cluster of tightly packed houses and winding alleys. It boasted a marketplace, theater, hospital, high school, city hall, Jewish quarter, and two churches (the Reformed church, where the Grimms' great-grandfather had been pastor, and the Lutheran church). The more spacious and meticulously planned New Town sported well-paved streets that crossed at right angles, uniformly built houses, and a canal to the Main River. In 1791 the combined population of the Hanau Old and New Town was just over twelve thousand, with a substantial majority living in New Town. Among the Protestant refugees were potters, diamond polishers, and gold- and silversmiths, trades for which Hanau soon became widely known. Other inhabitants were employed in the manufacture of silk, including velvet fabric and ribbons, in toy making, and in tanning.[13]

The young Grimm family prospered in this bustling setting. Philipp Wilhelm Grimm served first as court solicitor and then as *Stadtschreiber* for the Old Town and its surrounding administrative district. Dating to medieval times and growing in importance in the German lands in the late fourteenth and fifteenth centuries, the position of *Stadtschreiber* bore more authority than its literal translation of "town writer" or "town clerk" implies. Among the most influential figures in a municipality's administration, the *Stadtschreiber* stood at the head of the chancery and provided legal counsel to officials. In Hanau, the *Stadtschreiber* served alongside the Old Town's mayor and city council. Although Philipp Wilhelm served the Old Town, whose government remained separate well into the nineteenth century, he and his family lived in the New Town.[14]

The house in which Jacob and Wilhelm were born sat on a large square that had been created by Landgrave Wilhelm IX, who succeeded Friedrich II in 1785. As crown prince, Wilhelm IX had embarked on a building plan for Hanau that called for a moat separating the Old and New Town to be filled in to create an esplanade and Parade Square, so named because the military held their exercises there.[15] The Grimm family soon moved from their lodgings in this square to a house they rented in the nearby Lange Gasse (Long Alley), not far from the New Town city hall and across from a glove maker who occasionally gave Jacob leather remnants to play with. The house's exterior was light red with tan-colored doors, and its ground-floor drawing room was wallpapered with images of huntsmen, some of whose visages the Grimm boys naughtily augmented with penciled-in beards. Upstairs was their father's study and toward the rear of the house lay the nursery, from which Jacob and Wilhelm could look down on a narrow courtyard over whose walls fruit tree branches hung from the neighboring garden. Helped in the running of the household by the housemaid Marie and the nursery maid Gretchen, Dorothea Grimm could often be found knitting or sewing in the upstairs sitting room. There, by the large German stove, Jacob recalled her washing him with warm water to which she added a splash of wine. He also remembered that he happily submitted to having the lice picked from his scalp but resisted having his nails cut.[16]

A portrait from 1787 depicts the two-and-a-half-year-old Jacob standing amid trees, a rosebush, and flowering shrubs. A butterfly flutters nearby as he leans against a large hewn rock and holds a sprig of freshly picked flowers. Cherubic yet pensive, Jacob gazes at the viewer with his head slightly turned. His light-brown hair is combed forward, and his cheeks are full. For this formal portrait, he is dressed not in his everyday smock but festively in buckled shoes, violet-colored trousers, and a matching double-breasted jacket adorned at the waist with a large green sash and worn over a white shirt with a wide ruffled collar. The rocky outcrop, lush foliage, and even the butterfly are, with some variation, standard compositional elements in the portraits that artist Georg Carl Urlaub painted for his clients, who came from court society and the upper middle class. Not merely a likeness of Jacob as a toddler, the portrait testifies to both the Grimm family's rising socioeconomic status and the aesthetic tastes of the time.

Relatives from both sides of the Grimm family lived in Hanau. Jacob and Wilhelm were taken on the short walk into the Old Town a couple times a week to visit their maternal grandparents, who had moved to Hanau upon their grandfather's retirement from his distinguished career at the court in Kassel.[17] (Their daughter Henriette—the Grimms' maternal aunt and Dorothea Grimm's sister—remained in Kassel, where she served as first lady-in-waiting to the landgravine.) Jacob and Wilhelm recalled the tenderness of their grandparents during these visits. Philipp Wilhelm Grimm's eldest sister, Juliane Charlotte Friederike Schlemmer (known as "Charlotte"), also lived near the Grimms in the New Town. She had been widowed the year of Jacob's birth and was childless; decades earlier she had been the one to care for Philipp Wilhelm and her other siblings after the death of their mother. Nephews Jacob and Wilhelm visited her daily and often spent more time at her home than at their own. Although for a brief time they learned French from a language teacher in the New Town, most of their early education came

Jacob Grimm at the age of two and a half years (1787). Painting by Georg Carl Urlaub.
Courtesy of Staatliche Schlösser und Gärten Hessen.

from Charlotte, to whom they referred as Aunt Schlemmer. It was she who first taught Jacob to read by pointing to letters on a page with a needle or the ivory rib of a folding fan, such that the texts soon had tiny holes poked into them. So close was Charlotte to the Grimm family that when they moved in January 1791 from Hanau to Steinau an der Strasse, she sold her house and moved with them. Jacob had just turned six, Wilhelm was almost five, Carl was four, Ferdinand three, and Ludwig one.

A small town in the Kinzig River valley around fifty kilometers upstream from Hanau, Steinau an der Strasse had been Philipp Wilhelm Grimm's birthplace four decades earlier. He returned to it as district magistrate (*Amt-mann*), a position for which he had applied at the end of 1790. In the preface to their fairy-tale collection, the Grimms attributed Hessen's preservation of its customs and heritage to its remoteness from major thoroughfares; like Hanau, however, Steinau an der Strasse (Steinau on the Road) lay on the famous trans-European Via Regia (Royal Road) that extended from Santiago de Compostela to Kiev and whose main commercial stretch in Germany ran from Frankfurt to Leipzig. Steinau thus enjoyed considerable contact with the outside world despite its rural surroundings and small size. Although its residents numbered only between 1,200 and 1,400 in the second half of the eighteenth century, it boasted a particularly high concentration of inns, each of which bore a sheet-iron sign above the door with an image of the animal, object, or figure—swan, steed, eagle, lion, crown, knight, or angel—after which the inn was named. Known as the *Kumpen*, the marketplace took its name from the large water trough (*Kump*) that lay in the center of the square and quenched the thirst of travelers' horses. Next to the *Kumpen* lay Steinau's most prominent landmark, the sixteenth-century palace constructed on the foundations of an earlier fortress and used by the counts of Hanau as a secondary residence. In the church next to the palace, Philipp Wilhelm's father had served as pastor for forty-seven years, and there, too, the mother whom Philipp Wilhelm had known only in his earliest years was buried beneath the church floor. Wilhelm reflected later in life that his paternal grandfather—who died before Jacob and Wilhelm were born—had for twenty years walked over his wife's grave every Sunday as he strode to the pulpit to give his sermon.[18]

The spacious sixteenth-century magistrate's house into which the Grimms moved was close to this church, just past the town hall and a short way down the street now known as Brüder-Grimm-Strasse (Brothers Grimm Street). The home featured arched windows on the lower white stone story and exterior wooden brackets, each uniquely carved and painted, supporting the overhanging half-timbered upper story. To the right of the front door a rounded tower enclosed a spiral stone staircase that connected the Grimms' residence to Philipp Wilhelm's office above. Wilhelm and Jacob shared a bed in the same room as their parents, whose own bed lay behind a curtain. Next to this bedroom was the living room, where family portraits hung and cupboards displayed costly porcelain dishes, painted in the blue and white Dresden style. Outside, a barn with stalls for the horses and cows formed part of a large, enclosed courtyard. The family also kept ducks, chickens, rabbits, and sheep and grew hay and potatoes in the surrounding fields. The Grimms had at their disposal not only hired farmhands but also a cook, a coachman, and maids to help with the children and housework. Despite the handsome house in which they lived and the various benefits which Philipp Wilhelm's prominent position afforded him, his actual salary was rather modest.[19]

The most senior administrative and legal official in the district, Philipp Wilhelm was responsible for maintaining overall public order, presiding over criminal and civil lawsuits, carrying out notarial duties such as forming wills and contracts, and implementing and enforcing regulations pertaining to virtually all aspects of public life, including agriculture, education, religion, censorship, and construction. In German popular literature of the late eighteenth and early nineteenth centuries, the magistrate is portrayed as a well-respected father figure to the citizens in his district and an exemplary spouse and father in his household. The description of the district magistrate in Friedrich Wilhelm Haberland's novel *The District Magistrate of Reinhausen, or Frank's*

The magistrate's house in Steinau. Photo courtesy of Stadt Steinau an der Strasse.

Secrets (1812) is typical and could almost serve as a character sketch of Philipp Wilhelm Grimm:

> Imagine a vigorous forty-year-old, of moderate height and strength; a rounded masculine face on which joviality and quiet dignity alternately reign; a diction that is awe-inspiring, engaging, and moving; a gaze that instills fear in the villain and trust in the unfortunate; a warmth that awakens love and openness in social interactions; a proficiency and perseverance in every proceeding that arises, and which, because it is accompanied by an unusual perspicacity and genuineness of feeling, makes everything possible. He is a rare man!—And what a tender spouse and father he is!—How all love and honor him, and how truly just he is as an official![20]

Like this fictional description, Philipp Wilhelm turned forty in his first year as magistrate and was not very tall. He had, however, a lean, not rounded, face, with features described as serious, though he possessed a friendly disposition. Jacob, who extolled his father's diligence and orderliness, recalled the cabinets of neatly arranged books in his office. Many of these volumes bore Philipp Wilhelm's ex libris, featuring the intertwined crests of his parents' families and the motto *Tute si recte vixeris* (You live securely if you live justly).

Philipp Wilhelm was a thoroughly practical man who preferred the wool from the black sheep in the family's herd, since stockings made from cream-colored fleece showed too much dirt. He nevertheless cut a commanding figure in his Hessian uniform, which featured a blue tailcoat with red velvet collar and gold epaulettes. Before donning this official attire each morning and having his hair drawn into a pigtail and powdered by his coachman, he smoked and read morning prayers in his dressing gown. During the day, he worked in his upstairs office or went out on duties. The forest master and district doctor were among those in his social and professional circle. A loving father, he often allowed one of his children to ride along partway on horseback when he traveled to a nearby village on business, while another child rode with his coachman. He doted on his only daughter, the Grimms' sister Lotte, born in Steinau. Ludwig recalled his father tossing down a biscuit for Lotte from his office window as a maid carried her through the courtyard, and embracing her first among the siblings upon returning from his travels.[21]

As for the Grimms' mother, Dorothea, her official form of address in Steinau was "Frau Amtmännin" (Mrs. District Magistrate). Decades later, Jacob and Wilhelm gave a surprisingly personal tribute to her in the entry for "Amtmännin" (wife of the *Amtmann*) in their *German Dictionary*, noting that the residents of Steinau often elided "Frau Amtmännin" into one word: "our blessed mother [. . .] was addressed by the people just as the *framtmännin*." Dorothea's by all accounts happy marriage is evident in a poem she wrote to Philipp Wilhelm the year before they moved to Steinau, in which she described her husband as her "noble, warm friend with whom my heart is eternally united." In light of this devotion, it is perhaps not surprising that Samuel Richardson's epistolary novel *Sir Charles Grandison* was her favorite book, given that it presents "a man of religion and virtue; of liveliness and spirit; accomplished and agreeable; happy in himself, and a blessing to others."[22]

Contemporaries described Dorothea as having good sense and a gentle, nurturing, feminine disposition—traits conforming to the gender norms of the time. By contrast, her sister-in-law Charlotte Schlemmer, who lived with the Grimms, was known for her intellectual acumen and tough-as-nails temperament. Charlotte's strict, prudent demeanor intimidated the younger boys but benefited Jacob, her favorite nephew. Her fondness for him stemmed principally from the extraordinary intellect he showed already as a young child, as well as from his physical likeness to his paternal great-grandfather. Widowed and childless, Charlotte invested herself so thoroughly in the Grimm family heritage that she at times discounted the achievements of the Zimmer family into which Philipp Wilhelm had married. Jacob even later speculated that she was particularly unkind to his sibling Carl because Carl bore a striking resemblance to their grandfather Zimmer instead of to the Grimm lineage. Though Ludwig and Carl were, by Ludwig's own admission, the unruliest of the children, Jacob believed that his aunt—beloved as she was by Jacob—rejected Carl to the point of being cruel.[23]

Differences in age and personality at times led to frictions between Charlotte and Dorothea. Because Charlotte had served as a substitute matriarch to Philipp Wilhelm after the death of their mother and was twenty years older than Dorothea, her role was in some ways more like that of mother-in-law than sister-in-law. Any strife was nevertheless eased by their rather separate spheres of influence, as Dorothea ran the household while Charlotte managed the farm. The women's differences in character and responsibilities are starkly illustrated by Jacob's recollections of family life in Steinau: whereas the memory of his mother that most stuck with him was of her making dough for noodles, dumplings, and doughnuts, he remembered how his aunt methodically caponized young roosters, first castrating them with a knife, then dabbing butter into their incisions, and finally cutting off their combs and the spurs on the rear of their legs despite their struggles and cries.[24]

Charlotte applied her businesslike demeanor and mental fortitude to the management of not only the farm but also her long-standing physical ailments. To treat her ill health, she followed a regimen that included tablets, medicinal pastes of tamarind, and the practice of wet cupping, whereby the blood from incisions made on her back was collected via suction into small glass jars applied to her skin. In the mornings, Jacob routinely visited her in her yellow-painted bedroom as she sat in bed drinking warm beer and reading scripture after what was too often a restless night. She spent much of her day keeping accounts, writing letters, and receiving reports from the farm staff and day laborers she supervised as well as the occasional house call from Steinau's doctor.

Whereas in Hanau Charlotte had instructed Jacob and Wilhelm, in Steinau they went to the schoolhouse on the marketplace and received private tutoring from schoolmaster Johann Georg Zinckhan. Zinckhan taught his pupils arithmetic, writing, religion, and Latin, as well as violin and piano. He was in his fifties, broad-shouldered, and of short to medium height. He donned an unpowdered wig with thick curls at church or other social events and wore faded and shabby suit-jackets: a light blue-purple one in summer and a black one in winter. With his suits he wore an outmoded three-cornered hat, black or violet stockings, and shoes with large buckles. The Grimm siblings later recalled him as old-fashioned, strict to the point of humorlessness, and utterly lacking in pedagogical acumen. Jacob in particular found him woefully ignorant and pedantic. Later in life, merely gazing at his parents' wall clock led Jacob to recall marking time by the dreaded hour at which Zinckhan would arrive to tutor the Grimms and the moment of relief when he finally left. Ludwig described not only Zinckhan's large Spanish walking cane but also the canes and short leather whips (each of which Zinckhan had named) with which he punished misbehaving children, including the idle and inattentive Ludwig, who received almost daily thrashings.[25]

Separately from his instruction from Zinckhan, Jacob also learned some Hebrew from Jochil Strauss, a member of the Jewish community in a nearby village.[26] The Grimms' interactions with the local Jewish community were largely positive, though limited. As adults, however, Jacob and Wilhelm would evince anti-Semitic prejudice both in the choice of texts in their various collections and in numerous comments in their correspondence and other writings. Postwar commentators long remained silent on the issue of their prejudices or denied that the Grimms were anti-Semites: they noted that these comments usually appear as an aside and are not part of any longer diatribe against the Jews, and pointed out that the Grimms took issue with their friend Achim von Arnim's portrayal of the figure of the Eternal Jew in his play *Halle and Jerusalem.* More recent scholars, however, have begun to study the corpus of the Grimms' various prejudicial statements and rightly argue that the brothers' perpetuation of Jewish stereotypes should not be downplayed.[27]

The Grimms also had limited contact with members of other Christian denominations. Raised in the Reformed church with ministering ancestors, Jacob as a boy saw the more colorfully dressed Catholics in Salmünster as foreigners though they lived only an hour away. He also considered as strangers Steinau's few Lutherans, an unsurprising view given centuries of tension between the Lutheran and Reformed (Calvinist) strands of Protestantism. In the late sixteenth century, Calvinists had eliminated many feast days and removed the exorcism rite from baptism. In addition, they required the breaking of bread (*fractio panis*) during communion, since this act symbolized to them their belief that Christ was not physically present in the offering (whereas Lutherans banned the breaking of the bread precisely because of their belief in Christ's physical presence). Calvinists also destroyed altars, fonts, and other church images viewed as idols, believing that Lutherans had kept too much of what they viewed as Catholic idolatry. The church in Steinau where Jacob and Wilhelm worshipped bore witness to this destruction, since Calvinists had substituted a table with a black cloth for its altars and removed or painted over many of the images that had decorated its walls. In the eighteenth century, the Grimms' grandfather strictly adhered to and enforced Reformed teachings and during his long tenure as pastor in Steinau became known for his religious fervor. Although pious as adults, Jacob and Wilhelm did not share this fervor and tended to focus on what united Christian denominations instead of what divided them; nonetheless, later in life their *German Dictionary* was criticized as too Protestant in orientation.[28]

As for national and regional identity, the Grimms assumed as young boys that the rulers of Hessen-Kassel were superior to all others and that Hessen-Kassel was the most blessed of countries. Such assumptions likely went without saying, given their father's service to Hessen-Kassel as district magistrate, their grandfather Zimmer's career as councilman in the court of Kassel, and their maternal aunt Henriette Zimmer's position as lady-in-waiting to the landgravine in Kassel. Yet the brothers also developed an appreciation for local custom more particularly while in Steinau. Having previously worn their shoulder-length hair loose, for example, they soon adopted the Steinau fashion of wearing it in a pigtail. Jacob was troubled by his mother's inability to bind his hair as firmly as local fashion dictated, however, and envied friends whose mothers succeeded in creating pigtails so firm that the hair took on a wooden appearance. The lifelong appreciation of rural environs and local traditions that Jacob and Wilhelm gained in Steinau accounts in part for their idealized depictions of folk culture in their writings.[29]

The overall happiness that characterized the Grimms' early years in Steinau also shaped such depictions. Later, the brothers would fondly recall their dignified father with his powdered pigtail and blue frock coat adorned with gold epaulettes and their mother so often engaged in knitting or sewing. They remembered, too, the half-timbered magistrate's house with its walled courtyard and view of a neighbor's fruit trees, as well as their daily lessons and upbringing in the Reformed church. In the mornings, the siblings awoke to the sound of the teakettle. After the main meal, Philipp Wilhelm Grimm liked to inspect the livestock and garden. Young Jacob helped with grinding coffee, washing the porcelain, and collecting the eggs laid by the hens and ducks. The boys gathered acorn cups for their play, pretending that single cups were soldiers, two cups joined by a stem officers, and cups with gnarled or twisted stems drummers and trumpeters. Every December, the children looked forward to the holiday plates of nuts and fruits customary in German homes and the gold and silver apples that hung from the lighted Christmas tree. In spring, they awaited the return of the storks that nested atop the town gate, coped with the occasional flooding of the Kinzig River, and searched for Easter eggs in a garden the family owned in a meadow north of town. In summertime, they collected insects, butterflies, and flowers and often later made sketches of them. Their practice of collecting, analyzing, and saving specimens and mementos from their walks would continue throughout their lives and may have served as a foundation for their later collecting of texts and tales.

While in many respects idyllic, the first few years of the Grimms' childhood in Steinau were not untouched by social and political tumult. The guillotining of Louis XVI in Paris so frightened the eight-year-old Jacob that he wrote of it to his grandfather Zimmer in Hanau, who sought to reassure Jacob that God often allows one ill in order to achieve more beneficial aims. For Jacob, Wilhelm, and their siblings, the upheavals of the time were not just far away in Paris, but on regular display in Steinau during the French Revolutionary Wars. French, Austrian, Dutch, Prussian, Mainz, and Hessian troops marched at various times through Steinau on the road that ran between Frankfurt and Leipzig. A thousand Hessian soldiers marched through on one day alone in July 1792, with a total of six thousand more following at the end of the month. At times Saxon, Prussian, and Austrian units were quartered in Steinau, and on these occasions Steinau's inhabitants were required to provide food and lodging, albeit in exchange for some compensation. From November 1793 to the end of 1795, almost 479,000 troops passed through, accompanied by 235,000 horses.[30]

Steinau, with only some 1,400 inhabitants, was overwhelmed by this traffic. Rarely orderly, the troop marches led to frequent altercations between soldiers and townspeople, for which reason a fearful Dorothea Grimm kept her sons indoors whenever the regiments were present. Peering through a window, the Grimm siblings watched in fascination as cannons rolled by, each pulled by as many as ten draught horses. They beheld soldiers peddling stolen silverware, porcelain, and books and darting into alleys to plunder additional wares. Soldiers on horseback rode off with bread and sausage speared with their sabers from roadside stands. Slaughtered chickens, geese, and goats hung from their kit bags, and some soldiers even punctured holes in bread loaves and then braided them into their horses' tails. At every well and fountain, soldiers quenched their thirst. Drunken soldiers who could not keep pace with their regiments straggled alongside wagons carrying the seriously wounded and dying or heaped with slaughtered oxen, hogs, and calves. Shackled soldiers, many of them alleged spies, marched along with the regiments. Many soldiers were barefoot and disheveled and some had a bandaged head or an arm in a sling, but they nevertheless sang cheerfully to the music of violins. Pet squirrels, ravens, or magpies perched atop their kit bags. The soldiers took whatever wood they could find for their fires, including the railings enclosing the Grimms' flower beds. Townspeople were at times forced to give hay and straw to the livestock herds that followed the regiments. On one occasion, the Grimms' maid smoked out the barn with juniper in an effort to safeguard the family's cows from a cattle plague that broke out among the regiments' herds and spread rapidly to the local livestock. Until the contagion subsided, the Grimms avoided their cows' milk and drank only water or tea.[31]

Despite the tumult of the French Revolutionary Wars, the Grimm family led a joyful life in Steinau until the early hours of January 10, 1796, when at the age of forty-four Philipp Wilhelm Grimm died of pneumonia. Jacob had turned eleven only days earlier, Wilhelm was just over a month away from his tenth birthday, and their four siblings ranged in age from eight to two. Philipp Wilhelm had grown seriously ill shortly before Christmas, and Jacob described in a letter of January 5, 1796, to his grandfather Zimmer the bloodletting and medicaments with which two doctors tried to cure him. His condition appeared to improve, such that Jacob asked his grandfather to send a courier with a loaf of freshly baked multigrain bread from a favorite Hanau bakery for his father's growing appetite. But Philipp Wilhelm's condition again worsened, and the requested loaf arrived too late. Ludwig recalled how Aunt Schlemmer grew increasingly distraught as she watched over the Grimm children in their father's final hours. On the morning of Philipp Wilhelm's death, Jacob awoke to voices in the neighboring room. He allegedly opened the door partway to find a carpenter taking measurements of his father's body and remarking that the well-respected magistrate deserved a coffin of silver, not wood. Only a few lines into an autobiographical essay published in 1831, Jacob related that he could still see in his mind his father's black coffin and the pallbearers with lemons and rosemary in their hands.[32]

The Grimms' memories, however idealized, of the life lived before the death of their father would later serve as refuge and inspiration at times of hardship. Wilhelm's nightly dreams as an adult often took him back to the magistrate's house and its emotional and material comforts. Traveling in France in 1814 after the end of the French occupation of Hessen-Kassel but while battles continued to rage on French soil, Jacob sought to ease his homesickness by drafting an essay recounting his childhood and family. Yet the Grimms' later works also attest to the enduring psychological impact of their father's premature death, which ended their happy childhood. In an April 1818 letter to his mentor Savigny, Jacob, then thirty-three years old, attributed his inner unrest and extreme work habits to his assumption that he would die young like his father and thus needed to accomplish whatever he could before middle age. Not even teenagers when their father died, Jacob and Wilhelm at once understood that the trajectories of their personal and professional lives had abruptly and incalculably changed.[33]

CHAPTER 2

Transition to Adulthood, 1796–1805

The financial impact of Philipp Wilhelm Grimm's death was severe and swift. As a magistrate, he had received benefits such as in-kind rent, household staff, and the right to cultivate certain tracts of land in the district, all of which supplemented his salary. The forty-year-old Dorothea and her six children experienced a dramatic decline in their standard of living due to their meager savings and the sudden loss of these benefits. Within weeks they had to vacate the large magistrate's house in Steinau to make room for Philipp Wilhelm's successor. They moved first into the run-down and crowded almshouse next door, whose views of the magistrate's house afforded painful reminders of the family's emotional and economic loss. Now the family's eldest male, the eleven-year-old Jacob assisted Dorothea in selling a garden plot and billing the new magistrate for resources such as dung and hay that the Grimms had purchased for the farm. In the days after his father's death, a grieving Jacob wrote to his aunt Henriette Philippine Zimmer, first lady-in-waiting to Landgravine Wilhelmine Karoline in Kassel, to tell of his mother's suffering and receive counsel. Almost certainly influenced by Henriette, the landgravine issued a small annual pension for Dorothea of 100 Frankfurt guilders, effective the month of her husband's death. The annuity amounted to one-sixth of the Grimms' previous income. Scraping together the funds available to her, Dorothea bought the upper floor of a house at the opposite side of the town center from the magistrate's house; the purchase included stalls, a barn, and a small garden.[1]

In the years before Philipp Wilhelm's death, minor frictions had sometimes surfaced between the Grimms' mother and their paternal aunt Charlotte Schlemmer. Now, however, grief united the women, as did the challenges that lay before them. But this unity did not last long: Charlotte died on December 18, 1796, at the age of sixty-one, just eleven months after Philipp Wilhelm's passing. For Jacob, it was a particular loss. He and Aunt Schlemmer had long appreciated each other's mental acuity, and he tended to be quietly partial to her point of view when she and his mother disagreed (though in later years he felt he had been unfair to his mother). As eldest male sibling, Jacob had also been thrust into a role like the one Aunt Schlemmer had assumed decades earlier when, after her mother died, she became caregiver to her many younger siblings.

Although Jacob was now without Aunt Schlemmer's advice, he was not alone as he helped his mother and prepared to support the Grimm family financially in the years ahead. He could rely on the generosity of both his maternal aunt Henriette Zimmer in Kassel, who would come to play a significant role in the Grimms' adolescent years and early adulthood, and his grandfather Johann Hermann Zimmer. After his wife passed away in 1792, Grandfather Zimmer continued to reside in Hanau and was looked after by an unmarried daughter. His letters to Jacob after Philipp Wilhelm's death overflow with tenderly imparted wisdom and grandfatherly warmheartedness. When Jacob conveyed his outrage that a tailor had spoken ill of his dead father, for example, Zimmer responded that citizens often criticized administrators out of ignorance or spite. Instead of allowing himself to be rattled by the man's malicious words, Jacob should continue to be an example to his younger siblings, "such that in this way you will each bring joy to your Grandfather Zimmer, who loves you all so dearly, in the days that are left to him."[2]

Life settled into a new if doleful routine. After meals Dorothea and the children often walked north of town to their garden, which produced much of the family's food and yielded feed for their two cows. Ludwig remembered his mother seated on a bench in front of the garden hut, reading, knitting, or gazing at her children as they played while in the distance the church bells chimed on the hour. Indoors, the family kept pet blackbirds and linnets in cages as well as a pair of doves that nested under a bed. In the evenings, the boys did their lessons while Lotte darned stockings, practiced embroidery, or

spun flax with Dorothea and the family's maid. Though primarily educated
by Dorothea, Lotte also received summer tutoring from the schoolmaster
Zinckhan, who treated her more gently than he did his male students.

Jacob and Wilhelm for their part soon exhausted the limited instruction
Zinckhan could provide. In June 1798, two and a half years after their father's death, it was decided (with the aid and advice of Aunt Zimmer) that
they would attend high school that fall in Kassel, where Grandfather Zimmer
had been a councilman and Henriette continued to serve as the landgravine's
lady-in-waiting. Introspective and self-aware, the thirteen-year-old Jacob
knew this had to be, but he nevertheless cried and paced in anger at having
to leave his family and, as eldest male, fulfill his responsibility to them from
afar. In late September, he and twelve-year-old Wilhelm journeyed by coach
from Steinau to Kassel. The day before they arrived in Kassel, they ate their
noonday meal in Frankfurt with the kindly postmaster, who treated them
to an afternoon visiting a traveling menagerie of elephants, monkeys, tigers,
parrots, and other exotic animals and an exhibit of some fifty wax figures of
military generals and reigning monarchs.

Wonders far more imposing and enduring awaited them in Kassel. For well
over a century, the landgraves of Hessen-Kassel had lavished their fortunes on
monumental building projects in and around the capital city, which was regarded by admirers as "the German Versailles" and by detractors as "a gilded
bauble."[3] The Grimms' arrival in Kassel coincided with the completion of Landgrave Wilhelm IX's neoclassical palace Wilhelmshöhe (Wilhelm's Height), situated on the grounds of a vast mountain park six kilometers outside the city. The
park, whose construction began in the late seventeenth century, featured a colossal copper statue of Hercules and a water display that released 235,000 liters
of water down over 825 steps. Additional water features were built in the eighteenth century during the park's transformation into an English landscape garden, complete with artificial ruins of a medieval castle and a Roman aqueduct.[4]

Other royal residences included the Baroque-era Orangery Palace, which
lay between the south side of Kassel and the banks of the Fulda River, and
the Winter Palace on the enormous Friedrich Square at the center of Kassel.
Friedrich Square also featured an esplanade, the royal administration, and
the Fridericianum, founded in 1779 as the first museum in Germany open
to the public. The Grimms' school, the prestigious Lyceum Fridericianum,
was established by Friedrich II the same year as the museum in a nearby
street across from the Winter Palace. The school building housed ground-
floor classrooms, the headmaster's apartment and a hall for ceremonies on the

second floor, and teachers' apartments above that. The entrance was flanked by columns on which perched allegorical statues representing religion and diligence, to make concrete the dictum *ora et labora* (pray and work).

Much the same imperative was conveyed to the Grimms by their mother and grandfather. Just over a week after the boys arrived in Kassel to commence their studies, Grandfather Zimmer wrote to exhort them to fear God and study earnestly so that they could secure their future well-being and bring joy to their family. Upon learning that the school headmaster had examined the two boys within days of their arrival and found Wilhelm in need of remedial tutoring, Zimmer also wrote his daughter Henriette to express his concern that Wilhelm needed to study more and his dismay that Jacob appeared to gloat over having been assigned to a higher level than his brother. Dorothea, too, in a letter to Wilhelm urged him to work hard and take advantage of the opportunity that God had presented him, as it might not be afforded to his younger siblings. He and Jacob would need to forgo entertainment and eschew socializing with their classmates, lest they lose focus on their studies. In particular, she cautioned, they must not compare themselves to other students, whose parents likely were both still alive. Because she or Aunt Zimmer could die at any time, it was essential that Wilhelm and Jacob make the most of their studies so that they could support themselves and their siblings as soon as possible.[5]

When death struck just weeks after Dorothea's letter to Wilhelm, however, it took neither Dorothea nor Henriette but Grandfather Zimmer, who passed away without illness at the age of eighty-nine on November 22, 1798. Six weeks shy of his fourteenth birthday, Jacob now truly became the family patriarch. Within less than three years, he and his siblings had lost their father, Aunt Schlemmer, and their grandfather. In Steinau, Dorothea Grimm, forty-three years old, devoted herself to bringing up Carl, Ferdinand, Ludwig, and Lotte, secure in the knowledge that in Kassel her unmarried and childless sister Henriette, aged fifty, would provide emotional and financial support to Jacob and Wilhelm. Having enabled them to attend the Lyceum Fridericianum, Henriette also arranged room and board for the boys with the court cook, and upon their arrival in Kassel she had given them presents of calendars and silk money purses.[6]

Henriette was able to support her nephews due to the financial security and personal influence that her position as first lady-in-waiting conferred. Landgravine Wilhelmine Karoline, a Danish princess, was estranged from her husband, Wilhelm IX. He had for years installed a succession of official mistresses at his court, and his dissolute behavior had damaged the court's

Henriette Zimmer (1808).
Drawing by Ludwig Emil
Grimm. HGV-B0000.6470,
Städtische Museen Hanau.

reputation. As was the case for many consorts in Europe, Wilhelmine Karoline's household became a center of power separate from that over which the
landgrave presided.[7] Of her staff of eight, a chief adviser, two court ladies, and
two pages were aristocrats, while her chamberlain and two ladies-in-waiting
were commoners. In his youth, Wilhelm IX had been known for the modernizing and enlightened style with which he governed Hanau as regent, but as
landgrave he rolled back the reforms made by his father. Instead of spending
money on maintaining his court, he squirreled it away in private accounts.
The Winter Palace became spartan and shabby, offering little entertainment
and a shrinking number of courtiers. Despite the splendid building projects
on which Wilhelm IX and his forebears had embarked, Kassel itself and its
residents—numbering between eighteen thousand and nineteen thousand at
the end of the eighteenth century—did not appear particularly affluent during his reign. As one visitor observed, "Among the citizenry one sees little
that indicates commerce, good nutrition, or prosperity; one meets few well-
dressed people; and a carriage is a rare sight and even then not very elegant."[8]

Jacob remembered a particular emphasis on geography, anthropology,
natural history, physics, and philosophy at the lyceum, among subjects that

also included writing, mathematics, religion, Latin, Greek, and modern languages. Headmaster Karl Ludwig Richter was well-liked by his pupils but
weakened by old age. Jacob found other teachers not only lacking in pedagogical skill but also disdainful, and he noted with bitterness that one teacher
politely addressed students raised in Kassel with the formal second-person
pronoun *Sie* while addressing him with the pronoun *Er*—at the time already
an old-fashioned form of direct address used only with subordinates and then
as now, in lowercase, also the third-person pronoun for "he."[9]

Undeterred by such slights, Jacob and Wilhelm studied for over twelve
hours a day and quickly were counted among the school's best students. On
school days they received six hours of instruction at the lyceum and then four
or five hours of private tutoring by Dietmar Stöhr, master of pages at the court
and a man whose patience and love of teaching benefited the boys considerably, most notably in their studies of Latin and French. In their rare moments
of leisure, they sketched or went outdoors to search for butterflies and eggs to
add to their collections. They also enjoyed reading some of the popular literature of the day, including novels glorifying various events and figures in the
Germanic past. Heeding their mother's admonishments, they largely avoided
socializing with others, although they formed close friendships with the aristo-
crat Ernst Otto ("Otto") von der Malsburg, son of a Hessian officer who had
commanded a regiment to fight for the British in the American War of Independence, and with Paul Wigand, whose father was a professor at the cadet
school in Kassel and also served as court archivist. Although they were diligent
students, the Grimms were not entirely isolated from schoolboy culture; Jacob
even appears to have participated in the occasional brawl at the lyceum.[10]

Each of the four levels at the lyceum took eighteen to twenty-four months,
such that pupils normally devoted seven to eight years for the full course of
study. Jacob and Wilhelm finished in half this time and, like other talented
students, started university study without having completed the highest level.
The seventeen-year-old Jacob entered university first, matriculating in the
University of Marburg on April 30, 1802, followed a few days later by Otto von
der Malsburg, who like Jacob came to study law. Wilhelm and Paul Wigand
stayed in Kassel to continue their studies at the lyceum. Because Jacob and
Wilhelm had always shared not only the same room but also the same bed,
they found their separation from each other unnatural and alienating. Both
knew, however, that the family's precarious financial situation required that

Jacob begin and finish his university studies as soon as possible so that he could support his mother and siblings with an income. For Wilhelm, physical misery soon compounded the emotional distress of his separation from Jacob. First struck with scarlet fever in fall 1802, he then experienced severe asthma. Soon he found himself short of breath just walking to the lyceum and complained of the bitterly cold winds that blew across Friedrich Square and aggravated his breathing difficulties.

Wilhelm's sudden and protracted ill health was unexpected. Hit hard by smallpox as a child, Jacob had been regarded as having the weaker physical constitution, whereas the young Wilhelm enjoyed robust health. Wilhelm attributed his sudden frailty to the lack of exercise that resulted from spending virtually all his waking hours studying. Unable to attend school for six months because of his illness, he kept abreast of his lessons with informal tutoring from Paul Wigand. Wilhelm missed not only Jacob but also Otto von der Malsburg, to whom he wrote, "How can I help it if everything reminds me of you [. . .]? Whenever I am on the way to the lyceum, I still look up at your window, as that was my habit." Such effusive and intimate shows of emotion were standard components of male friendship at the time. Indeed, from Marburg Jacob wrote to Wigand with similar longing: "*Mon cher ami!* How much it delights me each time I see a letter from you, open it, read it, read it again, and then read it once more! So many strings are touched inside of me while doing so, so many memories awakened of happy and blithe days, hours, and moments that I spent in Kassel with you and which here I—cannot enjoy!" In other letters to Wigand, Jacob is more playful in tone, as when in one he recorded the time as "7 o'clock, 43 min., $\frac{1891065321100216787}{100000000000000}$ sec." In another, he drew a sketch of himself in bed and signed off, around quarter to eleven at night, with parenthetical stage directions and onomatopoetic words mimicking yawns: "iiha, iüaha. Good night! Uah! *(yawning)* Goo—ood—night—ight *(falling asleep and snoring)*."[11]

While Wilhelm coped in Kassel with physical illness, Jacob tried to adjust to the quite different surroundings of Marburg, a town nestled into a steep hillside overlooking the Lahn River valley some ninety kilometers by road to the southwest of Kassel. As the capital city, Kassel had experienced a flurry of building projects in the eighteenth century, but Marburg had changed little since the sixteenth century, when it had been the seat of the landgraves before Hessen's division into separate landgraviates. Architecturally, this meant that antiquated Gothic and early Renaissance structures still dominated Marburg, in contrast to Kassel's modern Baroque and neoclassical architecture. The towns' skylines offered perhaps the most dramatic illustration of shifting political power and contrasting architectural styles: whereas in Kassel the massive mountaintop statue of Hercules symbolized the landgraves' absolutist power, in Marburg the hilltop castle towering above the town served in the Grimms' time merely as a jail, despite having once been a main residence of Hessian landgraves and the site of the 1529 Marburg Colloquy.

The view of the Lahn Valley from the castle struck Jacob as picturesque, yet he held little esteem for Marburg itself. Describing to Wigand the town's steepness, Jacob observed that there were considerably more staircases out in the streets and walkways than inside the houses themselves, and that one house built on a slope even had to be entered through the roof. He also recounted his visit to the thirteenth-century Gothic cathedral in Marburg, which until the sixteenth century had served as the resting place for the Hessian landgraves. Jacob found their tombs downright eerie, but he marveled at the cathedral's stained-glass windows and paintings.[12]

View of the Castle and St. Elizabeth's Church, Marburg. Colored steel engraving based on the drawing by C. Reiss, 1842. Collection of the author.

As for the University of Marburg, Landgrave Philipp I founded it in 1527 as Germany's first Protestant university. Unfortunately, Philipp's incurious successors allowed it to fall into such neglect that by 1775 a government minister proposed (unsuccessfully) that it be moved to Kassel and amalgamated with another institution. Enrollments were low: in 1779 only forty-nine students were matriculated; while this number rose to 150 in 1786, it sank again. In only three years between 1796 and 1806 were there more than one hundred students at the institution. Marburg was not alone in these enrollment declines: the total number of students at German universities decreased from almost nine thousand students in the first half of the eighteenth century to below six thousand at the end of the century and below 4,900 at the conclusion of the Napoleonic Wars.[13]

Hessian restrictions on which socioeconomic classes could study at the university accounted in part for Marburg's low enrollments. In 1793, it was mandated that Hessian civil servants wishing to secure a university place for their sons must belong to one of the first seven civil service ranks, which directly impacted Jacob and Wilhelm, whose father, as a district magistrate, had belonged to the eighth rank. Although Philipp Wilhelm Grimm had studied at Marburg and Jacob and Wilhelm were excellent students, Dorothea Grimm had to obtain a special dispensation to enable first Jacob and then Wilhelm to secure a place at the university. The mandate also threatened to affect Paul Wigand, who upon attempting to matriculate in 1803 was told that he, too, could do so only with a special dispensation, because his father's position as professor at the cadet school was of too low a rank. Fortunately, Wigand quickly mentioned that his father also served as court archivist, and a scan of the list of ranks revealed this role to be high enough to enable Wigand to study at Marburg after all.[14]

Wilhelm matriculated at the same time as Wigand, having gone directly to the university on recuperating from his illness instead of returning to the lyceum. Even though the Grimms' widowed mother was raising six children, neither Wilhelm nor Jacob received state support for their university studies. Such aid in Hessen-Kassel was often awarded to sons of aristocrats and landowners as political favors, and indeed Jacob later claimed that Otto von der Malsburg, whose family belonged to the Hessian nobility, received "the fattest scholarships" for his studies in Marburg. Convinced that "indigence spurs diligence and work," Jacob believed that his and Wilhelm's privation as university students was nevertheless ultimately beneficial.[15]

While the more outgoing Wilhelm founded a reading society with twenty-eight members in Marburg, Jacob remained the more studious and solitary of the two. He at times declined invitations to go on walks with Wilhelm, Wigand, and Malsburg by saying he was obligated to saunter through literature instead. His friends often referred to him as "der Alte" (the Old One), since he was not only the elder of the two brothers but also the more serious and sharp-witted. But he, too, occasionally attended concerts and dances. The happy familiarity the friends shared is evident in notes Malsburg wrote to Wilhelm at the time. "Dear one! Do you want to come to my place around six o'clock? Otherwise, I'll go out," one slip of paper reads. "Dear Grimm! Please allow me to borrow a pair of white stockings," Malsburg wrote on another, "because all of mine—that is, two pairs—are in the wash."[16]

In later years, the Grimms' friendship with Malsburg grew more distant. They saw in his preference for refined society and his fixation on appearance an inauthenticity at odds with their own groundedness. Moreover, they did not think highly of the translations of Spanish literature and other writings that he produced alongside a public career as chamberlain, diplomat, and counsel. He died at thirty-eight. In contrast to their tepid relationship with Malsburg, the Grimms maintained a warm and lasting correspondence with Wigand. When his father died suddenly in July 1805, leaving behind few resources, Wigand was forced to quickly finish his studies and begin earning money for his widowed mother. He later presided over the municipal court in the Hessian town of Wetzlar, but his professional success was clouded by persistent sadness: his wife and children experienced mental illness, and the former was confined to a sanatorium.

That Jacob, Wilhelm, Wigand, and Malsburg all studied law at the university is unremarkable; of the handful of disciplines that dominated German universities at the time—principally law, theology, and medicine—law was quickly becoming the most popular. Jacob later related that he unquestioningly acceded to his mother's wish that he follow in his father's footsteps, but that he would have chosen botany if he had his choice. (The many botanical metaphors throughout the Grimms' writings are in keeping with nineteenth-century literary style, but Jacob's professed interest in the subject might further explain his penchant for such imagery.) In any case, law was second nature to him, since his father had often imparted to him legal definitions

from the *Corpus iuris civilis* (Body of civil law, also *Corpus iuris*), the title
given since the Renaissance to the codification of Roman law under Emperor
Justinian in 533 and 534 CE. This work formed the basis of Roman law as
practiced and interpreted in Europe for hundreds of years, and its study was
essential to German legal training.[17]

At the time that the Grimms were students in Marburg, Roman law was,
paradoxically, seen as emblematic of Germanness. The interpretation and application of Roman law had taken hold in Germany far more firmly than in other
European countries; in part due to this adoption, the German-speaking lands
had long regarded the Holy Roman Empire as the successor to ancient Rome.
Additionally, leading figures of the German Reformation had actively promoted Roman law in the 1500s, with the result that late eighteenth- and early
nineteenth-century legal scholars associated Roman law with the Reformation
and appropriated it to German cultural and political heritage. Roman law thus
became a point of German pride and promise as the German-speaking lands
fought against the French from 1792 to 1815. Indeed, because the sixteenth-century German reformers and legal scholars who had most vocally promoted Roman law saw in it a method of impartiality and peace, its study during and after
the Revolutionary and Napoleonic Wars was regarded by many in Germany
not as a diversion from but in some respects a solution to war-torn times.[18]

Unsurprisingly, much of Jacob and Wilhelm's coursework as law students
in Marburg was devoted to Roman law, as well as natural law, canon law,
logic, and the history of the Holy Roman Empire. Many lectures were still
delivered in Latin, and the overall pedagogical emphasis was on memori-
zation. The Grimms found some professors monotonous and limited and
others learned and cheerful. The only professor who truly stood out, however, was the brilliant young legal scholar Friedrich Carl von Savigny, who
distinguished himself from his professorial peers with his lively yet calming
lecture style, the clarity of his demeanor, and his warm interactions with his
students. Savigny quickly became the Grimms' mentor and close friend, ex-
erting a formative influence on their future scholarly endeavors. Just a few
years older than Jacob and Wilhelm, he had earlier been a student at the University of Marburg himself. He was born in Frankfurt, but after the deaths
of his parents and brother the orphaned teenager had moved to Wetzlar as
the foster son of an official at the imperial court of law. To supplement his
studies in Marburg, Savigny spent half a year in Göttingen and visited cen-
ters of learning including Jena, Halle, and Leipzig. In 1803, at the age of just
twenty-four, Savigny presented his landmark legal study *The Law of Possession*.

Friedrich Carl von Savigny.
Lithograph from *Borussia:
Museum für Preußische
Vaterlandskunde*, 1839. Collection
of the author.

Commentators compared him to a giant among dwarfs and rejoiced at the
appearance of a pathbreaking work after decades without any major scholarly
contribution to civil law.[19]

Because of the meteoric impact of *The Law of Possession* and related works,
Savigny is regarded today as the most influential jurist of nineteenth-century
Europe and the de facto founder of the historical school of legal scholarship, which instead of viewing law as simply issuing from reason emphasized
its historical underpinnings. "The historical school assumes," Savigny wrote,
"that the substance of law is given in the entire past of a nation, not arbitrarily—in the sense that this substance might coincidentally have been one
thing or another—, but proceeding from the innermost essence of the nation
itself and its history."[20] Savigny was the first to instill in Jacob and Wilhelm
an appreciation of the historical and cultural foundations of German law and,
concomitantly, to spark their lifelong interest in older German literature.

Almost half a century after their first meeting, Jacob dedicated an essay to
Savigny in which he described his mentor as a tall, slender, dark-haired man
attired in a gray jacket and brown silk vest with blue stripes. He recalled a
summer day in 1803 when he visited Savigny in his home, which lay on a hillside estate just beneath Marburg's castle. Situated between the estate's manor
and the gate to the property, Savigny's ivy-covered house struck Jacob as like
a bird's nest lodged among branches. In Jacob's sentimentalized description,

the house (and the library within it) became an intellectual extension of the surrounding natural landscape. Jacob described magical views through Savigny's windows of the Lahn River valley below and the opposing mountains, but more wondrous still was the panorama within of bookcases packed with volumes curiously alphabetized on some shelves from left to right and on others from right to left, a system Savigny endeavored in vain to justify to Jacob. Jacob recalled that when Savigny invited him to inspect his books more closely by climbing the library ladder, "my eyes then were afforded a view that they had never before beheld." Far back on a shelf, Jacob spied Johann Jakob Bodmer's collection of *Minnelieder*, medieval German songs whose exploration of courtly love, or *minne*, reflect the rise of the knightly class in secularized twelfth-century culture.[21]

Both in his autobiography and elsewhere, Jacob emphasized the significance of the moment in Savigny's library when he first beheld Bodmer's collection. To understand why his first encounter with this work was so pivotal for his and Wilhelm's future scholarly interests, it is important to consider both the collection itself and the state of German literature and literary scholarship in the eighteenth and early nineteenth centuries. Published in the late 1750s, Bodmer's volume presented the nearly six thousand verses from 140 poets that made up the Codex Manesse, a medieval manuscript that is still the most comprehensive source of *Minnelieder*. Many texts in the codex would have been lost if patrician Rüdiger Manesse of Zurich and his son had not collected and compiled them into manuscript form between approximately 1300 and 1340. Over four hundred years later, Bodmer, a Swiss poet and literary critic, had the codex sent from Paris first to Strasbourg and then to Zurich, where he and collaborator Johann Jakob Breitinger studied and transcribed it.[22]

Bodmer's edition of the Codex Manesse texts supplied a blueprint of sorts for Jacob and Wilhelm's later scholarly work on literature and language. Like Rüdiger Manesse and his son centuries earlier, the Brothers Grimm would, in their collection of fairy tales, preserve literature that otherwise might have been lost. Similar to Bodmer in the eighteenth century, moreover, the Grimms often relied on established contacts, shrewd detective work, and sheer serendipity to obtain a manuscript or oral telling; like Bodmer, too, Jacob's linguistic work would draw attention to the beauty and richness of older forms of language.

Jacob was mesmerized in particular by the songs' Middle High German, a form of the language that had existed approximately between 1050 and

1350 and only half of which Jacob could readily understand upon first paging through Bodmer's edition. In his preface, Bodmer likened the work of literary scholars to that of naturalists: just as the naturalist's sharp eyes detect vestiges of the caterpillar in the body of the butterfly, the literary scholar sees traces of Middle High German in modern High German. But viewed in another way, Bodmer continued, just as the caterpillar in some ways possesses more subtlety and fineness than the glorious body of the fully metamorphosed butterfly, so, too, will the literary scholar find a latent beauty in the hitherto neglected poetry of Middle High German.[23]

And neglected it had been and would continue to be for some time. When, in 1784, Bodmer's friend Christoph Heinrich Müller dedicated an anthology of medieval German literature to Friedrich II of Prussia, the king famously dismissed its contents as not worth a shot of powder.[24] For much of the eighteenth century, German writers and intellectuals had disdained or ignored medieval literature and material from German legends, songs, and historical events, focusing instead on plots inspired by Greek and Roman mythology and history. They had also typically followed the strict literary principles promulgated by seventeenth-century French neoclassical critics. For instance, a drama was expected to adhere to the three unities: it should revolve around a single main action occurring in a single location and unfolding within the span of a single day. German authors did not concern themselves with celebrating or creating a literature that would reflect German culture, for the simple reason that there was, in their view, no German culture worthy of such reflection.

Resistance to French neoclassicism had grown in the 1760s and 1770s. It coincided with German intellectuals' discovery of and love for Shakespeare, whose plays they saw as a more genuine and natural form of poetic expression than what they now regarded as overly pompous and declamatory French drama. As they turned against French literary influence, German writers and critics were also influenced by British collections of folk songs. In the 1760s, Scottish writer James Macpherson published his translations of Gaelic poems purported to be written by the third-century Celtic hero Ossian. Suspicion arose that Macpherson had at best found only fragments of songs and stories and had fabricated the rest. The debate over the texts' authenticity endured for decades. (Jacob Grimm wrote in defense of Macpherson as late as 1863 and indicated that Wilhelm before his death had planned a book on Ossian.) The Ossianic revival that Macpherson's work spurred influenced several German writers and intellectuals. In 1773, Johann Gottfried Herder published

"Ossian and the Songs of Ancient Peoples," in which the term *Volkslied* (folk song)—adapted from the English "popular song"—appeared for the first time. Herder saw in the folk song the most authentic expression of poetry.[25]

Against this background, the Romantic movement (which began in the late eighteenth century) increasingly turned to the Middle Ages for inspiration. Around the time that Jacob first encountered Bodmer's edition of medieval songs, the Romantic writer Ludwig Tieck published a selection of *Minnelieder* in modernized German. Jacob was captivated by Tieck's depictions of poetry as an unachievable and incomprehensible ideal, which can be only partially glimpsed as we try to comprehend it. In poetry, Tieck posited, past and present continually inform and enhance one another; thus, temporal distance might enable a modern reader to understand ancient texts more deeply, in some ways, than their contemporary authors and readers. To Tieck, this renewal implicitly justified textual modernization.[26]

In a sense, Bodmer's and Tieck's work provided the Grimms with two different models for how to reinvigorate an appreciation of medieval literature. Bodmer had presented texts in their original form but with detailed explanation and analysis, whereas Tieck had chosen to modernize the texts to make them more accessible to a broader audience. In the years and decades ahead, Jacob would prove to be closer to Bodmer than to Tieck in this respect. By contrast, Wilhelm was more open to adaptation in his editing of texts, including the brothers' collected fairy tales. Both were nevertheless profoundly influenced by Savigny's conviction that "all Laws depend more on the ever-changing wants and opinions of those who obey them, than on the mere fiat of any legislator."[27] This emphasis on the role of the people, and not merely the powerful, in shaping law, literature, and language would inform the Grimms' views of themselves as recorders of the folk record, as restorers of folk texts to an allegedly uncorrupted state, and as rejuvenators whose prudent edits enabled readers to appreciate the literary heritage from bygone eras.

During the Grimms' studies in Marburg, Savigny further spurred their appreciation of this heritage by introducing them to the Romantic writer Clemens Brentano. Brentano in turn introduced them to his friend and collaborator Achim von Arnim a few years later. Through their friendship with Brentano and Arnim, the Grimms deepened their interest in Germany's literary and cultural past, particularly as this past manifested itself in folk culture, since Brentano and Arnim saw in folk songs, fairy tales, legends, and related genres a continuation of older German poetry and literary expression. Indeed, Jacob and Wilhelm's friendship and scholarly collaboration with Brentano and Arnim would prove to be the catalyst for what became the fairy tales of the Brothers Grimm.

Originally from Lombardy, Brentano's family had settled in Frankfurt in the seventeenth century, where they engaged in trade. Brentano's grandmother was the celebrated author and salon hostess Sophie von La Roche, in whose home he was born in 1778. After a tumultuous childhood, Brentano went first to Bonn to study minerology, soon left to help with the family trade in Frankfurt, and later studied cameralism and medicine for a time at the universities in Halle and Jena. In Jena, he became acquainted with Romantic writers and intellectuals including Tieck and the brothers August Wilhelm and Friedrich Schlegel. There, too, he met Savigny; their friendship led him to move in fall 1803 from Weimar to Marburg, where Savigny introduced him to the Grimms. Accompanying Brentano was the writer Sophie Mereau, whom he married in November of that year, and her daughter Hulda. Sophie had divorced her first husband, the lawyer Karl Mereau, after the death of their son. During her marriage to Mereau, she had had various affairs, including an on-and-off relationship with Brentano. At the time of Brentano's move to Marburg his sister Kunigunde Brentano (known as "Gunda" or "Gundel") was engaged to Savigny, and they married in 1804.

As for Brentano's friend Arnim, whom the Grimms would meet later, he was born Karl Joachim Friedrich Ludwig von Arnim in 1781 in Berlin into an aristocratic family. His father was director of the Royal Theater; his mother, a baroness, died just weeks after his birth, after which Arnim was raised principally by his grandmother. He studied law at Halle and there also delved into philosophy, mathematics, and science. In Halle, Arnim met Tieck and traveled with him to Leipzig. In 1800, Arnim went with his only brother to Göttingen, where Arnim studied mathematics and met well-known cultural figures including Johann Wolfgang von Goethe. Arnim's friendship with Brentano began there in 1801 and led not only to fruitful literary collaborations but also to Arnim's marriage in 1811 to Brentano's sister Bettina, with whom the Grimms enjoyed a decades-long friendship.

Brentano, inspired by Tieck's adaptations of *Minnelieder*, had hoped to partner with Tieck on a collection of songs, but Tieck proved uninterested in the venture. Separately, Arnim proposed to Brentano that they found an academy with the mission of reconciling high culture and folk art through the teaching of folk forms of music, dance, art, theater, and literature. Such a reconciliation, Arnim believed, was essential if the German-speaking lands were to realize a national German culture and achieve national political con-federation. Arnim also wished to establish a press that would publish folk songs and to set up a network of hostels where members could learn directly from minstrels and street performers. Brentano questioned whether Arnim's socially elevated family would countenance work that strayed so radically from the strictures of high culture; he instead proposed that they collaborate on a collection of poems and songs. Having previously begun to assemble manuscripts for the collaboration he had pitched in vain to Tieck, Brentano already had many songs to contribute. Influenced in part by the fascination of German intellectuals and writers a couple decades earlier with British folk song collections, he and Arnim were convinced that German-language songs, legends, and tales from the Middle Ages to the Baroque demonstrated a "spirit of the people" (*Volksgeist*) that had flourished before the corrupting influence of the Enlightenment and French neoclassicism.[28]

Jacob later recalled sitting in Brentano's green upstairs room in Marburg, listening to him read from his work while Savigny poured red wine into the tea. Accustomed to relative privation, Jacob regarded such interactions as a luxury in which he should not indulge too often, and he felt a strange mix of pleasure and fear whenever he visited Savigny or Brentano. These visits soon ended, however. Brentano and his wife left Marburg in 1804, first traveling to Frankfurt and then living in Heidelberg. There, Brentano and Arnim worked intensively in May and June 1805 on their folk song collection, which they titled *The Boy's Magic Horn*, after the name of the opening song. The first vol-ume was published at the end of 1805 (although its title page listed the year of publication as 1806). In the years ahead, Jacob and Wilhelm would help Arnim and Brentano compile a second and third volume of songs.[29]

Meanwhile, beginning in 1804 Savigny was away from Marburg on ex-tensive travel, researching medieval legal traditions in libraries across the German-speaking lands and in France. These studies would culminate in his multivolume *History of the Roman Law during the Middle Ages* (1815–31). Ja-cob suddenly found himself invited to join Savigny in Paris to assist with this work. The invitation was occasioned in part by scholarly misfortune: Savigny had arrived in Paris with his pregnant wife and her sister in early December 1804 to find that luggage containing papers and manuscripts he had assembled in the preceding months had been stolen from the back of the coach. In vain, he reported the loss to the police and offered monetary rewards for the items' return. To aid him in reconstructing what he described as a thousand notes of importance and to help with his archival research more generally, Savigny called on Jacob to serve as his assistant, offering to pay for his travel and room and board. After seeking permission from his mother and Aunt Zimmer, the twenty-year-old Jacob left Marburg at the end of January and arrived in Paris on February 12, 1805. He never completed formal studies at Marburg, though in Germany at the time attending a university for a year or more was the functional equivalent of obtaining a baccalaureate degree.[30]

Wilhelm felt as if his heart were being torn to pieces upon seeing Jacob depart. The first two decades of their lives had been marked by familial happiness and grief; by their status as academic and socioeconomic underdogs whose persistence and diligence, aided by family and scholarly mentors, helped to fuel their academic success; and by the political uncertainty in the world around them. Although formally students of law, they already felt particularly drawn to languages and literary traditions, their personal study of which progressed rapidly thanks to their quick minds and intense work habits. Their desire to immerse themselves in books at times superseded the need for social interaction, particularly for Jacob. As they increasingly devoted themselves to the study of older languages and texts, they grappled with questions of how to study the past, what traces of earlier eras could be discerned in the present, and how to preserve or reconstruct such vestiges without corrupting them. They had begun, too, to ponder what it meant to be Hessian and German, and which aspects of the texts they studied were unique to a particular locality and which part of a transnational context. These considerations would further shape their scholarly work and cultural outlook in the tumultuous years ahead.[31]

CHAPTER 3

Contributions to Scholarship, 1805–1808

"Last week I slaughtered my pig," Dorothea Grimm wrote matter-of-factly to Jacob, then newly arrived in Paris, on February 24, 1805. "Just think, it weighed 250 pounds, and from it I made really fat salvolat sausages that you shall consume with us in Kassel—God willing that you find me there on your return trip." While Jacob helped Savigny in Paris and Wilhelm continued his studies in Marburg, Dorothea spent spring and summer 1805 preparing to sell her house in Steinau and move to Kassel with Lotte. Steinau had afforded the Grimms happy memories as a family before the death of Philipp Wilhelm; but it was also the place where Dorothea had mourned her husband's passing and despaired over how to provide for her children, for whom the town was simply too small and provincial to offer any long-term opportunities. Her move to Kassel, the city of her birth and upbringing, would be a welcome return for her. "The thought of spending an hour with your dear aunt and having my children with me fills me with an unending joy," she wrote brightly to Jacob.[1]

Such a reunion would have to wait some months, however, since only Ferdinand and Ludwig were in Kassel, studying at the lyceum where Jacob and Wilhelm had been pupils. Whereas Jacob and Wilhelm had been praised for their academic achievements, teachers noted that Ferdinand's and Ludwig's lack of diligence hindered their academic progress. Ferdinand evinced no sustained passion whatsoever and was bluntly described as having limited talents; by contrast, Ludwig's apathy toward schoolwork stemmed from his growing love of drawing and painting. While at the lyceum, he began to receive instruction at the art academy in Kassel. Alone among the Grimm boys, Carl did not attend the lyceum; he apprenticed in Hanau and subsequently worked in Kassel for banker Carl Jordis, the husband of Clemens Brentano's sister Ludovica ("Lulu"). Dorothea and Lotte moved to Kassel in August 1805.[2]

In Paris, Savigny tasked Jacob with comparing manuscript versions of *Corpus iuris* texts. Jacob found the work interesting, insofar as variations among the texts not only yielded penetrating insights into the development of Roman law through the centuries but also informed eighteenth- and early nineteenth-century debates over the origins of certain manuscripts. Jacob also copied passages from the glossators, eleventh- and twelfth-century legal scholars who held that the entire *Corpus iuris* was true and valid despite apparent contradictions; they maintained that these could be resolved through interpretation. Their "glosses" were notes originally written in the margins of *Corpus iuris* texts and later compiled into freestanding editions.[3]

Jacob proved an ideal research assistant to Savigny. Several years after their trip to France, Savigny ended the preface to his *History of the Roman Law during the Middle Ages* with gratitude for Jacob's loyal assistance and for the exactitude and diligence with which his pupil approached archival work. Jacob's mastery of this painstaking research is of manifold importance to his and Wilhelm's subsequent scholarship. Because much of their work on fairy tales and legends involved comparisons of several tellings of the same basic story, Jacob's attentiveness in Paris to deviations among legal texts most certainly benefited him. Jacob was also likely influenced by Savigny's view of the glossators not as cloistered intellectuals divorced from practical affairs but as educated reformers whose achievements, albeit centuries old, were of continued social relevance.[4]

Although Jacob was intellectually engaged in his work in Paris, both he and Savigny disliked the city and longed for Germany. Savigny denigrated Parisians as egotistical and unimaginative, found the city's theatrical productions boring despite their excellent reputation (an assessment Jacob largely shared), and complained that the relentless Parisian dampness was causing his family's perpetual illnesses. With some 160,000 manuscripts, the collection in Paris was tremendous, but Savigny initially found his progress hindered by the lack of a general catalog of these holdings, insufficient opening hours, and even the librarians themselves, whom he derided as lazy, ignorant, and unhelpful. It was nevertheless a momentous time to be in Paris: when Jacob arrived in February 1805, less than three months had passed since Napoleon's coronation as emperor in the cathedral of Notre-Dame.[5]

At the beginning of March, Jacob moved with Savigny's family into a house where Otto von der Malsburg was staying. Jacob's connections with Malsburg, while friendly, had already weakened considerably, and they did not interact much despite their shared address. Malsburg's presence in Paris thus did little to ease Jacob's homesickness; nevertheless, when Malsburg returned to Hessen-Kassel a few weeks later, Jacob lamented his absence. An anxious mood hung over Savigny's family at this time, as Savigny's heavily pregnant wife had been in fragile health. Worried that the birth might not go well for mother or child, Jacob was relieved when a healthy baby girl arrived in April.

Back in Marburg, Wilhelm felt lost without Jacob and Savigny. While Malsburg was still in Paris, Wilhelm penned a letter to him in which he expressed his wish that he could have studied under Savigny for even six months longer, gushing that Savigny was the only person to whom he would entrust his life. "The separation from my brother still pains me so greatly," he further confessed, "that only now do I truly see how isolated I am here." Jacob began to regard his need to live with Wilhelm as an existential matter. "We shall never part from each other," he wrote to Wilhelm about their future professional careers, "and if someone should want one of us to go somewhere else, the other would need to resign at once. We are now so accustomed to each other's companionship that separation could distress me to death." In a subsequent letter, he shared his vision for their future life in Kassel, where "we will presumably at last live quite withdrawn and isolated, for we will not have many friends, and I do not enjoy acquaintances. We shall want to work with each other quite collaboratively and to cut off all other affairs." These declarations are among the most quoted of Jacob's pronouncements to his brother. While they might seem self-absorbed and needy on Jacob's part, they represent the sense of inseparability, common purpose, and scholarly discipline that the brothers shared. To cheer up Jacob and advance their scholarly goals, Wilhelm encouraged him while in Paris to see if the library held works of medieval or early modern German literature that might be unusual or unknown. Jacob took particular joy in consulting the Codex Manesse, from which Bodmer had compiled the edition of medieval German songs that had so mesmerized Jacob at Savigny's home in Marburg.[6]

Because of the movements of Napoleon's forces, Savigny and Jacob had to travel through Metz instead of Strasbourg on their way home. They worked at the library in Trier, among other stops, and arrived in Frankfurt at the end of September 1805. Jacob proceeded to Kassel, where Dorothea Grimm and her children—now ranging in age from twelve to twenty—rented an upper floor of a house in the Marktgasse (Market Alley). Upon arriving at the apartment, Jacob was comforted by the sight of the family clock in the parlor. His mother had gone out to spend the evening with her sister, and Jacob hurried to surprise her on her way.

In December, Ferdinand and Ludwig left the lyceum with plans to serve as copyists. One month later, Jacob became a secretary at the War Board (Kriegscollegium), the government agency charged with administering military justice, recruiting and equipping troops, and providing for soldiers with injuries. Jacob found the work tedious and uninspiring, especially compared to his scholarly work in France. Moreover, now accustomed to Parisian fashions, he hated having to wear a uniform and outmoded powdered pigtail at the War Board. He devoted whatever time he could to furthering his studies of older German literature.

Hessen-Kassel had, at least nominally, achieved greater status as a political entity in the three years Jacob had been away from its capital city. Under pressure from France, in 1803 the Holy Roman Empire underwent mediatization and secularization, whereby the larger, more powerful states subsumed the lesser ones, including free imperial cities and ecclesiastical principalities. Rulers of mediatized or secularized states no longer directly served the Holy Roman Emperor; rather, they were subservient to the ruler who now served as their intermediary in Holy Roman Empire affairs and to whose territory their own now belonged. In contrast to the scores of smaller states that lost their sovereignty, Hessen-Kassel was elevated from a landgraviate to an electorate and became known as the Electorate of Hessen (Kurfürstentum Hessen), or more concisely Electoral Hessen (Kurhessen). It was still often referred to as Hessen-Kassel, or simply Hessen. Landgrave Wilhelm IX of Hessen-Kassel became Wilhelm I, Elector (Kurfürst) of Hessen, and was styled His Royal and Serene Highness.

From the thirteenth century on, electors had served as members of the electoral college of the Holy Roman Empire. Because with only one exception all emperors since the mid-fifteenth century had been Habsburgs, the electors in reality merely ratified the Habsburg succession. The "elector" title had thus long been more formal than functional, but it would soon become even more anachronistic. After Napoleon's victory in the Battle of Austerlitz in early December 1805, the ensuing Peace of Pressburg forced the Habsburg emperor Franz II to sharply reduce his authority in Germany; in 1806 the Holy Roman Empire dissolved when Franz II abdicated his title as Holy Roman Emperor and became Franz I, Emperor of Austria. With the end of the Holy Roman Empire there was no longer an emperor to elect even in a merely formal sense, so the rulers of Bavaria, Saxony, and Württemberg shed their "elector" title and, as a reward for supporting Napoleon, were granted the title of king, while several other electors became grand dukes. Together they formed the Confederation of the Rhine, which Napoleon created in summer 1806. By contrast, upon the fall of the Holy Roman Empire Wilhelm I of Hessen clung to his recently gained elector title even though it was now quite antiquated.[7]

Soon the Hessian elector would find the country he ruled conquered by the French. Napoleon professed a desire to spare the "impoverished land" of Electoral Hessen from war and pretended to respect its neutrality in the War of the Fourth Coalition (1806–7), but at the same time he made preparations to occupy it.[8] Having defeated Prussia in the battles of Auerstädt and Jena on October 14, 1806, French armies invaded Hessen from the south in late October 1806. They took only five days to reach Kassel, during which time their marshal deliberately deceived the Hessians into thinking that the French were merely passing through. So unconcerned were Kassel residents that many gathered early in the streets to seek out the best spots to observe the spectacle of the marching troops, and vendors set up food stands to cater to the growing crowds.[9]

On the evening before the French takeover of Kassel, Wilhelm Grimm had warily observed the French sentry fires off in the distance, but he, too, did not foresee that the next morning French regiments would occupy the city. "Soon everything changed from the ground up," he later wrote. "Foreign people, foreign customs, and in the streets and on walks a foreign, loudly spoken language." When it became clear that French troops were mounting an unprovoked invasion and occupation of Hessen, Elector Wilhelm I fled with the crown prince, eventually choosing Prague as his place of exile while the crown prince settled in Mecklenburg. His estranged wife made Gotha her home in exile (and thus so, too, did the Grimms' aunt Henriette Zimmer, as the electress's first lady-in-waiting). With no hope of resisting the French,

Hessian soldiers were ordered by their superiors to disarm. "The hardest days of my life," Jacob later recounted, "were those on which I witnessed a haughty and jeering enemy take over my fatherland and throw down onto the cobblestones the courageous Hessians' rifles, the proper use of which was not granted them." All of Electoral Hessen was under French control by the end of the first week of November; French martial law was declared, and General Joseph Lagrange served as governor. Napoleon now disingenuously justified the invasion by proclaiming that Electoral Hessen had been operating in service to Prussia, though he knew full well that it had remained neutral in the War of the Fourth Coalition. He also insisted that the Hessians would be happier under French rule.[10]

This was not the case. In the immediate weeks and months after the invasion, Hessians found ample reason to chafe under the French yoke. Napoleon ordered the disarmament of the Hessian people, forced them to bear the costs of quartering French troops who now occupied their land, and conscripted soldiers into newly formed Franco-Hessian regiments. Moreover, they executed over six hundred Hessian civilians during the period of martial law, primarily in response to uprisings among the rural lower classes in late 1806. Kassel saw a steady stream of captured soldiers from various regions, as well as soldiers pressed into service to fight for the French.[11]

By mid-November, the War Board at which Jacob worked had become a commission tasked with provisioning French troops. Jacob complained to Savigny of meetings day and night, clueless functionaries, and the tumult quartered soldiers were causing at the Grimms' apartment. He confessed, too, that the public tragedy unfolding in Hessen was making him bitter, spiteful, and incapable of focusing on his scholarship.[12]

But more upheavals were to come. In 1807, France announced the annexation of Electoral Hessen into the French vassal state designated the Kingdom of Westphalia, which also included conquered Prussian territories west of the Elbe River, the Duchy of Braunschweig (Brunswick), and portions of the Kingdom of Hanover. Jacob lamented the forced substitution of the name "Westphalia" for "Hessen" that made neither geographical nor historical sense: the region known in German as "Westfalen," which lay farther to the west, did not encompass the majority of the nearly two million inhabitants living in the Kingdom of Westphalia's 195 towns and cities and over four thousand villages.[13] Having previously appointed his brother Joseph King of Naples and his brother Louis King of Holland, Napoleon in July 1807 announced that his youngest brother, twenty-two-year-old Jérôme Bonaparte, would serve as Westphalia's king.

Born Girolamo Buonaparte in Corsica on November 15, 1784, Jérôme had as a young man grown accustomed to the life of luxury and indolence afforded him as the brother of Napoleon Bonaparte. By his teens he had already established himself as a womanizer, a role that came naturally to the charming and handsome youth but proved hazardous when a duel with a rival suitor left Jérôme with a bullet wound in his breastbone. He later joined the French navy and sailed to America, where in 1803 he fell in love with and married the daughter of a prominent Maryland family. Outraged at this union, Napoleon refused to allow Jérôme's wife, now pregnant, to enter France, whereupon she traveled to England and there gave birth to a son.

Napoleon in 1806 arranged Jérôme's betrothal to Katharina, the daughter of the king of Württemberg. The ruler of Württemberg had only recently been elevated from elector to king as a reward for his support, and Jérôme's betrothal to the king's daughter further solidified this alliance. Jérôme was still wedded to his American wife when he and Katharina were married in August 1807. Katharina was besotted with her husband, whereas Jérôme treated her with courtesy but found her unattractive and continued his womanizing. Husband and wife arrived in the Kassel area in December 1807 and proceeded first to the great palace, gardens, and water displays of Wilhelmshöhe, which the French had spared no time rechristening "Napoleonshöhe." They had also renamed prominent squares in Kassel, removed a statue of Landgrave Friedrich II and erected an obligatory statue of Napoleon, and substituted a new Westphalian crest for that of Electoral Hessen. Not everything was to Jérôme and Katharina's liking, however: they discovered that both Napoleonshöhe and the palace in the Kassel city center had been thoroughly looted and remained in disrepair.[14]

At the end of 1807, Westphalia received not only its new king but also a constitution. Written by leading French jurists and modeled in part on the constitution that the French had imposed a few months earlier on the Duchy of Warsaw, it was the first written constitution in German history. Napoleon chose to announce it on Jérôme's twenty-third birthday (November 15, 1807) and to have it officially come into force on December 7, to coincide with Jérôme's and Katharina's first visit to Westphalia. The constitution established Westphalia as a member state of the Confederation of the Rhine, proclaimed which territories belonged to Westphalia (soon further augmented by the annexation of Hanover), and divided Westphalia into administrative departments, which, as in France, were named after rivers and mountain ranges.

The constitution was traditional in its proclamation both of Westphalia as a hereditary monarchy within the Bonaparte dynasty and of Jérôme as Westphalia's king, but it also featured many modernizing and emancipatory elements. It introduced new systems for measurements and coinage, and it rescinded the nobility's exemption from taxation and the preferential treatment given to nobles in the allocation of government positions. Most strikingly, it promised freedom of religion (including Jewish emancipation), the abolishment of serfdom, and the equality of all subjects before the law, which it specified would be the Code Napoléon effective January 1, 1808, the same day as Jérôme's official coronation. In a speech that day, the justice minister for the Kingdom of Westphalia described the Code as "the loveliest of gifts, having afforded equity and judiciousness to human beings" and serving as the best guarantee of German property and contracts. In Napoleon's eyes, the constitution and Code would establish Westphalia as a model state and thus engender a loyalty from Westphalian subjects that would serve, he told Jérôme, as a more powerful barrier to Prussia than even the Elbe River (which separated Westphalia from Prussia).[15]

Such loyalty was not forthcoming. The judicial equity promised by the Code's champions was questionable, since in practice the law led principally to the transfer of wealth from aristocrats to the state. In addition, the constitution contained provisions that set the kingdom on a precarious financial path. It laid out the kingdom's war debts, announced that half of the territory's allodial estates were to be surrendered to Napoleon, and directed that Westphalia was to contribute to the Confederation an army of 25,000, with half of the troops provided by France and half by Westphalia but all paid for by the Westphalians.[16]

Jérôme tried in vain to convince Napoleon that Westphalia was suffering financially under the strain of forced war contributions and the effects of Napoleon's Continental System, which blocked British imports. All the while, Jérôme's own lavish spending only exacerbated the kingdom's financial woes. He had no previous administrative experience and was clearly in over his head. To his subjects, he was a man solely interested in parties, music, and theater. However, those who met him found him affable and well-intentioned. Although untrue, rumors that he bathed daily in red wine furthered his reputation for self-indulgence and underscored his foreignness in a region accustomed to white wine. Whereas Jérôme's brother Louis enjoyed some measure of popularity among the Dutch, Jérôme was regarded as too impetuous, self-indulgent, vacuous, and dismissive of German culture to endear himself to his subjects. To the Hessians, he was officially "Hieronymus," the Latin form of Jérôme commonly used in Germany, but he soon received a less exalted moniker. Ignoring his advisers' pleas that he study the language of his subjects, Jérôme never learned more than a few words of German. His repetition of three of these words—*morgen wieder lustig* (tomorrow jolly again)—strung together into an awkward catchphrase, captured his cheerful disposition but lack of depth and led to the derisive nickname "König Lustik" (King Jolly), the *k* reflecting his French pronunciation of *lustig*.[17]

Remarkably, it was this man to whom the studious and introspective Jacob would later serve as personal librarian, but only after Jacob experienced substantial personal and professional upheavals. Already in January 1807 he confided in Savigny that he wished to devote himself to scholarship, acknowledging, however, that he could not possibly leave his employment at the commission amid the turmoil and uncertainty of the French occupation; in March, he further confessed to Savigny that he had some time ago decided to give up his studies of jurisprudence. Jacob had come to prefer language and literature as a student in Marburg before the French occupation; as he reflected later in life, the introduction of the Code Napoléon made much of his legal training obsolete and thus further spurred him to pursue these scholarly interests.[18]

Jacob's inaugural publication—an essay titled "On the *Nibelungenlied*" ("Über das Nibelungen Liet [*sic*]")—appeared in April 1807 and began his decades-long engagement with the *Nibelungenlied* (*Song of the Nibelungs*), the Germanic epic written anonymously around 1200 that had been rediscovered by eighteenth-century scholars. The *Nibelungenlied* is known today primarily through Richard Wagner's *The Ring of the Nibelung*, but Wagner's operatic cycle is based largely not on the *Nibelungenlied* itself but on Old Norse sources.

The plot of the *Nibelungenlied* is as follows: Siegfried, son of a king whose court is at Xanten on the Lower Rhine, arrives at the court of the Burgundians in Worms on the Upper Rhine, with the goal of winning as his bride Kriemhild, sister of the Burgundian king Gunther. Gunther's vassal Hagen recognizes Siegfried as the man who received the sword Balmung from two brothers. Siegfried was to divide for the brothers the treasure previously owned by their father, Nibelung. Hagen recounts how Siegfried won the treasure and killed the brothers in an altercation, forced the dwarf Alberich to guard the treasure, and then stole from Alberich a cloak that confers invisibility on its wearer. Siegfried then slew a dragon and bathed in its blood, which made him invincible save for (as Hagen later learns) a small patch of skin on which a leaf had fallen.

Siegfried travels with Gunther to Iceland, where he helps Gunther win the fierce Icelandic queen Brunhild as his bride by pretending to be Gunther's bondsman and performing tasks for him, but in Worms the recalcitrant Brunhild ties Gunther up and hangs him on a nail on their wedding night. Siegfried again assists Gunther by subduing Brunhild. Donning his cloak of invisibility and pretending to be Gunther, Siegfried steals Brunhild's ring and belt and later reveals this to Kriemhild, whom he has married. Years later, the two women quarrel, whereupon Kriemhild produces the ring and belt and calls Brunhild Siegfried's concubine. When Brunhild demands vengeance for this insult, Hagen cunningly kills Siegfried during a hunt by hurling a javelin between his shoulders on the vulnerable spot where the leaf had fallen. The treasure of the Nibelungs is sunk in the Rhine. Kriemhild later marries Etzel, king of the Huns, and avenges Siegfried's murder by inviting the Burgundians to his court. In the bloodbath that follows, she and the Burgundians perish.

Jacob saw in these characters and events a national epic without parallel in modern literature, and he regarded the *Nibelungenlied* as proof that a German literature had blossomed before the influence and imitation of French chivalric poetry. The importance of such views at a time of French occupation cannot be underestimated. During the Napoleonic period, interest in the *Nibelungenlied* and other older German literature and folklore increased greatly among the wider populace. As the writer Henriette Herz recounted in her memoirs, for example, Berliners eschewed French literature in the winter of 1807–8 in favor of Germanic legends and epics; even the educated classes, who would typically disdain the puppet theater, flocked there when performances based on these works were staged.[19]

At the time of Jacob's essay, over fifty years had passed since a manuscript of the *Nibelungenlied* had been found in a library in Austria. Although knowledge of the Nibelungen stories had survived through the centuries, the *Nibelungenlied* itself had fallen into obscurity. Interest in the epic had grown in the second half of the eighteenth century, with scholars regarding it as the German equivalent of the *Iliad* and the product of an entire epoch's collective genius. In his essay, Jacob delved into intellectual debates concerning the authorship of the *Nibelungenlied* and the dating of various extant manuscript versions. Like many of his contemporaries, he believed that whoever authored or compiled the *Nibelungenlied* could not be known; he insisted that this was usually the case with national poetry, because it more rightly belongs to and issues from the people of a nation. Drawing, perhaps, on the skills he had honed while comparing manuscript versions of the *Corpus iuris* texts in Paris, he pointed out that scholars too frequently focused on what they regarded as the oldest known manuscript instead of acknowledging that subsequent variants can facilitate our understanding of how the same literary work is modified over time. Because in Jacob's view the extant manuscripts were written in a language that modern Germans could understand without too much effort, he felt that the *Nibelungenlied* needed only critical commentary, not linguistic modernization.[20]

Jacob's other early published work included essays on German lyric poetry from the twelfth to sixteenth centuries and the characteristics of epic poetry. In view of his growing scholarly work and aspirations, in summer 1807 he asked to be relieved of his duties at the commission overseeing provisions for French troops and that fall he formally resigned. For several months in 1807 and 1808, he did not know how he would provide for his mother and siblings. Noting his need to provide for his family and listing as qualifications his studies in Marburg, archival experience in Paris, and command of several languages, he unsuccessfully requested a position as librarian in December 1807. Wilhelm, too, was unemployed and remained so until 1814. Unlike Jacob, who had left Marburg without formally completing his studies, Wilhelm had taken his university examinations in May 1806. He subsequently asserted that he likely would have obtained a government position had the French not occupied Hessen.[21]

Both Jacob and Wilhelm later cited the occupation as a turning point in their professional lives. Amid so much uncertainty, they pursued their burgeoning interests in language, literature, and folk culture in part by contributing to the folk song project on which Clemens Brentano and Achim von Arnim had embarked. Having published the first volume of *The Boy's Magic Horn* at the end of 1805, Brentano and Arnim were now at work on second and third installments and had enlisted the Grimms' help.

On October 19, 1807, Brentano sanguinely wrote to Arnim that the additional volumes would proceed more rapidly than work on the first volume had in Heidelberg "because here I have two very dear, dear friends named Grimm who are well-versed in things old German and whom I some time ago interested in older poetry." For Brentano, Arnim, and the Grimms, the designation "old German" (*altdeutsch*) encompassed not only medieval and early modern German literature, language, and culture but also more recent folk literature, since they saw in it a continuation of older German poetry and literary expression. Brentano expressed astonishment over how many works of older German literature the Grimms had grown familiar with in the two years since he had last seen them. He was all the more impressed and humbled by their knowledge since poverty often forced them to hand-copy manuscripts and books instead of buying them.[22]

Toward the end of 1807, Arnim met the Grimms in person when he traveled to Kassel with Clemens Brentano, Brentano's sisters Bettina and Meline, Savigny and his wife Gunda (who was also Clemens's sister), and the composer Johann Friedrich Reichardt. Several members of this party continued on to the Savigny family estate near Hanau, but Arnim and Brentano stayed in Kassel to work on *The Boy's Magic Horn*. Arnim soon described Jacob in terms similar to those Brentano had used: "There is here a very learned scholar

Clemens Brentano and Achim von Arnim. Woodcut by Hugo Kaeseberg based on a drawing by Hans Speckter and a portrait of Arnim by Peter Eduard Ströhling. In Theodor Storm, ed., *Hausbuch aus deutschen Dichtern seit Claudius: Eine kritische Anthologie* (Leipzig: Wilhelm Mauke, 1875), 81. Courtesy of University of Illinois Library Special Collections.

of German language and literature, *Herr* War Secretary Grimm, who has the most complete collection of older poetry," he wrote to Ludwig Tieck. As such pronouncements indicate, the Grimms' lifelong love of collecting books and manuscripts and their practice of copying texts in whole or in part by hand was evident already at this early stage of their scholarly development.[23]

The Grimms quickly became friends with Arnim. Due in part to similarities in outlook and disposition, this bond proved more solid and lasting than their relationship with Brentano. Although Arnim hailed from an aristocratic family, he found luxury and privilege unattractive. The grandmother who raised him had instilled in him a devotion to thrift, earnestness, and hard work. Brentano's sister Bettina described the stark differences in appearance between Arnim and Brentano: whereas Brentano was elegantly dressed, one of Arnim's armhole seams was coming unstitched and the lining of his cap was frayed. Shabby clothing aside, he impressed everyone with his tall, handsome appearance, exuding a sense of stability, confidence, cheerfulness, and trust so unlike Brentano's tendency toward moodiness, impulsiveness, and despondency.

Brentano had experienced considerable tragedy in the years since the Grimms first met him in Marburg. His wife, Sophie, died giving birth to a stillborn child in 1806, after which he too hastily married seventeen-year-old Auguste Busmann in 1807 and moved with her to Kassel, where his sister Lulu and brother-in-law Carl Jordis, now banker for the Westphalian court, were living. The Grimms did not care for the pomp on display at Jordis's home or for the French officers who socialized there. Brentano's marriage to Auguste rapidly soured, and he often sought diversion at the Grimms' home, which further expedited work on *The Boy's Magic Horn.*

The Grimms graciously offered to share all the songs in their possession with Arnim and Brentano. Many were mere fragments, but Jacob hoped that Arnim and Brentano might come across other texts that would enable them to be made whole, like pieces of a jigsaw puzzle. The Grimms' siblings also contributed to the endeavor: Ferdinand served as copyist, and Ludwig, whose artistic abilities continued to grow, completed the frontispieces for volume 3 and the children's songs appended to that volume. Even Wilhelm contributed to the collection's illustrations by drawing the frontispiece for the second volume, the idea for which came from Brentano. The drawing combined elements of seventeenth-century engravings to depict the famous drinking horn of the northwestern city of Oldenburg, but instead of Oldenburg it was the southern city of Heidelberg (with the imposing hilltop ruins of its castle) that

Ludwig Emil Grimm, self-portrait
(1815). Illustration based on the
etching by Ludwig Emil Grimm,
in L. E. Grimm, *Erinnerungen
aus meinem Leben,* ed. Adolf Stoll
(Leipzig: Hesse & Becker Verlag,
1913), n.p. Collection of the author.

was depicted in the background. Wilhelm's finished drawing was engraved
by Adam Weise, an artist in Heidelberg under whom Ludwig Grimm would
soon study with the support of Arnim and Brentano, who provided for his
lodging there.[24]

The substitution of Heidelberg for Oldenburg was a tribute to the city in
which Arnim and Brentano had collected many of their songs and published
The Boy's Magic Horn, and it is no surprise that Ludwig traveled there to
pursue his artistic aspirations. This famed university city on the banks of the
Neckar River was a source of immeasurable inspiration to nineteenth-century
writers and artists. In *Jane Eyre,* for example, Charlotte Brontë described her
heroine tracing, in the embers of a fireplace, "a view, not unlike a picture I
remembered to have seen of the castle of Heidelberg." Arnim described the
city in idyllic terms, noting that he and Brentano had during one stay lodged
near the castle in a beer pub, from which they delighted in hearing the songs
of washerwomen and, in the distance, the soothing flow of the Neckar.[25]

Although not a formal movement, Arnim and Brentano's literary efforts
and approach later became known as "Heidelberg Romanticism"; figures such
as the writer and political journalist Joseph Görres and eventually the Grimms,
too, became associated with the term, although the Grimms spent little time

in Heidelberg itself. Less theoretical than the early phase of Romanticism whose center had been the city of Jena, Heidelberg Romanticism focused on uncovering the Germanic past and the folk literature it had produced—a corpus that had endured, in their view, despite the encroachment of high culture. Whereas an individual, subjective worldview permeated the creativity of early Romanticism, the Heidelberg Romantics celebrated folk and heroic literature because they saw in it the collective experience of a people. Although not a mere reaction against French domination and occupation, Heidelberg Romanticism was in any case profoundly shaped by this experience. Heavily damaged by French forces in the 1690s, the ruined Heidelberg castle served as a symbol to the Heidelberg Romantics of the need to assert German identity against French hegemony. The promulgation of folk culture and older works of literature that captured the collective experience of a people in some respects conveyed a belief that thwarting the individual genius of Napoleon would require the collective efforts of the German people.[26]

Joseph Görres's experience and early writings shed light on the development of this belief. Through his collaborations with Arnim and Brentano, Görres became a long-standing friend of the Grimms. He was born in 1776 in Koblenz, the son of a wood merchant. As a young man, he enthusiastically supported the republican ideals of the French Revolution and even hoped for the annexation of the Rhineland into the French Republic. He saw no contradiction between cosmopolitan republicanism and pride in German identity, but he soon became disillusioned with France and the Revolution and found living in French-occupied Koblenz unbearable. His disgust with Napoleon further fueled his interest in German nationalism, and his interactions with Arnim and Brentano in the early years of the nineteenth century spurred his interest in German folk traditions and medieval literature. He not only was a prolific journalist but also published an edition of German popular tales, or "folk books" (*Volksbücher*).

The early awakenings of Heidelberg Romanticism are inseparable from both Arnim and Brentano's folk song project and this project's catalytic effect on the Grimms' future collections. Already while compiling the first volume of *The Boy's Magic Horn*, Arnim and Brentano had themselves planned to augment their folk song collection with fairy tales and legends. Instead of adding these to the song collection itself, however, they ended up addressing these genres principally in contributions to journals. For example, Arnim's *Journal for Hermits* included Romantic artist Philipp Otto Runge's retelling, in Hamburg dialect, of the grisly fairy tale "The Juniper Tree," in which a stepmother murders her stepson, makes her daughter believe that the daughter had accidentally killed him, and feeds the son's flesh to her unknowing husband in a meal. The boy is reborn as a bird, sings of his stepmother's treachery, kills her by dropping a millstone around her neck, and is transformed back into a boy. As for Brentano, his essay on the seventeenth-century statesman and satirist Johann Michael Moscherosch in the *Baden Weekly* contained a version of a tale about a bird, mouse, and sausage who set up house together and live harmoniously only as long as they follow roles appropriate to their respective traits and strengths. These and other texts fueled the Grimms' enthusiasm for collecting and studying folk narratives.

The Grimms' sources and inspiration as they began to collect fairy tales included not only seventeenth-century written texts that afforded them insights into German culture and customs during and after the Thirty Years' War, but also tales imparted to them by several women they knew. These informants—a term in folklore studies used to describe persons interviewed by the folklorist—then included Marie Hassenpflug, daughter of government official Johannes Hassenpflug; pharmacist's daughter Gretchen Wild and her mother, Dorothea; and Friederike Mannel, a pastor's daughter who also contributed several songs to *The Boy's Magic Horn* and to whom Brentano introduced Wilhelm in September 1808. As would largely be the case over the coming years, these early Grimm informants were literate, middle-class, young adult townspeople, and thus they did not conform to the prevalent image of the storyteller as an uneducated, older peasant woman from the countryside. As for the stories the Grimms collected and later published, not all were what one might conventionally regard as fairy tales (if by fairy tales we mean a tale that contains enchantment in some form, often portrays a magical helper figure or villain, and focuses on the fortunes and misfortunes of a hero or heroine before typically culminating in a happy ending). The Grimms were collecting *Märchen* (the diminutive form of *Mär*, a narrative in prose or verse), which in its specific use is equivalent to the English "fairy tale" but can also refer more broadly to popular stories including fables, animal tales, and other folktale genres.[27]

In spring 1808, Jacob sent several tales he had collected to Savigny for his toddler daughter Bettina. These included "Snow White" and a variant of "Rumpelstiltskin" called "Rumpenstünzchen." A comparison of these early manuscript versions to the tales as later presented in various editions of the Grimms' *Children's and Household Tales* yields striking differences: for example, whereas in the published version of "Rumpelstiltskin" the miller falsely boasts that his daughter can spin flax into gold and she is magically helped by Rumpelstiltskin in fulfilling this task, "Rumpenstünzchen" begins with a maiden who is asked to spin flax into regular yarn but who despairs when her spinning produces only gold. Her sadness over not being able to spin actual yarn may suggest the high value given in preindustrial times to a woman's ability to spin, since this skill is prized more highly in "Rumpenstünzchen" than gold itself. But the Grimms also later suggested the possibility that spinning gold in "Rumpelstiltskin" and variants such as "Rumpenstünzchen" may have referred to the arduous task, typically given to women, of spinning metallic thread.[28]

The tales as presented in the manuscript sent to Savigny are also more like sketches than fully developed stories. Instead of trying to remedy deficient narration in the tales he sent, Jacob merely provided commentary, such as noting to Savigny that the beginning of such stories was often their strongest part, since storytellers tended to remember the beginning more precisely than other parts. In this way, the tales he sent served the dual purpose of engaging Savigny's interest as a scholar and entertaining his young children. This twofold aim would continue to be evident as Jacob and Wilhelm published tales in the years ahead. From the beginning of their collecting, the Grimms were expressly interested in tales deriving from the oral tradition, even though many of these were no longer retained in the memories of storytellers but had survived through the decades or centuries only because they had been written down at some point (and, in turn, these written-down versions at times further influenced subsequent oral tellings). The Grimms were not interested in polishing material mined from the oral tradition into stylized literary creations of their own making. They aspired to be scholars and editors, not authors of fictional works.[29]

But the Grimms had not yet truly emerged as scholars in their own right. Instead, they were still principally assisting with their friends' scholarly endeavors. Jacob had served as research assistant to Savigny in Paris, and both he and Wilhelm were sharing folk songs from their growing library of books, manuscripts, and notes with Arnim and Brentano. Four years would pass between Jacob's sending of tales to Savigny and the appearance of the first volume of the Grimms' collection. During this period, the Grimms would collect numerous other tales, refine their view of the origins and evolution of folk culture, deepen their knowledge of medieval literature, and cope with further familial crises and political upheavals.

CHAPTER 4

❦

Wilhelm's Journey, 1809

On May 27, 1808, the Grimms' mother died at the age of fifty-two from a sudden respiratory illness. The weekend before her death, she had experienced a severe headache, side aches, and shortness of breath, for which the family doctor prescribed bloodletting and a chest poultice. By midweek her condition appeared better, but then her breathing grew labored and she became weak. Leeches were applied and medicines administered. On the night of Dorothea's death the Grimm siblings served her coffee and wine, attempted to warm her cold hands, and gathered together around her bed. In letters to their aunt Henriette Zimmer, Jacob and Wilhelm portrayed their mother as knowing she was near death, trying to speak with them as much as she could, and retaining consciousness until just before she drew her last breath. But she had also hallucinated as she lay dying, envisioning that the French had lost the war and the triumphant Hessians were ascending to the heavens on a cloud.[1]

The Grimm siblings had lived in Kassel with their mother for not even three years, and twelve years earlier they had mourned the death of their father. At the time of her passing, Jacob was twenty-three and Wilhelm twenty-two. Lotte, the youngest, had celebrated her fifteenth birthday just two and a half weeks earlier. Aunt Zimmer wrote from Gotha (where she resided with the Hessian electress during the French occupation) to encourage Lotte to accept the loss of her mother as God's will. She insisted that God would stand by Lotte if she proved diligent, orderly, and a support to her brothers, and instructed her to dedicate herself to cooking, sewing, and other housekeeping skills. Such counsel from a benevolent older woman to a younger female would be right at home in the fairy tales the Grimms later published, and indeed Aunt Zimmer more than ever became a sort of fairy godmother to the parentless Grimm siblings.[2]

The emotional impacts of their mother's death were acute. For weeks, nightmares disrupted Wilhelm's sleep, although with time these softened into recurring dreams in which, even twenty years later, she reached out to him with a gaunt yet tender hand and inquired why he had been absent from her company for so long. Newly arrived in Heidelberg to study under engraver Adam Weise, Ludwig felt extreme homesickness as he grieved the loss of his mother. Before departing Kassel, Ludwig had begun to make drawings and etchings of the Grimm family, and his drawing of his mother—completed just days before her death—captured what Jacob described as her self-sacrificing devotion to her children and the withdrawn nature that each Grimm sibling to some extent shared. Jacob lamented that she had died without seeing even one of her six children in a proper career, for it was a couple months later—in early July 1808—that he received the position of librarian to King Jérôme.[3]

Dorothea Grimm (1808).
Drawing by Ludwig Emil Grimm.
HGV-B0000.5744, Städtische
Museen Hanau.

Jérôme was just a year older than Jacob, but their closeness in age could not bridge the immense differences in their characters and stations. The intellectual and unsocial Jacob was the eldest in his family and now responsible for providing for his parentless brothers and sister; the party-loving and self-indulgent Jérôme was the youngest Bonaparte sibling and used to being luxuriously provided for. Added to such differences, of course, was the fact that Jacob was endeavoring to promote German cultural self-confidence through his scholarship while directly employed by the French occupier (and at the same time, too, that their aunt continued to serve as lady-in-waiting to the exiled electress). Despite such incongruities, Jacob found Jérôme's demeanor toward him friendly and decent. Jérôme, too, must have found Jacob's performance impressive, for in February 1809 he added to Jacob's duties the position of auditor of the state council. Jacob soon realized that his attendance at state council sessions was necessary only if Jérôme himself was presiding, which was rare due to the king's frequent and extended travels. When in residence, Jérôme seldom requested books from the library. As a result, Jacob spent only a few hours each day in the library or attending cabinet meetings. Because Wilhelm remained unemployed, both brothers were able to devote themselves principally to studying older German literature and developing scholarly works for publication.

In their published works from around this time, Jacob and Wilhelm set forth their notion of the differences between what they and their contemporaries termed "natural poetry" (*Naturpoesie*) and "artistic poetry" (*Kunstpoesie*), with poetry here used in an expansive sense to encompass various literary genres. The Grimms designated epic literature such as the *Nibelungenlied* as "natural," since in their conception the deeds and histories presented in epics resonated organically through an entire people as a collective good. They included in natural poetry genres such as folk songs, legends, and fairy tales that were grounded in a tradition of oral recitation and had, in their view, descended from the epic tradition. In contrast to natural poetry, artistic poetry expressed the unique viewpoint and experience of a single person. In an essay published in 1808, Jacob claimed that this uniqueness meant that artistic poetry could not resonate as widely through the collective experience of a people as could natural poetry. Whereas he saw in natural poetry purity, innocence, and collective experience, he associated artistic poetry with cultivation, education, refinement, and subjectivity.[4]

Jacob further argued that a split had occurred in more recent times when the educated classes began to neglect the stories of the common people. Folk songs, legends, and national epics had continued among the people, albeit in constricted circumstances and without defense against the inevitable influence of the cultivated classes. The same basic folk narrative might be told and retold in various locations and times and with different names, but it nevertheless retained its essence. The proliferation of these variants might impede our ability to determine the precise origin of a specific tale, but to the Grimms this was offset by the joy of finding ever older traces of the narrative.

Jacob extolled ancient literature's depiction of a deeper truth beyond that recorded in certificates, diplomas, and chronicles. Whatever might be regarded as factually untrue in epics merely presented, in his estimation, ancient peoples' views of nature's wonders; thus he insisted that truths about the natural world could be discerned even in fanciful depictions of spirits, dwarfs, and magic. He likened epic poetry to green wood, fresh water, and pure tone, in contrast to the dryness, tepidity, and cacophony of recent history, in which political artifice and machinations reigned instead of what he termed the free battles of ancient peoples.

Wilhelm expressed similarly idealized views in an essay published in 1808 on the origins of medieval German literature and its relationship with Nordic literature and culture. He suggested that nothing could be more charming than the image of a medieval city, whose walls safeguarded art-adorned churches and public buildings, verdant squares, and beautifully dressed citizens proud of their freedoms, generous in their gift-giving, honorable and upright in their familial relations, worshipful of God, and industrious and lively whether engaged in joyful dance and play or in preparations for war. The almost childish sentimentalism of these and other pronouncements stood in sharp contrast to the Grimms' view of modern society as beset by ills on a scale not experienced in medieval times.[5]

Indeed, the Grimms' conception of natural poetry reveals both their idealization of past epochs and biases against their own age, sentiments undoubtedly influenced by the political upheavals of their time, their personal losses, and the rural upbringing that led in part to their defense of those lacking formal education against the disdain of the learned. As Wilhelm later attested, the Grimms' eagerness to study and transmit older German literature was heightened by the political events unfolding around them. Britain and Sweden had remained at war with France, and Austria and Britain had formed the Fifth Coalition in 1809. These and related events were not faraway abstractions but seeped into daily life. During a stay in Halle in May 1809, Wilhelm witnessed a squadron of Prussian hussars passing through as part of Prussian major Ferdinand von Schill's revolt against Napoleonic forces; weeks later, Schill was killed at Stralsund and his corpse decapitated. Still in Halle at the end of July, Wilhelm also saw the march through the city of the Black Brunswickers, a volunteer corps led by the Duke of Braunschweig-Wolfenbüttel in opposition to the Napoleonic occupation, and he found the skull-and-crossbones badges on their caps arresting. Upon witnessing captured peasants being led through Kassel on a wagon after an uprising in April 1809, Jacob felt heartbroken that Germans in French service were capturing fellow Germans.[6]

The Grimms not only sought refuge in their scholarship amid the French occupation, but also hoped their work on older literature would aid in the transition to a better time. Their intellectual outlook was shaped by contemporaries like Johann Gottlieb Fichte, who in 1807 and 1808 had delivered his *Addresses to the German Nation* as a series of lectures in Berlin. In the *Addresses*, Fichte had characterized shared language, not arbitrarily drawn political borders, as constituting the natural or inner frontiers of a state. In a letter to Wilhelm in Halle, Jacob expressed his wish that the scholarly *Addresses* could also be issued in a popularly accessible format so that everyone could read and profit from them.[7]

Wilhelm had traveled to Halle in 1809 to receive treatment for his fragile health, which had worsened in 1808. He now suffered not only from the asthma that had plagued him at the lyceum but also from a heart ailment assumed today to be paroxysmal tachycardia. His heartbeat would suddenly accelerate to two to three times its normal rate; this racing pulse would last from a few minutes to several hours and leave him exhausted and lightheaded. He also experienced frightening chest pains that he described as like having fiery arrows pierce his heart. These episodes, and the anxiety they provoked, took an extreme toll on his mood and his scholarly pursuits. A few weeks before departing Kassel for Halle, he told Savigny that "the influence of the body on the soul" was preventing him from working as he wished he could, and "despite my best intentions and my very cheerful nature, it is nevertheless at times difficult for me to overcome a certain despondency."[8]

Wilhelm's traveling companions to Halle in 1809 were family members of the musician Johann Friedrich Reichardt, who was known for having set to music numerous poems by Goethe. As a young man, Reichardt had been music director to the Prussian court until his sympathy for the French Revolution led to his dismissal. He then oversaw the salt mines near Halle before briefly holding a musical post in Kassel. His house and gardens in Giebichenstein near Halle served as a gathering place for artists, poets, and intellectuals.

En route to Halle Wilhelm stopped briefly in Gotha. He surprised Aunt Zimmer in bed at six o'clock in the morning and spent an hour catching up with her on political events before traveling on.

The city of Halle had been part of the Duchy of Magdeburg until the French dissolved the duchy in 1807, and in 1815 it would become part of the Prussian province of Saxony. In Halle, Wilhelm spent several months in the spring and summer of 1809 under the care of Johann Christian Reil, a professor of medicine at the University of Halle and the city's official physician. Reil first prescribed an elaborate daily regimen of salves, pills, and powders, including medication given to Wilhelm by Johann Wilhelm Heinrich Conradi, his doctor in Marburg. Wilhelm described this program as follows in a letter to Jacob in May 1809:

> When I get up in the morning, I rub my throat at half past seven with a mercury salve, and after that I wash my chest with spirits. At nine o'clock I take an extremely abhorrent powder that I receive each month when the moon is waning. Because it makes me feel so awful, I take a bitter essence half an hour later to restore my stomach and appetite, then at eleven o'clock Conradi's pills, and from twelve to two o'clock I wash my chest again and take the pills and essence, which this time makes me quiver with such a strong hunger, though my hunger is satisfied after eating just a little. At four o'clock, pills and chest washing, and then pills and chest washing again before bed. This medical treatment costs me a lot, twenty to thirty talers already, because the spirits are so expensive and a prescription often comes to a half Louis d'or.[9]

In other letters to Jacob, Wilhelm described the magnet, bath, and electric shock therapies Reil prescribed. He reported experiencing strange effects upon first wearing a magnet, which was sewn into a black band and placed over his heart: he had a metallic taste in his mouth, his heartbeat grew irregular, and he felt sweaty, dizzy, and nauseous. He also told of sitting halfway in hot water while holding a very cold sponge over his heart, a treatment intended to change the direction of his bloodstream. In a modification of this treatment, Reil at one point tried to activate a rash on Wilhelm's body with iron and brine baths before the application of the cold sponge. As for electric shock treatment, Wilhelm initially sat halfway submerged in water while wearing a chain around his neck through which shocks were administered, but later in his treatment he would first bathe and then receive shock therapy. "A splendid large machine made of mahogany wood is turned, and I must sit on a cutty stool atop a table with glass legs, and I am then attached to the machine with chains and the electricity streams through me," he explained to Jacob. He complained that this treatment made his skin blister, but he tolerated it better than some of the other patients. In a detail revealing anti-Semitic prejudice, he noted that two Jewish patients screamed and jerked terribly as the electric current streamed through their bodies.[10]

Regardless of how pseudoscientific, ineffective, and even risky these various treatments now appear, Reil was no quack doctor. He was a leading internist and physiologist recognized today as one of the founders of the field of neurology and the originator of the term "psychiatry." Early in his career he had espoused a materialistic and mechanistic conception of physiological processes, arguing that digestion and reproduction, for example, are functions only of the basic chemical structure and makeup of the body. By the time he was treating Wilhelm in Halle, his views had shifted to a Romantic conception that emphasized the body's striving for the ideal in its individual form and as part of the universal organism that is nature. Bizarre as they might seem by modern standards, the various treatments Wilhelm underwent in Halle were in keeping with this Romantic conception of physiology and medicine, which preferred an organic restoration of the body's equilibrium with internal and external forces to mechanical or surgical intervention into the body.[11]

As described by Wilhelm, Reil possessed a penetrating intellect and uncanny depth of speculation. His speech was clear and measured yet his voice mild and friendly as he spoke of various physiological concepts, such as what Wilhelm described as a "terrible and brazen" stasis that Reil had detected in certain physiological processes around midnight. "I had a strange experience when he placed one of his hands on my bare chest and his other hand on my back," Wilhelm also related. As Reil pressed ever so slightly on Wilhelm's chest after detecting his heartbeat, Wilhelm was so overcome with fear and unable to stand the experience that Reil himself was surprised. Wilhelm's description is thoroughly Romantic in its invocation of the alleged stasis of certain physiological processes around midnight, the terror that he felt when Reil applied the slightest pressure to his chest, and Reil's extraordinary perspicacity. He found in Reil an odd and even fantastical person, and in his portrayals Reil appears similar to the magical helper figures in the fairy tales that the Grimms would later publish.[12]

But there was no cure, magical or medical, for Wilhelm's heart troubles. Hypothesizing that glandular issues in Wilhelm's throat were a secondary cause of his heart ailment, Reil told Wilhelm that while these could be treated, the heart trouble itself would never be cured. Wilhelm in any case continued to report in late summer 1809 that Reil's treatment, however unpleasant, seemed to be helping. For the first time in two years, he found that he could fall asleep quickly and calmly, whereas at home he had gone to bed "as if going to torture, where in the silence and the long wakefulness I would feel the strange coursings of my blood and fear for my heart," he wrote Jacob. He told Savigny of his happiness at being able to sleep without nightmares now that his heart trouble had somewhat subsided: "I feel of course that I cannot fully be helped, and that I must die of it," he acknowledged, proceeding to add (with words that can be read literally and metaphorically) that he was "thankful to God with all my heart" for the improvement in his condition. And in a letter to Brentano, he shared his relief at no longer suffering from a recurring nightmare in which he beheld his heart, burst open and with blood spurting out, lying before him outside his body.[13]

Wilhelm's tendency toward active dreams nevertheless continued with respect to other troubles. On the anniversary of his mother's death he had two dreams, one of her and one of Jacob. In the latter, Wilhelm confusedly made his way through several rooms, taking items out of cupboards and cabinets as if he were packing for travel. A stranger whose hands Wilhelm felt too afraid to touch helped him organize these items. Suddenly, Wilhelm found himself journeying high up a mountain that reminded him of the Gotthard in Switzerland, and he recalled that the corpses of people who had frozen to death on the alpine pass were temporarily put in a fenced enclosure there. In his dream, Jacob sat in such an enclosure, peering at Wilhelm with bloodred eyes, telling him in a weak voice that he had been frozen for two days and scolding him for not having come sooner to save him.[14] This nightmare, which Wilhelm shared with Jacob in a letter, captured the guilt he felt over their separation and his knowledge that Jacob's interactions with brothers Carl and Ferdinand were proving difficult, since neither seemed to have any direction in life. Ludwig alone among their brothers did not cause them worry. He, too, had been adrift before discovering his passion for art, but he now seemed well-situated. With financial and logistical assistance from Savigny, Brentano, and Brentano's sister Bettina, he had moved from Heidelberg to Landshut and begun to study at the art academy in nearby Munich.

Wilhelm also knew that the costs of his room, board, and medical treatments in Halle placed a significant financial burden on the family. After only a few months as librarian, Jacob's salary of 2,000 francs had increased to 3,000, and he received another raise in February 1809 when Jérôme appointed him auditor of the state council. The Grimm family finances remained tight, however, because the pension Dorothea had received ceased with her death, Wilhelm remained unemployed, and the economic situation in Westphalia led to widespread hardship. The Grimm siblings often rationed their food, at times sharing portions among themselves, skipping meals, going without wine, and cutting out evening tea when the price of sugar rose too high. Their letters to Aunt Zimmer, who continued to help them financially, detail these and other budget-cutting efforts and speak of the effects of Westphalian inflation and taxation on their household.[15]

Besides straining finances, Wilhelm's stay in Halle took a psychological toll on the brothers. The two were so accustomed to each other's presence that, when apart, even their experience of physical spaces proved disorienting. Wilhelm found himself imagining another chair in his room in Halle, with Jacob sitting in it and conversing with him. In the evenings he closed his eyes and envisioned every detail of their study at home, including Jacob poring over their books. For Jacob, too, working beside Wilhelm's empty desk was unsettling, and his usual productivity slowed. Even Kassel itself seemed foreign to him in Wilhelm's absence. Jacob now felt at home in the city only because their mother was buried there; he yearned to move to a small town of two to three thousand inhabitants where he and Wilhelm might enjoy a lower cost of living and devote themselves to their studies.[16]

Jacob also reflected, in Wilhelm's absence, on his dislike of most social gatherings. He preferred conversation with Wilhelm and a small circle of close friends, and he wrote to Wilhelm of the tedium and vacuity he experienced in other social settings. Wilhelm supportively replied that he knew that Jacob had never enjoyed public events such as the theater, firework displays, fairs, and pageants, but he also gently reminded Jacob that others' love of such gatherings was just as natural to them as Jacob's preference for solitude was for him. Jacob had further confessed to Wilhelm that he regarded the modern penchant for teatime socializing as understandable enough as long as the participants were interesting; on the whole, however, he found such activity akin to the vogue for modern journals, which were no substitute for actual books and contained at best a few useful articles scattered among

inferior contributions. His comparison of tea parties to periodicals starkly illustrates how scholarship and the printed word served as a frame of reference
through which the introverted Jacob sought to understand the wider world.
As ever, printed matter was more immediate and relatable to him than people
themselves, and he preferred to express himself in writing. Vaguely, he wrote
Wilhelm that "there is much of which I cannot speak, and at best could write
about, to those whom I hold dear, because I have an inner shyness. However,
just writing about this to you makes me feel as though you'll now be absent
for even longer."[17]

A rare argument between the brothers arose over this cryptic passage. Wilhelm implored Jacob to tell him straight out what was bothering him. Was
Jacob disturbed by the length of Wilhelm's stay? Jacob fired back, demanding
to know how Wilhelm could think he was attacking him and characterizing
Wilhelm's interpretation of the passage as hasty, mistaken, and uncharitable.
He underscored his worry that the length of Wilhelm's stay in Halle might
indicate that Wilhelm was not telling him just how serious his illness truly
was, while Wilhelm for his part expressed his concern that Jacob might feel
that he was staying in Halle so long purely for entertainment and not out of
medical necessity. The rift, however brief, revealed fundamental differences
in personality between Jacob and Wilhelm that typically complemented each
other but in this instance led to considerable tension. Jacob appears to have
feared that Wilhelm, more outgoing than himself, did not need his companionship in the way he needed Wilhelm's, and that the social events and
interactions in Halle were a fine substitute for, or even surpassed, daily life
in Kassel. Jacob's fears were likely also compounded by his bafflement over
the German practice of seeking extended courses of treatment at spa towns,
localities he once described as the "pinnacle of the depravity of modern social
life," since he could not fathom being in such close proximity to so many
people with whom one presumably had nothing in common and could not
get away from.[18]

Any such fears that Wilhelm preferred life in Halle to Jacob's company
were unfounded. When not in treatments, Wilhelm walked in the countryside or pursued scholarship that included translating Danish songs and Icelandic sagas and studying Thucydides, Herodotus, and Plato. He described the
many social events taking place around him not as an engaged participant but
as a dispassionate and even skeptical observer. He was, for instance, doubt-
ful of Reil's efforts to transform Halle—known for its dilapidated streets and
smog-filled air—into a spa destination where patients would enjoy various

entertainments and amenities (including a newly built dance hall) alongside their medical regimens. Wilhelm rarely attended the daily social gatherings and outings Reil organized, finding that they only heightened his loneliness. As for the musician Reichardt, with whose family he had traveled to Halle, Wilhelm considered him arrogant and desirous of high society, rather than intellectual company, as he related in a letter to Brentano.[19]

Wilhelm also did not enjoy his lodgings. He boarded at the same house, owned by Reil's sister, as Henrik Steffens, a professor of science and natural philosophy at the University of Halle and Reichardt's son-in-law. Born in Norway to a Danish mother and a father whose German parents had immigrated to Surinam, Steffens lived in Norway and Denmark as a child and then studied at the universities in Copenhagen and Kiel. Through his work in the fields of medicine, philosophy, literature, and geology, he grew acquainted with Goethe, the philosopher Friedrich Schelling, Romantic writers such as Novalis, Tieck, and Friedrich and August Wilhelm Schlegel, and the Danish poet and dramatist Adam Oehlenschläger. Having traveled widely in Germany, in 1804 he began his appointment in Halle, where his social circle included Reil and the theologian and philosopher Friedrich Schleiermacher. While the individual members of Steffens's family showed Wilhelm kindness, they did not function at all well, in Wilhelm's view, as a family unit. As for Steffens himself, Wilhelm found him vain and temperamental. At times Steffens effusively praised those around him and even excitedly gripped another's hand until it turned blue, but after a few glasses of wine he became noticeably negative and caustic and wept easily. Wilhelm doubted that Steffens had any true friends, only a coterie of sycophantic followers. Steffens for his part seems to have liked Wilhelm; he described him in his memoirs as having a quiet, calm, and gentle disposition.[20]

Nevertheless, Wilhelm benefited in Halle from Steffens's connections with Danish scholars and his considerable knowledge of Nordic languages and literatures. Between medical treatments, Wilhelm was laboring to translate centuries-old Danish songs and tales into German. He finished this work, titled *Old Danish Heroic Songs, Ballads, and Tales* (*Altdänische Heldenlieder, Balladen und Märchen*), in 1809 but did not publish it until 1811.[21] Dedicated to Arnim and Brentano and published in Heidelberg, the work featured fourteen heroic songs and ninety-one ballads and tales, all in verse. Wilhelm based it on a collection of one hundred heroic songs first published in the late sixteenth century, as well as on an additional one hundred heroic songs and thirty love songs that had appeared in two seventeenth-century collections.

In his preface to *Old Danish Heroic Songs*, Wilhelm approvingly pointed to recent scholarship acknowledging the intertwining of the native and the foreign in literature. Although much of this scholarship focused on the influence of classical antiquity and the East on German culture, he noted that some scholars had also begun in earnest to articulate the importance of the North. Insisting that the elements of a nation's poetry were nowhere more purely expressed than in its folk songs, he lamented that, like all folk culture, folk songs had too often been viewed with disdain by those who sought to promote and perpetuate high culture, and that as a result folk songs' survival was now in jeopardy.

Indeed, Wilhelm noted that the preservation of literary expressions of folk culture was so precarious that many of the Danish songs he translated into German had survived only by the coincidence of a storm. Toward the end of the sixteenth century, rough weather had forced Queen Sophia of Denmark to lengthen to a third day her stay on the tiny island of Hven, where she was visiting the astronomer Tycho Brahe. (Wilhelm either misunderstood or embellished these circumstances, writing in his preface that Queen Sophia was forced to travel to Hven because of bad weather while on the open sea, when in reality she was already there and merely had to stay a day longer because of the storm.) Brahe suggested that the queen pass the extra time by calling on famed historian and translator Anders Sørensen Vedel. During this visit, the queen encouraged Vedel to publish his collection of heroic songs, which he did in 1591. Significantly, Wilhelm used the image of surging water not only when telling of the storm that led the queen to meet Vedel but also in denouncing modernizations of folk literature. Whereas the original *Nibelungenlied* texts had the power of naturally rushing water, he wrote in the preface to *Old Danish Heroic Songs*, modern adaptations were like fountains that constrain or control this power by forcing it into narrow pipes. With this metaphor, Wilhelm sought to defend his decision to translate, instead of adapt or modernize, older Danish songs.

Jacob for his part came to criticize *The Boy's Magic Horn* for reasons that echo those Wilhelm gave for rejecting modern adaptations of older literature. Although he and William had contributed songs to Arnim and Brentano's collection, Jacob saw too much artifice in the finished product. The central problem for Jacob and others stemmed from the fact that Arnim and Brentano had substantially revised and rewritten many of the seven-hundred-plus songs in *The Boy's Magic Horn* (at times even adding or deleting entire verses)

and also included six works of their own creation. Such reworking had always been their intent: upon pitching his idea for the collection to Arnim, Brentano had suggested that "the better folk songs could be fortified and new ones could be composed for inclusion." Instead of viewing the folk song as a static historical artifact to be preserved, Arnim and Brentano saw in it a living part of national culture that was to be constantly renewed and revitalized, and they regarded their revisions and additions as part of this process.[22]

Jacob, by contrast, believed that Arnim and Brentano had engaged in an unscholarly modernization of the songs that was not true to the source texts and diminished the songs' natural beauty. Just as Wilhelm had compared the original *Nibelungenlied* texts to the raw power of surging water and described modern adaptations as akin to stylized fountains, Jacob drew on imagery evoking misguided attempts to tame the power of nature. Captured lions and tigers pace sadly in their cages, and kangaroos would suffer unbearably if transplanted from Australia into the European environment, he wrote to Wilhelm in Halle, just as older poetry will wither if taken out of its historical context. Arnim and Brentano "do not allow the old to remain old," he opined, "but wish to transplant it entirely into our time, where it simply does not belong." Significantly, Jacob acknowledged that he was even more resolutely against modernizations than his brother, and that Wilhelm sometimes found his stance on the issue too rigid. In the years to come, Jacob frequently reiterated his stance against the modernizing of texts, while Wilhelm came to engage in an editing of fairy tales not unlike Arnim and Brentano's editing of the songs in *The Boy's Magic Horn*.[23]

Principally unsettling to Jacob was the fact that Arnim, and especially Brentano, typically gave no indication in *The Boy's Magic Horn* that a song had been revised. Their undocumented revisions produced the false impression that the songs came directly from the people. This led their most unmerciful critic—the writer, translator, and Heidelberg professor Johann Heinrich Voss—to describe the collection as "a shoveled-up heap of willful forgeries"; he lambasted volumes 2 and 3 in particular as "an incurable mishmash of all sorts of lumpy, sulky, dirty, and useless street songs [. . .], plus a few stale church hymns." Born in 1751, Voss was considerably older than Arnim and Brentano, and his late Enlightenment ideals clashed with their youthful Romanticism. Enraged by Voss's criticisms, Brentano pledged in a letter to the Grimms "to shut this shithead up at once" by issuing literary notes to accompany *The Boy's Magic Horn*. But because Brentano lacked notes for many of the songs he and Arnim had collected, he tried to pass this task off to the

Grimms, imploring them to write a scholarly study that would examine *The Boy's Magic Horn* in particular and the history of the German song more generally. "Oh, Jacob, don't wrinkle your nose!" he pleaded, rightly guessing that the Grimms would decline his entreaty.[24]

After declining Brentano's request, Jacob and Wilhelm did not hear from him for several months. Jacob suspected that he was not simply upset at the rejection but had come to regard the Grimms as mere acquaintances, to be exploited as convenient, rather than true friends. In July 1809, however, Brentano wrote to Wilhelm of his plans to visit him in Halle and apologized for his silence, which he attributed to his melancholy and always unsatisfied nature. He planned to continue from Halle to Berlin to visit Arnim and suggested that Wilhelm join him. Significantly, Brentano also asked that Wilhelm and Jacob share with him any fairy tales they had collected; although his earlier aim to augment *The Boy's Magic Horn* with fairy tales and legends had not come to fruition, Brentano now planned a separate edition of fairy tales. Upon hearing of this latest request, Jacob generously affirmed that he and Wilhelm should by all means support Brentano in his endeavor, despite misgivings about the nature of their friendship and concerns that Brentano might not produce the type of collection the brothers envisioned. As this indicates, Jacob assumed that Brentano would radically rework any tales they might give him.[25]

Brentano arrived in Halle in August 1809 and spent six weeks there, after which he and Wilhelm traveled on to Berlin to visit Arnim. Wilhelm left Halle feeling that his heart condition had improved, but he remained certain that it would eventually kill him. "I just always fear that it will return," he wrote to Jacob, "and how thankful I would be if God could prevent that, so that I would not have to lead such a fear-ridden life before I die." Years later, he acknowledged that he could not really know whether his improvement in Halle had been effected more by the treatments themselves or by Reil's advice that Wilhelm change his daily routines to minimize stress, which led him to lighten his workload and take frequent walks in the countryside around Halle. Though some of Wilhelm's symptoms recurred during his stay in Berlin, Arnim found him more vigorous than he had been in Kassel, marveled at his healthy appetite, and enjoyed his animated conversational style and knack for caricaturing social acquaintances.[26]

Wilhelm for his part clearly enjoyed Berlin, describing it to Aunt Zimmer as the most beautiful city he had ever seen and marveling, too, at nearby Potsdam. He, Brentano, and Arnim spent each day working on their respective writing projects and then ventured out to lively social events in the evenings. At one such event he met Friedrich Schleiermacher, whom he found to be a difficult conversationalist, although in later years he described the philosopher in far more congenial terms. Wilhelm enjoyed Berlin intellectual society on the whole, but his prejudice showed itself in his complaint to a friend that Jews were a dislikable people impossible to avoid in Berlin. He added that so many Jews were converting to Christianity that upright Christians would soon have to convert to Judaism to avoid Jews. It is possible this remark was influenced by Wilhelm's interactions with Arnim, whose anti-Semitic views were far more pronounced than those of the Grimms.[27]

Aware that Jacob was having difficulties with their siblings back in Kassel, Wilhelm engaged Brentano and Arnim in brainstorming a vocation for Ferdinand. Their efforts to help proved fruitless. After Ferdinand failed to respond to Wilhelm's suggestion that he learn the book trade with a leading publisher in Heidelberg, Wilhelm had a dream in which he stood on a bridge with Ferdinand, who showed him his last three coins and happily but foolishly threw one after another into the water below. Ferdinand seemed so lost that Jacob hesitated to even share with him news of Ludwig's growing success as an artist. In October 1809, Jacob endeavored to persuade Ferdinand to pursue a vocation outside the Kingdom of Westphalia, lest he be conscripted into the Westphalian army or the Grimms have to pay for a substitute for him (the going rate for which was 1,000 talers, a huge sum). Neither Wilhelm's nor Jacob's efforts helped, however, as Ferdinand continued to show little inclination to support himself and seemed incapable even of interacting appropriately with those around him. He often spoke not a single word for days, appeared to take joy only from the dovecote he had installed in one of the Grimms' rooms, and proved difficult to engage with during mealtimes. To make matters worse, Ferdinand was the cause of a scandal that occurred in late 1810, to which Jacob alluded in a letter to Arnim while imploring that Arnim never ask him about it. The nature of the incident remains unknown. Ferdinand was finally persuaded in 1812 to stay with Ludwig in Munich, although there, too, he was without steady employment and continued to require the Grimms' financial aid.[28]

It is telling in view of these emotional struggles that Wilhelm later recalled a nightmare he had had about Ferdinand while still living in Steinau after their father's death. In the dream, Ferdinand stood before an organ, but it was more like an iron maiden than a musical instrument. Ferdinand did not try to defend himself or even so much as let out a sound in pain or protest as the monstrous instrument cut him apart with thousands of knives. Just when Ferdinand was all lacerated and bloodied, he suddenly appeared whole again. But he looked at Wilhelm with a visage that appeared pale, mournful, and submissive, whereupon one of the knives took hold of him again. This disturbing nightmare captures Wilhelm's concern, already as a teenager, for Ferdinand's well-being, and possibly his early sense that Ferdinand lacked the agency and assertiveness of the other Grimm siblings.[29]

As for Carl, Jacob put the blame squarely on him when his work for the banker Carl Jordis ended in November 1809. Jacob and Wilhelm both presumed that their brother's lack of interest in much of anything meant he would never be an independent businessman and would always need to work for others. Their efforts to find steady employment for Carl were unsuccessful, and in January 1811 he left for Hamburg, where he seems to have found a traveling position with a merchant firm. Precise details are unknown, and indeed relatively little is known about either Carl or Ferdinand compared to the other Grimm siblings.

Lotte had also proved somewhat disappointing: not only did her upright but hardened character make her impervious to the tenderness her brothers attempted to show her, but Jacob and Wilhelm also faulted her for her disinclination to manage housework or productively contribute to their efforts to assist Brentano with his collecting of fairy tales. They tasked her in August 1809 with persuading an old woman in Marburg, renowned for her storytelling, to divulge fairy tales, but Lotte failed to bring back a single story. The woman had allegedly first told Lotte she needed time to remember her tales, but the next day she insisted that she no longer knew any. Jacob and Wilhelm were adamant that someone more capable than Lotte would have successfully persuaded the woman to divulge tales, since that same woman had previously told Brentano several stories.[30]

That fall, on November 20, 1809, Wilhelm left Berlin, having spent two months visiting Arnim. Brentano remained in the city until July 1811, almost two years since traveling there with Wilhelm. Savigny, who accepted a position at the newly founded University of Berlin while Wilhelm was in the city, joined Brentano and Arnim in 1810.

On his way home to Kassel, Wilhelm stopped first in Halle and then planned to proceed to Weimar, where he hoped to meet Goethe in person. After enduring blustery weather in an uncovered carriage, however, he was forced to stop in Naumburg and wait two days for the next covered mail coach. While there, he visited the prolific author and translator Benedikte

Naubert, who twenty years earlier had published a collection of legends and tales that she had worked into longer stories. He alighted in Weimar on December 11, 1809, armed with a letter from Arnim praising Jacob and Wilhelm's scholarship and requesting Goethe's help securing access to manuscripts that could benefit Jacob's work.

Goethe, recovering from an illness, was unable to meet Wilhelm on the day he arrived but arranged for him to attend the theater that evening and sit in his loge. The following day, Wilhelm was invited to Goethe's home, where they spoke about subjects ranging from the *Nibelungenlied* to nineteenth-century Danish literature. Wilhelm shared his translations of Danish songs; although Goethe expressed interest in the project, Wilhelm's hope that Goethe would write a preface or provide other scholarly support was not realized. Their conversation resumed the next day over goose liver pâté, rabbit, and a bottle of red wine (to which Goethe pointed Wilhelm with a friendly "ahem" whenever he felt Wilhelm's glass needed replenishing). The following week, Wilhelm took a brief side trip to nearby Jena, where he was disappointed to be afforded little access to the materials he wished to study. His frustration grew when Goethe indicated that Jacob would need to submit a formal request to consult manuscripts held in Weimar. Despite these setbacks, Wilhelm enjoyed his stay and his interactions with Goethe, whom he found generous, dignified, and kind. Goethe for his part ensured that Jacob's request was successful; in accordance with widespread library practices that frequently included the loan even of rare materials, the manuscripts in question were sent to Kassel in mid-January, where Jacob and Wilhelm kept them for five months. Wilhelm left Weimar on Christmas Day 1809, stopped briefly in Gotha to visit Aunt Zimmer, and arrived in Kassel on January 4, 1810, Jacob's birthday.[31]

During the many months they had been apart, Jacob endured struggles with his siblings, continued to discharge his library duties, and pursued scholarship on medieval literature. Wilhelm had coped with the side effects of his medical treatments in Halle, worked on his translations of Danish songs, and profited from his time in Berlin with Arnim and Brentano and his meetings in Weimar with Goethe. The Grimms had pledged to share fairy tales with Brentano, but they now set their sights on publishing their own collection as well.

CHAPTER 5

Collecting Tales, 1810–1812

The Grimms made good on their pledge to share fairy tales with Clemens Brentano. In October 1810 they sent him a packet that, with one more tale sent in December, formed a manuscript of forty-six stories. Twenty-five were in Jacob's handwriting, fourteen in Wilhelm's, and seven written down by a total of four other informants. Brentano never returned the manuscript after consulting it. Fortunately, the Grimms had made their own copy, and this served as the basis for some of the tales they later published. Although their copy is lost, the manuscript they sent Brentano ended up in the Ölenberg Abbey in Alsace. In 1953, collector Martin Bodmer purchased it for his Bibliotheca Bodmeriana in Cologny on the outskirts of Geneva, where it is still held.[1]

The Grimms did not intend the Ölenberg manuscript for publication. Its renderings give the overall contours of each tale but without the fullness of narration that a storyteller would have provided. In their later published collection, the Grimms fleshed out these skeletal versions by either using extant oral or written renditions or augmenting such tellings with their own edits. The version of "Snow White" in the Ölenberg manuscript illustrates this spareness. Unlike many Anglophone versions, the tale begins when Snow White's biological mother is still alive. Its opening lines read as follows in Jacob's handwriting:

Once upon a time it was winter & snowed down from the sky, and a queen sat at a window of ebony wood & sewed. She really wanted to have a child. And while she thought about this, she accidentally pricked her finger with the needle, so that three drops of blood fell in the snow. Then she made a wish & said: Oh, if only I had a child as white as this snow, as red-cheeked as this blood, and as black-eyed as this window frame. Soon after she had a beautiful girl, as white as snow, as red as blood, and as black as ebony & the daughter was called Snow White.

In the first edition of the Grimms' fairy tales, the narration is much improved:

Once upon a time it was the middle of winter, and the snowflakes fell like feathers from the sky. A beautiful queen sat and sewed at a window that had a frame made of black ebony. And as she sewed and looked up at the snow, the needle pricked her finger and three drops of blood fell in the snow. And because the red looked so pretty against the white, she thought: Oh, if only I had a child as white as snow, as red as blood, and as black as this frame. And soon after she had a little daughter as white as snow, as red as blood, and as black as ebony wood, and thus she was called Snow White.[2]

Similarly, the tale "All Fur" in the Ölenberg manuscript is no more than a thumbnail sketch of the plot: "All Fur is banished by her stepmother, because a strange man disregards the stepmother's own daughter & gave the stepdaughter a ring as a token of his love. The stepdaughter flees, goes to the duke's court as a shoe shiner, secretly and unrecognized goes to the ball and in the end cooks the duke a soup with the ring under white bread. In this way, she is discovered and becomes the duke's wife."[3] Whereas this plot overview is brief, the version of "All Fur" published in the first edition of the Grimms' fairy tales spans several pages.

Like "All Fur" and "Snow White," tales such as "The Brave Little Tailor," "The Frog King," "The Straw, the Coal, and the Bean," "The Virgin Mary's Child," "Hansel and Gretel" (recorded in the Ölenberg manuscript as "The Little Brother and the Little Sister"), "Briar Rose" (a version of "Sleeping Beauty"), and "The Little Louse and the Little Flea" later appeared in all seven editions of the Grimms' fairy tales that appeared in their lifetimes, albeit in revised form and typically influenced by additional sources and tale variants. Some tales in the Ölenberg manuscript were never included in the Grimms' published anthology, while others appeared only in certain editions.

Jacob and Wilhelm knew that the packet of tales they sent Brentano gave only a glimpse of a vast corpus that was vanishing as traditions ebbed. A case in point was the elderly woman in Marburg whom Lotte had visited in 1809. Wilhelm traveled to Marburg in September 1810 in a renewed attempt to obtain stories from her, but like his sister he experienced difficulties. The caregivers in the woman's nursing home had convinced her that it would damage her reputation to go around telling tales, and only after Wilhelm met someone with family connections to the home's administrator was "the Oracle," as Wilhelm dubbed her, persuaded to recount some of her tales to a group of children. The woman's reticence points to a wider perception of fairy tales and related folk genres as shameful, inferior, and undeserving of serious consideration. Orally transmitted tales were often deemed unworthy of being written down and published unless radically revised to reflect literary standards.[4]

In view of these challenges and the threat that folk culture would be lost forever as older storytellers died, in December 1810 Jacob shared with Brentano his idea of founding a journal that would contain only legends and tales collected orally from the common people, for which he proposed the title Old German Collector (Altdeutscher Sammler). Brentano regarded the idea as problematic and suggested that it would have to be done carefully, with someone responsible for overseeing collection in each part of Germany. In the tentative call for contributions, titled "Request Issued to All Friends of German Poetry and History," Jacob wrote of the customs, stories, and beliefs that live on, untouched by a "false enlightenment," on tall mountains and in isolated valleys.[5]

Jacob emphasized, however, that folk culture was not stagnant, but rather constantly rejuvenating itself. He spoke of tales told in the nursery, in evening conversation, and in spinning parlors as well as the tales of hunters, manual laborers, and soldiers. He would welcome all German dialects, and he hoped for help from pastors, schoolteachers, and especially German women, who, he noted, might be shy about and not used to writing, but whom men could assist in transcribing tales. Nothing came of Jacob's idea for the journal. The draft call for contributions nevertheless sheds light on the Grimms' associations of folk culture with naturalness and authenticity, as well as their metaphorical conception of it as a precious hoard in need of exhumation and celebration. Indeed, alluding to legend, Jacob compared folk culture to golden treasure at the bottom of the ocean, saying that while some riches were forever lost, many precious rings could be found, undamaged, in the bellies of fish.[6]

But Jacob could not devote himself exclusively to recovering such treasures. Although not overly taxing, his position as Jérôme's librarian pulled him away from scholarly pursuits more than he would have liked. When, in November 1811, a fire broke out at the palace, Jacob had just minutes to work with soldiers to move thousands of books to safety. The shelves and cabinets burned, so until new ones could be installed the evacuated books were housed, along with a few thousand items from the queen's library, at Napoleonshöhe. In the months after the fire, Jacob undertook the tedious work of sorting through the jumble of books and accounting for individual volumes. In a further complication, he was given only a small room, already lined with mirrors and other fragile objects, in which to store and sort the collection. Jacob was particularly irritated whenever someone requested an item from the unsorted piles, since it might take him hours or even days to find it.[7]

The Grimms nevertheless made progress on their various scholarly pursuits. In 1811 and 1812, they each published reviews of editions of older German and Norse literature. In addition, in 1811 Jacob published a book on the *Meistergesang* (master song), a tradition of German lyric poetry cultivated by guild poets from the fourteenth to the sixteenth centuries. In this and other works, Jacob fleshed out the conceptual distinctions between natural poetry and artistic poetry while recognizing the historical connections between the two. In conceptualizing such distinctions, he and Wilhelm were influenced by Johann Gottfried Herder, Friedrich Schiller, and the Grimms' Romantic contemporaries.[8]

Because the Grimms viewed the epic as the foundation of natural poetry, they insisted that all other genres of natural poetry possessed an epic quality. Emphasizing his view of the epic as a collective product of a people, Jacob asserted that only a rare individual poet could alone command epic power in a manner that would transform personal experience into something universal and thus marry artistic poetry with natural poetry. Wilhelm for his part often described natural poetry as an unseen whole of which we glimpse partial manifestations, and he ascribed to it a divinity he regarded as the same for all peoples and having just one source. To him, all instances of natural poetry thus bore a secret interrelationship: like descendants of a common ancestor, they had developed from a shared origin and in analogous ways, even if the precise family tree was now lost.[9]

Notably, Wilhelm's belief in the power of literature and language to connect the human to the divine also enabled him to cope with his ongoing health concerns. Although he initially believed that Johann Christian Reil's treatments in Halle had alleviated his symptoms, his ailments soon returned. Sudden chest pains often interrupted his scholarly work and served as a terrifying reminder of his weak heart. Despite such interruptions, he reported to Achim von Arnim in 1811 that he had immersed himself in his studies in part because his heart condition made so many other activities impossible: "What should someone do whose heart beats so rapidly that his feet can no longer walk far, who can hardly make it to a forest in order to stroll through the green, who cannot hang on to a bough with his arms in order to climb it, sit in the branches, and pick the fruit himself," he asked rhetorically. "What should he do other than turn his attention to the word, and hold before his eyes the consolation that God, too, is the word?"[10] Here, Wilhelm references not only scripture but also the literary word in which he and Jacob saw the interface of the human and divine. As philologists ("lovers of the word"), the brothers sought to illuminate the overall nature, development, and manifestations of language and literature, not to serve merely as literary historians for a particular epoch. For them, philological work necessarily involved understanding the epic as a foundational genre and probing its interactions with other genres. Wilhelm thus emphasized that his initial interest in older Danish songs had lain in their interrelationship with the *Nibelungenlied* and other epics, and he celebrated literature's ability to bring to life glorious images from previous times.[11]

But Jacob and Wilhelm occasionally differed over the way scholars should preserve and transmit older literature. Reviewers criticized Wilhelm's translations in *Old Danish Heroic Songs* as clumsy and stilted, and Jacob himself opined that Wilhelm should have published a critical edition of the original texts instead of a translation. Writing to Savigny, Wilhelm defended himself against Jacob's views by emphasizing the need for literature to be transmitted, and, in this case, translated, so that it can be understood and appreciated, lest it in effect cease to exist. Jacob, however, dismissively compared translated poetry to a dried plant affixed to a piece of paper (as in an herbarium) while likening original poetry to the juicy fullness of a cherry. Original texts should not be tampered with, he insisted, for every addition or emendation is "a lie or an error"; in his view, poetic goodness is "made lame" by translations. Conceding that few readers would purchase an edition of older poetry that did not include a translation, he suggested that any such translation would ideally be in Latin, to signal to readers that it was merely a dictionary-style rendering of the content and not an attempt to recreate the work's poetic form. This and related pronouncements reveal Jacob's sometimes narrow-minded assumption of his readers' abilities and interests. After all, if older literature and traditions were as foundational to a culture as he claimed, why would one not want to ensure that they could be understood by a broad readership? Such a sentiment more closely aligned with Wilhelm's view.[12]

Jacob further insisted that if older poetry must be translated into modern German, it should be in prose rather than verse. This is the format he and Wilhelm settled on for their edition of the *Lay of Hildebrand* (*Hildebrandslied*) and the *Wessobrunn Prayer* (*Wessobrunner Gebet*), published in one volume in 1812. They supplemented the original language of the poems—still the earliest known poems in Old High German—with both scholarly commentary and a literal translation in modern German that did not seek to replicate the original texts' alliterative verse (a form in which alliteration, not rhyme, supports the meter). Although interest in the Grimms' edition of the *Lay of Hildebrand* and *Wessobrunn Prayer* was confined to scholarly circles, the publication is more broadly significant as the first of their works to bear on the title page the designation the "Brothers Grimm" (*Brüder Grimm*).

The Grimms' work on the ninth-century *Lay of Hildebrand* was particularly noteworthy, insofar as they made scholarly breakthroughs in understanding the Germanic past. In part because the manuscript has the appearance of prose, with continuously written words instead of line breaks for verse, scholars before the Grimms had not even understood that the *Lay of Hildebrand* was a poem. These readers saw it as a mere fragment of a medieval chivalric romance in prose, thus bolstering their view that the earliest German literature lacked poetic form. By contrast, the Grimms recognized that the *Lay of Hildebrand* provided evidence that epic poetry had existed in early medieval Germany and was therefore of substantial significance to the German cultural heritage.[13]

For the Grimms, deciphering the *Lay of Hildebrand* entailed not only identifying the alliterative verse but also decoding hard-to-read passages of the physical manuscript, determining the correct divisions between individual words, grappling with the text's limited punctuation, and understanding the meaning of obscure terms. In their published edition, they presented a transcription of the manuscript followed by a verse rendering with word and line breaks inserted and the alliteration marked, lest anyone doubt their finding that the work was a poem. They then provided a translation in modern German. The verse rendering of the opening lines of the text read as follows in the Grimms' edition, except that instead of indicating alliterative letters with boldface as below, the Grimms ensured that in every copy of the published book a hand-drawn red vertical line was painstakingly inserted before each alliterative letter:

Ik gihorta that seggen, that sih urhettun änon muotin,
Hildibraht enti Hathubrant untar heriuntuem.
Sunu fatar ungo; iro saro rihtun.
garutun se iro guthhamun, gurtun sih iro suert ana,
Helidos, ubar hringa, do sie to dero hiltu ritun.[14]

I heard it told that two challengers, Hildebrand and Hadubrand, met alone between two armies. Father and son prepared their armour. They put on their breastplates and girded their swords, the heroes, over their chainmail, as they rode to combat.[15]

The Grimms' penetrating insights pertained not only to the form of the *Lay of Hildebrand* but also to its meaning. They discovered that previous scholars had misread the words "sunu fatar ungo" in the opening lines as referring to cousins (*Vetter*), when instead they referred to a father (*Vater*) and son. The text thus tells of a son who tragically does not recognize his father on the battlefield, with the result that the father must either kill his own son or be killed by him—and his choice remains unknown, since the end of the manuscript is missing.[16]

These were stunning scholarly breakthroughs. But not every aspect of their engagement with the *Lay of Hildebrand* benefited posterity. In the course of his decades-long work on the poem, which included publishing a facsimile in 1830, Wilhelm and other nineteenth-century librarians treated the manuscript with acid-based reagents, which revealed some parts of the faded medieval ink but further obscured others.[17]

The question of whether or how to translate older works of literature became still more palpable for the Grimms as they labored on an edition of the Old Norse *Poetic Edda*, which they would publish in 1815. Increasingly, however, they also applied their views concerning allowable and unallowable editorial interventions to their collecting of fairy tales.

Their compilation had grown to include tales from several additional informants beyond those whose tales appeared in the manuscript they had sent to Brentano in 1810 or in the smaller packet Jacob had sent Savigny in 1808. The Grimms' collecting was aided by a weekly evening reading group they hosted from winter 1811–12 to the end of 1813. Among those who gathered in their Kassel apartment were several young women from the Wild, Ramus, and Hassenpflug families. These women told the Grimms tales that they had likely heard growing up or read in chapbooks, including the French *bibliothèque bleue* ("blue library") tradition of popular literature.[18]

Known as "Dortchen," Henriette Dorothea Wild—Wilhelm's future wife—was the daughter of pharmacist Rudolf Wild, originally from Bern, whose pharmacy lay in the same street as the Grimms' apartment. Dortchen's maternal ancestors included a prominent professor of poetry and oratory in Göttingen. Her sister Gretchen and their mother, Dorothea, had previously told tales to the Grimms, but Dortchen soon became the most significant Wild family contributor and was so close to Jacob and Wilhelm that they regarded her as a sister. She was a teenager when she began telling them tales, and among the many she contributed are "Mother Holla," "The Singing Bone," and "The Six Swans," all of which, in typical fairy-tale fashion, convey a strong sense of right and wrong through rewarded obedience and punished misdeeds. In "Mother Holla," for example, the supernatural title character rewards a hardworking girl with a shower of gold and punishes her lazy stepsister by covering her with pitch. Dortchen's younger sister Marie (known as "Mie" or

Dortchen Grimm, née Wild (1829). Illustration based on the drawing by Ludwig Emil Grimm, in L. E. Grimm, *Erinnerungen aus meinem Leben,* ed. Adolf Stoll (Leipzig: Hesse & Becker Verlag, 1913), 385. Collection of the author.

"Mimi") played a lesser role in contributing tales: the only known story she imparted is "Godfather Death," in which Death serves as godfather to a physician and gives him the power to foretell which patients will live and which will die; after the physician twice abuses this power, Death takes the physician's life.

As for Julia and Charlotte Ramus, their father was pastor of the French Reformed congregation in Kassel—a sizeable community given that Kassel was second only to Berlin in the German-speaking lands in the number of Huguenot refugees who long ago had fled France. Like Marie Wild, the Ramus sisters contributed only one tale to the Grimms' published collection: "The Twelve Brothers" depicts a princess who must remain mute for seven years in order to free her twelve brothers from a spell that transformed them into ravens. Julia and Charlotte appear to have heard this story from Dorothea Viehmann, the daughter of an innkeeper and wife of a tailor, to whom they later introduced the Grimms. Viehmann's repertoire of tales would prove indispensable to the second volume of fairy tales.[19]

Like the Ramus sisters, the Hassenpflugs had Huguenot ancestry. Before moving to Kassel in 1799, they had lived in Hanau, where their father, Johannes, served in the government of Hanau's New Town. The eldest daughter in the Hassenpflug family, Marie, was among the earliest contributors to the Grimms' collection. She suffered from ill health, and it has been speculated that necessary periods of rest may have afforded her the time to reflect on and transmit the tales she knew.[20] Though she imparted more tales than her younger sisters, her contributions long went unrecognized. Later in the nineteenth century Wilhelm's son Herman incorrectly attributed tales for which Wilhelm had made the handwritten notation "Marie" in his personal copy to a Wild family servant known as "Old Marie." This misattribution supported the long-held notion that these tales had come directly from the lower classes and from older women.[21] Marie probably told her tales orally to Jacob, as did her sisters Jeanette and Amalie. Notably, the Hassenpflug family spoke French at home well into the nineteenth century, and their repertoire of tales was shaped in part by the many French stories they heard as children. As a result, most of the tales in the Grimms' collection with a strong connection to those of the Frenchman Charles Perrault came from the Hassenpflugs. They also contributed tales that they had heard in Kassel, including one that an older female servant in another family told to Jeanette.

It appears, too, that it was Marie Hassenpflug who introduced the Grimms to the elderly sergeant of dragoons Johann Friedrich Krause. Born in Hoof near Kassel in 1747, Krause was a retired widower of little means and in poor

Portrait of Marie Hassenpflug.
Artist unknown. Städtische
Museen Hanau.

health; he told tales to the Grimms in exchange for some of their used clothes. Given his military background, it is not surprising that tales such as "Old Sultan," "Herr Fix-It-Up," and "The Tablecloth, the Knapsack, the Cannon Hat, and the Horn" speak directly or implicitly to the experiences of soldiers. These and other tales appear in a notebook that Krause handwrote, in an uneven orthography that suggested he received little formal education. The document contains tales, anecdotes, and jokes purportedly told at spinning parlors in Hoof.[22]

It has been suggested that Krause may have wanted to lend the tales further legitimacy in the Grimms' eyes by describing them as having been told in spinning parlors, since the Grimms idealized what they regarded as the authentic and wholesome telling of tales by village women as they spun. Held primarily during months when agricultural work was at a lull, spinning parlors were gatherings at which women engaged in spinning, knitting, sewing, lace-making, and other textile arts. A seventeenth-century description of Hessian customs indicated that in the wintertime sixty or more villagers would gather in a spinning parlor to pass time singing and conversing. In many regions of Germany, men also attended and partook in singing, dancing, drinking, and

games. The Grimms' idealization of spinning parlors went together with fears
that growing urbanization (and what they regarded as the dissoluteness of city
life) was threatening rural institutions.[23]

Such fears were shared by the Haxthausens, a large Catholic aristocratic
family whose estates Abbenburg and Bökerhof lay northeast of Paderborn.
Indispensable contributors to the Grimms' efforts, the Haxthausens likely collected many of their tales from their servants and from villagers in the region
surrounding their estates. Jacob and Wilhelm met Werner von Haxthausen
in Kassel toward the end of 1807, and the three shared a lively interest in
folk songs. Werner was one of fourteen children born to Werner Adolf von
Haxthausen and his second wife, Maria Anna von Wendt-Papenhausen. In
1811, he introduced the Grimms to his younger brother August, whose love
of older German culture, literature, and traditions included his penchant,
while a student at the University of Göttingen, for dressing in old-fashioned
German attire. Most of the tales the Haxthausens gave to the Grimms were in
August's handwriting, but the narratives themselves were collected by family
members including his sisters Ludowine and Anna. Just ten years of age at the
time, Anna had told Wilhelm a tale while on a walk with him at Bökerhof in
August 1811.

Now in possession of dozens of tales beyond those earlier sent to Brentano, the Grimms were determined to publish their own collection. But they
realized that Brentano's planned volume might appear in print at the same
time as theirs. Brentano's edition would presumably include some of the very
tales they had sent him in 1810, and they knew he would probably substantially augment them, just as he and Arnim had reworked the songs in *The
Boy's Magic Horn*. How then, they wondered, would his reworkings stack up
against the Grimms' versions? Jacob avowed to Arnim that every day he grew
more convinced of the importance of fairy tales to the history of poetry, and
more convinced, too, that his and Wilhelm's fidelity to preserving the texts
as they had collected them was superior to Brentano's revisionist practice.
Arnim, for his part, urged the Grimms to publish without delay, concerned
that waiting until more tales were acquired might jeopardize the entire project. Many years later, Wilhelm described Arnim pacing back and forth in
a room at the Grimms' home, a pet canary perched in the curls of his hair,
while approvingly reading manuscript versions of some of the tales Jacob and
Wilhelm had collected for the first edition.[24]

Arnim had at the time of reading the manuscript been married to Bettina for over a year. With Brentano's sister Gunda married to Savigny and his

sister Bettina now married to Arnim, Brentano thus enjoyed ties of friendship, scholarship, and kinship with Savigny and Arnim. Brentano had fleet-
ingly hoped that marriage might also come to bind him more closely to the
Grimms; he wrote to them in early 1811 of his desire—never realized—that
Hulda, the daughter of his first wife, Sophie, might someday marry Jacob. As
for Brentano's marriage to Auguste Busmann, it had by this point irretriev-
ably deteriorated. The two divorced in 1814; Auguste remarried a few years
later and committed suicide in 1832.[25]

Although he encouraged the Grimms to publish their tales, Arnim rebut-
ted some of Jacob's harsher criticisms of Brentano's literary practice, and in
particular Jacob's at times too rigid distinctions between natural and artistic
poetry. As Arnim pointed out, Jacob had, as a scholar, skillfully traced the
evolution of various aspects of older literature across several centuries, so why
could he not see that modern writers such as Brentano, too, were participating in, instead of disrupting, this larger evolution? Further challenging Jacob's
inflexible and subjective demarcation between authenticity and artificiality,
he pointed to artist Philipp Otto Runge's dialect version of "The Fisherman
and His Wife," which the Grimms were including in their collection and
viewed as an exemplary folk text that preserved the voice of oral storytellers:
when Runge told the tale to some skippers, Arnim said, they protested that
he was telling it wrong, "and they were just as dissatisfied with him as you are
with Clemens." Arnim posited that a rigid cementing of narratives—in the
sense of stipulating which changes are permissible and which not—would be
the death of the entire world of fairy tales.[26]

Sidestepping some of Arnim's central arguments, Jacob responded that he
esteemed modern authors such as Shakespeare and Goethe, but that he was
far more interested in the epic literature of ancient times and the traces he believed it had left on folk literature. Indeed, as he had proclaimed to Arnim in
September 1812, "I am now fully of the epic religion." To Arnim's suggestion
that any distinction between natural and artistic poetry ultimately becomes
mere drollery, Jacob retorted with gravity that "all of my work, I feel, rests
on learning and showing how a great epic poetry lived and prevailed across
the earth, but was with time forgotten and squandered by human beings—or
not even fully that, but instead how humans nevertheless still draw on it."
Employing biblical imagery, he argued that just as paradise was lost, so, too,
had the gate to the garden of older literature been closed, but everyone car-
ries a small bit of paradise in one's heart and thus also a small bit of older
literature. As evidence of the epic poetry he believed had spread to all cultures

everywhere, he pointed to the way various remnants of older literature revealed what he regarded as an amazing inner correspondence; he saw, too, the development of language through the ages as stemming from an inner poetic perfection.[27]

These views enabled Jacob to defend the more imaginative aspects of older literature against stereotypes of inferiority or unseriousness. That which is marvelous is not mere fancy, illusion, or falsehood, he claimed; instead, it is part of the epic's presentation of a history of humankind that is far more divine and mythological than that which historians write in modern times. It was in view of this divine and mythological nature, he asserted, that one ought not speak of a definitive author of an epic; all the author has done is to prepare a new channel for a stream of water, under whose waves his name will and ought to be subsumed. While Jacob conceded that he should not judge Brentano's fairy tales themselves—not least because he admitted that he had not read them—he suspected that he would find in them not only a depravation of poetry but also a defilement of "children's truth." Crucially, Jacob believed that an individual's early childhood mirrors the incipient stages of an entire people. Therefore, he considered the "children's truth" in fairy tales equivalent to the truth he saw in ancient mythologies. He was convinced, too, that the fairy tales he and Wilhelm had collected were without exception all told in various forms centuries ago. In this sense, he regarded fairy tales as both unchangeable and yet, because they appear in endless variation, always changing.[28]

Arnim congenially suggested that he and Jacob had more in common than they each thought. He noted that he would continue to insist that older writers were not without artistic poetry, just as modern writers were not devoid of natural poetry. Thus, he challenged Jacob's tendency to equate oldness with authenticity and modernity with artifice. To temper Jacob's assessment of the glory of epic literature and humans' subsequent squandering of this wondrous heritage, he pointed out that even Homer speaks of a decline of the human race and that the *Edda* is similarly mournful. Jacob for his part saw his and Arnim's approaches as proceeding from different emphases, with Arnim upholding the humanity of poetry more than its divinity and Jacob doing the opposite. Despite their intellectual arguments over Brentano's approach and its implications for the gathering and preservation of folk literature, Arnim and Jacob, as close friends, tried to find points of agreement.[29]

The Grimms need not have feared that Brentano would publish a competing edition of fairy tales. While Wilhelm, Brentano, and Arnim were in

Berlin together in 1809, Brentano had confessed that he often felt like some-one standing high on a mountaintop holding a tiny ship that could not be launched into water. His poetic ideas went unwritten, he explained, because each appeared more promising than the next, like a succession of waves, with the unfortunate result that each dissipated before it could ever reach the shore. Brentano's fairy-tale collection soon proved to be among these forever-incomplete ideas. By contrast, the Grimms would publish seven complete and ten abridged editions of their *Children's and Household Tales* over forty-five years. Having, with Arnim's help, secured a contract with a publisher in Berlin, the Grimms sent the manuscript for the first volume off in September 1812 so that the book would be available in time for Christmas.[30]

CHAPTER 6

❧⦿☙

Reception of *Children's and Household Tales*, 1812–1814

Jacob and Wilhelm were just under twenty-eight and twenty-seven years of age, respectively, when in December 1812 Georg Andreas Reimer issued the first volume of their fairy-tale collection, titled in full *Children's and Household Tales: Collected by the Brothers Grimm.* Eighty-five tales were supplemented by a preface, an appendix with scholarly notes, three pages of quotations about fairy tales from figures including Martin Luther, Walter Scott, and the ancient Greek geographer Strabo, and a dedication of the volume to Bettina von Arnim "for little Johannes Freimund"—the infant son born to Bettina and Achim von Arnim in May 1812. The collection was supposed to contain eighty-six tales; however, Reimer inadvertently omitted number 86, "The Fox and the Geese," though the appendix included notes for it. Referring to the tale's portrayal of geese who annoy a hungry fox, Wilhelm quipped that, because of Reimer's mistake, this "tale of vexation" had proved more vexing still. To allow the error to be rectified, the bulk of the edition of nine hundred copies was not released until early 1813.[1]

Like "The Fox and the Geese," dozens of tales in the volume are little known today. These include "The Hand with the Knife," which depicts a girl who can cut peat unusually quickly because her lover, an elf, has a magic knife; "Princess Mouseskin," in which a princess clothes herself in a mouse-skin dress and pretends to be a male servant at another court after her father unsuccessfully orders her death; "The White Snake," in which a servant magically understands the languages of animals after eating part of a white snake and uses this skill to gain the hand of a princess; and the four Dummy tales, in which a character considered unintelligent accomplishes feats that others cannot. But the volume also contains well-known tales such as "Rapunzel," "Hansel and Gretel," "Snow White," "Rumpelstiltskin," "The Frog King or Iron Heinrich," "The Brave Little Tailor," "Briar Rose," "Cinderella," and "Little Red Riding Hood" (given in the Grimms' collection as "Little Red Cap").

Today's readers may find the *Children's and Household Tales* version of some of these tales surprising. In the Grimms' "The Frog King or Iron Heinrich," for example, the frog turns into a prince not with a kiss, but when the daughter hurls him against her bedroom wall in anger over her father's order to keep her promise. Another difference is the loyal servant Heinrich, whose appearance at the end accounts for the tale's two-part title: upon his master's transformation into a frog, the servant had had three iron rings placed around his heart so that it would not burst from grief. Deviating from the Perrault version that is better known through Disney and other modern tellings, "Cinderella" does not include the pumpkin that magically becomes a coach or the rodents turned into horses and coachmen, but instead features an enchanted tree planted atop the grave where Cinderella's mother is buried. Also, whereas Perrault's version begins after Cinderella's mother has already died, the Grimms' version opens with the mother on her deathbed, changing it from a story of "rags to riches" to "riches to rags to riches"—a trajectory, incidentally, that parallels the Grimms' experience of modest comfort in their childhood, followed by the crisis of their father's death and years of working their way back to relative stability.

Many tales also differ from how they appear in subsequent editions of the collection. For example, in some tales in the first volume female characters exhibit greater independence and have more direct speech than in later Grimm versions of the same tales. This difference reflects the Grimms' edits, principally after the first edition, to make the tales conform more strictly to nineteenth-century gender norms. Such norms are nevertheless palpable in the first edition, where female characters are typically rewarded for piety, obedience, and self-sacrifice, whereas male characters are rewarded for their cheekiness, subterfuge, and risk-taking. Men are not only protectors, as fathers, suitors, and husbands, but also underdogs who must use their cleverness to prevail—not unlike the Grimms themselves, whose intense study habits proved particularly important after their father's death imperiled their socioeconomic status. Thus, Thumbling uses his diminutive size to outwit others, Dummy succeeds despite being underestimated, and the Brave Little Tailor, who brags about killing "seven with one blow" (misinterpreted by those around him as seven humans instead of flies), overcomes giants, a unicorn, and a wild boar, and eventually becomes king.

In addition, numerous tales appeared in more rudimentary form in the first volume. While they were typically more developed than corresponding versions in the Ölenberg manuscript from 1810, the tales in the 1812 volume were short and the narration lean compared to subsequent editions. This spareness resulted from the Grimms' pronounced intention to be true to the form in which they had received a tale, which also accounts for their inclusion of a couple tales in dialect form instead of standard German.

The desire to preserve the tales as they were imparted is emphasized in the preface, which Wilhelm wrote with some contributions from Jacob. The preface's organic imagery, implicit reaction against industrialization and urbanization, and idealized constructions of folk culture and the Germanic past reveal the influence of Heidelberg Romanticism on the Grimms' assessment of the social and political changes unfolding in the early decades of the nineteenth century. Expressing the urgency of collecting fairy tales before they might be lost forever, the Grimms opened the preface by describing a storm that has destroyed almost an entire planting of crops, save for a few stalks protected by a hedge. Once the sun emerges, they wrote, these few surviving stalks will grow unnoticed until late summer, when "poor, pious hands" will find them, gently bundle them together, and carry them home. The meager harvest will provide sustenance over the winter and well into the future, for it bears perhaps the only remaining seeds for future plantings. It will thus be treasured more than if whole sheaves had been harvested. "So it is for us," Jacob and Wilhelm observed, wistfully and nostalgically, "when we consider the richness of German poetry in early times and see that so much of this is no longer alive, and that even the memory of it has been lost, with only folk songs and these innocent household fairy tales remaining."[2]

Although they received most of their tales from educated young townswomen, the image of peasants gathering crops served to ground their collection in rural folk culture. This association continued throughout the preface as the Grimms portrayed kitchen conversations, holiday celebrations, the stillness of the meadows and forests, and even fantasy itself as a protective hedge that preserved a small number of fairy tales. Because these stories' survival was now threatened by the waning custom of oral storytelling and the mortality of the few storytellers who remembered them, the Grimms explained that they had taken it upon themselves to safeguard tales by collecting and printing them. The protective theme is emphasized by the hand metaphor that appears not only in the first paragraph's mention of "poor, pious hands" that harvest stalks, but also in the last paragraph: there, the Grimms announce their delivery of tales into the "benevolent hands" of readers, as well as their hope that the volume will escape the hands of anyone dismissive of folk culture. As for their own editorial approach, they portrayed this as essentially hands-off: "No circumstance has been poeticized, beautified, or altered," they proclaimed. "In this respect, no such collection has previously existed in Germany, for one has almost always used fairy tales as material from which to form larger stories." Such adaptations had "gratuitously expanded and changed the tales" and "grabbed what belonged to children out of their hands, giving them nothing in return."[3]

This passage not only continues the hand metaphor but also conveys the Grimms' view that, by poeticizing tales, other authors and editors had produced texts of interest solely to learned audiences. They believed that *Children's and Household Tales* would be of interest to young and old alike because they had not engaged in stylistic embellishment. This mindset distinguished the Grimms from many of their predecessors and contemporaries. At the time that they published their collection, the fairy tale in its various forms had a long history as a published genre. But this lineage often underscored the view that the oral tale, unless heavily revised into something more cultivated, was unworthy of publication. Early published European fairy tales were often presented within a frame narrative, where a character recounts a tale as part of a larger story. For example, in Apuleius's *Metamorphoses* (also known as *The Golden Ass*), a Latin novel from the second century CE, an elderly woman tells the story of Cupid and Psyche to comfort a kidnapped young woman. In Gianfrancesco Straparola's *The Pleasant Nights* (1550, 1553), characters in a palace on the island of Murano near Venice share stories, including several fairy tales, as entertainment in the evenings during Carnival. The first European attempt to place within a frame narrative an entire collection of fairy tales based on oral folklore was Giambattista Basile's *The Tale of Tales* (1634; also known as *Pentamerone*), which contains early variants of "Cinderella," "Snow White," "Sleeping Beauty," and "Beauty and the Beast."

The salons of late seventeenth-century France spawned a rich corpus of literary fairy tales written by female authors such as Madame d'Aulnoy, Mademoiselle de La Force, and Marie-Jeanne L'Héritier. Emblematic of the influence of the French literary fairy-tale tradition on the development of the genre is the term "fairy tale" itself, which is a translation of the French *conte de fées*. (Since relatively few fairy tales depict fairies, the term is somewhat of a misnomer, for which reason "wonder tale" is sometimes preferred to "fairy tale.") Fairy tales had long been described in France as "Mother Goose tales"; it was through the translation, in 1729, of Charles Perrault's *Tales and Stories of the Past* (1697), subtitled *Mother Goose Tales*, that the fictional Mother Goose persona came to the Anglophone world. Perrault's collection contains eight tales, including "Cinderella," "Sleeping Beauty," "Little Red Riding Hood," and "Puss in Boots," each told in a skillful blend of poetic and popular diction and ending with a moral in rhymed verse.[4] To advance the notion that peasant women had told and retold fairy tales through the ages, Perrault presented on his collection's frontispiece an old woman telling tales to children while spinning with a drop spindle. The French vogue for fairy tales continued in the eighteenth century; highlights include the "Beauty and the Beast" versions of Gabrielle-Suzanne de Villeneuve and Jeanne-Marie Leprince de Beaumont as well as Antoine Galland's French translation and adaptation of the centuries-old Middle Eastern collection *One Thousand and One Nights*.

Eighteenth- and nineteenth-century German writers of literary fairy tales were often influenced by tales rooted in oral traditions, but they felt obligated to point to the learned style they employed in crafting their tales. Christoph Martin Wieland portrayed literary tales as capable of imparting Socratic wisdom; by contrast, "tales told in a nursery tone may be propagated through oral transmission, but they must not be published." For that reason, he had made the style and language of his three-volume *Dschinnistan* (1786–89), which comprised mainly his translations and reworkings of late seventeenth- and early eighteenth-century French salon fairy tales, classical instead of childlike.[5] Similarly, Wieland's contemporary Johann Karl August Musäus emphasized in the preface to his five-volume *Folk Tales of the Germans* (1782–86) that fantasy and reason can go hand in hand, and that not all fairy and folk tales should be narrated in a childlike tone. Like Musäus's collection, Benedikte Naubert's anonymously published *New Folk Tales of the Germans* (1789–92) included many legends that she developed into longer stories. Whereas eighteenth-century German authors had been strongly influenced by French salon tales and the Enlightenment emphasis on reason and wisdom, toward the end of the eighteenth and beginning of the nineteenth century the deeply psychological fairy tales written by Romantics such as

Ludwig Tieck, Novalis, E. T. A. Hoffmann, and Friedrich de la Motte Fouqué gained influence.

In short, the fairy tale had for centuries been regarded as something to be dressed up with additional morals, intellectual content, psychological depth, or literary stylization to make it respectable. Influenced in part by the teachings of Savigny and the historical school of legal study, the Grimms' approach was decidedly different: they saw the fairy tale and related folk genres as worthy in and of themselves. These stories were a testament both to the German culture, customs, and language of past times and to the enduring influence of this cultural and linguistic heritage on the present. In their preface, likening the innocence of fairy tales to the bright eyes of children, the Grimms lauded the simple depictions that appear in many tales. As examples they gave the parents who have no bread and the fearful siblings in the big woods in "Hansel and Gretel"; the sister in "Little Brother and Little Sister" who seeks herbs and moss for her brother after he is transformed into a fawn; the sister in "The Six Swans" who sews shirts of asters for her brothers to release them from the witch's magic that transformed them into swans; and even the many cruel stepmothers who torment their stepdaughters. They described fairy tales as presenting a shining world of gold and pearls, but also a world of darkness and evil. In the fairy tale, kings, princes, loyal servants, and honest handworkers live among nature, whose enchantment is revealed in talking animals, plants, and stones and in fanciful creatures such as dwarfs and nixies. In essence, they portrayed fairy tales as imbued with the "children's truth" that Jacob, in his correspondence with Arnim, believed Brentano had sacrificed.[6]

Because of fairy tales' depictions of universally relatable situations, the Grimms also declared that there was likely no people on earth that did not tell them; however, they implicitly endorsed nineteenth-century assumptions of European cultural and racial superiority when they remarked that "even the Negroes in Western Africa entertain their children with stories." Alongside mention of Scandinavian, Welsh, Scottish, and Irish traditions, they praised the tales of the Frenchman Perrault and the Italians Basile and Straparola. Their emphasis on the transnational spread of fairy tales may explain why the Grimms did not include the word "German" in the title *Children's and Household Tales.*[7]

That tales are told and retold by storytellers across time and space may also account for why the Grimms did not acknowledge their informants, apart from mentioning Philipp Otto Runge in the appendix and indicating the source for tales taken from printed works. These works included German sources from the sixteenth through the early nineteenth century as well as a volume published in London in 1811 from which Jacob, despite his misgivings regarding translation, had rendered a Scottish tale into German. In keeping with their notion of natural poetry as the collective product of a people, the first volume of *Children's and Household Tales* thus almost without exception neither named nor provided even general characteristics of individual informants who had contributed oral or handwritten tellings. In the preface, the brothers insisted merely that all but a few of their tales had been collected "through oral transmission" in Hessen. Wilhelm, however, left handwritten notations in his copy of the first edition which, for many of the tales, have enabled scholars to identify which informant supplied the tale and on which date.[8]

Based on the preface, a reader would likely assume that the Grimms had personally collected the ensuing tales from the mouths of the common people—and not, as was actually the case, primarily from educated young women. This incorrect assumption was perpetuated in numerous works of scholarly and popular literature in the nineteenth and even twentieth centuries. According to a popular English edition published in the late nineteenth century, the Brothers Grimm had "travelled through Hesse and other parts of Germany for thirteen years, persuading the poor people to tell them all the stories that they had heard from their grandparents, and then writing them down." The idea for *Children's and Household Tales* "seems to have come to them almost without thinking," a scholar wrote in 1915, since "folk tales could be picked up anywhere in Hesse, at their very doors." Another specified in 1951 that the Grimms "obtained their folk tales from the lips of peasant women, shepherds, waggoners, vagrants, old grannies, and children in Hesse, Hanau, and other areas." As these and other erroneous pronouncements indicate, the Grimms' silence over when, by whom, and from whom their tales had been collected through oral transmission made this transmission appear more connected to the ordinary rural people than it actually was.[9]

While omitting such identification supported the Grimms' claim that no tale could be attributed to a single voice, it also enabled them to skirt the fact that they did not collect most of their tales from peasants. Together with the Grimms' substantial editing of the tales—which becomes pronounced after the first edition—this led some twentieth-century scholars to accuse them of deliberate fabrication and even to dub the Grimms' tales "fakelore."[10] A neologism coined in 1950 by folklorist Richard M. Dorson, "fakelore" is "the presentation of spurious and synthetic writings under the claim that they are genuine folklore"; it applies to texts "not collected in the field but [. . .] rewritten from earlier literary and journalistic sources in an endless chain of regurgitation."[11] But branding the Grimms' tales "fakelore" is misleading and reductive. Folklore as a scholarly enterprise was too new in the nineteenth century to constitute a discipline with established scientific norms (as underscored by the fact that the English word "folklore" was first coined in 1846 to describe the various stories and traditions collected by the Grimms and their contemporaries). Moreover, denigrating *Children's and Household Tales* as fakelore might erroneously imply a standard of folkloric purity that did not in reality exist, regardless of the Grimms' own efforts to differentiate authentic from adulterated tales. Despite long-standing attitudes that oral folk tellings needed stylistic enhancement to attain literary worth, for centuries high culture and low culture had been produced not in entirely separate silos, but on a dynamic spectrum. Oral and written traditions had been interdependent, with oral tellings influencing written versions and vice versa.[12] As for the versions the Grimms' informants provided, it is difficult to know whether or how much the Grimms revised these for the first edition, because they did not retain manuscript versions for most of their published tales. But even in cases where a manuscript for a particular tale does exist, as for example in the Ölenberg manuscript, the manuscript version may simply be an abbreviated sketch and not intended as a word-for-word transcription. That is, deviations from a manuscript source may signal an effort to restore the richness of a storyteller's rendition.

In any case, the Grimms' notion of authentic folklore rested on unstable demarcations between oral and written traditions, the "folk" and educated classes, and natural and artistic poetry. Although they shied from providing details that would have complicated their account of the tales' rootedness in peasant environs, to accuse them of falsifying folklore misses the point that folklore was already built on tenuous assumptions.

It is notable that, after discussing questions of authenticity with Jacob during the creation of *Children's and Household Tales*, Achim von Arnim revisited these topics when the Grimms surprised him with a copy to give as a Christmas gift to his wife, Bettina. Arnim wrote to the brothers to thank them for dedicating the volume to his wife and son and to share some observations. Although he did not regard the tales as falsifications, he was skeptical of the Grimms' claim in the preface that there had been no substantive editorial interventions. He found it impossible that they could not have exerted any such influence on their tales, while judging this influence as not negative, but productive. As he had done in rebutting Jacob's harsh criticisms of Brentano, Arnim implied that the Grimms, too, were part of a rich storytelling tradition; they should neither claim nor aspire to be detached observers and recorders of this tradition but instead view themselves as active participants in it.[13]

Jacob retorted that storytelling is not mathematical, so of course a tale will change from one recounting to the next. To retell a tale with flawless fidelity to the original is as challenging as breaking open an egg without leaving any white on the shell; what matters is keeping the yolk intact. In keeping with the Grimms' preference for natural poetry over artistic poetry, Wilhelm for his part told Arnim that any influence he had had on the tales was spontaneous rather than deliberate.[14] While it is true that the Grimms did not use the tales they collected as a springboard for their own literary creations (in contrast to their Romantic contemporaries and eighteenth-century forebears), their admission of such influence suggests that they did shape and rework the tales even in the first edition.

As for Clemens Brentano, he asserted that the Grimms' had engaged in far too little editing. In his view, their insistence on remaining true to the form in which they received their tales produced tedious and impure narration. Insisting that he and Arnim were far superior in their editing of *The Boy's Magic Horn*, he compared the effect of the Grimms' volume to dirty children's clothing: "If you want to display children's clothes, you can do that with fidelity without bringing out an outfit that has all the buttons torn off, dirt smeared on it, and the shirt hanging out of the pants." Given that most of the Grimms' tales did not come to them from old women or children, it is ironic that Brentano also claimed that Jacob and Wilhelm should have prefaced each tale with a psychological account of the child or old woman who had, in his view, told the story so negligently.[15]

Brentano also criticized the appendix, which struck him as an assemblage of posthumously discovered notes that a hapless heir had thrown together. Far more useful, in his view, would have been a learned treatise, or what he called "a physiology of the fairy tale"—an interesting criticism given the Grimms' refusal to write a treatise on the folk song for Brentano a few years earlier. In fact, the Grimms' appendix deserves more credit than Brentano gave it: in addition to indicating the specific source for tales that had already appeared in print, the Grimms' notes to each tale typically point to parallel themes and motifs in myths, legends, sayings, songs, and chapbooks and provide information about regional and international variants, including French, Italian,

Nordic, Scottish, and Jewish tales. The appendix, like the Grimms' preface, was thus original for its time in approaching fairy tales from an interdisciplinary and comparative perspective. To Jacob, the variants referenced in the appendix enabled the reader to appreciate the fairy tale's widespread and long-standing oral tradition; moreover, it lent scholarly respectability to tales whose publication might otherwise be dismissed.[16]

Whereas Jacob worried that scholars would not see the tales as worthy of serious study without the appendix, Arnim feared that the book's contents were too scholarly to appeal to a popular audience. In his feedback to the Grimms, he conveyed his dismay over the edition's lack of visual appeal. Pointing out that illustrations would have supplied a needed counterbalance to the scholarly preface and appendix, he fretted that the public would not regard *Children's and Household Tales* as a children's book, despite its title. The Grimms agreed with the need for at least a frontispiece and asked that Reimer add one (with their brother Ludwig as the suggested artist) during work to rectify the omission of "The Fox and the Geese." Reimer demurred, meaning that the first volume remained without illustrations.[17]

Arnim worried, too, that the book's appeal would be limited by its more gruesome tales. He cited a mother who had complained that she could not share the volume with her children because the tale "How Some Children Played at Slaughtering" depicted siblings who see their father butchering a pig and then imitate this, with one child butchering the other. Similarly, he expressed concern over the implied obscenities in "Of Mrs. Fox," in which an old fox with nine tails, suggestive in folklore of penises, tests his wife's fidelity. In light of such tales, Arnim advised that Jacob and Wilhelm should have subtitled the volume "For Parents to Select for Retelling" or something similar, to indicate that adults should use discretion in choosing which tales to read to children.[18]

Unfazed, Wilhelm acknowledged that parents might object to some of the tales, but he underscored that his mother had herself told him "How Some Children Played at Slaughtering" when he was a boy. Rejecting Arnim's cautionary subtitle, Jacob countered that anyone so afraid that children's innocent eyes could fall on something they might dangerously imitate might as well just blindfold them so they could not see at all. As for the tale about the fox with nine tails, he swore that it was innocent and should not be interpreted as obscene; he also noted it was among his most favorite tales from childhood. Above all, he insisted that the collection's tales were not solely for children, and that even the oldest and most serious readers would find them captivating. If

children were more responsive to fairy tales than adults were, it was because
their innocence made them more open to the natural poetry rooted in ancient
epics. Jacob's stance differs starkly from that taken by A. L. Grimm, an author
of no relation to Jacob and Wilhelm who had published a volume of children's
tales just a few years before. Addressing parents in his preface, A. L. Grimm
had written of the tales in his collection, "I deliver them to you, because I
would rather see them in your hands than in the hands of children."[19]

Jacob and Wilhelm remained baffled by the notion that their volume
could not appeal to both scholarly and public interests. They saw no contradiction in dedicating the volume to Bettina von Arnim and her infant
son while including meticulous scholarly notes about tale variants. Their impetus for compiling the collection nevertheless stemmed first and foremost
from their sense that fairy tales were part of a vast corpus of folk literature
in desperate need of protection. In view of the substantial political upheavals of the time, the sense of loss, preservation, and regeneration they convey
in the preface is not surprising, and neither is their impatience with what
they regarded as petty concerns over whether children would be led astray by
specific tales or passages. Indeed, Jacob later observed that the Grimms had
completed the preface, dated October 18, 1812, exactly one year before the
Battle of Leipzig—until World War I the largest battle ever fought in Europe,
with some six hundred thousand soldiers and almost one hundred thousand
casualties.[20] Notably, the December 1812 publication of the first volume coincided with the end of Napoleon's disastrous campaign in Russia, which
marked a turning point in the Napoleonic Wars. In between the campaign in
Russia and the Battle of Leipzig, the many advances and setbacks in what in
Germany became known as the "Wars of Liberation" affected Jacob and Wilhelm's outlook. In a passage that recalls the opening lines of the preface to the
Grimms' fairy tales, Wilhelm invoked the image of a storm in describing the
psychological impact of the war after the French victory in Bautzen in May
1813: "We are like wayfarers who have experienced rain, storms, and sunshine
one after another," he wrote to Paul Wigand, "and even when the clouds cover
all the mountains we have remained steadfast in our knowledge that above
them the sun was still shining—and just when it would come out again was
in God's hands. In between, we have gone on working whenever possible; in
one's external life there is nothing better than a solid vocation, which is how
I view our work."[21]

At the time, the Grimms' work included gathering additional fairy tales for the planned second volume of *Children's and Household Tales*, a task greatly helped in summer 1813 by Dorothea Viehmann, a storyteller in her late fifties. The wife of a tailor and daughter of an innkeeper, she lived in Zwehrn (also "Niederzwehrn," or lower Zwehrn), a village near Kassel. Her crucial role in the Grimms' collection of fairy tales is memorialized in a German magazine illustration published in 1892, decades after the Grimms' deaths. It portrays the Grimms visiting Viehmann at her cottage. There is a tiled stove, a canopy bed, a wall clock whose hands show just after five o'clock, and a table and bench laden with fruit, a loaf of bread, and a coffee pot and cup. Three chickens strut and peck about the floor. Gathered around Viehmann are two children, a young woman holding an infant, and the Grimms. With her knitting resting on her lap, Viehmann tells them a fairy tale.

Jacob and Wilhelm Grimm visiting the storyteller Dorothea Viehmann in Niederzwehrn. Woodcut based on a painting by Ludwig Katzenstein, in *Die Gartenlaube* (1892), 505. Courtesy of the Julian Edison Department of Special Collections, Washington University Libraries. In contrast to this imaginary scene, Viehmann told her tales to the Grimms at their apartment in Kassel.

This rustic scene did not actually take place. The Grimms obtained many tales from Viehmann and regarded her as an ideal storyteller, as their prefaces to their collection and inclusion of a frontispiece depicting her would come to show. But there is no evidence that they visited her home in Zwehrn. Instead, to supplement her family's meager income, Viehmann went to Kassel once or twice a week to sell produce from her garden. Introduced to the Grimms by the Ramus family, she would visit their apartment, where there were neither children nor chickens. The Grimms typically gave her coffee, a glass of wine, and a small amount of money as thanks for telling her tales, all but one of which she shared in summer and fall 1813. (The remaining tale was told in September 1814.)[22]

The magazine illustration is striking in other ways. It was based on a painting by Kassel artist Ludwig Katzenstein, who, in what might be compared to today's photoshopping, had copied the heads and poses from two well-known portraits of the Brothers Grimm. However, the portraits depicted the Grimms as they had appeared as men in their sixties, when they were only in their late twenties when Dorothea Viehmann told them her tales. Katzenstein had painted a couple different versions, one of which formed part of a series depicting scenes from Hessian history. He used only gray and brown pigments for this series and then had the paintings photographed, so that they would approximate the look of nineteenth-century photographs.[23] Similar to Katzenstein's copying of heads from other depictions of the Grimms, the brothers themselves would (especially in later editions) combine elements from multiple tellings of the same basic tale to create a version they believed represented it as it might be told in rural communities. With their revisions the Grimms sought to bring fairy tales back to what they regarded as a truer form, efforts not unlike Katzenstein's attempts to make his historical scenes (however imaginary) appear as real as a photograph.

In the late nineteenth century, the illustration's cottage setting further fueled the myth that the Brothers Grimm ventured into rural environs to gather fairy tales directly from peasants. In reality, most informants had continued to be educated young women. In January 1813, Wilhelm sent Ludowine von Haxthausen the first volume accompanied by a letter asking for any additional tales or variants she and her family could collect. That summer, he traveled to the Haxthausens' estate. He met with not only the Haxthausens but also Jenny and Annette von Droste-Hülshoff, who were visiting with their mother and siblings from their estate near Münster. The Haxthausen siblings were Jenny and Annette's aunts and uncles, though the eighteen-year-old

Jenny and sixteen-year-old Annette were around the same age as their aunt Ludowine and older than their aunt Anna.

Like the Haxthausens, the Droste-Hülshoffs were aristocratic and Catholic. Despite differences in class and religion, Jenny seems to have quickly developed a crush on Wilhelm. She described him as having expressive eyes, dark hair, and a nice nose and mouth, and gushed that he was one of the most attractive and fascinating people she had ever met. Wilhelm for his part found Jenny kind and likeable, though he was not fond of her younger sister Annette, who always wanted to dominate the conversation. In keeping with long-standing medical lore, Wilhelm attributed Annette's precocity to her having been born at seven months' gestation. It seems he found her intimidating, as shown by a nightmare he had several months after his visit in which a malevolent Annette, bedecked in dark purple flames, pulled out strands of her hair and hurled them at him. The strands magically transformed into arrows, and Wilhelm felt during the nightmare that they could have blinded him. The highly gifted Annette later distinguished herself as a writer of poetry and prose. Her novella *The Jew's Beech Tree*, inspired by an actual account of the murder of a Jew in a rural community, remains a masterpiece of German literature for its riveting psychological ambiguities and powerful exploration of social ills including anti-Semitism, alcoholism, spousal abuse, poverty, and criminality.[24]

His dislike of Annette aside, Wilhelm enjoyed his stay with the Haxthausens immensely. His accounts paint a picture of a cohesive and congenial family committed to preserving the cultural traditions Jacob and Wilhelm held dear. The Droste-Hülshoff and Haxthausen women sang folk songs in the evening and the men played the flute and horn. Wilhelm excitedly wrote to Jacob that he would need four to six weeks to note down all the tales, legends, and sayings the Haxthausens and Droste-Hülshoffs knew; since he could not stay so long, he diligently recorded as much as possible. In keeping with Romantic interests in dream symbolism, Wilhelm also kept a diary of his nightly dreams that summer, whose fairy-tale-like qualities are unusually explicit. On July 17, 1813, for example, he dreamed that a sorceress in Hanau was transforming him into various animals, including a white bird and a horse. While in his own eyes he retained his human form, he could tell from the conversations of people around him whenever she had turned him into another animal. He felt fearful throughout this experience and begged the sorceress to lift the curse, protesting that he had done nothing to deserve it.[25]

Wilhelm left the Haxthausens and Droste-Hülshoffs with their assurances that they would continue to collect for him. His own collecting during the trip was not over, however: en route home, he climbed a couple hills and atop one found a shepherd pasturing his flock. Wilhelm and his traveling companions prevailed on the man to tell them any stories he might know and were delighted by the tales and legends he imparted. The next spring, Ludowine von Haxthausen sent Wilhelm more tales that she and her family had gathered in the intervening months. She praised her sister Anna, in particular, for the trustworthy disposition that enabled her to get people to freely divulge their stories.[26]

In addition to continued collecting for *Children's and Household Tales*, the Grimms' work in 1813 included publishing the first volume of *Old German Forests* (*Altdeutsche Wälder*), a journal dedicated largely to medieval German literature, language, and culture, although it also contained Italian and Dutch folk songs and an Indian fairy tale. The sole scholarly contribution not authored by the Grimms was an essay by Georg Friedrich Benecke, a librarian and professor in Göttingen, on the old German umlaut, which Jacob supplemented with added commentary. Wilhelm contributed an essay on medieval heroic literature, while Jacob's essays addressed grammatical topics, flower and leaf symbolism, the lives of medieval tradesmen, the *Lay of Hildebrand*, and Wolfram von Eschenbach's medieval Grail romance *Parzival*, based on Chrétien de Troyes's *Perceval, le Conte de Graal*.

The journal is largely forgotten today and (as would be true of many of the Grimms' works) did not sell well. It nevertheless yields important insights into the Grimms' developing notions of folk culture and medieval literature. For example, in keeping with his views on the interactions of various forms of natural poetry, in one essay Jacob made connections between *Parzival* and some of the fairy tales in the first volume of *Children's and Household Tales*. Relating a passage in which Parzival likens drops of blood on snow to the fair complexion and rosy cheeks of his beloved, Jacob compared this to the mother in "The Juniper Tree," who wishes for a child as red as blood and white as snow after she cuts her finger and blood falls on the snow. He linked such wishes, which in *Children's and Household Tales* also appear in "Snow White," to descriptions in myth of individuals born of blood and milk. In his interpretation, the mother's wish for a child with red and white complexion symbolizes the child's receipt of her blood as nourishment in the womb and her milk as an infant. In exploring this connection, Jacob also saw folk notions of the body in the frequent appearance of black (at times represented by a raven) alongside red and white, asserting that this color trio pervades folklore because "in them and in their intermixing the human body appears: the white in skin, nerves, tendons, and bones; the red in blood; the black in hair and in the sight of the eyes; and all three colors express themselves in particular in the chyle and in the red and black blood."[27] Here, Jacob expressed his continued belief that even the more fanciful aspects of folk literature were rooted in truths about the human and natural world.

But the method used to decide just what these truths were and how folk literature conveyed them seemed suspect to the Grimms' critics. In his review of the volume, the Romantic poet, translator, and scholar August Wilhelm Schlegel took aim at Jacob's analysis of *Parzival*. He sneered that Jacob had amassed all the snow in the literary world on which drops of blood had ever fallen, but that since that covered only the colors white and red Jacob had also selectively included texts in which "some raven or at least a crow must come flying by." As for the etymologies in the various essays in *Old German Forests*, Schlegel complained that Jacob too readily claimed, without providing rules or patterns, that letters such as *b*, *k*, and *d* could be substituted for one another, which gave him free rein to arbitrarily switch one for another in a manner that led to spurious claims regarding root words. To Schlegel, these and other methodological deficiencies lay bare Jacob's too hasty desire to see an interconnectedness among various texts and traditions where often none existed, as well as his penchant to overemphasize collective cultural output at the expense of individual creative accomplishment. Jacob seemed to suggest that anything meriting admiration had arisen spontaneously from folk culture, whereas Schlegel posited that what we prize from previous epochs is, on closer observation, always the product of individuals. As an example, Schlegel noted that upon beholding a beautiful tower, we of course realize that many workers contributed to putting its stones in place; but the stones are not the tower, which Schlegel regarded as the creation of the master builder.[28]

Schlegel's criticism of *Old German Forests* can also be leveled against the edition of Hartmann von Aue's *Poor Heinrich* on which the Grimms embarked in 1813. *Poor Heinrich* is a medieval narrative poem from around 1190 in which the title character is told that his leprosy can be cured only by the blood of a virgin who willingly sacrifices her life for his. When a maiden expresses her willingness to die for him, he refuses to allow her to do so, whereupon God miraculously cures him. In December 1813, the Grimms announced their intent to publish an edition of *Poor Heinrich* that would include a translation into modern German, noting that "a translation into today's language will make this ancient German tale into a universally readable folk book." Just a year earlier in his review of Johann Gustav Büsching's 1810 edition of *Poor Heinrich*, Jacob criticized Büsching for his "fatal manner of modernizing old poetry" and in particular for attempting to replicate the poem's verse form at the expense of its content and meaning. Jacob identified three main types of readers: true lovers of poetry who will take pains to read a text in its original language and form, dilettantes who are capable of understanding the original but seek an easy read instead of an intellectual challenge, and readers who simply do not have the skills to read the original regardless of effort. For this third category of readers (whom he identified mainly as female), he found it appropriate to modernize the form of the work, but not at the expense of its content; thus in his view Büsching should have retold *Poor Heinrich* as prose instead of trying to maintain its verse.[29]

The Grimms' edition therefore was to include Wilhelm's translation of the Middle High German poetry into modern High German prose alongside a critical edition of the original medieval text. Notably, the Grimms justified their prose translation on the grounds that modern language would make *Poor Heinrich* accessible to readers as a "folk book" (*Volksbuch*). In announcing their planned edition, the Grimms set the stage for their interpretation of Hartmann's work as folk literature, when it is in fact a courtly poem that illustrates Schlegel's notion of individual creative achievement. Also notable is that the Grimms sought to link the poem's content with contemporary events. Emphasizing the maiden's willingness to sacrifice herself, the Grimms spoke in their announcement of the appropriateness of issuing a new edition of *Poor Heinrich* "in this happy time in which each individual is sacrificing for the fatherland," and they indicated that subscriptions to the edition would benefit those serving Hessen in the Wars of Liberation. Indeed, Wilhelm donated 194 talers that he brought in from subscriptions for *Poor Heinrich* to a Hessian women's association for the care of wounded soldiers.[30]

The "happy time" the Grimms name in the subscription announcement referred to the end of French occupation. In the aftermath of the Battle of Leipzig in October 1813, the French were at last driven out of Electoral Hessen, over which Jérôme Bonaparte had ruled as King of Westphalia since 1807. As the war turned against them, the French ordered that the most valuable books in libraries in Kassel and at Napoleonshöhe (soon to be known again as Wilhelmshöhe) be packed up and transported to France. At the same time that Jacob and Wilhelm were working to preserve fairy tales and other texts they believed were in danger of dying out, Jacob was endeavoring to prevent the looting of Hessian books. He managed to save the manuscript collection by strategically downplaying its importance, but other works were plundered.

Westphalia was to have been a model state, with its customs system, use of the decimal system for currency, educational reforms, proclamation of Jewish emancipation, and modernizing constitution. Influenced by Prussian national ideology, however, nineteenth-century historians and society at large judged Jérôme, Westphalia, and the constitution negatively. Only in recent decades have scholars begun to acknowledge the significance of the kingdom's innovations and aspirations. Nevertheless, even these more balanced appraisals cannot escape the fact that Westphalia was from the start an unwelcome French satellite state that faced dire financial challenges. Under these circumstances, the self-indulgent Jérôme never endeared himself to his subjects. He fled Kassel on the night of October 25 with his bodyguards. Just a few weeks later, on November 8, the electoral prince of Hessen returned from exile, followed by his father, the elector, on November 21. The Grimms' aunt Henriette soon returned, too, from living in exile in Gotha with the electress. Jacob shared the jubilant mood of the crowds who welcomed the Hessian rulers home, but he also felt "that in my heart I have become somewhat more republican-minded than most were, or perhaps that I am too attached to Germany as a whole" instead of merely to Hessen.[31]

On December 11, 1813, Wilhelm requested that the newly returned elector appoint him to the museum library staff. He hoped to fill the open position of second librarian, but considering the elector's anticipated worries about the library's budget he was advised to apply for the less prestigious title of secretary. Wilhelm explained in his petition that he had expected to serve the elector in an official capacity after completing his law studies at Marburg, but the French occupation had intervened. He had wished neither to relearn jurisprudence under the imposed Code Napoléon nor to be in the employ of the Westphalian government, so he had worked as an independent scholar. His long-standing health issues, he further noted, had prevented him from serving in the war against the French. In early 1814, Wilhelm received a secretarial position at the library, but the salary was disappointingly small. "A salary of *one hundred talers*," he reported, dejectedly, to Paul Wigand, "which I am spelling out in letters lest you think that I accidentally wrote it wrong."[32]

As for Jacob, he petitioned the elector on December 16, 1813, for an appointment as secretary to a diplomatic legation, which he was granted on

December 23. He left just days later for Paris as secretary to the Hessian legation taking part in peace negotiations. En route, he wrote Wilhelm about the
glockenspiel at the palace in Darmstadt, how he found Heidelberg so lovely
he wished he could live there, the beautiful minster in Freiburg, and a brief
sighting of the Austrian emperor while in Basel. But he lamented having to
spend so much time with Dorotheus Ludwig von Keller, a German count and
experienced diplomat whom the introverted Jacob found unbearably loqua-
cious. The pair rode together in a carriage and often had to share a room.
Meals were a particular challenge: they usually lasted between one to three
hours, and Keller routinely chose expensive inns that Jacob could scarcely
afford.[33]

Though French victories in February 1814 dimmed Jacob's outlook, he
tried to stay optimistic. "In this war we have so often seen that what appears to be a misfortune becomes the foundation of a greater fortune, and
by the time you read this letter, the circumstances might be much different,"
he wrote hopefully to Wilhelm.[34] But whenever he thought of greatness and
joy, he confessed, he felt that one side of him was warmed while the other
remained cold, just as if he were sitting before a fireplace. The scenes he witnessed in France stunned him. He passed through looted villages in which all
the windows were shattered and the doors broken in, saw people lying dead
in the streets, and came upon fleeing villagers starved out of their homes. At
night he heard cannons or saw the flames of a burning village lighting the sky.
He told Wilhelm of German and Russian soldiers' rape of women and girls
in Chaumont, a pestilence that had arisen in Bar-Sur-Aube because so many
corpses remained unburied, and a wounded Austrian soldier whom people
simply walked past as he lay dying on a road near Combeaufontaine. In Van-
doeuvre, he gave some coins to an ill Bavarian soldier begging for soup, and
in Troyes he spoke with three Prussian soldiers who had lain ill in a field hospital. As he engaged with soldiers and witnessed their hardships, he thought
of his brothers Carl and Ludwig, who in February had joined the volunteer
forces fighting the French. Ludwig became an officer, while Carl served in the
volunteer infantry. Having left Hessen in 1811 for Hamburg, Carl had traveled around northern Germany before returning to join the volunteer forces,
whereas Ludwig had been studying art in Munich. Jacob believed that Ludwig, with his substantial artistic talent, was potentially sacrificing the most
by serving in the military, and he prayed that God would keep him safe and
protect his right hand from injury.[35]

Ferdinand told his siblings that he, too, would fight in the campaign against the French. Wilhelm, who had been ashamed of Ferdinand for not previously joining the campaign, brightened at this prospect. He and Jacob not only regarded it as a patriotic duty to fight against the French if one could but also believed that military service might be a fitting vocation for their wayward brother. Toward the beginning of March 1814, Ferdinand wrote Wilhelm that he had been in bed with a fever for fourteen days but had finally convalesced sufficiently to travel with the Bavarian forces. Wilhelm insisted that he wait until he had fully regained his strength, since an illness in the field could prove dangerous and Ferdinand was known to have a delicate constitution. Although Wilhelm assumed this pause would be only temporary, as the weeks passed he began to wonder if Ferdinand had joined the military at all. Several months later, a disappointed Wilhelm told Arnim that "because of circumstances, illness, and also surely his own fault," Ferdinand had not fought the French and still lacked a means of supporting himself.[36]

Wilhelm meanwhile struggled to make ends meet on his meager salary, and in April 1814 he sought a raise from the elector. He mentioned in his petition that he had gone without a salary during the years of French occupation and added that Jacob could hardly cover even his own costs on his salary as legation secretary, let alone help the family. Wilhelm had also paid for equipment and travel for two of their brothers now fighting for Hessen against the French, and he had two other younger siblings to support. The elector nevertheless denied his petition.[37]

Around the same time, Wilhelm asked his landlord to lower the rent for the Grimms' apartment in Kassel. When this request was rejected, Wilhelm decided they would have to move. This pained him greatly: the Grimm siblings had fond memories of living with their mother in the rented apartment in the Marktgasse, and it was there she had died. In addition, the Grimms had for years been close with the neighboring Wild family, from whom they had collected some of their fairy tales, and neither the Wilds nor the Grimms wished to be apart. Wilhelm also bemoaned the considerable time it would take him to pack up their belongings; indeed, he ended up having to devote three solid weeks to sorting through possessions, including family correspondence and records going back to their great-grandfather. Although he boxed up many materials for the move, for eight days he was able to heat the apartment solely from the many books and papers he tossed into the fire. At the end of April, he moved to lodgings in a building owned by the elector in the street known as Wilhelmshöher Tor (Wilhelmshöhe Gate), so named because it lay at one end of the long road that led to the palace and gardens of Wilhelmshöhe. Although missing the Marktgasse apartment for sentimental reasons, Wilhelm enjoyed the semirural tranquility of the new location.[38]

In France, Jacob tired of having to pack and unpack as he and Keller moved from place to place in spring 1814. His suitcase needed patching, his clothes were dirty, and on the occasions he could get clothing laundered it was not always ready by the time of their scheduled departure. The hectic schedule also left him little time to pursue his scholarly work. Homesick, he dreamed of Wilhelm and their siblings not only at night but also during naps in the carriage, and he longed for news of them. He had begun to number his letters so that Wilhelm would know if any did not reach him, and he instructed Wilhelm to be careful about what he wrote, since letters were routinely opened and read by censors. Due to constant travel and unreliable mail service, a letter Wilhelm wrote in January took five weeks to reach Jacob. When it finally arrived, Jacob responded by telling Wilhelm how alone he felt; he shared that when he thought of his siblings, different as they all were, he realized the commonalities that bound them through their upbringing. He wished in such moments that their parents were still alive, presuming that he would then have simply followed his father into the legal profession and known nothing but the joy of family and professional duty. Jacob's homesickness and nostalgia led him, when the legation fled to Dijon after several French victories and spent two weeks there, to write down his memories of his childhood and family. This writing was interrupted, however, by news of the surrender of French forces in Paris and Napoleon's abdication.[39]

The road to Dijon had cheered him somewhat. He took joy in at last passing through pleasant villages with people knitting and spinning, instead of seeing so many burned-out houses and dead horses. But when, a couple weeks later, the legation party proceeded to Paris, the sights were again depressing: he was shocked to see dug-up bodies in various states of contortion lying on the road and the hundreds of people walking past who did not bother to throw even a bit of dirt to rebury them. Typical of his idealization of the past, he contrasted this with the ancients' respect for the dead, noting Homer's descriptions of the gathering of limbs to take them home and the funereal burnings of bodies.[40]

During his stay in Paris from mid-April to mid-June 1814, Jacob took comfort in scholarship. He found ample time to consult archival materials, among them a Latin manuscript of the medieval beast epic *Reynard the Fox* that he copied by hand. His scholarly efforts in Paris were nevertheless consumed by his and Wilhelm's deliberations over whether to publish their work on the *Poetic Edda* prematurely or wait until they could do further work on it—an issue made more consequential by news that scholar Friedrich Heinrich von der Hagen was preparing to publish his own edition of the *Edda*. If he published before them, appreciation of their own scholarly insights would be diminished. The Grimms had initially agreed to partner with the Danish linguist and philologist Rasmus Rask on an edition of the *Poetic Edda*. They hoped not only to publish before von der Hagen but also to tap into German readers' fascination with the medieval past before this interest ebbed. Rask, however, proved unable to complete his part due to other scholarly commitments, so the project was delayed and reconceived.

In Paris, Jacob lived near the house in which he had lodged with Savigny in 1805; this proximity gave him occasion to reflect on all that had happened in the years since his first trip to France. His current duties included reclaiming Hessian books plundered by the French in the waning days of the Kingdom of Westphalia; the same French assistant who then had packed the books up in Kassel now handed them over to him in Paris to give back to the elector. In some ways, Jacob's dislike of Paris only grew. The noise of the city bothered him even more than when he had been there years earlier, and he despaired over its cost of living. More brightly, however, his brother Carl visited him while on military duty, and Jacob met with Werner von Haxthausen and August Wilhelm Schlegel, the critic who had rebuked his elucidations of motifs and etymologies in *Old German Forests*. Despite these scholarly and social interactions, Jacob longed to be back in Kassel with his siblings, and he was delighted when he could at last depart France in June.

En route to Kassel, he stopped briefly in Strasbourg and consulted archives there. He copied a fifteenth-century reproduction of a medieval Latin poem that became the source for the Grimm fairy tale "The Donkey," and he also studied a manuscript of *Poor Heinrich* that, together with a copy in the Vatican, served as the basis for the edition of *Poor Heinrich* the Grimms were assembling. He marveled that the Alsace region, over which the French king had had sovereignty since the seventeenth century, had managed, in his view, to retain German customs and traditions better than areas such as Baden and Württemberg that were still under German control. Expressing hope that a restoration of German traditions would flower in Swabia, Bavaria, Franconia, Saxony, Hessen, and Thuringia, he pondered "how much of what is good in the present depends on what was good in the past"—a sentiment, however idealized, that summarizes much of the Grimms' impetus to work on older Germanic literature and language.[41]

But this work continued to be hindered by Jacob's diplomatic duties. He had known before leaving France that any return to Hessen would probably be short lived, since he would likely be dispatched to assist Keller and the Hessian legation at the Congress of Vienna. The Congress arose from the Treaty of Paris signed on May 30, 1814. Within two months, the peace treaty specified, all powers engaged in the war would send plenipotentiaries to Vienna for an international assembly to complete provisions of the treaty. With respect to the German-speaking lands, key issues that needed to be settled included the future relationship of the German states (which the treaty announced would be independent but united in a confederation) and the extent to which individual entities might acquire or lose territory. Jacob looked forward to consulting archives in Vienna between his official duties, but he wished that he could first spend a year back in Kassel. The ongoing financial constraints he and his siblings faced required, however, that he remain in government employment. He was happy at least to return home before being posted to the Congress and grateful that his brothers had come back from the war without injury. He spent just a few months in Kassel in summer 1814 before proceeding to Vienna.[42]

CHAPTER 7

Unveiling the Second Volume of
Children's and Household Tales, 1815

Jacob left Kassel in September 1814, traveling by coach to Regensburg and from there by boat on the Danube to Vienna. From the coach, he delighted in the tall stone houses of Würzburg and Nuremberg, their beauty reminding him of the simple rhythm of a folk song. He wished Nuremberg, specifically, were in Hessen, "in order to live and die there," and regarded its medium size as superior to the larger populations of Berlin and Vienna, whose big-city atmospheres he associated with depravity and pretentiousness.[1]

Vienna would grow larger still during the Congress: its usual population of around two hundred thousand increased by over a third as foreigners streamed into the city to participate in the proceedings. (By contrast, having swelled to thirty thousand inhabitants as capital of the Kingdom of Westphalia, Kassel was rapidly shrinking, to around twenty thousand by 1820.) The most prominent visitors to the Congress were Czar Alexander I of Russia and the kings of Prussia, Bavaria, Württemberg, and Denmark, all hosted in Vienna's Imperial Palace by the Austrian emperor. The principal government figures were Austrian foreign minister Prince Klemens von Metternich, French statesman Charles-Maurice de Talleyrand-Périgord, Prussian chancellor Prince Karl August von Hardenberg, and Anglo-Irish politician Lord Castlereagh. Prominent attendees also included the Duke of Wellington and the Prussian philosopher, linguist, educational reformer, and diplomat Wilhelm von Humboldt, brother of the renowned explorer and naturalist Alexander von Humboldt. In all, more than two hundred heads of state and plenipotentiaries attended, along with their retinues comprising scores of noblemen, ambassadors, lesser diplomats, and servants. Cooks, tradesmen, artists, and musicians also descended on the city, whether to profit independently from the increased demands for their services or as part of official entourages. Viennese families squeezed into small spaces in their homes to reap the high rents they could charge to let out rooms to visitors, at times even throwing out their regular tenants to do so. The city was so crowded that Jacob had to lodge in a suburb and complained of walking half an hour for his noonday meal.[2]

Jacob was dismayed by the arrival of the elector, whose presence (fortunately brief) he regarded as unhelpful to the Hessian cause. Upon returning to Hessen from exile in 1813, Wilhelm I had rashly voided institutions and practices inaugurated under French occupation without examining which aspects might beneficially be kept in a rejuvenated sovereign Hessian state. He reclaimed properties sold off by the Kingdom of Westphalia without compensating owners and demoted Hessian government and military officials to the positions and pay they had had before the French occupation (even lowering some generals to the rank of lieutenant). Civil servants uniformly hated, and where possible ignored, his requirement that they resume wearing the outdated pigtail: one account of an electoral visit described how the sudden appearance of the "yard of horse-hair, powder, and pomatum dangling on the backs of the guards" made the elector's presence clear, while "the instant his back is turned, these cumbrous accoutrements are taken off." Jacob, given the poor state of his clothing, fretted that the elector might find him improperly dressed.[3]

Jacob understood the significant resentment caused by Wilhelm I's unconsidered reversals of Westphalian policy as well as the widespread anger toward an elector whom the Hessian people now found too old to change and too unconcerned with the fortunes and misfortunes of his country and its people. At the Congress, the elector requested that he officially be made "King of the Chatti," in reference to the people known as the Chatti who had settled Hessen in ancient times; his subjects, meanwhile, branded him the "two-headed monster" because of a large goiter that grew on the front of his neck. His request was refused both in Vienna and again in 1818 at the conference of Aix-la-Chapelle. Wilhelm I thus retained the title of elector; Hessen remained the sole electorate in Germany until 1866, when it was absorbed into Prussia after backing the losing side in the Austro-Prussian War.[4]

In early letters to Wilhelm, Jacob expressed frustration over the slow pace of diplomatic negotiations in Vienna. In particular, he derided the tendency for negotiators' questions to beget only more questions, leading to little headway on key issues. In the absence of concrete progress, he found inexcusable the numerous festivities for which the Congress became known. For this reason, he did not attend the opening masked ball at the Imperial Palace on October 2. While Jacob stayed away, some twelve thousand guests were welcomed into two colossal halls lit by eight thousand candles and a third hall that had been transformed into an orange grove. The unscrupulous reselling of tickets already collected at the door led to a surge of extra guests. Of the ten thousand silver teaspoons set out for the ball, a quarter were rumored to have gone missing.[5]

The Congress was not just about determining territorial reconstruction after more than a quarter century of revolution and war but also a months-long party celebrating the end of these decades of turmoil. Diplomatic negotiations were often deeply intertwined with the celebratory events. Four days after the opening masked ball, a public celebration of war veterans featured folk dancers in colorful regional costumes; competitions that included foot races, horse races, gymnastics, and sharpshooting; the release of a hot-air balloon; and illuminated representations of monuments in Berlin, Milan, and St. Petersburg. Mid-October brought a performance of Handel's oratorio *Samson* and a "Festival of Peace" held in commemoration of the Battle of Leipzig one year earlier. (Back in Kassel, Jacob's brothers took part in the festivities by fashioning a Napoleon out of pasteboard that they had hoped to add to the celebratory pyres, though it was not actually burned.) In November, Metternich hosted a masked ball at his villa, and Beethoven conducted a performance of his Seventh Symphony, *Wellington's Victory*, and the cantata "The Glorious Moment." The highlight of the month was the pseudo-medieval Carousel on November 23 at the Winter Riding School. Dressed as knights, aristocratic gentlemen speared rings with their lances and split falling apples midair with scimitars, cheered on by Europe's sovereigns and ladies in jewel-encrusted velvet costumes. The knights also propelled javelins at effigies of turbaned Moors' and Turks' heads, laying bare the spectacle's racialized nature. Other entertainments during the Congress included a requiem mass on January 21, 1815, for Louis XVI, who on that day in 1793 had been guillotined.[6]

The frequency of such extravagant events led the Prince of Ligne to quip that "le congrès danse beaucoup, mais il ne marche pas"—"the Congress dances, but it does not progress"—a bon mot that Jacob himself quoted to

Wilhelm. Jacob unsurprisingly preferred serious scholarship to the medieval-izing spectacle of the Carousel or the opulence of the balls. He had learned in October of a Frenchman in Vienna who owned a manuscript of the *Nibelun-genlied*, but who, he reported to Wilhelm in a witty reference to that story's monster, "is guarding it like a dragon and demanding three hundred ducats or more" for it. In November he succeeded in persuading the Frenchman to loan it to him, albeit for a mere three days. Jacob also continued to collect fairy tales in Vienna, worked on an edition of old Spanish romances with a preface he wrote in Spanish, and embarked on a mythological study connect-ing archeological pagan pillar structures to beliefs about the Milky Way.[7]

Most notably, he forged numerous connections with intellectuals in Vi-enna. Only days after his arrival, he visited Friedrich Schlegel, the German Romantic poet, linguist, and critic serving as war councilor to the Austrians. Schlegel's father had been a Lutheran pastor in Hanover, and his brother August Wilhelm Schlegel was the critic who had dismissed the Grimms' *Old German Forests* and met with Jacob in Paris. Friedrich and his wife Dorothea, the daughter of the prominent Jewish-German philosopher Moses Mendels-sohn, had together converted to Catholicism in 1808. Jacob's prejudices are palpable in his disparaging of the converted Jews in Friedrich Schlegel's Vi-ennese salon. He described a doctor he met there as someone "who, like all baptized Jews, has something impudent and untoward about him," and com-mented that Dorothea Schlegel "of course still has her Jewish face, too." As for scholarly conversation, Jacob was dismayed that Friedrich Schlegel (like Arnim earlier) felt that his and Wilhelm's efforts to appeal both to children and to scholars in *Children's and Household Tales* were irreconcilable.[8]

Jacob's collection of folk texts benefited from connections with bookseller H. Eckstein and librarian and bookseller Johann Georg Passy. Jacob was soon invited to Wednesday evening discussions of folk literature over what he called tolerable roasts and lousy beer and wine. Clemens Brentano, who had resided in Vienna from summer 1813 to May 1814, helped introduce him to Eckstein and Passy; although Jacob was grateful for his long-distance help with these scholarly connections, he was happy that Brentano's stay in Vienna did not overlap with his own. Jacob and Wilhelm's friendship with Brentano had become still more strained, and there were long stretches during which Bren-tano would not answer their letters. Candidly acknowledging these periods in a letter to Wilhelm in February 1815, Brentano attributed them to his tortured state of mind: "I do not know, dear Wilhelm, if I am still among your friends, for it seems so often—yes, most of the time—as if I am no longer among the living," he wrote. "I have lost my whole life, partly through delusion, partly through sin, partly through mistaken ambitions. The sight of myself destroys me, and only when I lift my eyes in supplication to the Lord does my quivering, hesitant heart have any solace." A few years later Brentano withdrew to the town of Dülmen in Westphalia, where he served as self-appointed scribe to the Augustinian nun, mystic, and stigmatist Anna Katharina Emmerick. Brentano's published works on her visions, sufferings, and divine insights are today regarded as containing substantial fabrication, which is not surprising given his penchant for embellishment.[9]

Jacob's scholarly pursuits in Vienna soon led to controversy. Back in Kassel, someone complained to the elector that he was neglecting his official duties. After hearing of this complaint from a confidant, Wilhelm defended Jacob by explaining that his brother's scant leisure time was better spent making scholarly connections than attending social functions. He informed Jacob of the issue in a letter sent in November 1814. An outraged Jacob responded that he had been to the library only three times in the preceding two weeks and had meanwhile drafted more official writings than any of his colleagues. His duties included completing a couple reports per week, the most recent two of which had spanned eighteen and twenty-four folio pages, respectively. Already deeply disillusioned with the Congress's lack of progress, he felt "the uselessness and perversity with every single page" that he wrote in his official capacity; he swore to Wilhelm that he could not endure his diplomatic duties much longer. His finances were tight, his fingers ached from writing so many official reports, and the diplomats continued to "thresh dead straw," he averred, "while I—God knows—bear such heartfelt concern for our fatherland and for Hessen."[10]

What would become of Poland and Saxony continued to be among Jacob's principal concerns. He fervently wished that Poland could obtain independence, both for its own sake and because he failed to see how adding a few million Poles (among them "ample foreigners and Jewish souls," as he disparagingly wrote Wilhelm) to Prussia could justify the continued oppression of the Polish people. He further objected to Prussia's annexation of part of Saxony, adamant that Saxons should not be punished for their king's loyalty to Napoleon. Regarding Hessen, he bristled over Bavaria's attempts to acquire the County of Hanau. Above all, Jacob fretted that such territorial disputes were pushing aside necessary planning for a German constitution. Jacob expressed these and other views not only in his personal correspondence, but also in essays, most of them published anonymously, in their friend Joseph

Görres's political newspaper *Rhenish Mercury*, founded in January 1814 to support the struggle against Napoleon. After lecturing at the University of Heidelberg and collaborating with Arnim and Brentano on the short-lived *Journal for Hermits*, Görres taught at a secondary school in his native Koblenz and served as director of public education in the Rhineland.[11]

Daily inconveniences exacerbated Jacob's despair over the Congress's lack of progress. As in France months earlier, he found Dorotheus Ludwig von Keller's loquaciousness intolerable, made worse by the thin walls separating their rooms. Jacob could not help but overhear Keller's many conversations with visitors and worried that Keller could overhear his. To make matters more unbearable, Keller persisted in his miserly ways with respect to Jacob: Jacob had to pay for meals and related expenses from his meager wages, when what he really needed was to replace his shabby shoes and clothes. Given his tight finances, he regretted having to have a new winter coat and a couple vests made for himself. Back in Kassel, Wilhelm similarly felt compelled to buy an inexpensive set of used furniture when the Grimms' existing furnishings became so broken that guests were warned of the peculiarities of each chair before taking a seat.[12]

Wilhelm had at least successfully renewed his request for a raise in salary on November 4, 1814, emphasizing in his petition the responsibility he bore, at the age of twenty-eight, for supporting his younger siblings. He also conveniently noted that a colleague's death had freed up two hundred talers from the library's salary budget. In other good news, in December Wilhelm secured a position in Berlin for Ferdinand with the publisher Reimer, for whom Ferdinand would engage in correspondence and manuscript corrections beginning in spring 1815. But as 1814 ended and 1815 began, Wilhelm suffered a recurrence of his heart ailment, found paying the household's bills a struggle, and was saddened that Jacob would once again be spending his birthday in January away from home. Worst of all, their close friend (and Wilhelm's future wife) Dortchen Wild, having already lost her mother in 1813, was now mourning the death of her father, who passed away on Christmas Day 1814. Hardship also struck storyteller Dorothea Viehmann. Describing her as "our fairy-tale woman," Wilhelm informed Jacob in December 1814 that Viehmann had been quite ill and had come to him, pale and shaking, worried about how to support her daughter's six children after the death of their father. He planned to help Viehmann by seeing if a couple of the children might be accepted into the local orphanage.[13]

Wilhelm was at the time completing work on the second volume of fairy tales, which featured contributions from Viehmann as well as from the Haxthausens and others. Whereas work on the first volume had spanned six years, the second volume had progressed more rapidly. Published in early 1815 while Jacob was in Vienna, the second volume contained seventy tales, most relatively unknown in the English-speaking world. Titles include "The King of the Golden Mountain," "The Water of Life," "The Old Woman in the Forest," "The Lazy Spinner," "The Ungrateful Son," and "The Six Servants." Some, such as "The Goose Girl" (contributed by Viehmann and featuring a macabre description of the talking head of the dead horse Falada), are still well-known in Germany today, although many others have sunk into obscurity.

Cognizant of the criticisms leveled against the first volume, Wilhelm in the preface to the second volume defended the inclusion of scholarly notes and the tales' overall suitability and pedagogical value for children. In subsequent editions the Grimms, and in particular Wilhelm, would enhance this appropriateness for children through substantial editing, but for this second volume they had continued to emphasize fidelity. For example, when Wilhelm wrote to Ludowine von Haxthausen in January 1813 asking for additional tales, he specified that they must be authentic and without embellishment.[14]

As with the first volume, however, this did not mean no editing occurred. Wilhelm explained to Savigny that he and Jacob had endeavored to present the origin of poetry as a collective possession of the common people, though they recognized that this origin could not actually be seen by "mortal eyes" and "therefore, as with everything living, is full of mystery." They thus had not wanted to cut into a tale "with a critical knife" in cases where they sensed the poetry was truly alive and of the people. This implies, however, that they did cut into a tale where they believed it had been tainted by highbrow literature. Because manuscript versions for most tales in the second volume do not exist, the extent to which the Grimms excised or augmented is in most cases unknown.[15]

A fascinating example of their editorial intervention does exist, however, in the tale "The Donkey." The tale in the Grimms' collection depicts a child born as a donkey to a king and queen. Although the king regards his son's animal form as God's will, the queen screams upon first seeing her donkey baby and suggests that he be thrown into the water so that the fish may eat him. The donkey nevertheless grows up to have cultivated sensibilities and becomes an accomplished lute player despite his hooves. Upon seeing his donkey form reflected in water one day, however, he grows downcast and decides to leave the kingdom with a loyal companion. An aging king at another court grants the donkey his daughter's hand in marriage and, to ensure that the donkey is mannerly to his daughter, instructs a servant to hide himself in their bedchamber on their wedding night. There, the servant witnesses the donkey's previously unknown ability to take off his donkey skin, beneath which he is a handsome prince in human form. The prince dons the skin the next morning, but the servant tells the king what he has seen. The following night, the donkey skin is surreptitiously taken and burned in a fire while the prince sleeps, ensuring that he will remain in his human form. He later inherits the kingdom after the old king dies. Folklorists have interpreted the ability to take the animal skin off at night as a vestige of ancient beliefs about metamorphosis; the Grimms suggested that the protagonist who can shed a skin must keep this ability secret as part of a curse.[16]

The source text for the Grimms' tale was a Latin poem, dated from around 1200, reproduced in a fifteenth-century manuscript that Jacob had examined in Strasbourg en route from Paris to Kassel in June 1814. He wrote a summary of the manuscript and transcribed a portion, from which "The Donkey" was formed as it appears in the second volume of *Children's and Household Tales*. In 1870, during the siege of Strasbourg in the Franco-Prussian War, fire destroyed the fifteenth-century manuscript that Jacob had consulted, but the Latin poem, typically titled "Asinarius," exists in other medieval manuscripts. In contrast to the Grimms' tale, "Asinarius" is highly literary, featuring references to classical mythological figures such as Jupiter and Juno and allusions to poets such as Virgil and Ovid. "Asinarius" is also overtly erotic: directly before telling of the donkey's entrance into the king's hall, the narrator points out that the growth of the princess's nipples and pubic hair indicates she is now ready to sleep with a man. The donkey's entrance into the hall thus symbolizes sexual penetration, unsurprising since the donkey has been associated with male sexuality since ancient times. Circulated among mimes and minstrels who performed at courts, oral versions presumably kept some of this erotic content.[17]

The Grimms excised not only the learned references but also the overtly sexual aspects of "Asinarius" as they cut into its artistic layers to reveal what they believed was an authentic folk text that lay beneath. But just as the donkey's sudden ability to peel off its skin seems like a contrived plot device, the Grimms' removal of what they saw as the highbrow content of the poem— which they believed had distorted the voice of the common people—only resulted in a folk text that was artificially constructed. The genesis of the Grimms' "The Donkey" from "Asinarius" is in this way emblematic of the broader inconsistencies in their notions of authenticity and artificiality.[18]

The brothers' choices about which tales should be included in the collection (and which excluded or relegated to notes) shed further light on these tensions. Notably, Jacob believed that Wilhelm should merely have summarized "The Donkey" in the appendix instead of including it in the text, as he told him in a letter of March 18, 1815. This might suggest that he did not regard it as sufficiently different from "Hans My Hedgehog," a tale that the Grimms collected from Dorothea Viehmann and included with "The Donkey" in the second volume of their tales. In that tale, a farmer's wife gives birth to a half-human, half-hedgehog child, who later also can secretly peel off his hedgehog skin. Jacob's view that "The Donkey" should not have appeared as a freestanding tale might also derive from his more conservative approach to editing and adaptation; that is, he may have felt more discomfort than Wilhelm over the considerable edits necessary to uncover the folk text the Grimms believed existed at its core. In any case, in the appendix to the second volume the Grimms acknowledged the tale's provenance in the Strasbourg manuscript; they even noted that the text of the manuscript was in verse form and provided a few lines of the Latin original. The preposition they used to indicate that the tale was drawn from the Latin manuscript was *nach* ("nach einem Lateinischen Gedicht," from a Latin poem), which in German also has the connotation "adapted from." They did not, in other words, suggest that the Latin poem and the published tale were identical in content. Instead of engaging in the deliberate fabrication of fakelore, if anything they are guilty of confirmation bias, seeing in "Asinarius" validation of their view that works of natural poetry existed beneath a veneer of artistic poetry and could be excavated and recovered.[19]

The Grimms found the greatest validation of their notions of natural poetry in Dorothea Viehmann, whom they depicted in the preface to the second edition as an ideal Hessian peasant storyteller. After acknowledging that the second volume had proceeded more swiftly than the first because of friends' contributions and what they described as sheer good luck, Wilhelm described Viehmann thus:

> One such happy coincidence was our acquaintanceship with a peasant woman from the village of Zwehrn not far from Kassel, from whom we received a considerable portion of the tales included here (which

are thus genuinely Hessian), as well as various supplements to the tales in the first volume. Still vigorous and not much over fifty years of age, this woman has the name Viehmann. She has a sturdy and pleasant face, her eyes gaze clearly and sharply, and she was probably pretty in her youth. She safeguards these old tales firmly in her memory, a gift, as she herself notes, that not everyone has been granted, as many would not be able to retain anything. She recites her tales with thought, certainty, and an uncommon liveliness, taking her own delight in the telling. She first tells a tale freely, and then, if one wishes, she will tell it again more slowly, so that with some practice one can write it down as she speaks. In this way, much has been retained word for word and is unmistakable in its truth. Anyone who believes that there might be, as a rule, slight adulteration in the transmission [of a tale] and negligent preservation [. . .] should hear how exact she always remains in telling the same tale and how intent she is on accuracy. When repeating a tale, she never alters anything substantial in it, and she corrects a mistake as soon as she notices it, even in the middle of her telling. For people who continue in a mode of life that has remained unchanged, the adherence to that which has been handed down is stronger than those of us inclined toward change may comprehend.[20]

The Grimms proceeded to give examples of fairy tales such as "Snow White" and "Briar Rose" that feature events or motifs they believed to be directly relatable to passages in Germanic and Nordic epics. In this way, a storyteller such as Viehmann became for the Grimms a steward not only of fairy tales in particular, but also of a primeval Germanic mythology that lived on, in their view, in fairy tales and other manifestations of natural poetry.

Scholars have differed over how much the Grimms exaggerated their portrayal of Viehmann, including her socioeconomic class. The Grimms referred to Viehmann as a *Bäuerin*, which in a general sense can mean country- or peasant woman, and in more specific usage means farmwoman. Whereas they saw her as representative of the rural common people and their natural poetry, some commentators have claimed that she belonged more to the middle class; others have persuasively countered that she lived in a farming village and her husband's work as a tailor was so unprofitable that the family lived in poverty.[21] In any case, Wilhelm's letter to Jacob regarding Viehmann's impoverished grandchildren provides further evidence of her financial hardship. It is clear, too, that their singling out of Viehmann by name shows that they saw in her an ideal representation of natural poetry; indeed, she alone is named in the preface among all the informants from whom the Grimms collected tales. By contrast, they did not refer by name to the Haxthausens there but mentioned only that friends had provided tales from the towns of Paderborn and Münster, and they praised in particular the preservation of these narratives in Low German dialect. In the published notes to the volume, the Grimms commonly listed the region from which they had obtained a tale but did not give the name of the informant.

Since Viehmann was of Huguenot ancestry on her father's side, scholars have also probed the influence of French cultural and linguistic heritage on the tales she told. Whereas the preface to the second volume describes her tales as "genuinely Hessian," it is significant that the Grimms removed this phrase in later editions. Her first language was nevertheless almost certainly German, and only a third of her tales reveal direct or indirect French influence. A more substantial source was likely the inn owned by her father, where in her youth she would have heard tales from traveling soldiers, wagoners, and salesmen. This could explain why most of the stories she shared with the Grimms feature male or animal main characters rather than female protagonists.[22]

While scholars have extensively discussed issues concerning Viehmann's class, ancestry, and upbringing, less attention has been paid to the Grimms' description of her robust cognitive abilities and physical appearance. The Grimms implicitly linked the health of the fairy tale as a genre to the ruggedness of the rural peasant culture that (in their view) had spawned and sustained it. Drawing on associations of the eye with the intellect, the Grimms thus placed particular emphasis on Viehmann's sharp, bright gaze, just as in the preface to the first volume they had described the childlike yet fully grown "eyes" of the fairy tale. Such descriptions point to the wisdom, innocence, purity, and truth the Grimms found in natural poetry.[23]

With her sharp gaze and seemingly magical ability to recount tales with unfailing precision and fidelity, Viehmann thus emerges almost as a fairy godmother who enabled the Grimms to succeed in their quest to enhance their collection. They emphasized that whenever she retold a tale, it was almost exactly the same as the first time she had told it to them, an ability they attributed to her simple rural life untouched by modern progress; moreover, they related that she told her tales with an "uncommon liveliness" and recognized that not everyone possessed such a gift. Though she is described in almost fantastical terms, it is striking that not a single witch or woman with magical powers appears in her tales.[24]

The Grimms' celebration of Viehmann's vitality was soon tempered by the fact that she grew ill and died in the same year as the publication of the second volume. Adjacent to the passage in which the Grimms extolled her sturdy features and clear gaze, Wilhelm wrote by hand in the margin of the Grimms' personal copy of their tales, "died on the evening of November 17, 1815." Later editions included a note after the description of Viehmann's sharp eyes that referred to the orphaning and illnesses suffered by her grandchildren and to her own illness and death. Upon first meeting Viehmann a few years earlier, the Grimms had described her in a letter to Ferdinand as "an old woman." Although she was only in her fifties, their description of her age is not out of place given the shorter life expectancy of their time, the fact that their own mother had lived only to the age of fifty-two, and the long-standing image of old women as storytellers.[25]

Her death corroborates the Grimms' sense that they had collected many of their tales just in time, before they otherwise might have been lost forever. This turned out to be the case not only for the tales Viehmann told them. Wilhelm admitted to Arnim that he was overcome with emotion whenever he read the tale "The Crows" because the soldier who told this tale to August von Haxthausen during a patrol one night in December 1813 was shot dead in battle, while standing directly behind Haxthausen, just three days after telling it. The Napoleonic Wars influenced the tales in other ways. Wilhelm had worked on the volume amid the din of boisterous Russian soldiers billeted in the house where the Grimms lodged in Kassel. At one point, Lotte had to vacate her room for seven Russians, who distinguished themselves principally through their "unbelievable appetite and even more unbelievable drinking." (A Russian shell also hit the library and reminded the Grimms of the precariousness of the rare manuscripts it held.) In addition, the Grimms attributed the hardships experienced by Viehmann and her family to the wars.[26]

Even though the Grimms received most of their tales from educated young women rather than soldiers in combat or older storytellers, their conviction that they had saved vital elements of folk literature from possible extinction was thus not unfounded. Their use in the preface of the metaphor of a destructive storm, and the subsequent need for renewal, aptly captured the physical and cultural devastation caused by the Napoleonic Wars. Wilhelm's serious physical ailments and the deaths of their parents further reminded them of life's fragility. Mortality and loss complicated, but also inspired, their efforts to preserve tales for their own time and for posterity. The sense of loss, preservation, and regeneration in the prefaces of the first two volumes

pervaded their lives and scholarly endeavors in the second decade of the nineteenth century. They sought to heal fairy tales that had been injured, in their
view, by urbanization, industrialization, and related factors imperiling the
rural culture they revered as the source and repository of folk literature.

These efforts continued in Vienna. Between his professional duties Jacob
sought to collect additional folk texts, including tales for a planned new edition of *Children's and Household Tales*. In the last days of December 1814, he
spearheaded the founding of the Wollzeiler Society, named after the street
near St. Stephen's Cathedral where he, Passy, Eckstein, Werner von Haxthausen, and others met at an inn. The society's goal was to collect and preserve
folk texts and traditions. According to the group's founding document, these
were to include folk songs sung in spinning parlors and at dances and other
celebrations; rhymes, animal fables, legends, children's tales, and puppet
plays; and descriptions of folk celebrations, customs, and superstitions. All
texts were to be collected through oral transmission whenever possible and
without embellishment. Members were to regard all variants as significant
and collect them even if other versions of the same basic text had already been
recorded; fragments, too, were not to be overlooked. Texts in dialect were
particularly welcome, and translations of texts from regions bordering the
German-speaking lands not to be ignored. Members were instructed to turn
especially to rural locales and seek out shepherds, fishermen, old women, and
children between seven and eleven years of age—particularly girls, since they
were believed to retain tales in their memory longer than boys. If necessary, a
collector could give small gifts to persuade people to tell tales, but he was in
any case to reassure them that he was seriously interested in rural stories and
customs and not ridiculing them. Pastors, traveling students, and schoolmasters could be of assistance because of their trusted relationship to rural folk.
Members agreed to write texts down on paper as soon as possible after hearing them, along with noting the year and place of transmission as well as the
name of the collector "and perhaps also that of the teller"—an interesting remark in light of the Grimms' omission of their informants' names apart from
Dorothea Viehmann. Members were to seek out friends and helpers through
all the German-speaking lands. However, the founding document expressly
rejected the admission of members who wished only to socialize; instead,
members were told to see themselves as "worker bees" who had pledged to
"honor the fatherland" through the "rescuing of our folk literature."[27]

The Wollzeiler Society's goals and methodologies were further elucidated
in a form letter that Jacob had printed in early 1815 for distribution to scholars

in Germany and beyond. Often referred to as his "fairy-tale circular," the letter referred to the Wollzeiler Society, albeit not by name, and solicited the recipient's membership in the society and assistance in collecting texts from his particular region. Some of the letter's phrasing was identical to that in the founding document of the Wollzeiler Society, but there were blanks provided where the sender could fill in his name, the date, and the geographical area the recipient was to cover. Jacob was convinced that the Wollzeiler Society and the letter, which he envisioned being sent to around a hundred acquaintances and locales, would enable far more collecting than he and Wilhelm could accomplish alone. In a sense, his strategy was to rely on a careful collecting of collectors. In February, he sent Wilhelm copies of the letter with instructions for distribution and indicated that he hoped they could also find support in Sweden, Norway, and Denmark for their collecting efforts.[28]

Like the founding document's welcoming of texts from Hungarian, Polish, Bohemian, and Wendish regions, Jacob's interest in engaging collectors from Scandinavian countries reflects his broader study of how folk texts could elucidate a people's history, whether in Germany or elsewhere, and how stories and motifs often transcend national and regional borders. In both his scholarly writings and his views concerning the political issues that dominated the Congress, he espoused the compatibility of national consciousness with local, regional, ethnic, linguistic, and historical identities. This conviction distinguished his and many of his contemporaries' views of nationalism from the more monolithic and exclusionary brand that prevailed later in the nineteenth century. During his stay in Vienna, Jacob also delved into Slavic languages and literatures, familiarizing himself with the work of linguist and philologist Jernej Kopitar and the language reformer Vuk Stefanović Karadžić. At this time, too, Jacob's book on Spanish romances appeared in print, as did the Grimms' edition of the *Poetic Edda* (titled *Songs of the Elder Edda*). Jacob instructed Wilhelm to send copies of the edition to several of the Danish and Dutch scholars with whom they had corresponded, a further sign of how wide the brothers' international connections had grown.[29]

As he continued his diplomatic work in Vienna, Jacob regretted that Wilhelm had to shoulder so much of the work for the second volume of fairy tales, *Songs of the Elder Edda*, the second volume of *Old German Forests*, and *Poor Heinrich*. Wilhelm had corresponded tirelessly with publishers, polished drafts into final manuscripts, and scrutinized proofs sent from printers. It was not only that Wilhelm had overseen so much of this work by himself, but also that Jacob's absence made it difficult to solicit his input on editorial decisions. Jacob sometimes remonstrated Wilhelm after the fact; for example, he asserted that Wilhelm should have incorporated more of Jacob's scholarly notes regarding various fairy tales into the second volume of *Children's and Household Tales*, and that Wilhelm should have had more foresight about the cost and time involved in having printers in Frankfurt cut special letters for the Grimms' work on medieval literature. Because of ongoing censorship and the unreliability of couriers and postal services, Jacob and Wilhelm also frequently worried that their letters to each other had gone missing; in fact, such delays in receiving mail from Jacob greatly slowed Wilhelm's work on texts such as *Poor Heinrich*.[30]

But Jacob's greatest regret of spring 1815 was being away from home when, on April 15, his aunt Henriette Zimmer passed away at the age of sixty-six. She had been feverish for three days but had not seemed dangerously ill. Just days after her death, the kindhearted electress she had served for so many years told Wilhelm that from now on he and his siblings should regard her as their aunt, and she generously provided money toward Ludwig's studies. Jacob berated himself for having been away on official duties for so much of the year and a half since Aunt Zimmer's return from exile with the electress and for not having written to her often enough. The Grimm siblings now had no remaining close relative, and Jacob predicted that in only a few years they, too, would "all sink together into a little hill of earth with all our love, worry, and toil." Aunt Zimmer's death also reminded him of how emotionally dependent he was on Wilhelm: "I am now so principally bound to you that I would not have a clue what to do if I lost you. But perhaps heaven will allow us to be together for a while longer." Wilhelm felt that the Grimms' connection to their family and upbringing was further severed when he learned that their childhood servant had died in Steinau that spring. As for Jacob, the futility of his diplomatic work in Vienna had made him pensive and melancholy, particularly because he realized that he would not be able to return to Kassel until late June.[31]

Jacob's last few months in Vienna were punctuated by the dramatic events of Napoleon's return from Elba, which unleashed the Hundred Days War. "At this moment news comes via Livorno that the resentful wolf has escaped from Elba and is heading for a landing with a frigate and soldiers," Jacob wrote Wilhelm on March 7 in a hurried postscript, noting that the Duke of Wellington had left the Congress that day to lead the fight against Napoleon.[32] In Kassel, Wilhelm's jubilance over news of the defeat of Napoleon at Waterloo on June 18 was tempered by the knowledge that German troops had suffered heavy loss of life. Just days earlier, an agreement had been signed in Vienna on the founding of the German Confederation. The three hundred or so German polities that had existed before the French Revolution and Napoleonic Wars were reduced to thirty-nine members of the new Confederation, which replaced the Holy Roman Empire that had been dissolved in 1806. Founded with the explicit purpose of ensuring the external and internal security of Germany while maintaining the independence of the states it comprised, the Confederation was weak by design and safeguarded Austrian and Prussian dominance over the German-speaking lands. Austria regained many of the territories it had lost in the preceding decades, and Prussia now reached to the Rhine but was bisected by Hanover and Hessen. The June 1815 agreement

The German Confederation, 1815.

signed in Vienna stipulated that the Confederation would have a federal assembly in Frankfurt, chaired by Austria and located in Frankfurt, to be opened on September 1 of that year. Among its first tasks would be attending to the Confederation's internal, external, and military relationships. Article 13 of the agreement specified that each member state would have a constitution, though some states ignored this stipulation in the years that followed.

During his nine-month stay in Vienna, Jacob had often found himself defending Hessen, even though he suspected that once home again he would be irritated by the political situation there. On a familial level, he also acknowledged that he would likely find daily life with his siblings annoying, despite having missed them so much while away. When in June 1815 Jacob readied himself to return to Kassel after having been gone since the previous September, much had changed for the Grimms and in the world at large. The Wollzeiler Society fizzled with Jacob's departure, and the letters he, Wilhelm, and others sent to potential collaborators met with little response. Nevertheless, his study of Slavic languages in Vienna would continue to influence his work and in particular his growing interest in grammar and linguistics. In addition, his collecting of more tales in Vienna had convinced him that the two-volume first edition of *Children's and Household Tales* should be revised to include his new insights, not merely reprinted. In the years ahead, the Grimms would undertake not only such a revision but also the collecting of legends, the publication of further works on medieval literature, and the readying of the first edition of Jacob's *German Grammar*.[33]

CHAPTER 8

∿⊙⊙∿

Exploring German Legends, 1816–1818

"Our entire fatherland has now cured itself, in its blood, of the French leprosy and reinvigorated itself with youthful life," the Grimms provocatively declared in the preface to their 1815 edition of the medieval narrative poem *Poor Heinrich*. This was far more nationalistic in tone than their 1813 statement announcing the project, which had linked the poem's theme of sacrifice to the hardships endured by Hessians during the Wars of Liberation. The published preface now more boldly compared the liberation of Hessen from French rule to the curing of the title character's disease. Unsurprisingly given this patriotic tone, the Grimms dedicated this edition to the Hessian electress and her daughter.[1]

The Grimms' comparison was far-fetched. In the poem, Heinrich learns that his leprosy can be cured only with the blood of a sacrificed virgin, but he would rather give his own life than see a maiden die for him. After he intervenes to prevent a young woman from sacrificing her life for his, he is miraculously cured. Author Hartmann von Aue (known as "Hartmann") thus used disease and cure in *Poor Heinrich* to explore Christian spirituality, suffering, faith, and redemption, not the miseries of war and occupation. The Grimms, by contrast, portrayed the French as a disease that the Germans had overcome through the bloodshed of war. The brothers' reutilization of blood symbolism in *Poor Heinrich* to make a patriotic appeal to their readers is striking: they associated blood not only with physiological and spiritual vigor and purity (as in the poem), but also with nineteenth-century constructions of national vitality.

Beyond this bombastic patriotism, however, the Grimms had serious cultural aims for their edition. Wilhelm's translation of Hartmann's Middle High German poetry into modern High German prose was meant to rejuvenate *Poor Heinrich*, a work whose medieval language and repellant subject matter had long made it obscure. But the Grimms' reading of the literary origins of *Poor Heinrich* was just as tenuous as their comparison of Heinrich's leprosy to the scourge of French occupation. Downplaying Hartmann von Aue's status as a learned knight and member of the nobility who wrote courtly literature for his patron, Wilhelm and Jacob recast *Poor Heinrich* as folk literature. This reconceptualization stemmed from their conviction that Hartmann had gently reshaped older folk texts and customs instead of authoring his own work from scratch. The Grimms thus devoted much of their scholarly afterword to showing that aspects of *Poor Heinrich* could be found in various legends, heroic epics, fairy tales, and folk beliefs. They linked the title character's name to the many characters in folklore named Heinrich, Hans, Hänsel, or Hanswurst. They also sought to connect Hartmann's suggestion of sacrificial blood as a treatment for leprosy to folk beliefs about blood cures. In the fairy tale "Bluebeard," for example, they interpreted the title character's strangely colored beard as a symbol of illness and claimed that his murdering of women—like the sorcerer's murdering of women in the fairy tale "Fitcher's Bird"—is an attempt to heal himself with their blood.[2]

The Grimms thus saw in Hartmann von Aue an author who faithfully transmitted folk material with little intervention, akin to their view of their own editorial practice. They assimilated Hartmann's medieval poem into the early nineteenth-century German cultural outlook by insisting that it had originated in German folk tradition and by transforming its themes of disease and cure into a metaphor for the rejuvenation of Germany after the Napoleonic Wars. *Poor Heinrich* had been translated into modern German in the eighteenth century, but it was principally the Grimms' edition that made the story of interest in the nineteenth century. Nevertheless, it was not a commercial success; purchasers were mostly the Grimms' friends and acquaintances, as well as others in Kassel.[3]

The Grimms' efforts with *Poor Heinrich* exemplify how German society drew on the traditions of the Middle Ages and the Reformation in the initial years of the post-Napoleonic era. Medieval literature offered a vision of a livelier and more unfettered German past populated by knights, traveling apprentices, minstrels, soldiers, and hunters. As such, it conveyed a sense of freedom that appealed to intellectuals who in the early nineteenth century had been subject to occupation, autocratic government, and censorship. The Grimms' attraction to medieval works was in any case not (or not merely) an attempt to take refuge in an idealized past; to them, uncovering pre-Enlightenment practices offered a path toward a more liberated future, in part because they believed the Middle Ages and the Reformation would afford Germans a self-sustaining sense of their heritage and identity.[4]

They were not alone in this belief. Their mentor Savigny continued to take inspiration from the Reformation and the widespread adoption of Roman law in sixteenth-century Germany as he and his colleagues articulated a way forward in the post-Napoleonic era. The Grimms, Savigny, and other intellectuals were in this way simultaneously backward- and forward-looking, and it is thus apt to regard the Grimms' position as that of "modern traditionalists."[5] Although Savigny and his followers have often been regarded as so nostalgic for the past that they opposed any progressive impulses, recent scholars have noted that such forward-looking liberalism hardly existed in the post-Napoleonic years; indeed, around the time of the Congress of Vienna, distinctions between liberal and conservative views were often blurry, with only the radical or reactionary extremes easy to pinpoint. Savigny and others saw the role of legal scholars and the professoriate as a middle ground between popular revolutionism and royal authoritarianism.[6]

The Grimms, too, supported change that would offer a slow but steady path forward. "The rulers have shown little insight into the lives of their peoples and little willingness to come to an understanding with them," Wilhelm wrote in August 1815 to Johann H. Christian Bang, a pastor in a small town near Marburg whom the Grimms had known for years. "Nevertheless, I am firmly convinced that a good seed has not only been sown but has also sprouted and can no longer be suppressed. If only it can grow slowly, it will grow that much more securely, just as nature manifests itself more nobly in plants that need a longer time to grow but are, as a result, more durable." Wilhelm's observation was apt. Restored to their thrones after the defeat of Napoleon, rulers across Europe realized that a return to order and stability would have to admit some reforms; however, the limits of such reforms became increasingly apparent as the second decade of the nineteenth century progressed.[7]

Wilhelm's optimism, too, soon began to wane. At times he felt as if a stifling fog that afforded only rare glimpses of blue sky hung over the German spirit, and he wondered if the many soldiers who had perished in battle believing in freedom for the Germans had died in vain. He worried, too, for Jacob, who wrote pointedly to the elector on August 10, 1815, to defend himself against allegations that he shirked his duties at the Congress. These accusations were spread by privy councilor Georg Ferdinand von Lepel; already while in Vienna a year earlier, Jacob had suspected that it was Lepel who had begun to speak ill of him to the elector.[8]

More positively, however, Wilhelm's health was improving. His chest tightness subsided to the extent that he could now read aloud at length, whereas previously he was out of breath after just one page. Although he still could not walk for hours on end as he wished, he could enjoy moderate strolls around Kassel, and he no longer appeared pale and gaunt. His condition improved further when, in August 1815, he traveled to the Rhineland to meet Ludwig, who wished to see more of Germany before leaving to pursue artistic studies in Italy.[9]

Sailing on the Rhine from Mainz to Cologne and back and then on the Neckar River to Heidelberg, Wilhelm reveled in the sight of what he later described to Ludowine von Haxthausen as "the sky, air, mountains, and the emerald-green water in such radiant splendor and grandeur from daybreak until into the night, when the moon and stars came out"; he effusively portrayed the Rhine as a river "that so singularly moves a German who sees it for the first time." Ludwig was less impressed, finding the scenery from the boat at best "somewhat decorative" and hoping that the views of the Rhine from atop the mountains might be more magnificent. During his stay in the Rhineland, Wilhelm visited with Savigny, Görres, and the Brentano family, and he also had occasion to meet with Goethe. On a stop in Hanau on his way home, he grew emotional upon seeing the house where he and Jacob had lived and visiting other locales from their childhood.[10]

While Wilhelm and Ludwig were in the Rhineland, Jacob received sudden orders to return to Paris to reclaim artworks, manuscripts, and books the French had plundered from Prussia and Electoral Hessen. While in Paris in 1814, he had already reclaimed some of what the French had taken from Kassel, but many stolen materials remained there. In Paris, he would be just one of numerous foreigners—among them Dutch, Austrian, and Italian officials—sent by their governments to recover artworks taken by Napoleon's forces. The pope had even dispatched the famous sculptor Antonio Canova to retrieve treasures belonging to the Papal States. In contrast to Jacob's earlier diplomatic travels, this time he was at least given a meal allowance and decent lodgings. While in Frankfurt on his way to Paris, he was also pleased to briefly see Goethe—the only time in his life when he would encounter the famous poet and thinker in person.[11]

But Jacob was just as disillusioned with his official duties as before. Now thirty years old and finding himself plagued with headaches, eye strain, and other minor ailments, he bemoaned the toll his years of diplomatic service were taking on his health. As he continued to shoulder the bulk of the Grimm family's financial burdens, he also recognized that he had undertaken his role as legation secretary largely out of loyalty and gratitude to his aunt Henriette Zimmer while she was still alive; this work had proved even more vexing and pointless than he had then anticipated. From Mainz, he wrote dejectedly to Wilhelm and Ludwig of his wish that he would have been able to accompany them to the Rhineland instead of finding himself on his third trip to Paris, which he now dubbed "that accursed place." He reflected on how his positions at the War Board, under the subsequent French occupation, and as part of Hessian diplomatic legations had for years left him always squeezing his scholarly work into his scarce leisure time. This had, he acknowledged, transformed him into someone with a persistent sense of haste and an intolerance of amusement.[12]

The mission of reclaiming artwork and other items might have seemed more suited to Jacob's scholarly bent than his previous government duties in Paris and Vienna, but this was not at all the case. For one thing, he disliked formal galleries, which meant that recovering objects taken from and destined for such spaces did not excite him. Such antipathy is not surprising given his overall dislike of high culture, conveyed a few years later in a letter to Ludowine von Haxthausen:

> Everything with which refined, worldly people entertain themselves has something avaricious, insatiable, and yet boring about it. A beautiful portrait, for example, belongs in the living room of the people who love and honor the person depicted; a holy painting belongs in church where one prays; a picture gallery, however, where the loved and unloved, beautiful and ugly, holy and unholy stand close together on a cold and foreign wall—that seems to me to be a perverse institution, where one object will disturb or even suppress the other. In the same way, it

seems to me, the opera commits an outrage against music, whereas church songs and folk songs grip us in a manner different from the opera, since they are sung and enjoyed one after another, but sparely and with contentment. [...] A waterfall made by human hands and all the fountains at Wilhelmshöhe might inspire our amazement that art itself can undertake and establish such things, but on closer consideration we perceive an emptiness therein, and that emptiness arises because nothing is in its true and natural place. A small stream in a meadow contains more truth and poetry, as does of course a magnificent current like the Rhine and its waterfalls like Schaffhausen.[13]

This extraordinary passage epitomizes many aspects of Jacob's worldview. It captures not only his abhorrence of taking texts, images, and objects out of the context in which he believed (at times mistakenly) they were created, but also his sense that humans themselves belonged in a more natural context than the artificiality of refined society. More personally, the passage helps to explain his feeling while in government service that he, too, had been extracted from his own natural context in the world of scholarship. At times his grumblings had a whiff of entitlement, as if he were somehow owed a position befitting his academic potential; more to the point, though, he found diplomacy at odds with his character, which made engaging in this work excruciating for him.

The work of reclamation was indeed frustratingly bureaucratic. Jacob's official reports chronicle the many obstacles he encountered. Within just days of his arrival in Paris, he learned that Hessen's most precious masterpieces, including paintings by Leonardo da Vinci, Claude Lorrain, and Paulus Potter, had already been sold by the French and sent off to Russia. Back home, Wilhelm was so outraged upon hearing of this that he published an anonymous article decrying the sale in Görres's political newspaper *Rhenish Mercury.* As Jacob soon discovered, much of the remaining fine art plundered from Hessen was held in French royal palaces and châteaux. However, gaining access to these spaces was a hassle, in part because allied statesmen had not yet agreed on principles for the restitution of stolen artwork. Having persisted through seemingly endless stonewalling, he was at last able to dispatch the Hessian painter Wilhelm Unger to Fontainebleau to reclaim a large Rubens painting and to Rambouillet to collect two paintings by the Dutch-German still life painter Abraham Mignon. Retrieving other works proved even more difficult, such as a Rembrandt in a Parisian mansion. In addition to corresponding with government officials over the recovery of such items, Jacob spent hours poring over catalogs in libraries, museums, and other archives to find out where missing pieces might have ended up. He tired of daily travel to and from these various sites and of waiting to be admitted to audiences with ministers and other officials. He found that the French tried to hamper his progress in every way possible. At least Quatremère de Quincy, a prominent French theorist of art and architecture, observed sympathetically to Jacob that the German states seemed more ashamed of asking for the return of plundered works than France had been in plundering them.[14]

Jacob's dislike of Paris and frustration with his duties only fueled his bitterness over the interruption of his scholarly plans. Just days before leaving for France, Jacob had solicited August von Haxthausen's help collecting legends, noting that he and Wilhelm aimed to publish an edition of legends before issuing a new installment of *Children's and Household Tales*. Whereas fairy tales typically take place "once upon a time," untethered from historical personages, places, or events, legends occupy a space between myth and fact; they typically tell of a historical person, place, or event that has become larger than life. (Thus, the fairy-tale Frog King was not a real person, but the legendary king and emperor Charlemagne was.) Utilizing imagery both organic and scientific, Jacob described legends as less beautiful than fairy tales but still attractive in their own way: "Fairy tales are like flowers, whereas legends are like fresh herbs and shrubs that often have their own particular scent and breeze," he wrote Haxthausen. "We would welcome your contributions to our botanizing." The freshness and authenticity Jacob so glorified in his description of legends and other manifestations of folk culture differed markedly from what he regarded as the unending bureaucracy of diplomatic work. He wished to serve as a steward of the natural poetry he found in folk literature and medieval works—regardless of how constructed his notion of natural poetry actually was—but in Paris he saw himself as forced to serve art and artifice.[15]

Following Napoleon's escape from Elba and defeat at the Battle of Waterloo, the Allies set forth stricter conditions for France in the 1815 Treaty of Paris compared to the more lenient terms of the 1814 peace settlement. In the lead-up to the signing of the second treaty, Jacob's official reports conveyed not only his progress in collecting various artworks but also the status of negotiations over France's payments of indemnities, the stationing of allied troops in France at French expense, and the territories that France would cede to German states such as Prussia and Bavaria. To his deep dismay, he learned from

Hessian privy councilor Carl Friedrich Buderus von Carlshausen that the elector had named Buderus representative to the federal assembly in Frankfurt and that Jacob would go with him. At the end of October, Jacob wrote the elector to request that he be released from diplomatic service. He cited his feeble health, his desire to work in a setting where he could more beneficially apply his knowledge, and his belief that after a decade of service he deserved a position that would not require an unorderly and uncomfortable lifestyle that consumed his entire salary. Summoned by the electress, Wilhelm, too, learned of the elector's plans to dispatch Jacob to Frankfurt and explained to her that Jacob could not possibly be made to accompany Buderus. The kindly electress promised to do whatever she could, and a few days later she confirmed that Jacob would not be sent to the federal assembly after all.[16]

Jacob had been hoping to obtain a position at the library in Kassel where Wilhelm worked. However, genuine prospects for such a position opened up only with the unfortunate death of head librarian Friedrich Wilhelm Strieder just days after Wilhelm's return to Kassel from the Rhineland in early October. Jacob applied for and received the position of second librarian, effective April 1816. In the months between his departure from France in December and his assumption of his library position, he continued to receive his salary as legation secretary, although without new duties. He used this time to work with Wilhelm on projects including their collection of legends.[17]

With Jacob's appointment as second librarian, the Grimms entered the happiest period of their lives. Such was Jacob's joy at being back in Hessen that, in 1816, he turned down a professorial position at the University of Bonn, "because I imagined myself living and dying in Hessen," as he later wrote. The Grimms had previously found a move unthinkable while their Aunt Zimmer was alive, but Jacob's rejection of the position in Bonn points to their reluctance, even after her death, to leave their homeland. After years of being apart for extended periods, they now worked alongside each other in the library, which was open to the public for only three hours a day and thus afforded ample time both for professional duties and for their scholarship. Just weeks before Jacob assumed his new position, Wilhelm described himself to Ludowine von Haxthausen as "a very ordinary librarian": although he at times felt like a plant that sees the sun only through the window and forgets what fresh air is like, he found himself in a beautiful room every day except for holidays, speaking congenially with people seeking books and the information in them. He and Jacob got along well with head librarian Johann Ludwig Völkel, and their only persistent wish was for better pay: Jacob's annual salary was 600 talers, the same amount he had received as legation secretary.[18]

In March 1817, Jacob requested and received vacation time to travel to Heidelberg to consult some manuscripts. A few months later, Wilhelm visited the Haxthausens, from whom he collected still more tales and legends. It was his third time at their estate. The following winter, the Haxthausens sent Wilhelm more tales and a twig from a famous rosebush at the cathedral in Hildesheim. According to legend, during a winter hunt a ruler had lost a crucifix that bore a precious relic. He sent a servant to find it and vowed to build a chapel on the spot where it was discovered. Amid the snow, the servant found a patch of green and a wild rosebush growing out of the ground; the crucifix was hanging on the bush, and it was there that the Hildesheim cathedral was built. Wilhelm included the legend in the Grimms' collection, and one of their personal copies has a twig affixed to the page on which the legend appears along with a notation by Jacob that the twig came from the cathedral.[19]

While Jacob and Wilhelm entered a happy time as they worked together in the library and met with friends such as the Haxthausens, others in their social circle were not so fortunate. Arnim had grown quite ill in 1816, and Wilhelm visited him as he convalesced. More consequentially, Joseph Görres's *Rhenish Mercury*, having previously been banned in various individual German territories, was now definitively closed down by the Prussian king because of the newspaper's antigovernment content, which included demands for a constitution. Jacob wrote to Görres to express support and related that he and Wilhelm joked that at least now they could engage more efficiently in cataloging work, since previously this task had been deterred by the many library visitors who came to the reading room expressly to peruse *Rhenish Mercury*.[20] The government's suppression of the newspaper and removal of Görres from his post as director of public education in the Rhineland hardened Görres's antigovernment stance and inspired his return to Catholicism, the faith into which he had been born.

To further show their support for Görres, the Grimms commissioned an ornamental goblet for him. Wilhelm worked with the Kassel sculptor Johann Werner Henschel on the design, which featured a German emperor, a soldier, a Madonna and child, and an image of the Rhine (chosen because "it is the German river above all others" and is associated with the mythical treasure of the Nibelungs). Plants and flowers were to adorn the goblet's stem, and its foot was to bear images from the legends of "The Knight of the Swan" and "The Mouse Tower of Bingen."[21]

The choice of these two legends is telling. In "The Knight of the Swan," a version of the story of Lohengrin, a swan pulls a small boat carrying a sleeping knight to the shore of the Rhine. The knight awakens, frees a young ruler from her enemy, and marries her, stipulating only that she not ask his name or origins. Although she initially stifles her curiosity, after a couple years she requests that he reveal his identity so that their children will know who their father is, whereupon he regretfully calls the swan to come and take him away, never to return. In "The Mouse Tower of Bingen," the evil bishop Hatto II, ruler of Mainz, tells starving peasants he will feed them if they go to a barn and wait for him. Once they are inside he has the barn locked and set on fire. After he dismissively compares their screams to the squeaking of mice, God has mice run over him and bite him day and night. To escape the mice, he builds a tower in the middle of the Rhine, but they swim to the tower and eat him alive. Relevant to the banning of *Rhenish Mercury* was not only the legends' Rhine setting but also their depictions of rulers' actions leading to suffering and misfortune. In addition to noting that Görres had published a version of "The Knight of the Swan," Wilhelm reflected that in Germanic mythology the swan symbolized a spirit sent by God to bring better times and whose work should not be interrupted by worldly cares.

The goblet never progressed beyond the design stage, because Henschel in the meantime embarked on a large sculpture for the Dutch queen. Significantly, however, versions of both "The Mouse Tower of Bingen" and "The Knight of the Swan" appeared in the Grimms' stunning *German Legends*, published in two volumes in 1816 and 1818. A few anthologies existed and writers such as Goethe and Schiller had incorporated German legends into some of their works, but the Grimms were the first to attempt a systematic collection of German legends.

Their attempt was compromised in several ways. Just as in *Children's and Household Tales* the Grimms had spoken of their collection as like the few stalks remaining in a field of crops destroyed by a storm, in *German Legends* they noted that this collection, too, represented only the meager remains of a once great hoard of ancient German folk literature lost through centuries of war and migration. Their efforts to preserve what remained were inhibited, in their view, by the younger generation's reluctance to help, which Jacob attributed to their merely faddish engagement with folk culture. While many youths followed the trend of wearing German folk costumes, he scoffed, not one had answered the Grimms' call to submit legends from their particular region. He and Wilhelm acknowledged, however, that such calls for collecting assistance were typically not successful at the outset of a project; only upon perusing a collection in print might readers typically feel inspired to send in additional texts. The most valuable assistance they received in compiling *German Legends* came from established friends such as August von Haxthausen and the writer and scholar Friedrich Wilhelm Carové, with whom the Grimms had corresponded for years, as well as their brother Ferdinand.[22]

Significantly, whereas many women had contributed to the Grimms' *Children's and Household Tales*, the individuals who helped with *German Legends* were overwhelmingly male. This is not surprising given the presence of legends in historical chronicles, with which the educated men in the Grimms' circle were quite familiar. *German Legends* thus relied far more on learned written sources than did *Children's and Household Tales*. Ancient sources included Tacitus's *Germania*, written around 98 CE, as well as the Venerable Bede's *Ecclesiastical History of the English People* and Paul the Deacon's history of the Lombards, both from the eighth century. Among thirteenth- and fourteenth-century sources were the collection of tales and anecdotes known as the *Gesta Romanorum*, Petrarch's *Letters on Familiar Matters*, and the *Sachsenspiegel* (Saxon mirror), a book of law. Sixteenth- and seventeenth-century sources included satires by Johann Fischart, Johann Michael Moscherosch, and Hans Jakob Christoffel von Grimmelshausen as well as a book of curiosities by the Frankfurt physician Johann Jacob Bräuner and works by writer and historian Johannes Prätorious. Chapbooks and early nineteenth-century journals and newspapers also served as important sources.

The result was an edition of 579 legends, divided into local legends in the first volume and historical legends in the second. The local legends told of spirits, events, and natural and built landmarks particular to a certain place. They featured magical objects along with creatures including the Devil, giants, kobolds, dwarfs, gnomes, hobgoblins, moss people, wild women, changelings, dragons, werewolves, mountain spirits, ghosts, will-o'-the-wisps, nixies, witches, and mermen. As for the historical legends, they portrayed events momentous to an entire people, telling of battles fought and won, the origins and migrations of peoples, the building of cities, the accomplishments of rulers and religious figures, and the rise of aristocratic families. They depicted Goths, Saxons, Bavarians, Thuringians, Merovingians, Franks, Hessians, Austrians, Swiss, Huns, Vandals, Lombards, Swabians, Frisians, and even Amazon women. Prominent historical figures in *German Legends* include Charlemagne, Martin Luther, Frederick Barbarossa, the Ostrogoth king Theodoric the Great, and Boniface, the Anglo-Saxon saint known as the "Apostle of the Germans." While it is often clear why the Grimms deemed a particular legend more local or more historical, at times the distinctions are blurry. For example, the second-volume legend of how a mountain in the Harz region came to be named the Rammelsberg after a hunter named Ramm would seem to fit more neatly among the local legends in the first volume; legends about figures such as Charlemagne also appear in both volumes.[23]

The Grimms sought to distinguish not only between local and historical legends but also between the legend and the fairy tale as genres. They described the fairy tale as more poetic and childlike and the legend as more historical and serious. They also asserted that any particular fairy tale can seem at home anywhere in Germany while legends are more regional, typically bound to specific places or figures. Despite the Grimms' efforts, scholars have noted that a clear delineation of the two genres remains difficult to articulate. The Grimms themselves drew attention to the affinity between the fairy tale, the legend, and history; they noted that of this trio, the fairy tale and legend have the most in common and are often intermixed. While in Paris in 1815, for example, Jacob had excitedly written to Wilhelm of finding that a depiction of a field of flax mistaken for a pool of water appears both in the fairy tale "The Beam," included in *Children's and Household Tales*, and in a legend from Lombardy; he cited this seemingly trivial detail as evidence for his view that folk literature is complete in itself and requires no artistic reworking.[24]

Jacob's conclusion regarding the field of flax exemplifies his tendency, criticized by his contemporaries and more recent scholars alike, to substantiate wide-reaching claims with details cherry-picked from multiple sources. He himself was aware of this inclination, and he acknowledged, too, that he overwhelmed his readers with tangents. Indeed, though he disliked galleries because of what he regarded as curators' juxtaposition of artworks taken out of their appropriate settings, he and Wilhelm, too, could be accused of similar behavior both in their compilations of folk texts and in their subjective determinations of what came from the people's collective voice and what did not.[25]

Although the Grimms' interest in legends extended far beyond the German-speaking world, in keeping with the tenor of the time they expressed markedly patriotic sentiments in *German Legends*. "Every time a man journeys out into life he is accompanied by a good angel who has been bestowed upon him in the name of his homeland, and who accompanies him in the guise of an intimate companion," the preface to the first volume begins. "This benevolent companion is none other than the inexhaustible store of tales, legends, and history, all of which coexist and strive to bring us closer to the

refreshing and invigorating spirit of earlier ages." They also expressed hope
that readers would welcome the legends as "purely German fare" and indicated that, while we may on occasion be dazzled by the foreign, "nothing
edifies and brings greater joy than that which hails from the fatherland."[26]

Sadly, in their efforts to elevate German culture the Grimms perpetuated
notions of Germanness that propelled centuries-old prejudices against Jews.
Two legends in their collection depict Jews who bought and then tortured a
child to death; another purports that a city once existed on Mount Matter
beneath the Matterhorn but, because of a pronouncement made by the Wan-
dering Jew, nothing but ice and snow exists there now.[27] *German Legends* was
not the first Grimm work with anti-Semitic content, however. The second
volume of *Children's and Household Tales* contained two tales, "The Jew in
the Thornbush" and "The Bright Sun Will Bring It to Light," that point to
long-standing European stereotypes of Jews; a third tale depicting a Jewish
character was added to the collection in 1819.[28]

The Grimms' appeals to their readers' patriotic sentiments in any case did
not translate into sales. Only one edition of the legends appeared during the
Grimms' lifetimes; the second was published posthumously in 1865 and the
third and fourth editions in 1891 and 1905, respectively. Although the Grimms
never realized their plan to supplement the two volumes of legends with a
third volume of scholarly commentary, in some respects Jacob's *German Mythology* (*Deutsche Mythologie*, 1835) took the place of that third volume.[29]

Regardless, several legends in the collection are still reasonably well-
known. These include not only the aforementioned "Mouse Tower of Bingen" and legends related to Lohengrin. They also cover Wilhelm Tell, the
Swiss countryman who, after defying Austrian authority, was forced to shoot
an apple off his child's head with his crossbow; Luther throwing his inkpot at
the Devil's head when the Devil tried to hinder his translating of the Bible;
the Pied Piper of Hamelin, who lured 130 children away when the town refused to pay him for getting rid of rats and mice; the knight Tannhäuser, who
missed the chance given to him by the pope to repent after spending a year
with Lady Venus in her mountain; and emperor Frederick Barbarossa, who
is said to be alive and secluded in Mount Kyffhäuser, waiting to return and
bring a better age.

But these and other legends have not taken hold in popular consciousness
the same way many of the Grimms' fairy tales have. Some of these legends are
remembered today not because of their appearance in *German Legends* but
because they were later incorporated into better-known literary or musical

works. Nevertheless, the Grimms' collection not only inspired many such adaptations, including numerous nineteenth-century ballads, but also had a catalytic impact on the field of folklore studies: between 1850 and 1950 over five hundred legend collections were published in German. Scholarly interest in the collection itself, however, has been narrower and more sporadic compared to that shown in *Children's and Household Tales*. The international appeal of *German Legends* has also been quite limited; for instance, the first translation of the collection into English did not appear until 1981.[30]

Similar to complaints regarding the fairy tales' first edition, the main criticism regarding the legend collection was the unevenness of the Grimms' editorial practice. They had reworked some texts while leaving others more or less untouched. As in their previous writings, the brothers in their preface to *German Legends* nevertheless differentiated between changes that falsify folk literature and those that support its natural self-regeneration. Asserting the truth value of folk literature, they rejected literary adaptations of legends as the artificial creations of a never-satisfied educated class. They also compared such reworkings to overly refined gourmet dishes as opposed to the more natural, wholesome fare of the people. Lastly, they blasted the cultivated classes for regarding folk literature as unpoetic.[31]

Thus, just as the Grimms believed that *Poor Heinrich* was the product of Hartmann von Aue's careful shaping of existing folk material, so, too, did they see their own editorial work in *German Legends* as that of gently nurturing the folk literature they had collected. The Grimms continued to espouse this philosophy as Wilhelm began work on the second edition of *Children's and Household Tales,* though in reality he was substantially revising many of the tales. It is with the second edition that these stories as known today take palpable shape.

CHAPTER 9

Revising *Children's and Household Tales*, 1819

During his stay in Vienna in 1814 and 1815, Jacob had become increasingly convinced that any new edition of *Children's and Household Tales* should take the form of a substantial revision and expansion. He and Wilhelm had voiced plans for a revised edition already in 1812, when they called on readers of the first volume to assist with improving it by sending them authentic tales, whether complete or fragmentary. After the appearance of the second volume in 1815, they had elected to focus first on *German Legends* before revising the fairy-tale collection; nonetheless, in preparation for a revised edition they had all the while continued to collect new tales and variants.

Jacob and Wilhelm wished in a new edition to add tales, discuss alternate versions more thoroughly in their scholarly appendix, remove certain tales altogether or replace them with better tellings, and in many cases synthesize two or more versions of the same tale into what they regarded as a more cohesive narrative. Because Jacob had begun to work in earnest on his linguistic studies, Wilhelm assumed the lead editorial role in preparing this second edition (just as he had assumed the lead role for the second volume of the first edition while Jacob was in Vienna). By contrast, Jacob had done substantial work for the original 1812 volume, and most pages in the Ölenberg manuscript they had sent to Brentano were in his handwriting.[1]

Wilhelm's editorial role included testy correspondence with publisher Georg Andreas Reimer. The publisher had announced a new edition of *Children's and Household Tales* in April 1817, but as time passed Wilhelm blamed Reimer for not solidifying the announcement into a firm commitment. Reimer countered that Wilhelm had failed to provide him with any updates. The situation must have been awkward for Jacob and Wilhelm since their brother Ferdinand still worked for Reimer. Wilhelm increasingly worried that the edition's appeal would wane with time, especially as competitors published similar collections. Pressuring Reimer, he related that acquaintances told of being unable to obtain the first edition of *Children's and Household Tales*, and he also indicated that a publisher in Breslau had shown interest in publishing the second edition if Reimer would relinquish his right to do so. Reimer caustically reminded Wilhelm that the second volume of the first edition had not been particularly successful: 350 copies remained unsold and, contrary to Wilhelm's claims, demand had ebbed. If Wilhelm wished to proceed with another publisher, Reimer would consent only if the publisher bought up all the remaining copies; Reimer himself would commit to publishing a second edition only if costs could be kept down and the volume offered at an attractive price. These stipulations are unsurprising given how the book market had weakened considerably amid inflation and widespread crop failures and famine (caused in part by weather changes stemming from the eruption of the Indonesian volcano Tambora in 1815). The Grimms agreed to Reimer's terms.[2]

The substantively revised two-volume second edition was published in mid-November 1819, in time for the Christmas gift season, with a print run of 1,500. Its production included proofreading aid by the philosopher Friedrich Schleiermacher. A third volume published in 1822 featured notes to the tales and extensive analysis of fairy-tale collections in various countries in Europe, the Middle East, and Asia through the centuries. The two 1819 volumes were sold only as a set. Both Reimer and the Grimms acknowledged that the second edition needed to be more visually appealing than the first; thus each volume of tales featured both a frontispiece and a title page on which a lush floral wreath encircled the title. Despite these enhancements, sales were sluggish.

Drawn by Ludwig Grimm, the first volume's frontispiece depicts siblings from the tale "Little Brother and Little Sister," who are shown innocently asleep in the forest despite the brother's having been transformed into a fawn by their wicked stepmother. An angel, who does not appear in the tale itself, floats above them. Wilhelm suggested in a letter to Jenny von Droste-Hülshoff that, considering the illustration's place at the beginning of volume 1,

Dorothea Viehmann.
Lithograph from the drawing
by Ludwig Emil Grimm for the
second and subsequent editions
of the Grimms' *Children's and
Household Tales*. Shown here
from the seventh edition (1857).
Collection of the author.

the angel also hovers over all the tales that follow. Complementing the angel
is storyteller Dorothea Viehmann, who now appeared in a frontispiece to the
second volume. Ludwig depicted her gazing to one side. The wrinkles on her
forehead and under her eyes convey her age, curly wisps of hair peek out from
under her bonnet, and her clothing is plain and modest. Her folded hands
rest on a table and hold two sprigs of flowers and leaves—a humble adorn-
ment in a depiction that conveys naturalness, rusticity, and purity.[3]

The addition of the frontispiece in some respects served as a memorial
to the storyteller whom the Grimms had first extolled, a few months before
her death in 1815, in the preface to the second volume of the first edition.
But the frontispiece in the second edition was also more than that. Its inclusion further casts Viehmann as a representative of the various storytellers
whose tales appeared in the volume; indeed, in later editions the illustration
bore the caption "MÄRCHENFRAU" (fairy-tale woman). As in the 1815 preface,
Wilhelm singled out Viehmann for praise in the 1819 preface. He noted that,
with the help of friends, he and Jacob had collected numerous other tales

for the second edition in addition to those from Viehmann but once again did not name other informants, whether from Hessen or elsewhere. Thus, the Haxthausens continued to go unmentioned in the preface, although they contributed many tales to the second edition. In all, the Haxthausens and their circle of acquaintances contributed about eighty tales; by way of comparison, Viehmann alone told around forty to the Grimms, of which almost half appear in the collection from the second edition on.

Later generations of Haxthausens told of August's pride over contributing the well-known "Bremen Town Musicians" (as well as his happiness that the Grimms retained the tale's mention of Bremen, since their tales only rarely invoke a particular place). Like other Grimm informants, the Haxthausens were otherwise silent on their role in shaping the collection. They seem to have endorsed the notion of Viehmann as foundational storyteller and themselves as mere collectors and intermediaries. This is not surprising given their elevated socioeconomic station and the association of natural poetry with the common people. Upon receiving a print from Wilhelm of the Viehmann illustration, Ludowine von Haxthausen felt compelled to pin it to her wall even before she could find a suitable frame. "It seems to me that she is looking very far into the future, deep in thought," Ludowine remarked, "but she is nevertheless so real and true that one might still guess what she is thinking, even though her mouth is firmly, firmly closed. She has clearly experienced many sad days and yet has retained a calm heart throughout." Although Wilhelm did not mention the Haxthausens by name in the preface, in December 1819 he sent a copy of the second edition to them with a letter in which he described the book's contents as "true household tales, that is, tales belonging to your house."[4]

The resilience and steadfastness Ludowine saw in Viehmann's gaze matches Wilhelm's description—added to the second edition's preface—of Hessians as vigorous, hardworking, handsome, tall, and made stronger by the region's rural culture and lack of frivolous comfort. Wilhelm further connected these traits to the Hessians' ancient ancestors, the Chatti. Despite Viehmann's Huguenot ancestry on her father's side, she became emblematic to the Grimms of a hardy and unpretentious Hessian heritage that stretched back through the ages.

Wilhelm's mention of the Chatti in the second edition would have resonated with the Grimms' Hessian readers not only for reasons of heritage. The elector of Hessen was at the time planning a new residence for himself that he designated the "Chattenburg" (Chatti Castle). Jacob attended the laying of the foundation stone in June 1820; however, construction was halted after the elector's death the following year. Although the Grimms celebrated the ancient Chatti in *Children's and Household Tales*, they offered no corresponding celebration of the elector. On the contrary, tacit critiques appear in the handful of tales that depict rulers' disgraceful treatment of discharged soldiers. These tales often begin at the end of a war, with a soldier given at most a few coins or some bread upon being discharged, despite having put his life on the line for king and country. The Grimms' inclusion of such tales was not mere coincidence: when their brother Ludwig and his regiment returned from fighting the French, they found that half of their pay had been cut. Perhaps because of Ludwig's experience, Wilhelm had criticized the elector's poor treatment of returning soldiers and overall neglect of the Hessian military in essays in Görres's *Rhenish Mercury* in April 1815.[5]

Wilhelm's celebration of Hessian rural culture and invocation of the Chatti did not come at the expense of broader German identity. On the contrary, in keeping with the Grimms' view of nationalism as compatible with regionalism, Hessians are depicted in the preface as embodying a pure, untainted Germanness. Moreover, Wilhelm explained that the Grimms had omitted first-edition tales that they regarded as too foreign in origin or corrupted by too many amendments. Viewed as too dependent on Perrault's version, Jeanette Hassenpflug's telling of "Puss in Boots" was thus booted, as was the Hassenpflug family's Perrault-influenced version of "Bluebeard." Similarly, the second edition did not include "The Hand with the Knife," the Scottish tale in the first edition that Jacob had translated. In place of these, the Grimms had added new tales from German-speaking lands, including some from Austria and Bohemia. Compared to the first edition, therefore, the second was meant to be more explicitly German in orientation.

Wilhelm also stressed in the preface that what was incomplete or lacking in the first edition had now been made whole: as a result of incorporating new passages many of the tales now appeared in better form and were told more simply and purely. Justifying the Grimms' edits, he further explained that some reshaping must occur in any transmission of folk literature, for without it even a faithful retelling would be "somewhat infertile and dead"; indeed, this accounted for why each region and each storyteller would tell the same tale differently. "But there is, of course, a large difference between this half-conscious unfolding which, similar to the quiet growth of plants, has drunk directly from the source of life," he wrote, "and an intentional alteration that arbitrarily ties and even glues things together. It is the latter that we cannot condone." The editor or author who unnecessarily polishes or reworks a tale becomes like Midas, Wilhelm claimed: every tale he touches turns to gold and cannot nourish us. In short, amendments that intervene too radically will make a fairy tale inanimate instead of restoring or preserving its innate vigor. The Grimms' editorial philosophy was akin to the Romantic medicine of Wilhelm's doctor Johann Christian Reil and others of his generation, who preferred to organically restore what they saw as the equilibrium of the body's internal and external forces instead of performing surgery.[6]

Wilhelm's idea of a "half-conscious unfolding" implies that a successful editor operates in a trancelike mode guided by mystical forces. But Wilhelm also noted the difficulty of determining whether any given passage is part of a tale's organic wholeness or an inauthentic addition, and he asserted that honing the ability to make such determinations takes time and practice. The editor in a sense had to operate, rather inexplicably, in a spontaneous and yet highly focused and skillful manner. Wilhelm thus espoused editorial purity while trying to justify how edits such as the merging of two or more tales did not violate this principle. He navigated between principle and practicality, knowing there were complaints that the Grimms had not sufficiently edited the tales in the first edition to make them suitable for nineteenth-century children or to improve their style and narration.

Indeed, despite the Grimms' earlier protestations in response to such criticisms, much of the reworking in the second and subsequent editions made the tales more suitable for nineteenth-century bourgeois children. Wilhelm's efforts to convey the tales' appropriateness for a young audience take many forms. Not only does the frontispiece depicting "Little Brother and Little Sister" visually emphasize children, but the first volume of the second edition also contained Wilhelm's essay "On the Essence of Fairy Tales," in which he extolled the purity of children's stories. He explained, too, that they are sometimes called household tales because their simple poetry can be enjoyed by everyone and they are shared within the family sphere. As for the second volume of tales, it included a prefatory essay in which Wilhelm examined children's songs, games, sayings, and holiday traditions; in addition, nine children's legends were appended to the volume.[7]

Further, Wilhelm took out the tale about children who play butcher that Arnim had found objectionable. But this does not mean the second edition eschews violence. On the contrary, to enhance the tales' pedagogical value Wilhelm added or intensified violent punishments for bad behavior. In the first edition, Cinderella's wicked stepsisters merely grow frightened and turn pale when the prince discovers Cinderella's identity and escorts her to his carriage; from the second edition on doves peck out the stepsisters' eyes at the end of the tale "and thus they were punished with blindness for their wickedness and deceit for as long as they lived."[8] Likewise, in the first edition the helper-turned-tormenter Rumpelstiltskin merely runs away in rage after the miller's daughter correctly guesses his name; in the second he angrily stomps his right foot into the ground and sinks up to his waist, then pulls his left foot so forcibly that he tears in two and destroys himself. There were many instances already in the first edition of evil characters suffering violent punishments, such as the witch in "Snow White" who is made to dance to her death in red-hot iron slippers, or the lazy daughter in "Mother Holla" who is covered with pitch, whereas her industrious and obedient sister is showered with gold. But the collection becomes more explicitly moralistic, admonishing bad behavior and rewarding good, in the second edition. This is particularly the case for children and women, whereas male characters continue to be rewarded for their cheekiness, deviousness, and subversion of authority. In part through Wilhelm's shaping of the tales, the teaching of lessons through extreme punishment became standard fare in nineteenth-century German children's literature. A notable example is Heinrich Hoffmann's *Shock-Headed Peter* (1845), which depicts a girl who burns herself to death when she plays with matches and a boy whose thumbs are cut off when he disregards his mother's admonishment not to suck them.

Wilhelm also sought to add or enhance Christian references. Ludwig's depiction of the angel in the frontispiece is a visual example of this, but many passages also make the second edition more overtly religious. Starting with this edition, for instance, in "Rumpelstiltskin" the first trio of names the queen guesses refers to the Three Wise Men. Similarly, "Cinderella" begins in both the first and the second edition with Cinderella's biological mother on her deathbed; only from the second edition does the dying mother instruct her daughter to "remain pious and good, so that the good Lord will always help you."[9]

Wilhelm also expunged or euphemized sexual references that went against bourgeois social mores. For example, in the first edition the sorceress in "Rapunzel" learns that a man has been in the tower when Rapunzel complains that her clothes have become too tight; in the second and subsequent editions this reference to pregnancy is removed, and Rapunzel instead blurts out that the sorceress is so much heavier to hoist up into the tower than the prince. Rapunzel still gives birth to twins later in the tale, but narration indicating that Rapunzel and the prince were as fond of each other as husband and wife makes their tryst somewhat more socially acceptable. In later editions, their relationship is made still more proper, insofar as the prince proposes to Rapunzel in the tower before their implied sexual encounter.

The references to incest in "All Fur," in which a king wishes to marry his daughter after his wife dies, also demonstrate Wilhelm's approach to sexual taboos in the second edition. Whereas in the first edition the narrator merely conveys that the king's advisers tried to talk him out of marrying his daughter and that his daughter regarded his wish as "godless," in the second edition the judgment against the king is far more pronounced. The daughter's indirect "godless" comment is removed; instead, the male advisers are given direct speech, in which they tell the king that incest is a sin forbidden by God. In neither version does the king actually marry his daughter, since she leaves home, but Wilhelm's edits serve the moral purpose of teaching children of the evils of incest. That Wilhelm puts moral judgment of the king in the mouths of men is in keeping with many other edits in the second edition that diminish the independence of female characters and reinforce patriarchal norms. A sharp drop in Cinderella's direct speech utterances and corresponding increase in male speech in the tale after the first edition are but one example.[10]

Wilhelm's moral and pedagogical aims throughout the second edition also routinely intersected with his efforts to enhance the tales' pictorial quality. In numerous tales, his edits served to convey a character's essential morality or immorality through added descriptions of the character's eyes. In "The Frog King or Iron Heinrich," the frog becomes a prince "with beautiful and friendly eyes," a description that first appears in the second edition. Similarly, the second edition adds mention that the wicked stepmother's biological daughter in "Little Brother and Little Sister" was "as ugly as the night and had only one eye." When the stepmother learns that her stepdaughter is now a queen, she uses magic to make her own daughter look exactly like the stepdaughter. This is done so her daughter can usurp the stepdaughter's royal status. But her evil magic is incomplete: in the second and subsequent editions, the narrator mentions that the wicked stepmother could not restore the missing eye. (And, as mentioned above, in perhaps the best-known addition of ocular symbolism, doves peck out the wicked stepsisters' eyes at the end of "Cinderella" from the second edition on.)[11]

Beyond endowing exemplary characters with beautiful eyes and diminishing the sight of immoral characters, Wilhelm made the tales more pictorial in other ways. In "Old Sultan," a tale that the Grimms had obtained from

Sergeant of Dragoons Johann Friedrich Krause, the cat who comes to the aid of the old dog is described as lame in the first edition; in the second and subsequent editions the narration more vividly portrays the cat as three-legged and holding its tail erect out of pain. Where such descriptions change between editions, it is in many cases impossible to know whether a detail originated with the Grimms or in another telling. For the second and subsequent editions of "Old Sultan," for example, Wilhelm incorporated elements from a version told by the Haxthausen family into the tale, so the added descriptive language may have come from that version. Regardless of the source, however, it was Wilhelm who chose whether to incorporate a specific element into a tale.

"How Six Made Their Way in the World" is a fitting example of how Wilhelm at times substituted one image for another. The Grimms received the tale from Dorothea Viehmann and added it to the second edition. It tells the story of a discharged soldier who wishes to revolt against the king. To help him, he assembles a group of men with unusual capabilities, from a man so strong that he can carry six trees at a time on his shoulder to a hunter whose eyesight is so sharp that he can shoot the left eye out of a fly from miles away. Among them is a runner able to sprint on his two legs as fast as birds fly and who can unbuckle one of his legs when he does not wish to move so swiftly. As the Grimms indicated in their published notes, Viehmann's version did not include the runner's detachable leg; she had the man attach a cannon to his leg whenever he wanted to slow himself down. A version of the tale from Paderborn included the detachable leg, and they substituted this image for the cannon. The runner has typically been interpreted as representing a soldier who has lost his leg in battle and now has a prosthesis. While the cannon serves as a visual reference to war's destructive capacity, the detachable leg accentuates the bodily effects of such weaponry. In substituting the detachable leg for the cannon, the Grimms made the runner's situation both more relatable to those who had seen or sustained bodily injury in war while also more fantastical, since the unbuckling of the leg is depicted as the runner's way of curbing his superhuman speed.[12]

These and other descriptive enhancements resulted in part from Wilhelm's growing understanding of the differences between oral and written storytelling. He understood by the second edition that an orally told tale benefits from the speaker's tone of voice, facial expressions, and hand gestures—elements missing from a written text that can be compensated for by enhanced pictorial descriptions, folksy sayings, and rhymes. Thus, the first-edition version of "Mother Holla" as told by Dortchen Wild was combined in the second edition with a variant in which the rooster speaks a rhyme. And in the first edition, "The Brave Little Tailor" had appeared in two different versions: one from a sixteenth-century text and another from a fragment supplied by the Hassenpflugs. Arnim had criticized the outdated language of the sixteenth-century text as inaccessible to children, so for the second edition Wilhelm mixed various versions and included idioms and humorous passages, such as indicating that the flies the tailor attempted to shoo away did not understand German. The tale also illustrates Wilhelm's understanding of number symbolism in folklore and mythology: whereas the Hassenpflug version had the tailor killing twenty-nine flies with one blow, Wilhelm opted for the seven flies specified in the sixteenth-century version. Similarly, to form "The Three Spinners" in the second edition, Wilhelm retained the three women deformed by spinning who appeared in a variant from Jeanette Hassenpflug in the first edition, but otherwise relied on the telling supplied by Paul Wigand, which had only two spinners.

Wilhelm's frequent mixing of two or more tales to form the version presented in the second edition illustrates what folklore scholars refer to as "contamination," a term that sounds negative but merely describes the process by which variants of a tale are synthesized to form a new variant.[13] He insisted in the preface that the Grimms had mixed two or more versions into one narrative "once they completed each other and there were no contradictions to cut out in uniting them." Only where there were contradictions among versions, he explained, did they choose the best one for the collection and give summaries of the other versions in their appendix. Similarly, in the volume of notes to the tales, the Grimms insisted that they had explicitly named cases in which they had incorporated something from one telling into another or merged two tellings; they avowed that "an actual commingling has not taken place and whatever has been added could easily be separated out again." In no instance had they exercised the freedom afforded to creative writers, they added, but had instead opted for scholarly precision.[14]

The tale "Brother Lustig" illustrates this philosophy well. It is one of the Austrian tales that had been added to the second edition. While in Vienna, Jacob had obtained "Brother Lustig" from the librarian and bookseller Georg Passy, who had collected it from an elderly Viennese woman around 1815. In the tale, the discharged soldier Brother Lustig is joined by a traveling companion who, unbeknownst to him, is St. Peter. Brother Lustig slaughters and cooks a lamb while St. Peter is out on a walk. Despite promising St. Peter that he will not eat the lamb, he consumes its heart and lies about this upon St. Peter's return; he even preposterously claims that lambs do not have hearts. Trying to force Brother Lustig to confess his guilt, St. Peter makes a body of water appear that rises to Brother Lustig's neck and almost drowns him as he attempts to cross it. In the appendix to their tales, the Grimms explained that while they viewed Passy's version as the most complete and liveliest of all the known variants, it did not contain the part about the water. They had taken this part from a shorter version from Hessen. "Brother Lustig" thus exemplifies Wilhelm's merging of tales to form what he believed was a poetically complete narrative.[15]

But not every merging of tale variants accorded so neatly with the principles the Grimms professed. Wilhelm's synthesis of variants of "The Maiden without Hands" is a case in point. As told in the second and subsequent editions, the tale depicts a poor miller who is promised riches by an old man in the forest if the miller gives him what is behind his mill. Thinking that the only thing behind his mill is an apple tree, the miller agrees and returns home. But his wife despairs, for she knows that the old man was really the Devil and meant not the apple tree but their daughter, who was standing behind the mill at the time the pact was made. On the day the Devil comes, the daughter washes and draws a circle of chalk around herself so that her purity will make it impossible for the Devil to claim her. When the Devil instructs the miller to take all water away so that she cannot continue to clean herself, she cries so much on her hands that they are purified and the Devil once again cannot take her. The Devil then commands the father to cut off his daughter's hands, claiming that he will belong to the Devil if he does not do so. After the father tells his daughter of the consequences if he does not carry out the Devil's command, she submits to having her hands cut off; however, she then cries so hard on the stumps of her arms that the Devil yet again cannot take her and finally gives up. Having kept the wealth gained from the Devil, the father pledges to give his daughter a life of luxury for the sacrifices she has made. But she insists on leaving home; a king takes her in, has silver hands made for her, and marries her. When the king must travel while his wife is pregnant, the Devil tries to take revenge on her by intercepting and falsifying letters between the girl's mother-in-law and the king. In the end God makes the girl's natural hands grow back and she and the king are reunited with the son she has given birth to in his absence.

In the first edition, this gruesome tale followed a version Marie Hassenpflug told to the Grimms in March 1811. For the second edition, however, the Grimms mixed Hassenpflug's version with one that Dorothea Viehmann told them two years later, which they found superior "in its inner completeness."[16] Viehmann's version did not include the Devil; instead it portrayed an enraged father who cuts off his daughter's hands and breasts when she refuses to marry him. Wilhelm chose to keep Hassenpflug's beginning and fuse it onto the body of Viehmann's tale, so that the Devil, not the father, is the instigator of the bodily mutilation and there is no reference to incest. After the maiden leaves home in the first edition, she enters the king's garden through a gap in the hedge and cleverly uses her body to shake the trunk of a tree so that some apples fall and she can bend over and grab them with her teeth; she has less agency in the second edition, where an angel helps her across a moat and she can conveniently eat the fruit (now pears) directly from the branch. In the first edition, she is jailed for eating the apples and later made to tend the king's chickens, and she does not receive silver hands; in the second, she is not thrown in jail, does not tend chickens, and receives the prostheses. Wilhelm also retained from Hassenpflug's version the Devil's interception and altering of correspondence between the maiden's mother-in-law and the king; in Viehmann's telling, it was the maiden's mother-in-law who intercepted and altered correspondence between the maiden (now queen) and the king. Wilhelm continued to revise the tale in later editions, but the principal edits were made between the first and second.

"The Maiden without Hands" provides a remarkable example of Wilhelm's editorial handiwork, insofar as he blended different versions to arrive at a form that aligned with his notions of bourgeois values and gender roles. In a statement that aligns with the editorial philosophy espoused in their preface, the Grimms claimed in their appendix that the tale is told "according to two tales from Hessen that on the whole agree with and complete each other." Unlike in "Brother Lustig" and "How Six Made Their Way in the World," however, Wilhelm's editing of "The Maiden without Hands" was more about cutting and pasting pieces that did not fit well together and therefore compromised the plot motivation, rather than finding a missing puzzle piece or substituting one suitable component for another. It is clear, for example, why the daughter would leave home if it is the father who has cut off her hands and breasts because she will not marry him; however, when the Devil is the instigator of violence against her, it is less clear why she—now handless— would venture out alone into the world, where the Devil may lurk. Female independence and agency are reduced through Wilhelm's edits, and the father's culpability is transformed into a literal case of "the Devil made me do it."[17]

Amid all the rearranging, adding, merging, and culling of tales that Wilhelm engaged in between the first and second editions (and to a lesser extent between all the subsequent editions), one curious fact remains constant: the opening tale in all seven complete editions of *Children's and Household Tales* published during the Grimms' lifetime is the "The Frog King or Iron Heinrich" and the last tale, save for the children's legends that appear separately at the end of the volume, is "The Golden Key." The two have in common a character's retrieval of a submerged golden object. In "The Frog King or Iron Heinrich," a frog fetches a princess's golden ball from a well, on the condition that she promise to be his friend and allow him to eat at her table and sleep in her bed. She reneges on the promise, but her father then forces her to honor it. The tale's position at the beginning of the collection may be attributed to the Grimms' belief, as noted in their appendix, that it is one of the oldest and most beautiful in the German fairy-tale tradition.

As for "The Golden Key," unlike most Grimm tales, it is a mere one paragraph long. It reads in full as follows:

> One winter, when the snow was very deep, a poor boy had to go outside and gather wood on a sled. After he had finally collected enough wood and had piled it on his sled, he decided not to go home right away because he was so frozen. He thought he would instead make a fire to warm himself up a bit. So he began scraping the snow away, and as he cleared the ground he discovered a small golden key. Where there's a key, he knew, there must also be a lock. So he dug farther into the ground and found a little iron casket. If only the key will fit! he thought. There are bound to be precious things in the casket. He searched but could not find the keyhole. Then, finally, he noticed one, but it was so small that he could barely see it. He tried the key, and fortunately it fit. So, he began turning it, and now we must wait until he unlocks the casket completely and lifts the cover. That's when we'll learn what wonderful things he found.[18]

In some respects, "The Golden Key" has the makings of a conventional rags-to-riches fairy tale, in which a character is rewarded for facing and overcoming challenges through a series of tests. The poor boy works hard despite the cold, and he succeeds at finding the casket and then the lock. Accustomed to fairy-tale conventions, readers might expect that the boy will uncover treasure in the casket or that something magical will happen once he lifts its lid. However, the narrator interrupts the normal storytelling flow to tell readers they must wait to see what lies inside until he opens it. The tale is thus both foreclosed and left open-ended. Its striking ending frees us to wonder what might be in the casket and to imagine our own adventure for the boy.

If the Grimms had placed "The Golden Key" first in *Children's and Household Tales,* the tale's open-endedness might have been read as inviting readers to see the tales that follow as akin to the contents of the casket. But its placement at the end is much more powerful. The Grimms must surely have viewed the tale's conclusion—the tantalizing notion that the casket is still to be opened and its contents discovered—as symbolizing the inexhaustible nature of fairy tales and folklore. The tale's position invites us to see the collection as merely a slice of a dazzling spectrum of folkloric creativity and expression. The book ends here, they seem to say, but fairy tales live on.

That both "The Golden Key" and "The Frog King or Iron Heinrich" depict the recovery of a golden object may point to the Grimms' retrieval and preservation of fairy tales that might otherwise have been forgotten. Wilhelm used gold as a metaphor for such activity in a letter he wrote to Brentano in 1810: "Only through so many tunnels and cloisters is the gold brought to light," he noted with regard to his efforts to solicit tales from the elderly woman in Marburg who had been reluctant to tell any. The gold motif also recalls the treasure of the Nibelungs, which according to lore lies submerged in the Rhine. In this way, the Grimms' collection represents a figurative reclamation of a portion of this treasure, especially since they so frequently conceived of the fairy tale as rooted in the tradition of epics like the *Nibelungenlied.* "The Frog King or Iron Heinrich" and "The Golden Key" stand as testaments to this retrieval at the beginning and end of the collection.[19]

Importantly, this bringing to light of forgotten stories differs starkly from what Wilhelm rejected in the preface as the Midas-like effect of overly zealous editors and authors. His goal was not to turn tales into stylized literary gold by incorporating them into refined works of literature, but to recognize folk literature itself as golden and not requiring extensive polishing or overhauling. It needed only to be exhumed from the depths of time and memory and gently restored. Wilhelm's intent in merging two or more variants into one or in choosing one variant over another was to restore the tales to a state of organic wholeness and equilibrium. Doing so required subjective judgments concerning which editorial interventions might rejuvenate a text and which might jeopardize its integrity.

The results of Wilhelm's editing might not always correspond with these aspirations, but his high ideals were not a dodge. Although some

Wilhelm Grimm (1822). Lithograph from 1898, after the drawing by Ludwig Emil
Grimm. Collection of the author.

commentators have accused the Grimms of willful deception, Wilhelm tried
to have the tales correspond with what he believed were their original mes-
sages.[20] He was not so naive to think that his revisions would fully restore a
tale to the state in which it existed at a particular time and place; while he

strove to approximate the "truth" of a tale, he realized that complete accuracy could never be achieved, in part because fairy tales were not static but always renewing themselves. But discerning the essence of a tale within its inherent mutability was a formidable and perhaps impossible task. After all, each tale contained within it a multitude of voices: those of the original creator(s), intervening storytellers, the oral or written source from which the informant obtained the tale, and the informant herself or himself.[21]

Moreover, there is of course the perspective the Grimms themselves brought through their edits, even if they saw their work as merely preserving a great storytelling tradition. While still seeking to justify their editorial stewardship, the Grimms had responded to criticisms of the first edition by modeling their editorial practice more on Brentano's method of restoring and reconstructing texts. Under Wilhelm's pen, this tactic included greater efforts to appeal to a nineteenth-century bourgeois audience. For him, the second edition served both to educate children and to convey the significance of the fairy-tale tradition.[22]

At the time that Wilhelm had been preparing the second edition for publication, Jacob was engrossed in work for what became *German Grammar*, the first volume of which, like the second edition of *Children's and Household Tales*, appeared in 1819. In January of that year, Jacob and Wilhelm learned that the University of Marburg had awarded them honorary doctorates. Jacob was not particularly pleased by this; he wished that instead of conferring honorary degrees the university would focus on shoring up its own intellectual standing and reputation, which had continued to dwindle compared to other universities. While their alma mater stagnated, the Grimms' renown would continue to grow in the years ahead, most immediately with Jacob's work on what came to be known as Grimm's Law.[23]

CHAPTER 10

❧⦅✿⦆❧

Grimm's Law and the Small Edition
of the *Tales*, 1820s

"I have neither the time nor the inclination to make rough drafts," Jacob declared in April 1821 to his friend Karl Lachmann, the great textual critic who at the time was a professor at the University of Königsberg in East Prussia. Jacob was racing to finish a revised edition of *German Grammar*, the first volume of which, published in 1819, had spanned seven hundred pages. Already while preparing that volume for publication he had come to regard it as woefully incomplete and immediately set his sights on a revised edition, which swelled to almost 1,100 pages and was published in 1822. The follow-up edition focused more on phonology, especially what came to be known as Grimm's Law, his groundbreaking detection of how sounds in the Germanic languages had in the distant past systematically shifted.[1]

Jacob himself did not call his description of this sound shift a law. Instead, in 1837 a German scholar referred to "the law discovered by Jacob Grimm," and one year later a British scholar first gave it the designation "Grimm's Law." Jacob's monumental articulation of what is now also known as the First Germanic Sound Shift built on Danish scholar Rasmus Kristian Rask's prizewinning 1818 study of Old Norse, which had not reached Jacob in time to inform his 1819 volume. Rask showed the relationship of Old Norse to other Germanic languages as well as to Greek, Latin, and Slavic languages. In probing the grammatical structures of these languages, Rask had given

hundreds of examples of how a certain sound in one language corresponded
with a different sound in another language. Others before Rask had pointed
to isolated correspondences: Friedrich Schlegel had noted that *f* in Latin often
corresponds with *h* in Spanish, for example, and that a Latin *p* often becomes
a German *f*. But Rask's insights went so far beyond this work that some subsequent scholars even suggested that "Grimm's Law" should have been more
properly dubbed "Rask's Law." However, although Rask spoke of rules for
letter shifts between languages, he had still conceived of these shifts largely as
individual letter-to-letter (or sound-to-sound) correspondences.[2]

In the second edition of *German Grammar*, Jacob incorporated Rask's
findings and, crucially, explained more fully than Rask had that these correspondences were not isolated phenomena but part of a systematic sound
shift undergone by Proto-Germanic, the postulated ancestor of the Germanic
languages. This systematic shift comprised subsystems of sounds that had
shifted in a circular chain; the assumption was that a change in one sound
was not an isolated occurrence but was interrelated with, or even resulted in,
a change in other sounds. In respective correspondence, the voiceless stops *p*,
t, and *k* had shifted to the fricatives *f*, *θ* (*th*), and *h* (given as *CH* in Jacob's
tables); the voiced stops *b*, *d*, and *g* had shifted to the voiceless stops *p*, *t*, and
k; and the voiced aspirated stops *bh*, *dh*, and *gh* (given in Jacob's tables as *F*,
TH/Z, and *CH*, respectively) had shifted to the plain voiced stops *b*, *d*, and
g. As the descendants of Proto-Germanic, the Germanic languages had inherited these changes, whereas other Indo-European languages had not. Thus,

griech.	P.	B.	F.	T.	D.	TH.	K.	G.	CH.
goth.	F.	P.	B.	TH.	T.	D.	..	K.	G.
alth.	B(V)	F.	P.	D.	Z.	T.	G.	CH.	K.

oder anders aufgefaßt:

gr.	goth.	alth.	gr.	goth.	alth.	gr.	goth.	alth.
P	F	B (V)	T	TH	D	K	..	G
B	P	F	D	T	Z	G	K	CH
F	B	P	TH	D	T	CH	G	K

Jacob's tables explaining sound shift in *German Grammar*. Except for what he labels *CH*,
each sound can be traced diagonally through the tables, always moving one step down
and one step over. Jacob Grimm, *Deutsche Grammatik*, part 1, 2nd ed. (Göttingen: In der
Dieterichschen Buchhandlung, 1822), 584. Photo courtesy of the Newberry Library.

French as a Romance language has *pied, trois, cœur,* and *dent,* while English as a Germanic language has *foot, three, heart,* and *tooth.* To explain this sound shift to his readers, Jacob graphed out a tripartite chain of subsystems using tables arranged in two different formats and with Greek, Gothic, and Old High German as examples.[3]

Using this sound shift theory, Jacob could explain why "father" was *pater* in Greek, *fadrs* in Gothic, and *vatar* in Old High German, or why "grain" was *granum* in Latin, *korn* in Old Norse, and *chorn* in Old High German. Jacob acknowledged that many words were exceptional in that they had not undergone a predicted shift in sound, though later scholars were able to explain some of these by detecting patterns underlying them. For example, Verner's Law, named after Danish scholar Karl Verner, revealed syllable accent as the determining factor underlying one such set of irregularities. In his tables and explanations, Jacob intermixed the First Germanic Sound Shift with what is now regarded separately as the Second Germanic Sound Shift, in part because he saw the Second Germanic Sound Shift as virtually preordained by the first.[4] Also known as the High German Consonant Shift, the Second Germanic Sound Shift refers to changes in Old High German that explain why modern High German has "Schiff" whereas English has "ship," for example, and why High German has "*Tür*" whereas English has "*door.*" In Jacob's tables, this set of correspondences appears in the differences between Gothic and Old High German.

German Grammar is known today principally because of Grimm's Law, although in the editions and volumes Jacob published in the 1820s and 1830s he explored grammatical gender, case systems, declensions, and myriad other components of word and sentence structure. The 1822 edition, moreover, explores not just the systematic consonant shift for which Grimm's Law is named, but also numerous other phonological aspects, including substantial attention to vowels. Beyond its constitutive parts, *German Grammar* was groundbreaking in the more fundamental sense that it helped establish linguistics as a science and did so through Jacob's historical approach to language study. Jacob aspired to present a history of the grammatical development of the Germanic languages and, in so doing, to trace their interrelatedness. His historical approach reflected the ongoing influence of Savigny's teachings, for which reason it is unsurprising that Jacob dedicated the 1819 and 1822 editions of *German Grammar* to his great mentor.

Jacob's goal was also inspired by a flurry of language scholarship in the early nineteenth century, including Friedrich Schlegel's study of Sanskrit, articulation of comparative grammar, and conception of language as an organism; Wilhelm von Humboldt's study of the Basque language; and Franz Bopp's work on Sanskrit and comparative Indo-European linguistics. Their work was spurred in part by Englishman William Jones, a judge of the Bengal Supreme Court who in 1786 presented a lecture to the Asiatic Society in Calcutta in which he noted that similarities between Greek, Latin, and Sanskrit were so pronounced that the languages must have sprung from a common ancestor. Johann Gottfried Herder's notion of the interrelationship of language, thought, and nation also exerted a profound influence on Schlegel, Humboldt, Bopp, and others in the first decades of the 1800s. To Herder, different languages did not just express the same universal thought using different words, sounds, and grammatical structures; instead, language and thought were intimately interrelated. Speakers of different languages might also form different attitudes and customs, which in turn left their imprint on language. The human being is a herd creature, Herder explained, but because humanity could not possibly remain one herd and retain just one language, diverse national languages had developed. He spoke of languages rich in flatteries and titles, nouns or pronouns dependent on class, or verbs dependent on whether the object was animate or inanimate. Each language was in its own way both "lavish and lacking"; for example, he pointed to a Caribbean language in which male and female speakers used different words for common objects such as bed, moon, sun, and bow, a plethora counterbalanced by the mere four words that the same language had for colors. Informed by Herder, language scholars in the early nineteenth century were thus fascinated not only by language itself, but also by the way speakers of a particular language expressed their unique collective identity through customs, mores, and stories.[5]

The notion that language and national cultural expression were interrelated helps to explain, too, why Jacob viewed translation with such trepidation. In the 1819 preface to *German Grammar*, he opined that a truly faithful translation necessitates that the source language is at the same stage of formal and intellectual development as the target language. This is almost never the case, he asserted, but the closer the affinities between the two languages the better the translation will be. Thus, he believed that a German translation of Shakespeare would be more faithful than a French translation, while an ancient epic might never be satisfactorily translated because of the chasm between the naturalness of epic literature and the refinement of modern society.

To demonstrate in *German Grammar* that all Germanic languages were interrelated and that their modern structures must be understood in terms of their historical development, Jacob meticulously explored Gothic, Old High German, Old Low German (comprising Old Saxon, Anglo-Saxon, and Old Frisian), Old Norse, Middle High German, Middle Low German (comprising Middle Saxon, Middle English, and Middle Dutch), and modern Swedish, Danish, High German, Dutch, and English. Because he delved into the historical development of so many Germanic languages, he would have preferred to title his work *Germanic Grammar*; he refrained from doing so in deference to Rask, who opposed subsuming the Scandinavian languages under the designation "Germanic."[6]

But the title *German Grammar* is misleading in another sense. To modern ears, it evokes starchy grammatical precepts, when in fact Jacob vehemently rejected rigid rule-making as imperiling the organic and ever-changing nature of language. He scorned the pedantic grammatical instruction practiced in schools as stifling children's natural development and appreciation of their native language. Such inflexible focus on rules yielded "unchildlike children" who might speak a cultivated version of their language, but who, as adults, would lack any nostalgia for their youth because their experience of childhood had been stifled.[7] Similarly, a true poet takes no inspiration from grammarians, Jacob insisted, and he opined that women and girls typically have a more natural command of their language than men and boys because they learn it without the stultifying influence of schoolmasters. (One detects here, perhaps, his residual disdain for the pedantry of Johann Georg Zinckhan in Steinau.) In alignment with his and Wilhelm's extolling of folk literature, he claimed that peasants centuries ago understood and employed the beauty of the German language far better than modern grammarians did. He found imperfections in every language, but he believed that even the humblest dialect had advantages over the more standard version of a language. He regarded dialects as crucial to his work because they revealed grammatical forms that had dropped out of standard usage. Similarly, though Gothic struck him as the most perfect of the Germanic languages, he found that it lacked some advantages of Old Norse and Old High German grammar. His careful reading of older Germanic sources had revealed to him exquisite linguistic features that grammarians arrogantly thought present only in Greek and Roman literature. Their inability to detect and appreciate such features stemmed not only from their highbrow biases, but also from their failure to study German from a historical perspective and to view language as akin to a dynamic living organism.

Indeed, some grammarians had belittled the oldest forms of Germanic languages as barbarian tongues characterized by harsh, monosyllabic words. Jacob retorted that older forms showed more grammatical complexity than newer ones, and that older words often had more syllables and softer pronunciations than did modern ones. The names of German rivers exemplified this latter point: the melodic *swalmanaha* became in modern German the harsher-sounding *Schwalm*, and *loganaha* became *Lahn*. But this did not mean Jacob privileged older forms over new ones. He agreed with August Wilhelm Schlegel's comparison of language to an iron implement that can be smelted anew whenever it breaks; Jacob simply maintained that language is ever-renewing and does not need grammarians to impose reforms. He knew, too, that it would be folly to try to freeze German in its nineteenth-century form. This acceptance of linguistic evolution aligns with the Grimms' belief in the inherent mutability of fairy tales and related stories as they are told and retold.[8]

Jacob's distaste for rigid rule-making also explains why, in the 1822 edition, he audaciously broke with the convention of capitalizing all German nouns and instead used lowercase for all but proper nouns and the first word of a sentence. In the preface, Jacob defended this self-described "banning of capital letters" by noting that the practice of uppercasing nouns had originated in the fifteenth and sixteenth centuries, a time when the essence of the German language was, in his view, poorly understood. More puckishly, he described his rejection of capitalizing nouns to Lachmann as follows: "Actually, I just wanted to show that I, who in principle avowedly detest all language reform, am not so *ultra* that I myself cannot make a liberal suggestion. In any case, it is nothing new." In other words, whereas others had sought to reform the German language in the fifteenth and sixteenth centuries in part by stipulating that nouns be capitalized, Jacob's rebellious counterreform was to strip this away and go back to lowercase letters. Although grounded in his sense that the capitalization of nouns was imposed on German by pedants who lacked a sufficient understanding of grammar and language history, his rejection of capitalization points again to the way he and Wilhelm often failed to acknowledge their own subjective judgments concerning what was an organic versus an artificial change. In any case, Jacob's rejection of uppercasing nouns became a feature of *German Grammar* and his subsequent published works, but it did not take hold more broadly: as even beginning students of German know, the capitalization of nouns has endured. But this would not necessarily have bothered Jacob much. His point was more to reveal how this hallmark of written German had taken hold and to show that it had, for most of the language's history, not been the convention it had subsequently become. His aim throughout the work was not to prescribe but to detect, analyze, and describe.[9]

German Grammar is thus in no respect a leaden manifesto of how German grammar ought to be, but it is nevertheless hardly easy reading. Jacob himself knew this as he worked on the second edition and fretted that its sheer size and detail might be off-putting to readers. He wrote to Ludowine and August von Haxthausen that they would surely wonder upon reading the volume what all his intricate "crocheting with letters and words" there amounted to. If tedious detail after tedious detail appeared in the work, he explained, this was because even the tiniest grain of sand can help us to understand the largest planet.[10]

Jacob's descriptions of his work as a form of alphabet crochet or an amassing of thousands of grains of sand are not far from the mark, given the density of information presented on each of the volume's 1,100 pages. But while he understood that many general readers would find the work inaccessible, he also rightly feared that scholars would detect many errors in his scholarship. This was unavoidable for two principal reasons. First, Jacob knew he was exploring uncharted territory. He had scarcely any scholarly reference materials on which to base his extensive analyses. Instead he had to glean grammatical usage from seemingly endless original texts spanning over a thousand years of development in various Germanic languages. It was, he observed, both easier and harder to be the first person to make discoveries in a particular field: easier because no one had been there before, but harder because others would build on one's work and in so doing discover its deficiencies.

Second, Jacob also knew that some of these deficiencies were the result of the tight timeline under which he worked. To print such a large volume in which so many foreign and archaic letters and symbols appeared, his publisher in Göttingen had insisted that typesetting begin in installments already in spring 1820, instead of all at once when the full volume was complete. The typesetter still had to painstakingly set each letter by hand, since mechanical typesetting would not take hold until the end of the nineteenth century. Because the manual typesetting of the second edition occurred in batches over two years, for Jacob the edition was more like a serialized work although the volume itself was not issued for sale until 1822. In 1820 and 1821, he worked feverishly on installments that he often looked back on with some embarrassment, knowing that his understanding had already progressed beyond what was now irrevocably set in type. This mode of operation nevertheless accorded with his tendency to produce scholarship at a breakneck pace and without much of a plan for organizing his findings. Wilhelm, by contrast, was more methodical.[11]

In a sense, Jacob treated many of his published works, including *German Grammar*, as mere drafts to be continually refined in subsequent printings. In working on the second edition of *German Grammar* he would quickly write and send off pages to his publisher without even rereading them. Upon receiving the typeset proofs back, he made far fewer corrections than he knew he should, because he did not want to create extra work for the typesetter. His publisher also imposed a quick turnaround for these edits—so quick, in fact, that Jacob lamented that the postal schedule left little time between the arrival of mail in Kassel and its departure back to Göttingen. Just as soon as he sent off corrections for an earlier installment or mailed a new one to be typeset, he had to turn to writing the next section. As a result, he was often just pages ahead of the "hungry typesetter," he told Lachmann; at times he fell so behind that he could submit only half of a typical installment and then had to catch up and send the rest in a subsequent mailing. Devoting whatever waking hours he could to *German Grammar*, he grew annoyed when library visitors or other professional duties took valuable time away from this work, and he also spent every evening before and after dinner immersed in it. His only diversion was his daily walk. A more sociable person, he knew, would be incapable of sustaining this strict regimen; fortunately, Jacob relished his solitude and interacted almost exclusively with his close family members and his scholarly correspondents.[12]

First among these correspondents was Lachmann. In his studies of Middle High German works such as the *Nibelungenlied*, Lachmann had sought to elucidate the interrelationship of various manuscripts of the same text, probing, for example, how deviations between versions might indicate which was the oldest. Although some of his theories about the dating of manuscripts have since been contested or discredited, his overall contributions to philology remain foundational. It was not only Lachmann's scholarly background and expertise that made him an ideal interlocutor for Jacob, but also his welcoming personality and fiery curiosity. In November 1820, Jacob asked his publisher to send Lachmann typeset pages of *German Grammar* so that Lachmann could give feedback as he hurried to write further installments. Like *German Grammar* itself, Jacob's letters to Lachmann are dense with details and punctuated by the occasional problem Jacob was attempting to sort out, such as this: "I still cannot satisfactorily explain to myself why the Gothic *magan* [may] is *magum* in plural and not *megum.*" Similarly, in a letter to Lachmann in April 1821, Jacob presented a draft table of the systematic consonant sound shift he had detected, a system that Lachmann in a follow-up letter deemed plausible.[13]

Lachmann's textual expertise and Jacob's vast linguistic knowledge enabled them to build on each other's strengths and insights, though, as Lachmann asserted, posterity would regard all their efforts as mere child's play. Lachmann at times reassuringly coached Jacob through his trepidation that the published work would not reflect the many insights he had gained after sending in particular installments to be typeset. When Jacob complained about the constraints which the lengthy typesetting schedule imposed on his work, Lachmann gently pointed out that, due to the variety of alphabets and characters used in the manuscript, the poor typesetter would often have to fetch multiple cases of type just to set a single word. He added that it would be impossible to lay the foundation for further scholarship, as Jacob was doing, without there being some mistakes.[14]

And this was indeed the case. Scholars not only soon uncovered specific errors but also criticized overall deficiencies, such as Jacob's preoccupation with Gothic, Old High German, and Middle High German at the expense of other Germanic languages. A further fault in Jacob's work is that he frequently conflated letters with sounds (as Rask, too, had done). Despite knowing that *German Grammar* was still incomplete, Jacob resolved not to be shy about having his name on it: he had built a "grammatical house," he said, that he and other scholars could move into, furnish, and expand. He himself contributed to this renovation work by publishing further volumes and editions of *German Grammar*, which resulted in a four-volume work that spanned four thousand pages. Like the languages and dialects of which he wrote, Jacob's *German Grammar* thus proceeded organically and dynamically.[15]

Although scholars continue to debate how much the various consonant changes in Grimm's Law depend on each other and the causes and chronology of the sound shift, the significance of Jacob's *German Grammar* to the humanities has been compared to that of Darwin's *On the Origin of Species* to the life sciences. More poetically, the Grimms' contemporary Heinrich Heine likened *German Grammar* to a colossal Gothic cathedral in which the various Germanic peoples sang together, each in their own dialects. According to Heine, Jacob had singlehandedly accomplished more for the language sciences than the entire Académie Française since its founding; he had been such a prolific scholar that Heine joked he must have sold his soul to the Devil. In the decades after the initial editions of *German Grammar*, other historical-comparative grammatical works appeared, including Friedrich Diez's grammar of Romance languages, Johann Kaspar Zeuss's Celtic grammar, and Franz von Miklosich's grammar of Slavic languages. In 1824, Jacob published his translation of Vuk Karadžić's Serbian grammar. Karadžić had visited Jacob and Wilhelm in 1823, and they had been impressed by his grammatical work and his collection of Serbian folk songs.[16]

Although accolades poured in for Jacob's trailblazing *German Grammar*, the Hessian electors hardly acknowledged the work. Upon receiving a copy of the 1819 edition from Jacob, Elector Wilhelm I dismissively said that he hoped Jacob had not neglected his official duties while compiling the volume. As a recent scholar has trenchantly observed, Jacob sought in a ruler not the paradigmatic philosopher king, but rather a "philologist king." Armed by scholars like the Grimms with an understanding of his nation's cultural and linguistic heritage, such a monarch would reign successfully over his people.[17] Wilhelm I, however, was utterly unappreciative of Jacob's erudite and impactful exploration of Hessians' linguistic heritage, and at times treated the past merely as a vehicle for pomp or self-aggrandizement. Beyond his unsuccessful attempts to be styled King of the Chatti, he also planned an elaborate pseudomedieval funeral for himself. After his death in February 1821, he was entombed in the crypt at the Löwenburg, the medieval-style "Lion's Castle" he had commissioned in the late eighteenth century in the forest overlooking the Wilhelmshöhe Palace. Carried to the Löwenburg at night, Wilhelm I's coffin was accompanied by soldiers bearing flaming torches, noblemen dressed as knights, and, at the front of the cortege, a herald riding a black charger, both man and horse covered in black armor with black plumes.[18]

Wilhelm I's death occurred while Jacob worked on the second edition of *German Grammar.* For several weeks, Jacob was unable to make much progress in his writing because of duties associated with the official mourning period. Like Wilhelm I, the newly crowned Wilhelm II had no appreciation of scholarly work. A contemporary account described him as "dissolute, extravagant, without character, and loaded with debt." At the time of his father's death, he had for several years been estranged from his wife, Auguste, the daughter of Friedrich Wilhelm II of Prussia. Their estrangement resulted from his long-standing affair with Emilie Ortlöpp, the daughter of a

The palace of Wilhelmshöhe near Kassel, with the Löwenburg visible in the upper left and in the background the pyramid and octagon on which the statue of Hercules stands. Copperplate print by Wiederhold in Göttingen, around 1820. Collection of the author.

goldsmith from Berlin. Wilhelm II wasted no time elevating Ortlöpp to the title of Countess Reichenbach after his father's death. The Grimms got along well with the kindly Electress Auguste but had little regard for Wilhelm II.[19]

Under the new elector's administration, the library had less autonomy over its budget and was micromanaged in other ways. Jacob, Wilhelm, and the library director Völkel were ordered to transcribe the entire catalog, an extremely time-consuming and, to Jacob, pointless task. The Grimms also chafed when other civil servants received much-needed bonuses in 1823 but they at the library did not. "On top of it all, we have to stuff ourselves into newly decreed, costly uniforms, of the sort that no one likes to wear," Jacob wrote Lachmann. "If only you could see how ridiculous I look in this garb." This utterance is typical of the style-conscious Jacob: though he sports dark attire in surviving portraits, he was actually fond of wearing bright-colored clothing and fashionable shoes. In view of the elector's disregard for the library and for scholarship, it is unsurprising that Jacob decided not to present him with the second edition of *German Grammar*, lest he, like his father, regard this as detracting from Jacob's official duties.[20]

Under both Wilhelm I and Wilhelm II, those responsibilities included serving on the elector's Censorship Commission with Völkel and a government official. Jacob detested this role. He had to shoulder most of the work and hated that it took time away from his scholarly pursuits. Above all, he found censorship objectionable in principle and unworkable in practice. In his written opinions for the commission, he emphasized that human beings do not take kindly to being told by a government agency what they can and cannot read. He also underscored the futility of banning works printed outside of Electoral Hessen from being sold by Hessian booksellers, since many readers could easily obtain such titles from neighboring territories— and he pointedly added that banning these works merely fueled perceptions of Hessen and its government as illiberal. Jacob further sought to curtail the broad scope of censorship in Hessen, arguing that the censors should stay away from moral and religious matters and concern themselves only with political texts aimed directly at the Hessian monarchy and its government. He insisted that it went against Protestant teaching to stifle theological debate, and that public condemnation, not government censorship, was the best tool against blasphemous or obscene works. Finding it ridiculous that the elector had included reading and lending libraries in the commission's purview, Jacob noted that the sheer volume of works made these libraries impossible to regulate. Although concerned that reading and lending libraries might facilitate readers' appetite for what he regarded as vapid books, he also realized that such readers might not be able to digest the scholarly works he himself deemed healthier fare.[21]

Jacob's efforts to narrow the scope of censorship in Electoral Hessen were in vain. The prospect of greater freedoms had diminished throughout the German-speaking lands due to the Carlsbad Decrees, which curtailed press freedoms, dissolved student organizations, and clamped down on reformers' constitutional goals. Threatened by burgeoning literacy rates, autocratic governments became still more zealous in controlling what people could and could not read. Although exact literacy rates for the period are hard to determine, they likely rose from around 25 percent in 1800 to about 40 percent in 1830. Basic literacy may well have exceeded 50 percent throughout this period, however, and the practice of reading aloud, whether for information or entertainment, would have enlarged the audience of published works still further.[22]

The constraints under which Jacob worked at the library and as a member of the Censorship Commission exemplify the many restrictions on public life in the late 1810s and early 1820s. But he and Wilhelm felt limited in other, more personal ways. Wilhelm's health woes periodically flared up; bouts of severe abdominal pain began in autumn 1821 and his heart ailment returned in early 1822. Jacob, often consumed with worry about his brother, reflected on how "my whole life would be destroyed" if Wilhelm died. Despite his ill-nesses, Wilhelm had not been idle. Between late 1820 and the end of 1822, he spent around three hours a week tutoring the teenaged crown prince Fried-rich Wilhelm, who would later reign as the last elector of Hessen. The prince lauded Wilhelm's pleasant demeanor and clear presentation of material, but Wilhelm found his well-intentioned pupil unintellectual and suspected he had never in his life read a book of his own accord.[23]

As for scholarship, in 1821 Wilhelm published a book on runes. Many of his assertions about runic alphabets in that book and in a second study published in 1828 are today known to be erroneous; for example, he wrongly assumed that the shorter runic alphabet was older than the longer one. His efforts to gather and compare centuries of manuscripts on runes were never-theless impressive for his time, as were his attempts to tease out relationships between runic alphabets in Scandinavia, Britain, and Germany. He had been inspired to study runes when friends from his student years discovered what they thought were runestones on an ancient burial mound on their property. Wilhelm, however, believed the markings in question were mere doodles; they were later shown to have been caused naturally by worms.[24]

In 1822, Wilhelm published the third volume of the second edition of *Children's and Household Tales*, which contained notes to tales in the first and second volumes as well as Wilhelm's lengthy overview of tale traditions and collections in Europe, the Middle East, and Asia and his study of the tales of the Italian Giambattista Basile. Although the third volume appeared under both brothers' names, Jacob had been consumed with *German Grammar* and, not wanting to interfere with Wilhelm's progress, made only occasional sug-gestions. He found that some observations in the notes lacked thoroughness and accuracy, but he knew that Wilhelm had been ill while working on it.[25]

Adding to Jacob's concerns for Wilhelm's health were uncertainties over their living situation. The Grimms were given notice in late 1821 that they would need to vacate their lodgings on Wilhelmshöhe Gate, where they had lived for seven years. The area's semirural feel had afforded them many daily pleasures. From his north-facing window, Jacob had been inspired by daytime vistas of the mountains and by nighttime stargazing that included views of his favorite constellation, Ursa Major. Wilhelm had proudly cultivated sun-flowers, vetches, and wallflowers on the apartment's balconies. It took several months to find a new place to live and prepare to move. From the start, their new apartment proved unpleasing. Downstairs was a blacksmith whose pounding of metal disturbed the Grimms' concentration, although Wilhelm delighted in learning several new technical expressions from him. Wilhelm's room faced newly built barracks, from which a trumpet major played music that "tears your brain to pieces," as he told a friend. Jacob's room was quite narrow and offered a view only of lawn and apple trees.[26]

Jacob was at least able to indulge his love of the outdoors during a walking trip from Kassel to Hanau, Steinau, and other locales in June 1823. With just a knapsack on his back, he traveled alone by foot for twelve days. He was overcome with joy and sadness upon returning briefly to Steinau, where he had not been since 1804. The trees, meadows, paths, and river remained largely unchanged from his youth. He found his grandfather's gravestone still upright, but his father's had been damaged during the French retreat in 1813. Jacob had hoped to see the town incognito, but the innkeeper, who years ago had attended school with the Grimms, recognized him at once.[27]

Fortunately, in 1824 the Grimms were able to move into a more comfortable apartment, located on the street known as Bellevue. Befitting the street's name, they once again enjoyed unhindered views of the sky, mountains, and trees; additionally, to Jacob's great relief, they heard nightingales and other birds instead of the pounding of the blacksmith's hammer. Wilhelm described a blissful daily routine of rising early to read a passage from the New Testament in Greek, drinking coffee with Jacob around eight o'clock, and interspersing afternoon work duties with reading classics such as Homer's *Odyssey*. The Grimm household at this time comprised only Jacob, Wilhelm, and Ludwig. Ferdinand remained employed in Reimer's publishing house in Berlin; besides his editing work for Reimer, he dabbled unsuccessfully in writing and scholarship, and in 1820 he published a now-forgotten collection of tales and legends. He continued to rely on his siblings for money and to their chagrin frequently requested additional funds. His behavior concerned not only his brothers back in Kassel but also his coworkers and acquaintances in Berlin. He went to great lengths to hide the location of his lodgings, even deliberately giving out a false address if someone wanted to visit him. When on one occasion he grew ill, his coworkers visited four different addresses before they found him. At times even Jacob and Wilhelm did not know where he lived, and he sometimes went a year without writing home.[28]

Carl, too, continued to struggle with emotional and financial difficulties working as a tutor of English and French in Hamburg. He had been in the employ of a Bordeaux wine merchant for a time, but this and other positions proved short-lived. In fact, he had spent a year and a half back in Kassel without steady work, despite his siblings' renewed efforts to secure a position for him. Jacob, Wilhelm, and Ludwig were relieved to see Carl return to Hamburg, since at home in Kassel they had struggled with his behavioral eccentricities. In Ludwig's description, Carl wandered aimlessly from one room to another throughout the day, rarely left the apartment, seemed obsessively to rub salves into his eyes and on his forehead and nose, and erupted over any dust he spied in the apartment but kept himself in a disheveled state. Wilhelm, too, found his idleness, hypochondria, and pedantry unbearable but nevertheless was moved to tears upon seeing a downcast Carl off to Hamburg on the postal wagon. Wilhelm found in Carl's features and expressions so much of his mother's family and reflected on how this resemblance made him their mother's favorite child.

Among the Grimms' brothers, only Ludwig gave them no difficulty, although establishing himself as an independent artist was not easy. His oeuvre now encompassed historical and religious themes as well as portraits, landscapes, caricatures, and scenes from daily life. A breakthrough came in 1825 when his oil painting of the Madonna and child with saints was exhibited to glowing reviews in Berlin and elsewhere. Nevertheless, his efforts throughout the 1820s to obtain a position at the art academy in Kassel proved unsuccessful.

As for Lotte, in summer 1822 the Grimms had celebrated her marriage to Ludwig Hassenpflug, a junior official at the Kassel court of law and a member of the family that had contributed to the Grimms' *Children's and Household Tales*. They had been engaged since 1816. Jacob and Wilhelm initially got along well with Hassenpflug, but in later years their relationship with him grew strained as he impeded liberal reforms in his role as minister of the interior and justice departments for Electoral Hessen. Jacob and Wilhelm had long had a relatively good relationship with Lotte, despite what they regarded as her stubborn nature and uneven management of the household. Typical of the women of her time, she had scarcely journeyed out of Kassel since the family's move there, traveling to Marburg in 1809, Frankfurt in 1817, and a Hessian spa town in 1818 to seek medical treatment. In Ludwig's drawings, she appears modestly attired with elaborate braids of hair coiled atop her head. Wearing her wedding dress and myrtle wreath, Lotte so resembled their mother that Wilhelm was brought to tears. She was twenty-nine when she married; at the time, the average age of marriage in Germany was around twenty-six years for women and twenty-eight for men. Her five brothers, all

Lotte Hassenpflug, née Grimm (1820). Illustration based on the drawing by Ludwig
Emil Grimm, in L. E. Grimm, *Erinnerungen aus meinem Leben*, ed. Adolf Stoll
(Leipzig: Hesse & Becker Verlag, 1913), 320. Collection of the author.

in their thirties, were still bachelors, and it would be three years until Wilhelm, the next to marry, wed Dortchen Wild.[29]

Wilhelm and Dortchen's long-planned engagement became official in 1824, and they married in May 1825. Wilhelm was thirty-nine years old and Dortchen days away from her thirty-third birthday. The Grimms had for many years regarded her as a member of their family, especially since her parents' deaths in 1813 and 1814. Jacob's Christmas gift to each of his siblings in 1820 was a small booklet listing important family dates; in its preface he addressed Dortchen directly, saying that he had included her because he loved her like a sibling. Wilhelm echoed this sentiment in March 1825, writing to pastor Johann H. Christian Bang not only that his fiancée was his dearest friend, but also that "without exception, we siblings have long loved her as a sister, and if anyone is suited to us and our nature, it is she." In the same letter, he humorously acknowledged the many puns that were arising as his friends contemplated his and Dortchen's marriage: "Just no innuendoes about the names Grimm and Wild," he implored, "I have heard them so often that the joke no longer makes any impression on me." But Wilhelm himself may have indulged in such punning in the tale "All Fur." In what has been interpreted as a nod to Dortchen in the second edition (1819) of *Children's and Household Tales*, the king asks his hunters to investigate what the wild thing (*Wild*) is in a tree, not knowing that it is the maiden he will later marry, whereas in the first edition he had instructed them to see what animal (*Tier*) is there. This tribute is particularly fitting, given that it was her version of the tale that the Grimms chose for their collection.[30]

For Jacob and Wilhelm, it went without saying that they would remain together even after the marriage. As they had articulated so many times through the years, they could not envision living apart. Dortchen and Wilhelm thus resided with Jacob and Ludwig in their Bellevue Street apartment, and in 1826 they all moved two buildings down to a different unit. Dortchen's joyful, sensible, and genuine disposition only reinforced the Grimms' close-knit household. Wilhelm told friends that there was no one else in the world he could have married or been so happy with.[31]

It was later suggested that Jacob and Wilhelm were so committed to their work that they decided Wilhelm should marry just to have a woman manage their household. Nearly three decades after Wilhelm and Dortchen wed, Alexander Wilhelmi (the pseudonym of actor Alexander Zechmeister) published the one-act comedy *Someone Must Marry!*[32] He depicts the characters Jakob and Wilhelm Zorn as brothers who are professors at an unnamed German university. Neither wishes to marry, and they are thus dismayed when their aunt insists that at least one of them take a wife. The brothers agree to draw lots to decide who should wed, whereupon Jakob draws the lot for marriage and Wilhelm tries to help him woo their cousin. But Wilhelm marries the cousin in the end while Jakob remains a bachelor. That Wilhelmi was thinking of the Brothers Grimm is clear not only in his characters' first names, but also in the choice of "Zorn" (anger) as a surname, synonymous with "Grimm" (wrath, fierceness). The play is nevertheless fictitious, and Wilhelmi appears to have used the Grimms' well-known bond and dedication to their work as a convenient vehicle through which to explore his subject matter. In truth, Wilhelm's marriage to Dortchen was not just practical but also founded on genuine attraction and love.

Ludwig married seven years after Wilhelm, in 1832, but Jacob, Carl, and Ferdinand remained lifelong bachelors. Jacob had never been seriously interested in matrimony or in progeny of his own, though of course he had been a father figure to his siblings and borne principal responsibility for supporting them. He knew he was too engrossed in his scholarship and too desirous of his solitude to marry. The death of his father at forty-four also frequently led him to wonder if his time, too, might be short, for which reason he devoted himself that much more to accomplishing whatever he could in his studies.[33]

In the early twentieth century, a descendant of the Bratfisch family, who were related to Jacob and Wilhelm through their mother, nevertheless shared a family story that Jacob had once proposed to the Grimms' distant relative, Luise Bratfisch. Luise is alleged to have rejected the proposal so that she could continue to serve one of the Hessian princesses. Some elements of the story do not align with established timelines and facts, however, so its veracity is unclear. Another purported marriage proposal is similarly opaque and indeterminate. In what has been interpreted as a possible marriage proposal or indication of a willingness to marry if a suitable wife could be found, Jacob had written the following lines in 1818 to Charlotte Ramus, who with her sister had contributed a tale to *Children's and Household Tales* several years earlier and was already engaged at the time of Jacob's writing: "Because the mice annoy me more each and every day and even nibble the books before I can review them, I find myself willing to take a cat into service. Could you perhaps procure a well brought-up and hopeful one for me? She would receive bread and milk from me her whole life long and be properly treated." Nothing came of the cryptic letter. As these lines suggest, the reclusive Jacob viewed a wife principally as a congenial household manager whose efforts would facilitate his uninterrupted devotion to scholarship. He was pleased that Dortchen, as Wilhelm's wife, could fulfill this role. Nevertheless, Jacob saw in Dortchen not just a manager but also a sisterly, motherly, and friendly figure.[34]

Neither husband nor solitary bachelor nor lothario, Jacob defied conventional gender roles. Although uninterested in marriage, he was for decades an integral part of Wilhelm and Dortchen's family; it was not their household alone, but his, too. In his will, he specified that all his belongings should go to Wilhelm or his children, since in effect nothing he owned was his alone. Throughout their lives, he and Wilhelm had shared all their material possessions; more significantly, Jacob also partook in the family's joys and sorrows as brother, brother-in-law, and uncle.[35]

Pronounced among such sorrows was the death of Wilhelm and Dortchen's firstborn child, a son named after Jacob, in December 1826 at just over eight months old. The Grimm family was already mourning the death of Lotte's infant daughter Agnes. Around the time of Agnes's death at the end of October, Wilhelm and Dortchen's son had grown ill with bilious fever, a diagnosis commonly used in the nineteenth century to describe a range of conditions resulting in fever, jaundice, and gastrointestinal distress. The baby had been in robust health, and since his teething had begun without difficulty—a milestone then thought to indicate that an infant had survived his most vulnerable period—the family believed his continued health was assured. The suddenness and severity of his illness surprised them. For seven weeks he lay seriously ill, and for all but a few moments Wilhelm had little reason for hope. On the night of his death, Jacob remained by the dying child's bedside for twelve hours. "I will never forget the night he struggled with death for eight hours and longer," Wilhelm wrote to Achim von Arnim two weeks later, "and I still feel how his poor heart quivered under the violent convulsions." He was buried next to the Grimms' mother in Kassel. At the funeral, Jacob picked a clover from his mother's grave and kept it, preserved, in the pages of one of his books.[36]

The infant's death replayed itself in Wilhelm's nightmares for a long time to come. In the same year as his son's passing he and Jacob had published a translation of Irish fairy tales that Jacob described as "mostly about dwarfs and house spirits." The volume included tales in which elves steal a human baby and leave a sickly, screaming changeling in its place. It is thus perhaps not surprising that Wilhelm now described his grief as so all-consuming that his self, as he had previously understood it, seemed like an elusive and invisible kobold, or house spirit, playing tricks on him: every time he thought he had caught the kobold, its mischievous voice would taunt him from another corner of the room.[37]

An added reminder of life's fragility soon surfaced. Wilhelm and Dortchen's second-born child, a son who received the first and middle names Herman Friedrich after the Grimms' grandfathers, fell dangerously ill as a three-month-old in 1828. For a time, Wilhelm was convinced that this child, too, would be taken from them. He also worried about Dortchen, who had been so overcome with sorrow that Wilhelm feared for her health—to the extent that he asked correspondents not to mention Herman's illness to her.[38]

Herman convalesced and soon proved to have a doting uncle in Jacob, who acted much like a second father to him. From the time Herman could first speak he called Jacob "Apapa," a babbled designation similar to "Papa" that the boy came up with himself and used in lieu of "uncle." Jacob's extant papers include paper animals and hearts that he cut out for Herman, and he interrupted one letter to a friend with the words, "The child is crying, and I must help attend to him." A female acquaintance recalled that her father, on an errand to bring a book to the Grimms, entered their apartment to find Wilhelm holding a diapered baby being spoon-fed by Jacob.[39]

While the Grimms experienced the private joys and sorrows of family life, in the broader world their professional and popular acclaim was growing. In the 1820s, references to the Grimms appeared in English-language works such as the *Edinburgh Review* and an English anthology of Dutch poetry. Jacob's *German Grammar* greatly expanded his scholarly reputation, and *Children's and Household Tales* also began to attract international interest. Danish and Dutch translations of various Grimm tales had previously appeared, but it was the publication of Edgar Taylor's English translation of a subset of the collection in 1823 that proved uniquely popular. The Grimms had not authorized Taylor's *German Popular Stories*, but upon publication it almost immediately caught their attention. They attributed the success of Taylor's book in Britain to its abridged, visually appealing format (with twelve illustrations by George Cruikshank) and the tales' freely translated style. Indeed, Jacob told Lachmann that he found the shortness and lightness of English words more suited to children's tales than the stiffness of modern High German; he also conceded that the Grimms had not paid enough attention to the style of narration in their own collection. This shows Jacob's softening stance on translation and may constitute an acknowledgment that the Grimms' early insistence on fidelity to a tale as they had received it had resulted in compromised fidelity to narrative smoothness and tone. It might also suggest that more tales should have been included in dialect form instead of in High German.[40]

Wilhelm wrote to Reimer in August 1823 of the popularity of Taylor's translation and proposed that a similar abridged edition be published in Germany. Other slimmed-down versions of German and European fairy and folk tale collections were already on the market, so Reimer would have been aware of the idea's commercial potential; however, Reimer rightly feared that such a publication would cause the remaining unsold copies of the 1819 edition to gather more dust. Despite such reservations, he allowed work on the abridged edition to go ahead. Containing fifty tales and seven illustrations by Ludwig, with no scholarly notes, the first "Small Edition" (*Kleine Ausgabe*) appeared in December 1825 in time for Christmas. An unillustrated version was also available and proved more popular because of its lower price. (The choice of illustrated or unillustrated version was in keeping with book publishing conventions of the time, in which customers might also be able to select the quality of paper that a book was printed on, the binding material, and even whether to purchase the book bound or unbound.) The Small Edition contained what would become some of the most canonical of the Grimms' tales from the unabridged edition (or "Large Edition," *Große Ausgabe*), including "The Frog King or Iron Heinrich," "Hansel and Gretel," "The Bremen Town Musicians," "Cinderella," "Briar Rose," "Little Red Cap," "Snow White," and "Rumpelstiltskin." Although the Small Edition was published ten times during the Grimms' lifetimes, it was not the immediate or catalytic commercial success that some scholars have suggested.[41]

In fact, it was not initially as popular in Germany as Taylor's volume was in the British Isles. The British interest in *Children's and Household Tales* reflected not necessarily a fascination with German culture and language in and of itself, but more specifically a construction of English identity as rooted in Germanic ancestry. Thus, in his introduction to *German Popular Stories* Taylor referred to assumptions that if the inhabitants of England and the Scottish Lowlands were of Germanic (or "Teutonic") ancestry, so, too, must tales from these regions be of Germanic origin: characters such as Tom Thumb or the giant-killing Jack from "Jack and the Beanstalk" must have landed on British shores from the same warships that had conveyed warriors such as Hengist and Horsa, the Germanic brothers said to have invaded Britain in the fifth century. It was for this reason, Taylor posited, that so many of the tales in the Grimms' collection seemed familiar to English readers. Taylor not only contributed to such constructions of Englishness but also further fueled the myth that the Grimms had collected their tales directly from the peasantry: *German Popular Stories* bears the subtitle "From Oral Tradition," and its preface stated that the Grimms had obtained their tales "for the most part from the mouths of German peasants."[42]

The Grimms' other works from this time included the first volume of Jacob's work on Germanic law, a subject inspired by his studies of medieval German literature, as well as Wilhelm's edition of a medieval narrative poem and his examination of the German heroic saga. Their scholarly reputations were recognized by memberships in academic societies in Germany and as far away as Iceland; Jacob also received honorary doctorates from universities in Berlin and Breslau. Apart from routine duties at the library, they had been free to pursue their scholarship, even if the elector did not appreciate its importance.

The brothers' situation changed abruptly in January 1829 with the death of head librarian Johann Ludwig Völkel. Jacob requested Völkel's position, and Wilhelm, still a secretary, asked that he be promoted to Jacob's post of second librarian. To their deep dismay, Völkel's office was given to royal archivist Christoph von Rommel and their own positions remained unchanged. Jacob found this snub humiliating after his twenty-three years of government service, and particularly since Rommel knew little about running a library. Jacob complained of having to fetch books for Rommel's research because Rommel had no clue how to find them himself. Jacob also found it abhorrent that Rommel had pursued and been granted an aristocratic title (hence the "von" in his surname). If a distinction between commoners and aristocrats still made sense in their time, Jacob insisted, then that difference should be maintained; to elevate a commoner to the aristocracy only diminished the strength of the middle classes and further skewed the relationship between the two groups.[43]

Avowing that they could not continue their service to Hessen, the Grimms in autumn 1829 accepted positions at the University of Göttingen, in the Kingdom of Hanover north of Hessen. In Göttingen, Wilhelm would serve as librarian at a salary of 500 talers, while Jacob would be both librarian and professor and receive a salary of 1,000 talers (whereas in Kassel they earned 300 talers and 600 talers, respectively). Even with a 100-taler bonus they had each received in early 1829, their wages in Hessen did not cover their expenses.[44]

Upon hearing that the Grimms had decided to leave, Elector Wilhelm II scoffed, "Big loss! They never did anything for me." It was a foolish rejection of two scholars whose acclaim had grown in Germany and abroad. The elector, however, could not appreciate the brothers' far-reaching achievements unless these brought him personal glory. The Grimms had remained steadfast in their loyalty to his estranged wife, Electress Auguste, despite knowing that this only deepened Wilhelm II's dislike of them. (The elector lived in Frankfurt with his mistress, the Countess Reichenbach.) Wilhelm wrote to the sympathetic electress to assure her that they had no lack of love for Hessen; indeed, generations of Grimms had served the state with untarnished honor. However, having been passed over for promotions and needing to think of their family and future, they were now leaving to become librarians "at the most famous and beautiful library in Germany."[45]

At the time, Göttingen's library held two hundred thousand volumes compared to Kassel's sixty thousand. But Jacob worried that he would have little opportunity to make use of the library's sizeable holdings. In Göttingen, he would need to devote at least thirty-two hours a week to library duties; in Kassel he had been able to spend only eighteen hours on such tasks and was otherwise free to immerse himself in scholarship. In addition, Jacob would be obligated to give lectures, a prospect he did not relish—both because of the time needed to prepare and deliver them and because he was still recovering from a recent chest illness that left him short of breath. If he wanted to continue his studies amid his increased library and lecturing duties, he feared he would have to cut out his daily sixty- to ninety-minute walks. Moreover, Göttingen itself held no appeal for him. He had occasionally traveled there over the years and had tended to complain of liking neither the environs nor the people, apart from trusted friends such as the librarian and professor Georg Friedrich Benecke.[46]

It was thus with a sense of foreboding that he turned in his keys to the Kassel library on what, he noted, was All Souls' Day 1829. The windows in the library's long hall reminded him of weepy eyes, and he doubted that he would ever step foot in the hall again. He was forty-four years old, and Wilhelm forty-three. Both found the prospect of leaving the life they had known for so many years difficult to face. They had lived most of their lives in Kassel; their mother, Wilhelm's firstborn son, and their closest relatives were buried there. Apart from Ferdinand, who remained in Reimer's employment in Berlin, all their siblings were in Kassel. Lotte's husband continued to work at the court of law, and Carl had left Hamburg in 1826 and was now scraping by in Kassel as an English and French tutor. (He allegedly owned just one suit of clothes, consisting of a light blue jacket and gray trousers, which he wore year-round regardless of the weather.) Their brother Ludwig would remain in their apartment in Kassel and continue his work in painting and etching as an independent artist. He had recently become engaged to Marie Böttner, a childhood friend of Lotte Grimm and Wilhelm's wife, Dortchen. Marie was the daughter of an art professor who had died many years before, and her widowed mother was the Grimms' lessor. The pregnant Dortchen would have liked to remain in the apartment in Kassel until after giving birth and recovering; however, Ludwig planned to marry soon so they needed to vacate and move to Göttingen. As it turned out, Ludwig and Marie did not marry until 1832, when he at last became an art professor at the academy in Kassel.

Although Marie's family was well off, Ludwig was determined to marry only once he himself earned a steady income.[47]

Jacob and Wilhelm thus knew they were leaving behind the family ties and heritage that were so important to them. It was too late when, at the eleventh hour, the elector's mistress Countess Reichenbach unexpectedly intervened. Through her efforts, Jacob was offered the first librarian position in Kassel and Wilhelm second librarian; Rommel was to run the museum. As the Grimms conceded, this was everything they would have wanted if the offer had been made in the first place. The elector was trying to make amends for having overlooked them, they were told, but they stood by their decision to leave. It would be dishonest to renege on their commitment to Göttingen, they said, and they had in the meantime rejected a competing offer from Munich. Still, they left Kassel with bitterness and regret.[48]

CHAPTER 11

The Göttingen Era, 1829–1838

On December 27, 1829, Jacob and Wilhelm made the eight-hour trip in bitter cold from Kassel to Göttingen. Among their possessions was a potted plant that Jacob anxiously shielded by holding it under his coat in the drafty carriage. He and Wilhelm had more serious considerations on their mind, however: they had left Kassel without Herman and Dortchen. Wilhelm's wife, six months pregnant, had started feeling unwell two days before the departure and could not travel. Because the Grimms had already sent off the bulk of their furniture, bedding, and clothing, they had to borrow items for Dortchen when it became clear that she would stay behind. On Christmas Eve, Wilhelm had sat on a packed suitcase near Dortchen's bed and lit candles bedecking a scrawny Christmas tree for her and Herman. Unable to delay his departure until Dortchen convalesced, he entrusted her and Herman to the care of their two maids and extended family. As Jacob and Wilhelm passed the library and museum in their carriage, the morning sun cast a red glow on familiar shelves of books, which Wilhelm regarded as long-standing friends to whom he and Jacob were now saying a final goodbye. Upon exiting through the city gate, Wilhelm identified himself to the Hessian guard as a Hanoverian librarian.[1]

Dortchen and Herman's travel to Göttingen was further delayed when Herman, too, grew ill. A few weeks after he and Jacob had first departed,

Wilhelm returned to Kassel so that he and Dortchen could transport the boy to Göttingen in a heated carriage. Shortly before Wilhelm, Dortchen, and Herman reached Göttingen darkness fell, the wind began to howl, and the carriage windows froze up. But Herman had withstood and even enjoyed the journey; he played in the carriage and gazed at the passing scenery with curiosity. In the days and weeks ahead Wilhelm, Dortchen, and Jacob continued to worry about both him and their relatives back in Kassel, for Lotte's children had contracted measles and Ludwig had been dogged by a respiratory illness.[2]

These family concerns compounded the difficulty of acclimating to their new home. Almost eleven thousand people lived in Göttingen, far fewer than the twenty-five thousand in Kassel. One might have expected Göttingen to offer more of the country feel the Grimms so often craved, but they did not find the town appealing. Nineteenth-century accounts tended to agree that Göttingen lacked charm. Visiting in 1833, English novelist Frances Milton Trollope described it as having "no beauty, either of situation or architecture, though some of the old towers are curious and venerable. The buildings of the University appear by no means splendid." Similarly, an American student commented on "the general tameness of the North German landscape," described the river Leine that ran through Göttingen as "a narrow, muddy stream, that would be called in America a creek," and found the houses unattractive and poorly built. Because the university buildings were not concentrated in one area, he also could detect "no visible sign of the university, no chapel, no huge buildings, whether we call them dormitories or quadrangles, no campus."[3]

And yet there was little of note in Göttingen apart from its university. The Georgia Augusta University of Göttingen—named after its founder George II, King of Great Britain and Ireland and Elector of Hanover—was established in 1734 and began offering classes in 1737. At the time of the university's founding, Göttingen still had not fully recovered from the destruction of three-quarters of the town during the Thirty Years' War a century earlier. The establishment of the university changed the town's fortunes dramatically. Göttingen quickly became known as a leading intellectual center. Benjamin Franklin traveled there in 1766 to consult professors with specialties in constitutional law and in the history of the Holy Roman Empire, Samuel Taylor Coleridge studied at the University of Göttingen for four months in 1799, and Henry Wadsworth Longfellow visited in 1829. These and other political and literary figures were drawn to the intellectual vibrancy fostered by the school's remarkably liberal charter: the university granted professors academic freedom and, unusually, did not put the theology faculty above others. These changes were introduced not just for enlightened reasons, however, but also to lure aristocratic, wealthy, and foreign students. Such applicants were attracted to secular study and repelled by the rigidly sectarian control at many German universities, and their enrollment contributed handsomely to the University of Göttingen's bottom line.[4]

During the early years of the Grimms' time in Göttingen, the university's reputation continued to grow thanks to scholarly and scientific achievements such as physicist Wilhelm Weber and mathematician and astronomer Carl Friedrich Gauss's development of the first electromagnetic telegraph in 1833. Coincidentally, a figure of titanic importance to Germany's political future was also in Göttingen at this time: Otto von Bismarck studied law there in 1832 and 1833, but he spent more time dueling and drinking beer than studying.

From the start, Göttingen's illustrious university gave the Grimms little joy. Five weeks after moving, Jacob wrote that life there "still doesn't taste right." As he had feared, library duties were consuming far more of their time than in Kassel. The Grimms also chafed at working with the head librarian, whom they found petty, obstinate, and moody. More than anything, the work at the library seemed menial and unfulfilling. These initial impressions persisted. By summer 1830, Jacob was convinced that it had been a mistake to come to Göttingen. He described the library to Lachmann as "an always revolving wheel in which I must tread for six whole hours each day, and without feeling any inner joy for this work. Because what do I do there?—I retrieve books and put others back, always while constantly running around, and I have to copy the entire subject catalog for English history word-for-word on slips of paper and then put them in order for a new catalog, which means I will then have to copy everything once again." His metaphor is particularly illuminating: the treadmill had been invented in 1818 by British engineer William Cubitt as a means of rehabilitating prisoners through labor, and in 1827 and 1828, just a couple years before Jacob's description, a publication and series of lectures in Berlin had explored the use of the penal treadmill in England, Germany, and Holland. Continuing the prisoner imagery, he now felt like a "servant in a yoke," he said, whereas in Kassel he had felt like a free man. In Kassel he had ready access to new books; in Göttingen the processing of new acquisitions entailed sending them to the library's bookbinder for half a year and then on to scholarly reviewers, which meant that three years might elapse before a new title was accessible to others. He also had no time to consult the library's extensive holdings of rare books.[5]

Jacob's litany of complaints extended to the many unwelcome demands on his scarce free time, such as the obligatory social events so at odds with his reserved nature. After a day's work in Kassel, he had routinely immersed himself in his thoughts while on solitary walks; in Göttingen he was always bumping into colleagues who wished to stop and chat. Late evenings were often interrupted by social visits. Living in Göttingen was also proving more expensive than in Kassel. "In short, I find the entire town dislikable," Jacob declared to Lachmann. Considering this difficult transition, it is no wonder that he described his years at the library in Kassel as the most tranquil and productive time of his life in an autobiographical essay he composed in 1830, during his first semester in Göttingen. He also chose to deliver his inaugural address at the university on the topic of homesickness for one's native land. As was customary, this first lecture was given in Latin, but Jacob made a point in it of criticizing Germany's centuries of reliance on Latin as the language of state and church institutions at the expense of its native tongue. The neglect of German and its literary expression had been part and parcel of Germany's failure to achieve the stature or national unity of Britain or France, he argued; only with Luther had esteem for the German language begun to be restored. The lecture thus gestured to Jacob's longing not only for Hessen, but also for a coherent German nation and identity that to his mind should, but still did not, exist.[6]

Wilhelm, too, found adapting to Göttingen challenging, although he was characteristically more tempered than Jacob in expressing this. During their first few months in the town, he, Dortchen, Herman, and Jacob were unable to settle into a domestic routine since they could not move into their permanent lodgings until Eastertime. This was particularly uncomfortable for the heavily pregnant Dortchen, who in March gave birth to a boy christened Rudolf (a prevalent Wild family forename). Whereas Herman was rather frail and delicate as a toddler, Rudolf was a chubby baby in robust health. The Grimms rejoiced in Wilhelm and Dortchen's expanding family, but a few months later they mourned the death in Kassel of Lotte's one-year-old daughter Bertha.

In Göttingen, Wilhelm had a hard time adjusting to the new surrounding landscape, while Dortchen, who had lived her entire life in Kassel, initially struggled to relate to the people around her. Early on, the Grimms nevertheless formed a close friendship with the historian and political theorist Friedrich

Christoph Dahlmann and his family. Dahlmann had moved to Göttingen just a couple months before the Grimms to assume a professorship. He grew up in Wismar on the Baltic Sea and had studied in Copenhagen, Halle, and Wittenberg. Before coming to Göttingen, he had been at the University of Kiel, a town then ruled by the king of Denmark; his work for the cause of unifying the duchies of Schleswig and Holstein with the German Confederation did not endear him to the Danes. Dahlmann was almost the same age as the Grimms (his birthday fell between theirs), and his temperament, too, lay somewhat between Jacob's strict introversion and Wilhelm's more easygoing nature. His wife, Luise, quickly befriended Dortchen, and their children grew close.[7]

Within weeks of their arrival, the Grimms also began socializing with the jurist Johann Göschen and his family. The legal scholar Gustav Hugo visited them around five o'clock each Sunday, and they formed friendships with the scholar of Greek art, literature, and mythology Karl Otfried Müller and his wife, Pauline, as well as with law professor Friedrich Blume. Their friendship with librarian and professor Georg Friedrich Benecke also continued, although Jacob's dislike of tobacco smoke made it difficult for him to be around the heavy smoker.[8] Beyond forming individual friendships, the Grimms occasionally attended social and cultural events in the small university town. Since Wilhelm's birthday was the same as that of the Duke of Cambridge, the Hanoverian viceroy, he spent that day in 1830 dancing the polonaise at a ball held in the viceroy's honor. In May 1830 the Grimms also attended Niccolò Paganini's concert in Göttingen.

Such interactions eased the Grimms' alienation, but they continued to find it difficult to adjust to university life. Wilhelm despaired that the students he met cared little for intellectual development and wished only to pass their examinations. As students in Marburg decades earlier, he and Jacob had eschewed much of student life to devote themselves to their studies; consequently, they could not empathize with students' attitudes and expectations in Göttingen. Like his work at the library, Jacob's professorial responsibilities proved vexing. Preparing lectures on German grammar was tedious and afforded him no new scholarly insights. Moreover, he branded having to appear at the lectern at a designated time too theatrical for his taste.[9]

While the Grimms grappled with these personal and professional concerns, the 1830 July Revolution in Paris was reverberating throughout the German-speaking lands. Incited by the censoring of an essay by a docent affiliated with the university, rioters in Göttingen took over the city hall and sentry points in January 1831; their goal was to obtain a liberal constitution from William IV, the Hanoverian and British king. They paraded through the streets wearing white armbands and brandishing sabers and guns. Several thousand troops were sent to quell the uprising, which lasted just over a week. Because the rioters threatened to set fire to the library, the librarians stood watch night and day. Jacob found the rioting in Göttingen "in all respects despicable" and blamed it for his brother's latest illness, which he believed had developed during Wilhelm's final night watch at the library.[10]

Wilhelm's illness initially seemed mild, but soon he began coughing up blood and developed a fever and an excruciating rash. By the time a doctor performed bloodletting, Wilhelm was so delirious that he thought the blood was spurting not from his own arm, but from that of an unknown woman. In his feverishness, he also grew obsessed with the idea that it might not be Dortchen and Jacob who were caring for him, but impostors. To verify their identities, he asked them questions that he knew only they could answer. Jacob helped to watch over him for several nights. At one point he sat down at Wilhelm's desk and gazed at his brother's neatly ordered books and manuscripts, despondent at the thought that at any moment his brother might die and their life together would be upended. Written in part during Wilhelm's illness, the third installment of *German Grammar* (1831) was dedicated to Wilhelm; in the text Jacob mentioned that he had feared Wilhelm might not live to read it. To make matters worse, news arrived during the most dangerous point of Wilhelm's illness that Achim von Arnim had died. His sudden passing occurred just days before he would have celebrated his fiftieth birthday. Fearing that Wilhelm was not strong enough to bear this news, Jacob withheld it from him for a week. When at last told of Arnim's death, Wilhelm broke down sobbing. It took many weeks for him to convalesce. He began feeling better shortly before his forty-fifth birthday on February 24, for which Jacob lit forty-five candles for Wilhelm in the parlor.[11]

Jacob had followed with great interest the July Revolution in Paris and its ripple effects in Germany, knowing that so much hung in the balance for Germany's political future. Alarmed at the unrest and at growing republican sentiments, rulers in Saxony, Hessen, and Hanover sought to pacify their subjects with constitutions. Called upon to assist with framing the Hanoverian constitution, Dahlmann spent extended periods of time away from Göttingen. Though they knew Dahlmann's integrity and insights would be invaluable to the writing of the constitution, the Grimms doubted he would be able to balance progressives' and conservatives' competing demands. Extreme oppositional stances, whether on the right or left, would lead only to the failure of reform efforts and to a dangerous revolution, the Grimms feared. They were also skeptical that constitutions would solve all the problems proponents claimed they would: poorly framed constitutions might neither work in practice nor allow for flexibility and iteration.[12]

Despite such concerns, the Grimms tried to remain optimistic about the drafting of constitutions, in contrast to their brother-in-law Ludwig Hassenpflug. In 1832, Hassenpflug was appointed to the dual roles of minister of the interior and minister of justice for Electoral Hessen. He soon became known for staunchly supporting absolutist rule and disdaining government modernization, stances he exercised through harsh censorship and attempts to undermine the 1831 Hessian constitution. Playing on his surname, his opponents nicknamed him "Hessenfluch" (Hessian curse). Wilhelm harshly criticized him for opposing free speech protections, privacy of correspondence, and tax reform. Insisting that absolute monarchies were in a tailspin from which they could not recover, Jacob told Hassenpflug of his hope that constitutions, however flawed, might with time heal divisions.[13]

Restrictions on freedoms nevertheless continued. In 1832, the Confederal Assembly issued articles aimed at reining in the rights of popular legislative assemblies in individual states and prohibiting political organizations, public speeches about politics, certain festivals, and the wearing or displaying of symbols deemed rebellious. In April 1833, there was an unsuccessful attempt in Frankfurt to start a revolution. Jacob attributed Germany's overall weakness to Prussian and Austrian dominance, which led to the political and geographical squeezing of other German territories. Historians have since cited Germany's territorial fragmentation and slowness to industrialize compared to Britain and France as factors in the more sluggish assertion of political rights among its citizens.[14]

Political unrest was not the only challenge at the time. In response to a cholera pandemic that spread to Germany in 1831, Prussia, Hanover, and other states closed borders and issued lockdown mandates to stop transmission of the disease, which was believed to spread through foul air. As the pandemic reached Göttingen, some students stayed away from lectures. Undeterred, in fall 1831 Jacob traveled to Switzerland and southern Germany. On his way home, he spent a few days in Frankfurt and met with Clemens Brentano, who had dedicated himself in his travels and writings to promoting the Catholic faith. During Jacob's visit, Brentano told him about the years he had spent with the nun Anna Katharina Emmerick in Dülmen before her death in 1824. It would be Jacob and Brentano's last meeting before Brentano's passing in 1842.

Back in Göttingen, Jacob continued to compare the library to a nonstop treadmill and to a beast that demanded constant feeding. Though he found his teaching duties distasteful, he came to savor the rare occasions when he was relieved of library work to prepare his lectures. He was not particularly adept at lecturing and expressed his ideas far more effectively in writing. His students portrayed him as a short man with a strong Hessian accent, standing at the lectern with only a small slip of paper on which he had written a few names, words, and dates to guide his incomparable memory (instead of reading from a notebook, as was usual). Nevertheless, when Dahlmann suggested that pedagogy should be more engaging and participatory than the conventional lecture format allowed, Jacob responded with a mix of bewilderment and horror: "Should the teacher ask questions and then allow them to be answered? Should students work collectively under his direction? The teacher's authority—which beneficially influences susceptible natures—would easily be weakened by such methods." With time, however, his lectures attracted more interest, and he half jokingly boasted that in one semester thirty-two students attended his lectures on grammar, which for him was a large number. Still, he hated having to spend time on faculty senate duties and conducting student exams.[15]

While Jacob had held a professorial appointment from the start of his tenure in Göttingen, Wilhelm initially had only a library position. He was not appointed to the faculty until February 1831, albeit at a lower rank than Jacob. Wilhelm's professorial duties, like Jacob's, came on top of his library role. Despite this added workload, he enjoyed lecturing more than Jacob did and was heartened to find that his classes on the *Nibelungenlied* included several outstanding and well-mannered students. These lectures were also well attended, but Wilhelm realized that this was partly because aspiring high school teachers now had to be examined in older German language. This requirement, he felt, exemplified how modern universities might make average students better through a prescribed curriculum but in the process stifle the natural curiosity and development of gifted ones. Among other accolades in the early 1830s, Wilhelm was named a corresponding member of the Prussian Royal Academy of Sciences in Berlin, with which Jacob had been affiliated since 1826. Wilhelm's scholarship on medieval German literature now included the facsimile he had published in 1830 of the *Lay of Hildebrand*, and he was writing a critical edition of a work by the thirteenth-century didactic poet Freidank.[16]

Familial happiness accompanied Wilhelm's professional gains. In August 1832, his last child and only daughter was born. She was named Auguste after the electress in Hessen, with whom the Grimms had kept in contact. At the time of Auguste's birth, Herman was four years old and Rudolf two. Herman's early childhood memories of his father and uncle in Göttingen included seeing Jacob often hunched over his desk, scribbling rapidly, while Wilhelm wrote more slowly and thoughtfully. Herman also recalled Jacob and Wilhelm's love of nature, even though they still found the environment around Göttingen inferior to the beauty of the Hessian countryside. Rocks and shells served as paperweights, pressed flowers and leaves were used as bookmarks, and their workspaces looked out onto gardens. They kept abreast of political matters back home by reading the Kassel newspaper, the previous day's edition of which was delivered to them each day at noon, in time to be perused during their midday meal.[17]

They also kept up regular correspondence with their siblings. Dortchen found the fashions in Göttingen outmoded and in her letters often asked Lotte to procure more stylish apparel and accessories for her in Kassel. For his part, Wilhelm asked Lotte to send items for him to give Dortchen as presents, such as a Middle Eastern shawl for her birthday and a fur collar for Christmas. Such requests went both ways; for instance, Lotte asked Dortchen to bring a special sausage from Göttingen when she visited Kassel. As time allowed, some or all the family members returned home each year.

A trip in May 1833 was marred by tragedy. Dortchen had traveled with the children to visit Lotte, who was due to give birth in June. During their stay, Lotte came down with what appeared to be influenza and became so dangerously ill that Jacob and Wilhelm hurried to Kassel to be with her. Lotte went into premature labor and gave birth one month early to a baby girl. Jacob and Wilhelm's plans to return to Göttingen were thwarted when Wilhelm, too, grew ill; Jacob departed alone, and Wilhelm hoped to follow a few days later. But then Dortchen also succumbed to the illness and began coughing up blood. As Wilhelm started to recover, he took care of both Lotte and Dortchen; for four straight days and nights he went back and forth between their beds to check on them. Dortchen began to recover, but Lotte's illness progressed to myelitis. No longer able to speak, she weakly kissed Wilhelm as she lay dying. He administered her last dose of medicine and was by her side to feel her final pulse. Jacob had traveled to Kassel a few times during her illness, but on the day she died he arrived too late to say goodbye. Lotte, the youngest of the Grimms' siblings, was also the first to die. She passed away on June 15, 1833, at the age of forty, leaving behind her husband of eleven years and four children. In 1837, Ludwig Hassenpflug took as his second wife Agnes von Münchhausen, then seventeen years old.[18]

The year after Lotte's death, the Grimms' brother Ferdinand was let go by Reimer's publishing house in Berlin, where he had been employed since 1815. Reimer had long been dissatisfied with Ferdinand's work and had on occasion complained about him to the Grimms. Jacob and Wilhelm encouraged Ferdinand to come live with them, since he had no immediate prospect of supporting himself and they could provide for him more cheaply in Göttingen than in Berlin. Although he had musical and artistic talent and an uncanny ability to do impressions of people, he had never found a vocation that held his interest.

Having nowhere else to go, Ferdinand stayed in Göttingen with Jacob, Wilhelm, and Dortchen for a couple years, but one day in summer 1836 he left out of the blue. After disappearing, he sent only a cryptic and unapologetic note to Dortchen from another town; he did not share his plans or destination. Wilhelm speculated that Ferdinand might pursue theater, but Jacob retorted that Ferdinand was too lazy to even learn lines. Although concerned about Ferdinand's well-being, Jacob was relieved by his absence. No longer burdened by Ferdinand's selfish and withdrawn nature, he enjoyed the restoration of domestic harmony.[19]

To Jacob's dismay, it was not long until Ferdinand reappeared, just as suddenly as he had departed. Jacob conjectured that Ferdinand had wanted to avoid Jacob and Wilhelm while Dortchen was away in Kassel, since he tended to get along better with her than with his brothers. Jacob had now had enough, however; he informed Ferdinand he was no longer welcome to live with them in Göttingen. Ferdinand left and eventually settled in the small town of Wolfenbüttel in the Duchy of Braunschweig, where he spent the rest of his life. The Grimms sent him a monthly allowance and responded to his periodic calls for additional funds. They saw in him an ingrate who failed to appreciate the financial and emotional burden he placed on them, and they derided his indolence and lack of discipline.

But Jacob and Wilhelm also realized that their parents' untimely deaths had exerted a profound toll on Ferdinand. Like Carl, he had had to sacrifice his own hopes for the benefit of Jacob and Wilhelm (as the family's eldest sons) even more than if their father had lived. Carl wished he could have studied music, while Ferdinand would have liked to be a writer or thespian. Whereas Carl had at last found some measure of contentment as a language tutor, Ferdinand's situation remained acute. Even his appearance stood out to Jacob and Wilhelm as a reminder of how different he was from the rest of the family: unlike his siblings, who had darker hair and more pronounced features, Ferdinand had a delicate face and hair of a lighter shade.

Remarkably, it was not Ferdinand's behavior that caused Jacob the greatest concern in the mid-1830s, but Wilhelm's. Beginning in late 1834, Wilhelm's physical state once again deteriorated. For over six months he was scarcely able to perform his professional duties, which Jacob (having just returned from a research trip to Brussels) shouldered on top of his own. Wilhelm's mood darkened more this time than during previous bouts of illness, and even after he recovered physically his mental health languished. For much of 1835 and 1836 he avoided social gatherings, although he masked his personal distress when callers visited. His promotion to a higher professorial rank did not pull him out of his depression (despite Jacob's hopes that it might), and he approached his library work mechanically. Even his scholarship, which at the time involved preparations for an edition of the medieval *Song of Roland*, brought him little joy. Jacob was grateful that Dortchen somehow kept a positive outlook during Wilhelm's prolonged mental crisis.[20]

In contrast to Wilhelm's sudden lack of scholarly interest, Jacob had made progress on several of his own endeavors. Despite the ongoing demands of his professorial and library duties, in 1834 he published a hefty comparative study of several European versions of the medieval beast epic *Reynard the Fox*. In telling of the trickster figure Reynard as he outsmarts the lion king, bear, wolf, and various other animal figures in and around the lion's court, *Reynard the Fox* satirizes the aristocracy and clergy. In his analysis, Jacob explored the mythological bases for the projection of human characteristics onto animals and the use of animal traits to describe humans. He claimed that ancient beliefs in the ability of humans to be transformed into animals and vice versa arose because earlier peoples were more embedded in nature and thus had a stronger connection to fauna than in modern times. To poetically invoke this ancient connection, fairy tales and related texts occasionally spoke of olden times when animals still could talk.

During Wilhelm's illness, Jacob also published the first edition of *German Mythology* (1835). As with *German Grammar*, Jacob meant for the "German" in *German Mythology* to be understood as "Germanic." He had expressed a desire to write a comparative study of Germanic mythology already in 1820, while working on *German Grammar*. Just as ancient languages could be reconstructed by studying their modern descendants, so, too, in his view could ancient mythology be reconstructed by studying medieval Germanic literature and surviving manifestations of folk culture such as ballads, fairy tales, and legends. Comparing such manifestations across cultures could yield insights into the overarching mythology from which variants arose; Jacob's work thus draws on beliefs from numerous Indo-European cultures and language groups, including Celtic, Baltic, Romanic, Italic, Greek, and Indic as well as Germanic. This comparative approach was further needed because, as Jacob noted, ancient Germans and Scandinavians had interacted with peoples such as the Romans, Celts, Slavs, and Finns.[21]

Jacob's breathtaking command of numerous mythological traditions, combined with the immense scope of his examination of myth, makes *German Mythology* stand out even today and provided great inspiration to other nineteenth-century mythographers. The nine hundred pages of the 1835 edition cover beliefs concerning gods and goddesses; temples, priests, and forms of worship; heroes and wise women; creatures such as elves, dwarfs, giants, devils, and ghosts; illness, cure, death, and the soul; trees and animals, the heavens and stars, day and night, summer and winter; and superstitions, magic, and fate. Reconstructing ancient beliefs pertaining to these topics was key to Jacob as he sought to rescue the Germanic past and its peoples from charges of barbarism. In his preface, he noted that in his earlier books he had shown that ancient Germanic peoples had spoken not crude but supple, refined, and well-formed languages and lived not in lawless hordes but had well-established senses of morality and legality. In *German Mythology*, his aim was to refute stereotypes of Germany's ancient forebears as engaging in idolatry and primitive nature worship instead of possessing a nobler sense of the divine. "How is it possible," Jacob expostulated, "when we take into account all the rest that we know of the language, the liberty, the manners, and virtues of the Germani, to maintain the notion that, sunk in a stolid fetishism, they cast themselves down before logs and puddles, and paid to them their simple adoration?"[22] Unfortunately, elsewhere in his writings this defense of the ancient Germanic tribes was at times overtly racialized. In a review published a few years before *German Mythology*, he had described fetishism as "a descending into dullness and coarseness, like that which rules the wild Negro. But it is essentially foreign to a people like our ancestors, which as soon as it appears in history, acts worthily and freely and speaks a finely wrought language that is closely related to that of the noblest peoples of antiquity."[23]

Like so many of his scholarly books, *German Mythology* is intended as a work of erudition, not entertainment. Jacob's writing sometimes reads as if he were principally engaged in a private conversation with himself, rather than clearly communicating his ideas to readers. Paragraphs are peppered with words and phrases from Greek, Latin, Gothic, Old Norse, Old High German, and other languages. Abbreviations and page references break up the flow of virtually every sentence. The text is made even more visually peculiar by Jacob's staunch rejection of capitalizing German nouns and even the first words of sentences, as well as his frequent italicization of various words and phrases for emphasis. These features of his style are exemplified in the following passage in which he explores the German thunder god Donar's throwing of stones instead of arrows:

> but here it seems to me that the portrayal of shooting *arrows*, as appears in German poems (doners *pfile* [thunder's arrows]; *Tournament of Nantes* 35.150), just imitates the Greeks and Romans; the Germanic Donar actually throws wedge-shaped *stones* down from the sky: into the high castle "ez wart nie *stein* geworfen dar, er enkæme von der *schûre*" [there was never stone thrown there, unless it came from the storm]; Ecke 203. Ein *vlins* von donrestrâlen [a *flint* of thunder streaks]; Wolfram 9, 32. *Schûrestein* [shower stone] Bit. 10332. *Schawerstein* [shower stone] Suchenw. 33, 83.[24]

According to modern folk belief, Jacob continues, a black wedge or stone travels with each lightning bolt down from the storm cloud and deep into the ground. Every time it thunders, the wedge will rise somewhat; after seven years it will have emerged fully from the ground and, if kept, will safeguard a house from thunderstorm damage.

Forming just one of hundreds of such passages in the weighty volume, Jacob's analysis of Donar's stone-throwing bears many hallmarks of his work as a mythographer. He plucks evidence from Konrad von Würzburg's thirteenth-century work *The Tournament of Nantes* and from authors such as the German knight and composer Wolfram von Eschenbach. References to Greek and Roman mythology bolster his comparative approach, and the nineteenth-century folk belief that black wedge-shaped stones travel from storm clouds deep into the earth supports his view that vestiges of ancient mythology endure; we are, in his view, shaped by the distant past in ways we cannot fully fathom.

Among those influenced by the book was the composer Richard Wagner, who confessed to being initially challenged by Jacob's erudite probings of even the slightest fragments of mythology from long ago. But Jacob's work soon led to what Wagner described as a rebirth of his creative abilities. The mythological fragments grew in his imagination into clearer forms and figures that he would draw on for his operas.[25] And when, in 1846, William John Thoms first coined the English word "Folk-Lore," he did so with direct reference to *German Mythology*, declaring that the nineteenth century had to date hardly produced a more remarkable book.[26]

Jacob's scholarship in the 1830s also included further work on *German Grammar*. He published the third part in 1831, followed by the fourth in 1837 and a revised edition in 1840. Each part spanned between eight hundred and a thousand pages. A notable section of the third part is Jacob's lengthy consideration of languages in which nouns have grammatical gender. Enlightenment thinkers had regarded grammatical gender as largely arbitrary and inscrutable, apart from its association with biological sex and from the tendency for words with certain endings to take a particular gender. Toward the end of the eighteenth century, scholars began to see grammatical gender as meaningfully associated with the noun to which it is assigned. This view is unsurprising given their emphasis on language and human experience as mutually constitutive. Jacob and others conjectured that in the distant past, language speakers had viewed the entire world in animated and sexed terms and conferred masculine or feminine grammatical gender even on inanimate objects and abstract ideas. These scholars saw the grammatical gender of a noun as reflecting its meaning and revealing how early humans understood the world through their notions of maleness and femaleness. This understanding was also culturally specific, since the gender of a particular noun might vary between languages. The sun (*die Sonne*) is feminine in German while the moon (*der Mond*) is masculine, for example, whereas in Spanish the sun (*el sol*) is masculine and the moon (*la luna*) is feminine. Even within the same language, a noun's grammatical gender can change over time, location, and texts, offering clues to the language's evolution and its speakers' customs and interactions.[27]

For some nouns, Jacob traced grammatical gender back to myth. For example, he pointed out that in Nordic mythology the earth (*die Erde*) is personified as the daughter of the night. Regardless of whether a specific gender designation was rooted in mythology, however, he insisted that grammatical gender was in any case principally tied to the characteristics of its noun. He considered masculine nouns to have strong, large, active, and initiating qualities and feminine nouns to have small, weak, passive, and receptive qualities. As for neuter (a grammatical gender not found in all languages), he viewed it as signaling that a noun had mixed, collective, or still undeveloped masculine and feminine traits.[28]

But Jacob had to engage in considerable fantasizing to get linguistic phenomena to fit his theory of grammatical gender. For example, he speculated that although trees are tall, nouns for trees are typically feminine because either trees are more passive than animals or their grammatical gender stems from myths that personify trees with figures such as dryads. As for abstract nouns, he stated that capabilities associated with the human soul are typically feminine, and then rationalized exceptions to this pattern by insisting that artists and poets routinely employed female figures to represent even masculine and neuter words such as *der Verstand* (understanding) and *das Laster* (vice). Jacob also posited that the feminine grammatical gender had arisen, like Eve from Adam's rib, from the masculine; the masculine gender was therefore original and primary, and feminine derivative and secondary. As with the Grimms' editing of depictions of female characters in their fairy tales, Jacob's theory of grammatical gender lays bare his patriarchal view that women are inherently dependent on and subservient to men.[29]

Whereas Jacob's studies of customs, folklore, and mythology were inseparable from his linguistic interests, Wilhelm focused more on fairy tales and medieval literature in and of themselves. As Wilhelm emerged from his physical and mental turmoil, he began to refocus on his scholarship. He completed an edition of *The Rose Garden* (a medieval poem featuring many characters from the *Nibelungenlied*) as well as the third Large Edition of *Children's and Household Tales*, published not by Reimer but by a scholarly press in Göttingen. Wilhelm noted in the dedicatory preface to Bettina von Arnim that it had been twenty-five years since her husband, now deceased, had presented her with the first edition of tales, which the Grimms had dedicated to her and their young son.

Published in 1837, the third Large Edition coincided not only with the twenty-fifth anniversary of the first appearance of *Children's and Household*

Tales, but also with the University of Göttingen's centenary celebration. In view of these milestones, Wilhelm meticulously attended to the collection's content as well as its physical size, the paper on which it was printed, the arabesques, angels, and witches that now enlivened its cover, and the interior illustrations, which included colored title pages. Despite these enhancements, the edition still did not achieve widespread commercial success.[30]

As for the tales themselves, several had not previously appeared in the Large Edition. Some of the added tales continue familiar themes of reward and punishment. In "Mother Trudy," for example, a witch turns a misbehaving girl into a block of wood and then throws the wood into the fire. In "Snow White and Rose Red," unrelated to the better-known "Snow White," two pious and diligent sisters help not only a bear who is actually a prince cursed by a malevolent dwarf, but also the dwarf himself. After killing the dwarf and breaking the spell, the bear resumes his human form. He marries one sister, while his brother marries the other, and they all share the dwarf's jewels.

Remarkably, "Snow White and Rose Red" is based on "The Ungrateful Dwarf," a tale by children's writer Caroline Stahl that Wilhelm revised so substantially as to create his own tale. The bear in Stahl's tale appears only at the end, is not under a spell, and is not befriended by the sisters, who are rewarded with only the dwarf's jewels, not marriage. Wilhelm had summarized Stahl's tale in the appendix to the second edition of *Children's and Household Tales* and indicated there that he believed it to be genuine and old. He had also included "Snow White and Rose Red" in the second Small Edition of the Grimms' tales in 1833 but not in previous Large Editions. In the 1856 appendix to *Children's and Household Tales*, he clarified that he had leveraged Stahl's version but told the tale in his own way—a striking admission given his decades-long insistence that he merely shaped tales through his editorial practice instead of creating new renditions himself.[31]

In Wilhelm's reframing, "Snow White and Rose Red" more explicitly perpetuates stereotypical gender roles by emphasizing the sisters' piety, goodness, and diligence and by rewarding their good behavior with marriage. More strikingly, the tale mirrors Jacob and Wilhelm's close relationship as siblings. Whereas same-sex siblings in fairy tales are often rivals, Snow White and Rose Red in Wilhelm's telling "were so fond of each other that they always took each other's hand whenever they went out together, and when Snow White said, 'We shall never leave each other,' Rose Red responded, 'Not for as long as we live,' and their mother added, 'Whatever one of you has, you shall share it with the other.'" The passage recalls Jacob's declaration to Wilhelm in July 1805 that "we shall never part from each other" and the way they had always shared their incomes, possessions, and household. In view of Jacob's and Wilhelm's personalities, it is also noteworthy that Snow White is characterized as quieter and more of a homebody while Rose Red is more outgoing. Finally, the tale refers to storytelling when the mother puts on glasses and reads to her daughters while they spin.[32]

Beyond adding tales to the third edition, Wilhelm continued revising tales that had appeared in previous Large Editions and incorporated revisions he had first introduced in the Small Edition. The style and substance of many tales are made stronger through his addition of new symbols and imagery, alliteration, and ending rhymes. One such change appears to be delightfully personal: to the end of the tale "Hans My Hedgehog" Wilhelm added the rhyme "Mein Märchen ist aus, / und geht vor Gustchen sein Haus" (My tale is done, and go now to Gustchen's house). A Steinau woman who told stories to the Grimms when they were young used to end her tales with a rhyme about visiting someone's house, changing the name in the rhyme each time. As Jacob explained, the instruction to go to someone's house after hearing a tale was a call to pass the story on to others. Wilhelm's choice of the name "Gustchen," an endearing form of Auguste, is presumably meant as an affectionate gesture to his five-year-old daughter.[33]

A more famous edit appears in the opening lines of "The Frog King or Iron Heinrich." In the second edition, the tale began with the sentence "Once upon a time, there was a princess who was bored and did not know what she should do." The third edition, however, begins as follows: "In olden times, when wishing still helped, there lived a king whose daughters were all beautiful, but the youngest was so beautiful that even the sun itself, which of course had seen so much, was amazed whenever it shone on the girl's face." Here, Wilhelm enhances the pictorial nature of the tale by describing the sun's amazement at the girl's beauty. This mention of the sun adds to the tale's light imagery: the sun is a golden orb shining above, and the girl plays with a golden ball that falls deep into a well and must be retrieved. Moreover, the words "when wishing still helped," taken from the "The Iron Stove," another tale in the Grimms' collection, invite the reader into an enchanted world that has been lost. These words not only set the tone for the many tales that follow but serve as a subtle tribute to Dorothea Viehmann, since it was she who shared "The Iron Stove" with the Grimms. But the phrase also imparts a wistful tone that, at least for Wilhelm's family, might well have brought to mind the despondency he had experienced in the years leading up to the publication of the third edition.[34]

Still greater challenges would confront the Grimms after the death in 1837 of William IV, King of the United Kingdom of Great Britain and Ireland and also King of Hanover. Because William IV had fathered only illegitimate children, his niece Victoria ascended the throne in the United Kingdom. Hanoverian succession rules forbade women from inheriting the throne, so in Hanover William IV was succeeded not by Victoria, but by his brother Ernest Augustus, Duke of Cumberland and fifth son of King George III of England. When Victoria became queen of Great Britain and Ireland and Ernest Augustus king of Hanover, the personal union that had been in effect between Britain and Hanover since 1714 ended.

Known in German as Ernst August, the new king was more familiar with the kingdom he was to rule than his forebears had been. Born in London, he was sent as a teenager with two of his brothers to receive tutoring and attend lectures at the University of Göttingen. There, under the orders of his father, he and his brothers were allowed to hear and speak only German at their residence. Ernst August reported in a letter home that this immersion was so complete that his native-language skills had declined, an observation corroborated by the Germanicized syntax of his written English. Upon leaving, he looked on his years in the university town with genuine gratitude. "I should be one of the most ungrateful of men if ever I was forgetful of all I owe to Göttingen & its professors," he wrote to his father in 1791, soon after being appointed an officer in the Hanoverian military. Over the next few years, he fought with the Hanoverian forces against the French, sustaining an arm injury, a disfiguring facial wound, and the loss of sight in his left eye. He then lived in London and Berlin for several decades. When he acceded the throne at the age of sixty-six he returned to Hanover and lived there throughout his reign. His predecessors, by contrast, had largely ruled from Britain with a governor general or viceroy representing them in Hanover.[35]

Despite Ernst August's familiarity with and residence in Hanover, many of his subjects would have preferred that their popular viceroy Adolphus (the Duke of Cambridge and Ernst August's younger brother) succeed the throne of Hanover instead. Ernst August's temper and scheming disposition were well-known. His own family members believed he always attempted to sow divisiveness among them. In particular, they were irked by his marriage to

the twice-widowed Princess of Solms-Braunfels, since she had been unof-
ficially engaged to, and was believed to have jilted, Adolphus between her
two previous marriages. So unpopular was Ernst August that he was dogged
by persistent but untrue rumors that he had murdered one of his valets in
1810. (In reality, it was he who had been attacked in his sleep by an assailant
with a saber; the deceased valet, presumed to be the assailant, is thought to
have committed suicide.) There were also vicious slanders that his wife had
killed her previous husbands, sordid allegations that he was having affairs,
and outrageous fears that he might plot to have Victoria murdered so that he
could become king of Great Britain and Ireland. Many of these rumors were
stirred up by the Whig government, whose officials recoiled at Ernst August's
staunch Toryism and vehement opposition to Catholic emancipation.[36]

Rumors aside, it was principally Ernst August's antiliberal sentiments that
made Hanoverians nervous. This antiliberalism manifested itself just days
into his reign. After taking power in June 1837, he swiftly dissolved the diet in
Hanover and issued a patent in which he expressed his intent to change the
form of government. He proclaimed that he was not bound to the constitution of 1833, which William IV had issued in response to unrest, and that
his government would amend the document as it saw fit. The 1833 constitution had not only acknowledged the provincial diets but also divided the
principal diet into an upper and lower house and gave the lower house the
exclusive power of initiating legislation. The constitution had also transferred
the Hanoverian Domains—similar to the Crown Estate lands and holdings
in the United Kingdom—from the sovereign to the state. This action diminished the monarch's power, since the revenues from the Domains had paid
the members of the royal household and covered administrative costs. One
reason for this transfer was that in 1826 King George IV had borrowed money
using the revenues from the Domains as security—without consulting the
Hanoverian Estates.[37]

Noting that Ernst August's only son was blind, some contemporary accounts asserted that he wanted to nullify a provision in the 1833 constitution
specifying that any heir to the throne who was morally or physically defective
would be barred from inheriting it. But this downplayed Ernst August's illiberal and reactionary nature, the full force of which soon became apparent. On
November 1, 1837, Ernst August issued a second patent in which he annulled
the 1833 constitution altogether, on the grounds that William IV had not
engaged the Estates in changing certain passages, which violated procedures
for constitutional amendments set forth in the Vienna Final Act of 1820. In

addition, he insisted that as male heir his approval of the proposed constitution would have been necessary according to agnatic law; he claimed that he had voiced concerns about the constitution at the time and had refused to sign off on it.[38]

Although Ernst August invalidated the entire constitution, he made clear that laws passed under it would remain in force unless duly amended or repealed. In addition, he announced that he was lowering taxes and declared that anyone who had sworn to uphold the 1833 constitution was now relieved of that oath. His patent also dissolved the previous annual diet for good and established a body that would meet only every three years. A Cabinet rescript on November 14 directed all government personnel—which included university professors—to swear allegiance to Ernst August.[39]

These actions enraged the Grimms' friend Friedrich Christoph Dahlmann, who had played a lead role in drafting the 1833 constitution. Dahlmann denounced Ernst August's hypocrisy in portraying King William IV as having self-servingly amended the constitution without engaging the Estates. In addition, because Dahlmann had received an official communication assuring him that the male heirs had agreed to the 1833 constitution, he doubted Ernst August's claim that he had not consented to it. Either Ernst August (or his representatives) were lying or the communication Dahlmann had been given was incorrect.[40]

On the night of November 17, Dahlmann quickly wrote a statement protesting Ernst August's revocation of the constitution and underscoring protesters' intent to stay true to their original oath of allegiance to it, instead of taking a renewed oath of allegiance to Ernst August as sovereign. The following day, six other professors signed Dahlmann's statement: the professor of jurisprudence Wilhelm Eduard Albrecht, the biblical scholar and professor of Middle Eastern languages Heinrich Ewald, the physicist Wilhelm Weber, the literary historian Georg Gottfried Gervinus, and Jacob and Wilhelm Grimm. Together with Dahlmann, they became known as the "Göttingen Seven."

Reacting immediately in support of the Göttingen Seven, students gathered to distribute the protest statement. In addition to flooding Göttingen with copies, they sent many outside the Kingdom of Hanover and requested that newspapers publish the statement in full. A furious Ernst August ordered an investigation to determine which members of the seven were principally responsible for the statement's dissemination. The university's judiciary committee held an inquiry on December 4, and all seven professors freely admitted they had signed the protest statement; Dahlmann, Gervinus, and

The Göttingen Seven. Row 1 from top: G. G. Gervinus; row 2: Wilhelm (*l.*) and Jacob (*r.*) Grimm; row 3: W. E. Albrecht; row 4: W. Weber (*l.*) and H. Ewald (*r.*); row 5: F. C. Dahlmann. From Hans Blum, ed., *Die deutsche Revolution, 1848–49: Eine Jubiläumsausgabe für das deutsche Volk* (Leipzig: Eugen Diederichs, 1897), n.p. Collection of the author.

Jacob admitted to very limited dissemination of it, stressing that they had not shared it with others before sending it to Hanover nor had they sent it to newspapers in or outside of Germany. A week later, Ernst August fired all seven professors and further decreed that Dahlmann, Gervinus, and Jacob would face juridical consequences and forcible removal from Göttingen if they did not leave the Kingdom of Hanover within three days. As news of the terminations and banishment spread, students poured into the streets in protest; some were jailed for not following orders to disperse. Under threat of arrest, Dahlmann, Gervinus, and Jacob hurriedly left Göttingen for Kassel. A couple hundred students walked through the night to show support for the outcasts at the Hessian border. Upon crossing into Hessen, Jacob overheard an elderly woman refer to him as a refugee and tell her grandson to give him a hand with his luggage. Recounting this incident in his pamphlet "Jacob Grimm on His Dismissal," written in January 1838, Jacob noted the irony of fleeing the Kingdom of Hanover to become a refugee in his own homeland. At least he *could* seek refuge there: whereas he was a citizen of Electoral Hessen, Dahlmann and Gervinus were not, and the police allowed the two of them to stay there for only twelve hours.[41]

In Kassel, Jacob moved back in with Ludwig in the home where Jacob, Ludwig, Wilhelm, and Dortchen had lived before Jacob's and Wilhelm's appointments in Göttingen. Not all their siblings were as generous. From Wolfenbüttel, Ferdinand selfishly beseeched the Grimms for more money, despite knowing full well they had lost their positions. When, in 1838, Ferdinand published a collection of tales and legends under a pseudonym, he had the audacity to send Jacob and Wilhelm a copy with postage due upon receipt.

Jacob turned to writing his pamphlet on his dismissal. Commenting there on the politics of the day, he expressed his profound dislike of factions and described himself as identifying with views across the spectrum of political parties. Over the years, he stressed, he had observed liberals behaving as conservatives and conservatives behaving as liberals. He himself gravitated to the middle, and he saw the task at hand as determining how to maintain the traditional order without renouncing or impeding progress. To his mind, those clamoring for liberal constitutions at times seemed to wish to make everything equal and uniform, behaving as if mountaintops could simply be flattened, ancient forests eradicated, and wildflower meadows tilled. They too hastily sought a lowering of the upper classes and a raising up of the lower classes. But on the other side, those who clung to absolutism wanted to maintain an unnatural constancy instead of embracing change. Without progress, the weathered or decayed parts of the established order could never be rejuvenated. He likened moderation to the warmth of the heart and factions to the coldness of the body's extremities, and further charged that political extremes on either side would yield only far-fetched theories instead of sensible, sustainable practice. He emphasized the need to preserve tradition while recognizing that tradition becomes fossilized without gentle change—a position that recalls his and Wilhelm's desired, if not always fulfilled, approach to the editing of fairy tales and legends.

As for views of the distant past, Jacob opined that whereas conservatives made too much of a show of their longing for the Middle Ages, liberals saw in it only barbarianism and feudalism. He admitted that his readers might well find within his own works on medieval literature and language weapons that would either vilify or endorse nineteenth-century German society and its institutions. Jacob himself chose one such weapon for the title page of his pamphlet, a quotation from the *Nibelungenlied*: "war sint die eide komen?" (What has become of the oaths?), from a passage where Siegfried reminds King Gunther that he had promised Siegfried Kriemhild's hand in marriage.

Regarding Ernst August's revocation of the 1833 constitution, Jacob reminded his readers that William IV had agreed on the constitution with the Estates. If every successor could simply undo the agreements of his predecessor, there would be no certainty in the land. This did not mean that constitutions should be immutable, but that amendments should happen with the same parties at the table as before. Jacob emphasized that he was not defending the 1833 constitution itself. He acknowledged that some viewed it as too liberal and others as not liberal enough. But the constitution had been the law of the land, civil servants had sworn an oath to uphold it, and the king should not be allowed to relieve them of this oath unilaterally. Some might brand as naive the notion that political oaths should mean something, and opponents of the liberal constitution would excuse Ernst August's actions on the grounds that the ends justified the means. Others might simply want to distance themselves from political controversy. But to Jacob, an oath was an oath. In the last lines of his pamphlet, he vowed to remain proud of having defied the king "for as long as I can still draw a breath, [. . .] and I feel consoled that whatever of my work outlives me will not lose but instead gain because of this action."[42]

Jacob realized as he wrote the pamphlet that the censors would thwart its publication. Several of the other Göttingen Seven were also writing essays on the protest, and together they strategized about where they might be able to publish these works. They considered not only local censorship laws but also geographical location, knowing that publication in one region almost assured that the work would make its way into adjacent regions regardless of censorship. In the end, Jacob published his pamphlet in Basel to elude the German censors but allow for underground dissemination into southern Germany. As it happened, the published pamphlet was allowed in more territories than Jacob anticipated and was widely sold and circulated, although the Grimms were disappointed that it did not have a greater impact.[43]

Its publication also could not repair the hurt Jacob felt in the aftermath of his and Wilhelm's dismissals. Although several professors had publicly proclaimed support for the Göttingen Seven in the Kassel newspaper, the Grimms were dismayed by the unwillingness of many friends and colleagues to defend them openly. Some of their acquaintances quietly believed that Jacob and Wilhelm had made a stupendously self-destructive mistake, while others suspected them of having self-aggrandizing motives for engaging in the protest. Jacob was particularly unsparing in his criticism of those who had made careers out of teaching law, justice, and morality but whose characters had faded like autumn leaves after a frost the moment Ernst August revoked the constitution. He was especially disappointed at Savigny's tepid reaction to the protesters, which led to tension between the two long-standing friends.[44]

In Göttingen, Wilhelm faced a gamut of responses from acquaintances, ranging from outright coldness to simpering praise devoid of supportive action. Like Jacob, he was troubled that many assumed that he and Jacob had acted out of factionalism, instead of a principled desire to uphold an oath they had taken. With Jacob now living in Kassel, Wilhelm and Dortchen found their house in Göttingen eerily empty, and Jacob's absence only intensified the hollowness Wilhelm felt as he contemplated the future. He emphasized in correspondence that he had no idea where he and Jacob would find employment and that his only plan was to trust in God. He and Dortchen took to spending evenings in a back room; when, on his fifty-second birthday in February, they had sat in the front parlor, they saw that the police were watching them and were still there the next morning. Only the most loyal friends now came to visit.[45]

The Göttingen Seven were, however, not without defenders and benefactors. Spearheaded by a committee in Leipzig, philanthropic groups formed in cities around Germany to collect donations to support the dismissed professors while they sought other university positions—a difficult task now that governments saw them as dangers to absolutist rule. Supporters also unsuccessfully tried to get the professors' positions in Göttingen restored. Most memorably, the mathematician and astronomer Carl Friedrich Gauss asked Alexander von Humboldt to prevail on Ernst August to restore physicist Wilhelm Weber's position; at a banquet the king rebuffed Humboldt by shallowly boasting, "For my money I can have as many ballet dancers, whores, and professors as I want."[46]

Though the boast may have held some truth, Ernst August failed to recognize that the seven protesters were among the most eminent in their fields in all of Germany. His money could indeed buy more professors, but not of the caliber of those he had so angrily dismissed. And his money also could not buy the university's reputation, which suffered a tremendous blow. The dismissals left the Göttingen faculty seriously deficient and enrollment dropped precipitously. It took half a century for the university to recover its prestige.[47]

This reputational damage was particularly ironic given that in September 1837, three months before the professors' dismissals, the university had celebrated with great fanfare its hundredth anniversary. Visitors included dignitaries from other German governments, representatives from several German universities, and renowned alumni such as Alexander von Humboldt. In Göttingen for the celebrations, Ludwig Grimm found parades of students in the streets and a grand ball at which there was hardly room to dance amid the two thousand guests. To feed the visitors and strangers who came to their home from morning until late at night, the Grimms set up a table in their foyer laden with sausage, ham, roasts, and wine. During the festivities, Ludwig also spied King Ernst August—whom he described as a tall, stiff man with unpleasant features, white hair, and a white mustache—dressed in his military uniform.

Just a few months later, it was this man who, despite his vow never to forget the positive effects of Göttingen's professors on his own education, dismissed the Grimms and their five colleagues. The University of Göttingen had since its founding distinguished itself for affording academic freedom to professors. But the king had decisively reminded his subjects that academic freedom did not mean professors could refuse to comply with government directives, even if in this case the refusal rested on the premise that the king had had no right to revoke the constitution. Jacob found it reprehensible that a published account of the jubilee celebrations omitted any mention of the Göttingen Seven protest that had ensued shortly thereafter.[48]

With time, Ernst August's reign was regarded as surprisingly successful. Unlike many other rulers, he dodged the revolutions that swept across Europe in 1848. His success is partly attributed to Hanoverians' sense that they had no choice but to support their king or be engulfed by Prussia, but their eventual respect for him also came from his proven dedication to the kingdom. He continued to view himself as principally British, however. Although he later reconciled with some in his family and with London society, he and Queen Victoria disliked each other; making matters worse, he despised Prince Albert, whom he characterized as "a terrible Liberal, almost a Radical" and "still more dangerous than a Roman Catholic."[49]

In the aftermath of the Göttingen Seven protest, the technicalities of whether Ernst August's revocation of the constitution had been legal were of far less concern to many than the question of whether German states such as Hanover might ever achieve the freedoms enjoyed in Britain and America. The Englishman John Mitchell Kemble, who had studied under Jacob, sought to explain the Göttingen Seven protest to his British readers by emphasizing that visitors to Germany were typically astonished to find it so lacking in civil freedoms despite its civilized veneer. As for the dismissed professors, Kemble portrayed them as principled scholars, not political provocateurs.[50]

When friends and acquaintances tried unsuccessfully to get the professors' positions restored, Jacob and Wilhelm continued to act with principle instead of provocation in mind. The brothers made it clear they appreciated such good intentions but had no desire to return to Göttingen. Not only had they never really liked it there, but they also feared that a return would falsely signal that they had signed the protest to bring attention to themselves and engage in performative agitation; in fact, they had signed it out of conviction that Ernst August had been wrong to nullify the constitution and that time would vindicate their actions.[51]

Indeed, the Göttingen Seven are today a point of pride for the University of Göttingen and for the state of Lower Saxony, which includes Hanover and Göttingen. Although on legal grounds some commentators have found their position shaky, the protesting professors have most commonly been championed for contributing to the movement toward greater liberties in Germany by standing up to the absolutist Hanoverian king. Several memorials attest to their enduring legacy. The foyer of the Lower Saxony state parliament in

Hanover features a memorial plaque, and outside the building a set of bronze sculptures by Italian sculptor Floriano Bodini commemorates the Göttingen Seven. Installed in 1998, the set depicts the three professors banished from the kingdom outside a large gate, while inside are the four professors who lost their positions but were not exiled. Included among the statues are also figures of Ernst August and a student. Bodini did not seek to create likenesses of the actual historical figures, but instead modeled the statues on people he knew. In a symbolic representation of the Grimms' brotherhood, Jacob is modeled after Bodini himself, and Bodini's brother served as model for Wilhelm.[52]

Not surprisingly, Göttingen boasts the most memorials to the professors. The University of Göttingen auditorium bears a memorial plaque, the central campus area has long been named Göttingen Seven Square, and in 2011 a commemorative weathered-steel sculpture of an intertwined G and 7 designed by the Nobel Prize–winning German writer Günter Grass was installed in the square. Upon its unveiling, many pooh-poohed the sculpture as unbearably simplistic; others have pointed out that Grass insightfully distilled the intertwining of writing and history into a minimalistic conjoining of the letter and number, and that the 7 visually cuts through the G in a way that further draws attention to this historicity.[53]

The most provocative memorial by far, however, was erected in 2015 near the Göttingen train station. The work of German sculptor Christiane Möbus, it consists of a forty-ton granite pedestal that intentionally copies a pedestal in front of the train station in Hanover. The Hanover pedestal bears a sculpture unveiled in 1861 of Ernst August atop his horse. Unlike that pedestal, however, Möbus's in Göttingen is bare. Instead of the king and his horse, there are only hoofprints sculpted into a flat bronze plate affixed to the horizontal surface of the thirteen-foot-tall monument—and, because of the monument's height, the hoofprints cannot be seen by viewers. The empty pedestal suggests that the king who banished three of the seven fired professors has now himself been banished, with only his horse's hoofprints left behind. The Hanover and Göttingen pedestals also differ in their inscriptions: whereas the pedestal bearing the sculpture of Ernst August reads "To the Father of the State from His Loyal People," Möbus's empty pedestal states "To the Father of the State from the Göttingen Seven."

But the most controversial feature is Möbus's addition of her own name to the list of the Göttingen Seven professors carved into the pedestal. By boldly adding her name alongside, and in the same font as, those of the Seven,

Möbus did not simply sign her work as artist but also—to her critics—misleads viewers into thinking she, too, was one of the 1837 protesters. Interpreted in another way, Möbus's addition of her name encourages viewers themselves to sign on to protests against abuses of power. Similarly, Bodini's decision to depict his own likeness in his sculpture of Jacob could be seen as the artist's identification with the Grimms' cause. Upon its unveiling, Möbus's empty pedestal in any case provoked derision from some Göttingen citizens, who expressed concern that passersby would neither understand the empty pedestal nor realize that Möbus was not one of the protesting professors.[54]

While such critics have found her memorial too esoteric, it is striking that Wilhelm left his own subtle memorial to the Göttingen Seven protest in the fourth edition (1840) of *Children's and Household Tales,* the next edition to appear after the protest. He cleverly alluded to Jacob's banishment in the edits he made to "The Blue Light." The tale in the fourth and subsequent editions begins as follows:

> Once upon a time there was a soldier who had faithfully served the king for many years. But when the war came to an end and the soldier could no longer serve because he had suffered many wounds, the king said to him, "You can go home now. I no longer need you, and you shall receive no more money from me. I give wages only to those who can serve me." The soldier did not know how he would scrape by, and he went away full of worries and walked the whole day until he came to a forest.[55]

In earlier editions of *Children's and Household Tales,* the soldier is discharged because of his advanced age. He has no wounds, and there is no direct speech in which the king denies him a wage and tells him to leave. By contrast, Wilhelm appears to have altered the wording beginning in the fourth edition to include a crypto-political jab at Ernst August for his banishment and figurative wounding of Jacob. As in other Grimm tales, the forest to which the soldier walks is both an enchanted place where magical forces, whether benevolent or malevolent, appear and a liberating space where protagonists can use their skills and character traits to prevail. In the forest, characters can free themselves from rigid social norms, expectations, and judgments. For Jacob, the pursuit of scholarship back home in Kassel would be this symbolic forest.[56]

Jacob's pamphlet remains the most famous account of the Göttingen Seven protest, but it is not the only published work in which he commented on his dismissal. The opening lines of his preface to the first volume of the Grimms' *German Dictionary* (*Deutsches Wörterbuch*, 1854) also present a bold account of both the protest and the birth of the dictionary project in the months of unemployment that followed. Had he not been dismissed from his post, Jacob candidly acknowledged in the opening lines of the dictionary, he most certainly would not have undertaken the monumental task of writing a comprehensive dictionary of the German language with his brother. It was this groundbreaking project to which much of their attention would now turn.

CHAPTER 12

Aftermath of the Göttingen Seven Protest, 1838–1841

Ten months after Jacob's dismissal, Wilhelm and family moved to Kassel to reunite with him. They had surprised Jacob in Kassel on his birthday in January 1838, weeks after his banishment, and had also seen him briefly in April. Such visits, however, did little to alleviate the toll of separation on the close-knit family. Jacob and Wilhelm knew being together would help them weather the uncertain times ahead, but even so, Wilhelm struggled emotionally as he packed to leave Göttingen; he found it unbearable just watching the pictures in his study being taken down from the walls. Walking pensively through the apartment one last time, he stopped to sit alone in Jacob's room.[1]

Dortchen had already left Göttingen with the children, followed by Wilhelm a few days later. It was dark by the time he arrived at the home he had left eight years earlier; as he stepped over the threshold he was surprised to see Bettina von Arnim, who had traveled to Kassel to help Dortchen. Bettina memorialized her visit to the Grimms in her epistolary novel *Ilius Pamphilius and the Ambrosia*, gushing that Wilhelm's cheerfulness and Jacob's warmth and genuineness made it hard to believe that they were now (what she rather dramatically described as) beggars. Although the Grimms' relationship with some friends had grown strained since the Göttingen Seven protest, Bettina would continue her strenuous advocacy for them in the months and years ahead.[2]

Three large wagons loaded with the Grimms' possessions had also arrived, bearing among other items the books and papers Jacob had dearly missed since his forced exit from Göttingen. It took him a week to unpack and arrange all his books, and he wrote of his happiness at holding them in his hands again and rediscovering the various bookmarks he had tucked into their pages. He was also immensely relieved to reunite with Wilhelm. When an apartment became available in the building where Ludwig and his wife lived, Jacob moved there with Wilhelm and his family.[3]

Although the Grimms were back in the city they had so long regarded as home, their lack of employment made their time there seem disorienting and transitory. After all, Wilhelm had served in the libraries of Kassel and Göttingen since 1814 and Jacob since 1816. They did not know how long they would be back in Kassel or where they might eventually land. Many rulers of German territories regarded the Göttingen Seven as firebrands who would further destabilize the social order; moreover, many felt that hiring any of the Göttingen Seven professors would signal a betrayal of King Ernst August. Beyond this, the Grimms' insistence that they must stick together as brothers further complicated their search, as it was nearly impossible to find a university or library where not one, but two, suitable positions would be available.

Now in their early fifties, Jacob and Wilhelm had individually or together made their mark in linguistics, literary history, mythography, runology, folklore, and medieval studies, and soon they were to be known for their contribution to lexicography. The grand dictionary project on which they would work for the rest of their lives had started in the aftermath of the Göttingen Seven protest, while Jacob was in Kassel and Wilhelm still in Göttingen. A publishing house and classics scholar in Leipzig had pitched the dictionary idea to them early in 1838. The press was co-owned by Karl August Reimer (son of the Grimms' erstwhile publisher in Berlin) and Salomon Hirzel, both of whom were members of the Leipzig committee that had collected donations for the Göttingen Seven. The idea was not entirely new to the Grimms since a few German publishing firms had approached Jacob in the 1820s and 1830s about various lexicographical projects. But the Grimms were hesitant. Not only was Jacob busy with projects including a revised edition of *German Grammar*, but he also questioned whether the public really had an appetite for a comprehensive dictionary of the German language. Lachmann insisted that it was irrelevant to ask at the outset about readers' desires, since they were sure to want the dictionary once it was published. But Lachmann had also been among those who had counseled the Grimms to go to Göttingen years ago, and they of course had not liked it there.

The Grimms in any case accepted the dictionary project, knowing that it would afford them needed financial security while they sought other scholarly positions. They acknowledged, however, that writing a dictionary was an immense undertaking, which might force them to decline any employment that could impede their progress on it. But they put their best face forward in their announcement of the dictionary in a Leipzig paper: "Jakob [sic] and Wilhelm Grimm, simultaneously impacted by the same fate, and after a long and unfruitful hope that a German land would take them in its service, have mustered the courage to refresh, strengthen, and ensure their future themselves." Human nature, the announcement reminded readers, always hopes to discern something sweet in that which is bitter, and this is what the Grimms had endeavored to do. Their dictionary, they proclaimed, would capture the richness of modern German as used by great thinkers and writers from Luther in the sixteenth century to Goethe, who had died in 1832. In taking this historical approach, the Grimms distinguished themselves from Johann Heinrich Campe, whose dictionary published between 1807 and 1811 had focused on current usage. In their announcement, they also emphasized that Johann Christoph Adelung's *Grammatical and Critical Dictionary of the High German Language*, first published in the 1770s and 1780s and last updated in 1811, lacked comprehensiveness and had preceded advances in the grammatical understanding of German (including Jacob's own in *German Grammar*). Although in other countries royal academies had supported the production of dictionaries, the Grimms' dictionary would emerge from their work as private scholars and with assistance from friendly collaborators, they noted. Their Göttingen Seven colleague Gervinus also picked up on this irony, observing that the Grimms, having been spurned by Ernst August, were now writing a dictionary that in other lands would have been sponsored by royal patronage.[4]

In taking on the dictionary project, the Grimms entered their names into the long history of European lexicography. Medieval European lexicography had produced not only freestanding dictionaries but also glosses of words, typically in the margins of individual texts, which could later be gathered into a separate glossary. Jacob was of course intimately familiar with medieval lexicography from his early work on the glossators for Savigny in Paris. Whereas most bilingual medieval dictionaries had paired Latin with a vernacular

tongue, in the early modern period dictionaries increasingly paired two vernacular languages. The rise of the monolingual dictionary in Europe dates to
the end of the sixteenth century and by the eighteenth century included such
landmark dictionaries as Samuel Johnson's *Dictionary of the English Language*
(1755). The dictionaries produced by various national language academies in
the seventeenth and eighteenth centuries had sought to prescribe correct usage, but Johnson made a point in the preface of his dictionary of calling
out the folly of such attempts to control language. In the early nineteenth
century, the historical method of lexicography took hold; lexicographers now
viewed their work as not prescriptive, but descriptive. Quotations from various authors, texts, and periods could illustrate the meanings and usage of a
particular word through time, and thus contribute to an understanding of
a language's development and the culture(s) that produced it. It was in this
historical spirit, and drawing on their extensive knowledge of German grammar, folklore, and medieval literature, that the Grimms embarked on their
dictionary project.[5]

As in their earlier scholarship, the Grimms brought their insatiably in-
quisitive mindset to their practice of lexicography. They had long eschewed
prescribing German language usage and instead devoted themselves to uncovering and accurately describing the full spectrum of the language's forms
and conventions, which they found endlessly fascinating. When Dahlmann's
daughter Dorothee asked whether the word for grain (*Getreide*) ought to be
spelled with an *ai* or an *ei*, for example, Jacob responded that while both
forms were equally acceptable, "I prefer the former out of sheer pity [. . .],
because we have so little *ai* in our language and so much *ei*." He then related
the etymology of the word from the German verb *tragen* (to carry), explaining
that grain is that which is carried (harvested) from the earth. Having devoted
so much of his life to studying the development of Germanic languages, Jacob
would by this time have been able to decode virtually any word or utterance
in similar fashion. As the Victorian translator of Jacob's *German Mythology*
aptly observed, Jacob's scientific approach to philology "enabled him to trace
a word with certitude through the strangest disguises."[6]

The interconnectedness Jacob and Wilhelm saw in linguistic, cultural,
literary, and folk expressions pointed to a grand unity, however distant and
unknowable it might be, that might serve as both a substitute and a catalyst
for the political unity the German-speaking lands lacked. This perspective is
evident in the Grimms' repeated goal of providing a dictionary that would
be comprehensive not just with respect to words defined, but also in terms

of cultural heritage. Indeed, at times mapping this cultural heritage seemed to take precedence over presenting a complete alphabetical listing of the German language, as exemplified in their greater emphasis on covering Luther to Goethe than *A* to *Z*. The mention of these figures in their announcement of the project was not an isolated occurrence, but often repeated as they sought collaborators. Implicit in their invocations of Luther and Goethe—as masters of modern High German who served as bookends for the general span of time the Grimms were covering—was the importance of High German to the German cultural heritage and therefore to the goal of German political unification. Definitions would include not just a brief explanation of the word's meaning but also passages from authors in which the word was used. Foreign loan words would not be included, except in cases where they had long since been incorporated into German, but regional words were to be covered. At the same time, to aid non-native speakers, entries would include Latin and, if needed, French translations to supplement the definition in German.

By the end of 1838, the Grimms had enlisted around thirty contributors to help with the project; by autumn 1839 this figure had nearly doubled. With time, over one hundred contributors were engaged in the task of supplying examples of word usage on slips of paper, a process that spanned much of the 1840s. These then needed to be alphabetized, assembled, and scrutinized for gaps. By the 1850s, the Grimms had amassed some six hundred thousand slips. At home in his study, Jacob felt as if he were snowed in by words everywhere he turned. It had been costly to hire so many collaborators, but they saw no other way to accomplish their task. However, working with the collaborators was itself time-consuming, since the Grimms had to train each one and then badger them to keep on schedule. The Grimms were scholars, not project managers, and they resented having to devote so much time to reminding contributors of their commitments.[7]

But apart from these managerial issues, even their own scholarly work on the dictionary proved arduous and unfulfilling compared to the other projects they had pursued over the years. "For a few hours every day I chop wood," Wilhelm told Dahlmann, "which is to say that I work on collecting for the dictionary." The tedium involved in compiling words, meanings, and examples of usage had long been felt by lexicographers through the ages. Samuel Johnson had captured this tedium most memorably in the entry for "dull" in his *Dictionary of the English Language*, for which he supplied the example "to make dictionaries is *dull* work"; similarly, his entry for "lexicographer" includes the phrase "a harmless drudge." For the Grimms, the drudgery of compiling the dictionary was an added professional sacrifice on top of that which they had already made as members of the Göttingen Seven. If the work were to succeed, however, it would be "the fruit of our banishment, which we will lay at the altar of the fatherland," Jacob grandiosely avowed. As tedious as the dictionary work could be, he acknowledged that it was nevertheless more fulfilling than their positions in Göttingen, where so much of their time had been wasted on mundane tasks like compiling catalogs. It soon became clear to them that they would not be able to finish the dictionary in their lifetimes if they assumed a position at a university or library. But Jacob also recognized that regardless of whether they remained in Kassel as independent scholars focused on the dictionary or accepted a position somewhere in Germany, he had more ideas for scholarly works than he would ever have time to complete.[8]

As they settled back into life in Kassel, the Grimms became choosier about prospects for scholarly positions. Jacob proclaimed himself too proud and recalcitrant to give Prussia his academic service, since the kingdom had been timid in its response to the Göttingen Seven protests. His rebuff was moot, however, for any possibility of state-sponsored scholarly employment there was out of the question as long as Friedrich Wilhelm III—Ernst August's brother-in-law—was on the Prussian throne. At one point in spring 1838 it seemed the Grimms might go to Leipzig, but the Saxon government's initial support of the Göttingen Seven soon waned. When the Grimms learned of efforts to secure positions for them at the library in Paris, they were flattered but could not envision themselves leaving Germany. They would have been interested in positions in Jena or Heidelberg but would most have preferred the University of Marburg, whose faculty, too, would have welcomed them there. However, the Hessian elector opposed any appointment in Marburg, in part because he, like Friedrich Wilhelm III and many other German rulers, was related to Ernst August.[9]

Overall, the Grimms were content as independent scholars in Kassel, despite lingering uncertainties over how long they would be able to finance their lives there. Wilhelm attributed his improving health to being free to stroll in the fresh air whenever he liked, and he delighted in gazing out at the blue sky and smelling the scent of linden trees wafting in through his window. The Grimms received many visitors in Kassel; however, after the constant obligatory social and professional events in Göttingen, Jacob rejoiced in the relative seclusion of life back home. He hoped that the actions of the Göttingen Seven would, with time, inspire a more widespread assertion of German freedoms, but he himself did not want to take on a more public or political role. Still as close as ever, he and Wilhelm worked alongside each other without conversing as much as when they were young men; they only occasionally broke the silence to ask one another for thoughts on a particular detail. At mealtimes, Wilhelm and Dortchen's children carried the conversation. Dortchen grew ill with pneumonia during the winter of 1838–39, followed by a kidney infection. Jacob, too, experienced occasional ailments.[10]

Despite needing to devote themselves to the dictionary, Jacob and Wilhelm each completed other substantial projects. Jacob published the third, revised edition of the first volume of *German Grammar* in 1840; in the same year he also published the first two parts of a collection of historical texts related to German legal customs and guidance. Wilhelm not only completed more works on medieval German literature but also issued the fourth edition of *Children's and Household Tales*. Although most of his editing, adding, and rearranging of tales had already occurred in earlier editions, significant changes continued to appear. In addition to the subtle jab at King Ernst August that he added to "The Blue Light," a notable edit appears in "Hansel and Gretel," in which the mother is now referred to as the children's stepmother instead of their biological parent. In accordance with idealized bourgeois norms, Wilhelm thus implicitly suggested from the fourth edition on that a biological mother could not possibly abandon her children. Three years later, in the fifth edition, he edited the tale still further to indicate that a great famine had spread across the land, for which reason the father, a poor woodcutter, could not even procure his daily bread; Wilhelm in effect exculpated the father by providing an external reason for why he cannot adequately provide for his children. In the fifth edition, he also inserted more references to God, as when Hansel reassures his sister that God will not forsake them.

Wilhelm's work on these editions occurred at a time of rapid change in the German book market. Fueled by cheaper paper, faster presses, and a surge of new bookshops and lending libraries, German publishing expanded in the 1830s, with annual title growth exceeding 10 percent. Nevertheless, *Children's and Household Tales* not only still failed to become the bestseller that the Grimms had long hoped it would be, but also proved less popular than the fairy tales of emerging competitor Ludwig Bechstein. Bechstein's volume first appeared in 1845 and far outsold *Children's and Household Tales* during the Grimms' lifetimes, likely because of its lower price point, broader reach into markets in the Austro-Hungarian Empire, and wittier, more bourgeois style compared to the folksiness of the Grimms' tales.[11]

Wilhelm again dedicated the work to Bettina von Arnim, as he had in previous editions. His preface is a testament to the Grimms' enduring friendship with her. "I arrived in darkness and stepped into the same house that I had left eight years earlier in the bitter cold," he wrote, describing his arrival in Kassel after leaving Göttingen. "How surprised I was to find you, dear Bettina, sitting by my loved ones and giving succor and aid to my ill wife." He likened Bettina's unwavering support for the Grimms during their difficult period to the warmth of the sunlight streaming through his window. Moreover, he reflected on how fitting it was to return to *Children's and Household Tales* at a time when he felt reinvigorated by the "love and hate" he experienced during the Göttingen Seven protest.[12]

Of all their friends, Bettina was indeed the most tenacious in trying to secure employment for them. Jacob and Wilhelm appreciated her desire to help, but at times they worried her efforts would be counterproductive. Jacob complained to Dahlmann that Bettina was pursuing matters too relentlessly and intemperately, "like all women" were prone to do—a judgment against which, he confessed, his deceased mother and Dortchen would argue.[13]

But as Jacob himself knew, Bettina hardly conformed to the expected womanly behavior of the time. She was by all accounts a dynamo who had no time for etiquette and niceties. Already as a child, she had been a free spirit who loved to climb trees and was known for her talkativeness. While her mother attended to the needs of Bettina's younger siblings, Bettina used her effervescent personality to gain attention from adults and combat her loneliness. After the death of her mother, she was sent at the age of nine to an Ursuline convent. When her father died three years later, Bettina first lived with her grandmother, the author and salon hostess Sophie von La Roche, and later back at the Brentano family home in Frankfurt, where she developed meaningful friendships with the writer Karoline von Günderrode and with Goethe's elderly mother. Bettina idolized Goethe but was banned from his household in Weimar after falling out with his wife, Christiane. Wilhelm von Humboldt described her as someone whose thoughts and body were constantly in motion; he recounted that during one conversation she sat first on the floor and then atop the oven. Her appearance accentuated her impish behavior: she had a petite figure with small hands and feet, and her dark hair hung in curls around her pale face and sharp brown eyes. After she visited the Grimms at their apartment in Kassel for four days in October 1824, Wilhelm described her as possessing the most spirited personality and intellectual

Bettina von Arnim, née Brentano, depicted in 1838 seated in front of her design for a Goethe memorial. Illustration based on the drawing by Ludwig Emil Grimm, in L. E. Grimm, *Erinnerungen aus meinem Leben*, ed. Adolf Stoll (Leipzig: Hesse & Becker Verlag, 1913), 465. Collection of the author.

brilliance he had ever encountered. "God seldom sends the world a mind like hers," he later wrote to Lachmann. Jacob described her to Dahlmann as an "overflowing fountain" and faithful friend.[14]

Bettina's marriage to Achim von Arnim had been happy, despite their markedly different personalities and backgrounds. She was Catholic and he was Protestant. And whereas Arnim preferred to live at his family's rural manor house south of Berlin, Bettina spent most of her time with their children in the city, which caused the thrifty Arnim considerable anxiety over the cost of maintaining an apartment there. Arnim also fretted over their children's lack of learning and focus, while the always unconventional Bettina saw nothing amiss in their undisciplined behavior. Widowed with seven children upon Arnim's death in 1831, she suffered further loss when, in 1835, her eighteen-year-old son Kühnemund died in a swimming accident. That same year, she published *Goethe's Correspondence with a Child*, a poeticized rendering of her correspondence with the great writer. Meanwhile, at Bettina's request, Wilhelm was editing Arnim's collected works, the first volume of which appeared in 1839. Before his death, Arnim had acknowledged to Wilhelm that he had not been as prolific or renowned in his writing career as some might have hoped; he wondered how his life might have been different had the ringing in his ears been the sounding of trumpets heralding his poetic successes instead of annoying tinnitus. In later years, Bettina devoted herself to writing as well as to political and social issues that included poverty, labor conditions, and the emancipation of women. She was one of the first German women to directly engage with political matters.[15]

Given Bettina's energetic personality and passion for social advocacy, it was only natural that she enlist herself in advancing the Grimms' cause. Their plight, she divulged to Wilhelm, had hatched within her thoughts on how she could influence government officials—or in her words, "rule the state." Somewhat mystically, she described being able to draw the power out from the hearts of human beings and into herself, and then send it back into them; by this process, she sought to draw on their strength to in turn further empower them. She wished to see herself as mentor to the Prussian king and as someone who might cut through the bureaucracy that prevented rulers from understanding their subjects' true needs. Leveraging her considerable network of cultural and government contacts, she explored whether the Grimms might be able to take up residence in Weimar, but she principally aimed to see them established in Berlin.[16]

She had no patience for those who did not share this passion. Such disdain soon extended to her brother-in-law Savigny as well as to Lachmann (who like Savigny was now a professor at the university in Berlin). As a member of the Prussian State Council, Savigny held enormous influence; however, Bettina failed to realize that his position meant he had to exercise caution with regard to the Grimms' situation. She believed that Savigny—both as Jacob's foremost mentor during his student years and now as a person of power in Berlin—should have championed their cause. In his defense, Savigny had offered to explore whether funding from the Prussian Royal Academy of Sciences could support the dictionary project, but the Grimms had rejected this offer, at least for the time being. The success of the project was not at all certain, they said, and they knew it would be an embarrassment for the Academy if the dictionary failed. They also feared that accepting the support of a royal academy might make them appear penitential for their actions in Göttingen, whereas they had unwaveringly stood by their protest and stressed that they had acted out of moral conscience, not political aims. In addition, they were wary of finding themselves beholden to the Academy after their experience in Göttingen. Finally, for the near future they had sufficient resources to support the dictionary and to sustain their household, so they did not even necessarily need Academy funding.

Because he was a member of the Academy, Jacob would theoretically have been allowed to go to Berlin and give lectures at the university there, but he would have had to do so as an independent scholar, without state support. Lachmann warned Jacob that such permission might not actually be granted, however. Since the Academy was under royal patronage, government officials might consider royal approval necessary, and the king would not want to grant this, lest he appear to condemn Ernst August. Despite wondering whether Lachmann truly wanted to see them established in Berlin, the Grimms accepted such advice as well-meaning. According to Bettina, however, Savigny and Lachmann had complained that Jacob had grown too embittered and sensitive to accept help. Bettina's reports of these conversations to the Grimms exacerbated their feeling that Savigny had been too neutral in his stance on the Grimms' actions and that Berlin intellectuals had overall been too silent. They also bristled at suggestions that the Göttingen Seven should have been more tactful in their criticism of Ernst August. Nevertheless, they also felt that Bettina was judging Savigny and Lachmann too harshly.[17]

As an outsider, Bettina was uniquely able to see the hypocrisy, bureaucracy, cowardice, and small-mindedness of many government officials and institutions. She excoriated the Academy as an "old rats' palace" and dismissed its leadership as full of "little pasteboard guys." With bitterness and self-deprecation, she also conceded that Savigny simply would not listen to a "dumb woman's voice" like hers. As Savigny well understood, however, hasty actions and ill-considered pronouncements might unintentionally hurt the Grimms' prospects in Berlin. As for his neutrality on the Grimms' actions, while he had found Ernst August's handling of the situation reprehensible and had no doubt the Grimms' motivations were irreproachable, he averred that he could not judge whether the Göttingen Seven had taken the best course of action. Savigny also pointed to inaccuracies and embellishments in Bettina's long and declamatory letters about the Grimms' situation. He attributed these to what he deemed her lively imagination and likely intention to disseminate her correspondence to a broader audience, as she had done in publishing her highly fictionalized version of her exchanges with Goethe.[18]

Indeed, Bettina's letters to Savigny, sometimes dozens of pages long, overflowed with flowery descriptions of the Grimm family's idyllic life, the nobility of their actions against injustice, and their unwavering commitment to their values. After visiting the Grimms in Kassel with the young artist Julius Döring, she described how Jacob, his gray curly hair framing his pleasant face, patiently read and explicated passages from Anglo-Saxon poetry to Döring.

Whereas earlier in his life some had found Jacob rigid in tone and bearing, she was overcome by his melodic voice and warmth. It escaped her how anyone could not see and support his greatness. She charged that Savigny's renown within and beyond the German lands meant nothing if he failed to support his erstwhile student; while Jacob's intellect now towered over everyone around him, his heart still held youthful affection for Savigny as his mentor.

Bettina also appealed directly to Prussian crown prince Friedrich Wilhelm. In April 1840, she wrote to request help for two unnamed friends, praising the crown prince as someone who surely would recognize the goodness of their actions if he knew their identities and situation. Playfully punning on "Grimm," the crown prince responded that he had figured out the identities of Bettina's anonymous friends: "the fruit of my grim researching was—two researching Grimms!" He noted, too, that he had earlier attempted in vain to further their cause and was willing to try again to secure positions for them in Berlin. Indeed, Friedrich Wilhelm had written to Ernst August shortly after the Göttingen Seven protest to register his sentiment that the Hanoverian king had treated the professors too harshly, and he had already then hoped to see the Grimms established in Berlin.[19]

The situation changed with the death of Friedrich Wilhelm III in June 1840. Because Bettina knew that, as a crown prince, the new king had been sympathetic to the Grimms, she moved swiftly to mobilize governmental support for them. She wrote to Alexander von Humboldt, who exercised his influence by speaking with cultural minister Friedrich Eichhorn, whom Jacob knew from his work in Paris decades earlier.

The Grimms still feared that the embittered Ernst August would attempt to thwart any opportunity for them in Berlin, but their fears proved unfounded. In November 1840, Eichhorn offered Jacob and Wilhelm a combined salary of 2,000 talers per year, which they were free to split between them however they chose, as well as 500 talers for moving costs. Humboldt explained to a friend that one combined salary had been offered to the brothers "since they live like man and wife." In Berlin they would pursue their scholarship and work on the dictionary. There was no professorship vacant for Jacob, but he would be able to exercise his right to give lectures at the university as a member of the Royal Academy of Sciences. Since Wilhelm was a corresponding member of the Academy's historical-philosophical division, it would not be difficult to secure similar privileges for him.[20]

The Grimms were inclined to accept Eichhorn's offer, despite knowing that it would be difficult to live in Berlin on the proposed salary. They doubted they could secure a better offer anywhere else, particularly since they still refused to be separated. Bettina, however, beseeched them not to accept the positions too hastily. In an impassioned letter to Humboldt, she decried the salary as woefully insufficient. She cited Wilhelm's precarious health and his responsibility to his wife and children, highlighting their dependence on free rent in Ludwig's wife's building and the kindly support of Kassel residents who provided essential goods and services to them without charge. By contrast, their cost of living would soar dramatically in Berlin. Bettina carefully listed the expenses the Grimm family could expect to incur there, including rent, domestic help, heating materials, clothing, and even the glass of wine that Wilhelm required each midday to fortify his health. Humboldt in turn spoke with Eichhorn, who, after communications with Jacob, upped the offer to 3,000 talers. From the start, Jacob and Wilhelm had agreed that they would divide in half any salary offered to them. Jacob was delighted that he and Wilhelm would in Berlin finally be on an equal footing, since throughout their lives Wilhelm had always had the lesser position. Jacob knew, of course, that he himself was the more influential scholar, but it was important to him that Wilhelm's considerable contributions also be recognized.

Bettina was triumphant that, through her advocacy, the Grimms would be coming to Berlin and with a more livable wage than was initially offered. Acquaintances described her victory as twofold: not only had she done right by the Grimms, whose friendship she so valued and whose actions she had steadfastly defended on moral grounds, but she had also prevailed over what she viewed as the apathy, ineffectiveness, and even obstruction of her brother-in-law Savigny and figures such as Lachmann. She described Jacob to her brother Clemens Brentano as having transcended defamation and political rancor with the glow of a holy person; she saw in his facial features both the strength of a fighter and the transfiguration caused by suffering. At the time, the Grimms had not seen Brentano for many years, and only Ludwig remained in regular touch with him. He died in 1842 at the age of sixty-four.[21]

Bettina's efforts on the Grimms' behalf were not over. Jacob traveled to Berlin in December 1840 to search for housing, staying with his friend Karl Hartwig Gregor von Meusebach, a literary scholar, lawyer, and president of the Rhineland court of cassation. Bettina and Meusebach's wife insisted on accompanying Jacob in bitterly cold weather as he looked at over twenty apartments. Bettina also visited Jacob at the Meusebach home several times, routinely talking until midnight about topics as diverse as the Prussian king, homeopathy, and university students. Jacob found these evening social visits tiresome and worried about moving to such a big city, as he continued to prefer the far smaller Kassel and its proximity to rural environs. Fortunately, he secured an apartment in a building near the Tiergarten, the great public park in Berlin that had originally been hunting grounds for the Prussian royalty. He hoped this location would provide some respite from the hustle and bustle of the city. Ever the good uncle, he had also taken care to think of his nephews' education: their walk to school would take between fifteen and twenty minutes, which was typical for Berlin. In addition to finding an apartment, Jacob had an audience with the Prussian king before he returned to Kassel.

With housing and other details sorted out, Jacob and Wilhelm could at last envision starting a new life in Berlin. Their Göttingen Seven colleagues were also busy reestablishing themselves in the aftermath of their dismissals. Albrecht began to teach at the University of Leipzig and became a professor there in 1840. Weber had initially left Göttingen to pursue scientific studies in England and elsewhere; he later served as professor in Leipzig between 1843 and 1849, after which he returned to Göttingen. Gervinus first spent a year in Italy and later became a professor in Heidelberg, and Ewald traveled to England to visit archives in Oxford and London before returning to Germany to become a professor at the University of Tübingen. Dahlmann went to Leipzig and then to Jena, before receiving a professorship in 1842 at the University of Bonn. In the end, all were able to salvage their careers, but the scars of their experience remained.

The Grimms left Kassel early on the morning of March 14, 1841, and arrived in Berlin five days later. They were fortunate to have good traveling conditions for most of the trip, though near Bitterfeld flooding forced them onto a bumpy side road and across a meadow and in Wittenberg the Elbe, swollen with ice floes, looked like a lake. Just days before their departure, the electress of Hessen had died of influenza. She had stood by them after their dismissals and continued to regard them with fondness and familiarity; when caught in a sudden rain shower in May 1839, for instance, she and her daughter took refuge in the Grimms' nearby home and rested on Wilhelm's sofa until their carriage arrived. Wilhelm had visited the electress several times in the weeks and months before their departure for Berlin, and her passing marked a further closure on their years of service to the Hessian state. Berlin was where they would spend the rest of their lives.[22]

CHAPTER 13

Berlin Beginnings, 1841–1852

"It is surprising that the foundation of a town should ever have been laid on so uninteresting a spot," the *Hand-Book for Travellers on the Continent* aptly observed of Berlin in 1840, "but it is far more wonderful that it should have grown up, notwithstanding, into the flourishing capital of a great empire." Built on a flat plain of sand traversed by the sluggish river Spree, Berlin made up for its boring landscape with splendid museums, art galleries, theaters, an opera, a music academy, and a university. Contemporary travelers found Berlin less cosmopolitan than other European capitals, but they marveled at its cultural offerings, education system, and care for the poor. And whereas many European cities were a tangle of medieval alleys, Berlin's streets were spacious enough for pedestrians to stroll alongside the ubiquitous hackney coaches that transported passengers across town. Instead of Gothic structures that harked back to a distant past, eighteenth-century edifices dominated the Berlin cityscape, evoking a time that seemed only yesterday. Many of these buildings were clustered near Unter den Linden, named after its double avenue of linden trees. This boulevard culminated in the magnificent Branden-burg Gate, then as now an iconic landmark.[1]

By the time the Grimms arrived in 1841, the city had already expanded well beyond its historical core. Industrialization had brought factories to the outskirts of Berlin beginning in the late 1830s, and a rail line connected Berlin and Potsdam in 1838. The city's population in the early 1840s was over 330,000, up from around 265,000 in 1835. This rapid growth worsened infrastructure problems, not least the persistent water and waste issues caused by the flat terrain and insufficient drainage systems. The stench emanating from the streets and sewers was so bad, one writer quipped, that if the city's many statues of military heroes, winged angels, and Prussian two-headed eagles could smell, they would be depicted holding their noses instead of grasping their swords.[2]

The Grimms' apartment building had been constructed just a year earlier, a testament to Berlin's rapid growth. It was well out of the way of the stench and traffic, and some distance, too, from the city center streets that Jacob found disorienting because they were so long and straight he could not see their end. The apartment's location across from the immense Tiergarten park served as a suitable substitute for the rural stillness and natural beauty the Grimms so craved. Berlin's sandy soil made growing some plants difficult, but they found the Tiergarten lush nonetheless and well maintained. The park offered the Grimms not only idyllic sights of spring flowers and goldfish ponds, but also a playground for the children. Although their apartment was not as roomy as they might have liked, it was comfortable and well appointed, offering views of the Tiergarten, oak trees, and a neighbor's garden and newly built house. The Grimms also continued their lifelong habit of bringing nature indoors; they decorated their desks with rocks from their walks and vases of flowers and even kept a pet dove.

Amid these pleasant environs, Jacob and Wilhelm pursued their scholarly projects free of the time constraints their library duties in Göttingen had placed on them and without financial worry. Their many publications had not been particularly lucrative, but they could live in modest comfort on the salary afforded to them. Jacob was now fifty-six years old and Wilhelm fifty-five. Despite their continued work on the dictionary, Jacob managed to publish the third part of his collection of German legal customs and a second edition of *German Mythology*, while Wilhelm issued the fifth edition of *Children's and Household Tales* and further scholarship related to his studies of Middle High German literature. Both also periodically lectured at the University of Berlin: Jacob principally taught German grammar, legal customs, and mythology and Wilhelm medieval German literature. Their inaugural lectures in spring 1841 each attracted several hundred spectators.

While Wilhelm was known as an excellent lecturer and teacher, Jacob struggled at the lectern, as he had in Göttingen. Typically a mere two or three dozen students enrolled in his courses. Soon his familiar resistance to any professional duty that drew him away from his scholarship began to surface.

He grumbled that just traveling to and from the lecture hall took double the time as the lecture itself, and he chafed at his obligations at the Prussian Royal Academy of Sciences, where he had been elected to a board overseeing an edition of the works of Prussian king Friedrich II. "I would gladly forgo all external honors if I could just be left in peace to work as my heart desires," he told Dahlmann in 1841 with regard to the many honors and obligations bestowed on him, which now included being named a Knight of the French Legion of Honor. "I would happily don a homespun smock of the coarsest material and strive for nothing other than that." Instead, Jacob found himself beribboned the following year with the Prussian medal *Pour le Mérite* for his scholarly achievements. Within a few weeks of their arrival the king welcomed them, and his family thereafter issued occasional dining invitations.[3]

As ever the more outgoing of the two, Wilhelm partook more than Jacob in the many cultural attractions on offer. His diary is replete with entries listing his attendance at performances of *A Midsummer Night's Dream*, *Oedipus Rex*, *Hippolytus*, and *Antigone* in Berlin and Potsdam, for example, as well as his viewing of panoramic paintings of Moscow and St. Petersburg. He walked the botanic gardens and toured the palace's Cabinet of Art, where one could see historical collections featuring objects such as staves with runic carvings (which would undoubtedly have captured Wilhelm's attention), Luther's beer jug, a wax figure of Friedrich II on his deathbed, and Napoleon's hat. Wilhelm's social engagements were also so frequent that one finds him noting in his diary the "rare day without any visit."[4]

Unsurprisingly, Jacob found not only his professional obligations at the Academy but also many of his social interactions obtrusive. Just at the time each evening when he wished to engage in quiet contemplation or devote himself to his correspondence, Bettina von Arnim would arrive and annoy him with what he branded her "exuberant, never-ending, but nevertheless winsome conversation." Her inexhaustible energy made her oblivious to others' tiredness, and she persisted in trying to introduce the Grimms to people with whom they did not care to socialize. She became such a fixture in the Grimms' household that young Herman Grimm considered her a second mother, much like how Jacob had always been a second father to him.[5]

A lifelong bachelor like Jacob, Karl Lachmann, too, was a frequent visitor to the Grimm home. The Grimms also often saw Karl Hartwig Gregor von Meusebach, became friends with the philosopher Friedrich Schelling and the historian Leopold Ranke, interacted with the composer Felix Mendelssohn, and rekindled their friendship with Anna von Arnswaldt (née von

Haxthausen), who as a child had told tales to the Grimms with her older Haxthausen siblings. Having moved to Berlin at the end of 1840 to serve in the high court, Ludwig Hassenpflug and his family also regularly saw the Grimms, despite the Grimms' long-standing political and personal differences with him. During a stay in 1843 with his ten-year-old daughter, Ludwig Grimm described the Grimms' apartment as like a dovecote that birds flitted to and from all evening. Bettina came most days while Ludwig was there, and other visitors included Schelling, the Bremen mayor Johann Smidt (whom the Grimms had known for many years), and various professors and government officials.[6]

Savigny, too, occasionally came to see the Grimms. His friendliness had increasingly yielded to formality, however, especially after he became a government minister in 1842. He was obliged to hold almost nightly social events at his ministerial home for princes, counts, and visiting Britons, Frenchmen, and Americans. Jacob wondered how a man of Savigny's intellect could bear having to entertain stuffy dignitaries in trivial conversation night after night instead of engaging with serious scholars. At a dinner Savigny hosted in honor of the Prussian king's birthday, the simply attired Wilhelm felt like a crow amid peacocks upon seeing Savigny and others in their ornate uniforms. He marveled at the gas lighting in Savigny's home and was unaccustomed to having his coat removed by a servant in livery and being served exquisite dishes by white-gloved staff.[7]

Far more down-to-earth was the celebration of Wilhelm's fifty-seventh birthday in February 1843. As a sign of the esteem in which Wilhelm was held as a teacher, a group of university students formed a torchlight procession. The Grimms went out onto their apartment balcony to greet the students, who stood in a semicircle singing songs to celebrate Wilhelm. But a parade for Wilhelm's birthday the following year proved controversial because of the attendance of poet August Heinrich Hoffmann von Fallersleben. Born August Heinrich Hoffmann, he had added "von Fallersleben" to his surname to honor his hometown. Known today principally for writing "The Song of Germany," the third stanza of which is the official German national anthem, Hoffmann had been removed from his professorial position in Breslau in 1842 because of what Prussian authorities regarded as inflammatory rhetoric against the state in his *Unpolitical Songs*. The Grimms had known him since 1818, when he came to consult materials at the Kassel library, and they had kept in touch with letters and occasional meetings.

In Hoffmann's recounting of the birthday event that came to be known as the "Hoffmann Affair," he had ventured out around noon amid snow flurries. Upon learning from a friend that it was Wilhelm's birthday and the university students were planning a celebratory procession, he decided he would join in the festivities. The Grimm family warmly received him when he arrived at their home unannounced around eight o'clock in the evening. Soon after his arrival, the students reached the house. Wilhelm and others stood on the balcony and thanked the students for their good wishes and cheers, while Hoffmann stood near an open window in Jacob's unlit room. When Hoffmann drew closer to the window to better hear Wilhelm's words, the students spotted him and began to cheer him, too. Hoffmann claimed that he would normally have been delighted to hear his name cheered in connection with the Grimms, but he knew how precarious this was in Berlin. It was from this city that the Prussians had dismissed him from his professorship in Breslau and conversely provided refuge to the Grimms after their dismissals in Göttingen. Nevertheless, after Wilhelm went down to speak with the students and then came back upstairs, Hoffmann went down, too, believing that it was only polite to do so. The students began singing many of his songs and enjoyed a glass of punch with him. After receiving an invitation from Dortchen to come to the Grimms' home the next day for the midday meal, Hoffmann left with the students.[8]

The following afternoon, Lachmann arrived at the Grimms' apartment and was visibly surprised to see Hoffmann there. Lachmann went into another room first with Wilhelm and then with Jacob to speak with each brother in private. Hoffmann did not realize that Lachmann was there to warn the Grimms of fallout from the previous evening. Bettina arrived a bit later; despite her and Hoffmann's best efforts, the conversation was noticeably subdued and uncomfortable during the meal. After accompanying Bettina back to her apartment, Hoffmann went out for several hours with a friend. Early in the morning, a police official informed him that he had been ordered to leave Berlin by the end of the day. The students' cheers for him and his expressions of thanks had been deemed too dangerous in light of Hoffmann's writings and removal from his position.

Hoffmann insisted that he had not intended for the students to notice him, but the Grimms came to believe that he must have understood the predicament his presence at Wilhelm's birthday and involvement with the student parade would place them in. In light of the gratitude they owed the king for having supported them after their dismissals in Göttingen, any appearance that they had hosted a demonstration in support of a professor fired by the king's government was perilous. Beyond this, the king was no mere abstraction to them, but someone with whom they occasionally interacted at events and royal dinners. In their view, Hoffmann had purposely staged an appearance with them to use their reputations to regain some favor with the Prussian government.

After initially wavering on whether to comment on the scandal, Jacob and Wilhelm decided they should speak up out of respect for the king. As they wrote on March 6 in a Prussian newspaper, they had known Hoffmann for decades and valued his contributions to German literary studies. Though they had no intention of shunning him, they were not bound to defend his political actions or opinions, and they reiterated their hatred of unauthorized attempts to draw their names into political debates and partisanship. On the night in question, they pointedly observed, Hoffmann had been an uninvited guest whose presence ended up misappropriating the students' celebration of Wilhelm's birthday. A private celebration had regrettably become political.[9]

Many of the more liberal German newspapers found the Grimms' response tactless and sided squarely with Hoffmann. They criticized the Grimms for not supporting their friend, especially given their own experience as members of the Göttingen Seven, and they exhorted Jacob to reread the pamphlet he had written upon his dismissal from Göttingen and take a long look in the mirror. Although such papers understandably found the Grimms' actions hypocritical, the reality is more complicated than this. If one merely assumes they should have defended someone who, like themselves, had been dismissed from a professorial position on account of a writing, the Grimms were certainly guilty of the hypocrisy the papers accused them of. However, they had not invited Hoffmann to the event, did not agree with the political stances and provocations for which he had been removed, and felt in this instance more loyalty to the king whose government supported their scholarship than to the friend who had exploited their friendship for his own benefit.

Some of their friends privately backed them, but the Grimms were dismayed by the lack of open support. Their friendship with Bettina suffered greatly, as she championed Hoffmann's cause. She declared to her sister Gunda (Savigny's wife) that she could no longer in good conscience visit Jacob and Wilhelm. Instead, on one occasion she sought to speak with Dortchen by standing in front of the Grimms' house and calling out for her to come to the balcony; Dortchen instructed the maid to say she was not at home. When it later happened that the Grimms and Bettina attended one of Savigny's evening social events, Bettina spontaneously embraced Jacob and they spoke for a long time, but Wilhelm abruptly left to avoid speaking to her. The rift pained Herman, who remained close to Bettina and her family and, several months after Bettina's death in 1859, married Bettina's daughter Gisela. Jacob and Hoffmann later made amends, but Wilhelm remained estranged from him for the rest of his life.[10]

Apart from their strained relationship with Bettina and the charges of hypocrisy leveled against them by the press, the Hoffmann Affair did not significantly damage the Grimms' reputation. Students found the Grimms occasionally out of touch with the times but retained their affection for the brothers. The Grimms' scholarly reputations also continued to garner national and international acclaim. In 1844, Jacob was awarded the Swedish Order of the Polar Star and the Prussian Order of the Red Eagle (Fourth Class), and two years later he received the Order of the Red Eagle (Third Class). The scholarly societies to which they belonged reached across Europe and to America. Their correspondence with international scholars and writers had earlier included Walter Scott, *Children's and Household Tales* translator Edgar Taylor, the Irish writer and folklorist Thomas Crofton Croker, and the Serbian philologist Vuk Stefanović Karadžić. But it had now expanded to include the Norwegians Peter Christen Asbjørnsen and Jørgen Moe, who were inspired by the Grimms to publish a collection of Norwegian folk tales, as well as the Russian ethnographer Aleksandr Afanasyev, to name only a few of their international correspondents. The Grimms' reputation also captured the attention of rulers. In May 1845, Jacob had an audience with the crown prince of Bavaria, the future King Maximilian II. The interior walls of Maximilian's Hohenschwangau Castle, built in the 1830s, depicted scenes from history and legends, for which the Austrian historian Joseph Freiherr von Hormayr had drawn upon the Grimms' *German Legends* and consulted directly with Jacob.[11]

Among the many international scholars and writers who visited the Grimms was Hans Christian Andersen, the Danish author of "The Emperor's New Clothes," "The Little Mermaid," "The Ugly Duckling," and other tales. He had first tried to make the Grimms' personal acquaintance in 1844 but was unsuccessful when he arrived at their home without the customary letter of introduction. He had been assured that if anyone in Berlin would know of his work, it would be Jacob and Wilhelm. When the maid asked him which of the brothers he was there to see, he replied that he would like to speak with the more prolific of the two, whereupon she took him to Jacob. But Jacob recognized neither him nor his works, and Andersen left feeling quite embarrassed. To Andersen's surprise, just weeks later Jacob showed up in traveling clothes at Andersen's home in Copenhagen, assuring Andersen that now he grasped who he was. Andersen himself was packing for a trip, so their meeting was brief but friendly. In winter 1845–46 Andersen visited the Grimms again in Berlin, and Wilhelm also heard him read his fairy tales aloud at Savigny's home and saw him at a salon.[12]

Jacob had journeyed to Copenhagen as part of a larger trip to Denmark and Sweden. He marveled at the grass planted on the rooftops and the runestones and gravemounds that he described as jutting out of the earth. He found Scandinavian customs similar to those in Germany but noted that the Scandinavian languages had been more insulated from foreign influence than had German. Overall, he painted Scandinavia as foundational to the study of Germanic literatures. The previous autumn, Jacob had visited Milan, Rome, and Naples. He delighted in the Italian language and its dialects and found Italians refreshingly conversant and genial compared to Germans. He was grateful to have had the opportunity within the span of just a year to have viewed Gothic manuscripts in collections as far north as Uppsala and as far south as Naples. Over the next decade, his travels took him to Switzerland, the south of France, Venice, Vienna, and Prague.[13]

Unlike Jacob, Wilhelm never traveled internationally, though he enjoyed many trips within Germany. In 1841, just months after moving to Berlin, he and Dortchen returned to Hessen, where in Steinau he visited his grandfather's gravestone and also saw the same bakery from which the toddler Lotte had often fetched a fresh bread roll for breakfast. In Hanau, he stood outside the house in which he was born. He and Dortchen then moved on to the Rhineland, where they visited Cologne.

Wilhelm did not venture far in part because of his delicate health. His heart ailment flared up yet again in early 1842. He remained ill throughout most of the summer and lost so much weight that he looked emaciated. But Jacob, too, coped with declining health. An illness in 1841 had left him with such exhaustion "that I long for resolution in God, [. . .] who will take me as He created me, and who knows why He wishes that our eyes fade, our hands rest, and our hearts stop." That same autumn, he had written of his ailment to Hoffmann but avoided giving details because, as he put it, "I find graphic lament repugnant."[14]

On the eve of his sixty-first birthday in 1846, Jacob described himself to Paul Wigand, his friend from student days in Kassel and Marburg, as white-haired but intellectually undiminished. He hoped he would keep his mental acuity, because he still had so many plans for scholarly projects. Despite having thought as a young man that he would die an early death like his father, he now found he had outlived many of his and Wilhelm's schoolfriends from long ago. Their brother Ferdinand had passed away the previous year in Wolfenbüttel, after a restless and unhappy life. Upon hearing of Ferdinand's illness from a doctor, Jacob had hurriedly traveled to Wolfenbüttel and managed to see his brother just hours before he died. Carl and Ludwig continued to live in Kassel, and there Ludwig had remarried after the death of his wife, Marie, in 1842. In Berlin, meanwhile, Wilhelm's boys were already taller than Jacob, and Herman was almost old enough to begin university studies.

Needing more space now that the children were growing up, in 1846 the Grimms moved to an apartment near the Brandenburg Gate from which they had a view of another side of the Tiergarten. But it was a drafty corner unit; Dortchen complained that Jacob's room was so impossible to heat that he had taken to wrapping one of her old kerchiefs around his knees, and his niece Auguste had knitted him an extra wool blanket to place on his lap. Dortchen was thus hardly saddened when their lease was canceled just a year later, after Wilhelm forgot to pay the rent on time. They moved in April 1847 to a flat in a newly constructed neighborhood near the train station. This apartment—more comfortable than their previous one, though not as spacious—would be their home for the rest of their lives.

Wilhelm had forgotten to send in the rent because he and Jacob were attending a landmark conference of academics in Frankfurt. Two hundred scholars of German history, philology, and law gathered in September 1846 in the medieval Römer building, then as now an iconic landmark. They convened in the building's Emperor Hall, where, as some conference speakers noted, the portraits of German emperors lining the walls seemed to gaze approvingly upon the scholars and yearn to step out of their picture frames and mingle with them. The German poet and literary historian Ludwig Uhland successfully nominated Jacob to chair the conference. In his remarks as chair, Jacob described a people (*Volk*) as defined not by geographical boundaries such as mountain chains and rivers, but by a common language. Wilhelm, too, accentuated the cultural role of language when he spoke at the conference of the brothers' dictionary project. The following year, the German scholars gathered in the northern town of Lübeck, where Jacob again was voted conference chair. When participants toasted him for his extraordinary contributions to the study of German grammar, mythology, and law, he responded that soon he would be interred in the earth with grass growing above him; he hoped that after his death people would say he had never loved anything more than he loved the German fatherland.[15]

For the Grimms, such turgid expressions of patriotism were not as chauvinistic as they might sound today. Jacob articulated his view of a shared German heritage which (though not superior to other cultures) had been undervalued until the early nineteenth century. To him, this heritage pointed the way to a unified German political state. It is in this spirit that he understood and supported the burgeoning nationalism and liberalism of the 1840s, as Germans sought both a united Germany and constitutional rule. To Jacob's dismay, however, Friedrich Wilhelm IV had declared that he would not let a constitution come between him and his people, although he allowed a united Prussian Diet in 1847. The king had a childish fear of constitutions and representative government, Jacob wrote Dahlmann, and thus did not appreciate the spirit of the times and the evolving role of a king.[16]

The following year, the February Revolution in Paris sparked the March Revolution in Prussia and elsewhere. In Austria, Metternich resigned and fled to Britain, and in Bavaria King Ludwig I abdicated the throne to his son Maximilian II. Anticipating tumult, the Prussian authorities erected barricades in Berlin. On the day that uprisings erupted, students escorted Wilhelm from the university back to the Grimms' apartment half an hour away. From there, he fearfully waited out fourteen hours of fighting between soldiers and the crowds, with cannon fire and gunshots sounding into the night and fires breaking out. Wilhelm later saw troops arriving at the nearby train station and marching to the Brandenburg Gate. During the unrest, the Grimms occasionally provided meals to soldiers quartered in their neighborhood, who politely returned the loaned dishware and silver spoons.[17]

In the aftermath of the March 1848 revolution, Jacob was called to represent a voting district in the Ruhr region of western Germany at the Frankfurt National Assembly, the first freely elected parliament for the German-speaking lands. He was one of several professors who served as representatives, and among them were three other Göttingen Seven members (Dahlmann, Albrecht, and Gervinus). Protestants, Catholics, Jews, and atheists took part, but over half of the several hundred representatives were government employees; there was just one peasant, a handful of craftsmen, and no women (although many women attended as observers). The setting for the proceedings was originally planned to be the Römer building, where the Germanists had convened for their conference a few years earlier. That venue proved too small, however, so the Assembly instead took place at St. Paul's Church. It kicked off on May 18, 1848, but Jacob did not arrive until several days later.

Broadly speaking, the representatives aimed to create a unified German state out of territories that were deemed already culturally and politically interwoven, as well as to bolster civil rights with a constitution. Around the time of the Assembly, however, violence had broken out in the east, where the Prussians were suppressing Polish units in the Prussian-held Grand Duchy of Posen; in the north, where the contentious status of the Duchy of Schleswig had led to war between Germans and Danes; and in the south, where northern Italians were fighting for independence from the Austrian Empire. Against this background of competing national and ethnic interests, the Assembly faced an uphill battle from the start.[18]

This jarring reality was incongruent with the Assembly's iconography, which featured a newly created painting of the female allegorical figure of Germania that was affixed to the church organ for the duration of the proceedings. An imposing five meters tall, the painting depicts Germania wielding a sword and clutching the iconic black, red, and gold flag—Germany's symbol then and now. Her robe features a breastplate bearing the double-headed eagle of the Holy Roman Empire and German Confederation, and unfettered shackles lie at her feet. She projects strength, resoluteness, freedom, and the promise of a new and glorious beginning.

While Germania stood proudly above the representatives in her central position on the organ, Jacob—whom Gervinus later described in his autobiography as "the most German of Germans"—sat front and center below. Jacob was affiliated with the center-right Casino faction which, like other factions at the Assembly, took its name after the inn at which it met. Casino, the largest faction, advocated for a unified Germany supported by a constitutional monarchy that still acknowledged the distinct identities of individual member states. Jacob nevertheless showed his eschewal of rigid partisanship by sitting in the middle aisle between the rows of seats, directly before the podium.[19]

Like the allegorical Germania affixed to the organ, Jacob proved to be a largely symbolic presence at the Assembly. Whereas the towering painting projected youthful vigor, however, the sixty-three-year-old Jacob was to many

A session of the German National Assembly at Frankfurt am Main, 1848. Notice the painting of Germania that towers over the representatives. When present, Jacob Grimm sat in the middle aisle. From a lithograph by E. G. May after a drawing by F. Bamberger. From Hans Blum, ed., *Die deutsche Revolution, 1848–49: Eine Jubiläumsausgabe für das deutsche Volk* (Leipzig: Eugen Diederichs, 1897), n.p. Collection of the author.

a respected but out-of-touch elder. He spoke his mind on a few issues but did not otherwise actively participate. Comparing the aristocracy to a fading flower, he advocated unsuccessfully for the removal of all legal differences between the aristocracy, the middle classes, and the peasants. His motion on the first article of a draft German constitution also failed. Decades earlier as Hessian legation secretary at the Congress of Vienna, Jacob had viewed enshrining Germans' freedom as the essential starting point for any constitution. It is thus not surprising that in Frankfurt he proposed that the first article open with "All Germans are free, and German soil tolerates no servitude. German soil makes unfree foreigners who linger on it free." Representatives voted 205 to 192 against the motion, which had been slightly reworded to include mention of the German people (*Volk*). Between Jacob's original submission of the motion on July 4 and the ensuing vote on July 20, he had received a letter from Friedrich Wilhelm Carové, who decades earlier had helped the Grimms compile German legends. Carové suggested that Jacob add language

outlawing slavery and participation in the slave trade and specifying that because German soil included German ships, setting foot on a German ship
would make an enslaved person free. Jacob handwrote a version of the article
that incorporated Carové's suggestions, but he did not submit this for a vote.
Instead of adding direct mention of slavery and slaves, Jacob stuck with the
word *Knechtschaft* (servitude), likely preferring the Germanic word because it
encompasses concepts such as slavery, serfdom, and bondage. Presumably, he
also regarded language pertaining to ships and the slave trade as too detailed
for the opening article of a constitution and better left to law to specify. Thus,
too, his motion's reference to unfree foreigners could refer broadly to enslaved
people as well as the non-German peoples in territories claimed as German.[20]

Most fervently, Jacob spoke out on the "Schleswig-Holstein Question,"
which revolved around whether the duchies of Schleswig and Holstein should
be part of Denmark or a united Germany. The roots of the conflict reached
back centuries. In medieval times, Schleswig had been a Danish fief and
Holstein a subfief within the Holy Roman Empire. In the fifteenth century,
Schleswig and Holstein chose Count Christian of Oldenburg as their ruler.
Since Christian was also King of Denmark, Denmark came to be in personal
union with Schleswig and Holstein, although the duchies kept their semiau-
tonomous status and were not incorporated into the Kingdom of Denmark.
Holstein was more overtly German: lying to the south of Schleswig, it was
the northernmost territory of the Holy Roman Empire and later a member
of the German Confederation. German claims to Schleswig were not so clear
and rested in part on a sentence in a fifteenth-century charter that Dahlmann
and others interpreted as meaning that the two duchies were always to be
together, undivided. The southern areas of Schleswig had been Germanized
since the fourteenth century, and central Schleswig had become more German in the early decades of the nineteenth century; despite Danish being the
main language in northern Schleswig, German was used in courts, administration, schools, and some churches.

Difficult constitutional issues arose in the post-Napoleonic period, since
Holstein was part of the German Confederation but Schleswig was not.
While ethnic Germans in Schleswig upheld Schleswig's ties with Holstein,
Danish nationalists insisted that Schleswig be incorporated into Denmark.
Thorny succession issues threatened to further fuel the conflict because the
Danish king had no heirs. The various entanglements became so complex
that in Britain, Lord Palmerston remarked that only three people had ever
fully understood the Schleswig-Holstein Question: Prince Albert, consort

of Queen Victoria; a German professor who as a result of the issue's complexities had gone mad; and Palmerston himself, who averred that he had since forgotten all about it. For Jacob and Dahlmann, however, any questions about Schleswig-Holstein boiled down to a simple matter of cultural heritage. Steadfastly against Danish demands for Schleswig's annexation, they claimed that it was not merely Danish territory inhabited by Germans, but rather originally settled by Germanic tribes centuries prior to Danish migration. To them, the Schleswig-Holstein Question revealed a misalignment of cultural nationhood with national political borders that German intellectuals of the nineteenth century wished to rectify. The grounds on which they justified such fixes were nevertheless often shaky and inconsistent.[21]

Looming large over the Assembly's proceedings was another question, this one regarding Austria. Representatives advocating for a "Greater Germany" wanted a Germany united with Austria, whereas those in the "Little Germany" camp wished to see Prussia elevated and Austria diminished. Some wished to see all of the Austrian Empire incorporated into a united German state, while others proposed that only the ethnically German areas be incorporated—a division unacceptable to the Austrian government. Its work impeded by the uprisings and related events in various territories, the Assembly spent months wrangling and eventually offered Friedrich Wilhelm IV of Prussia a "Little German" imperial crown in 1849. But he refused it, on the grounds that only the other German princes had the authority to offer it to Prussia, not the "man-donkey-dog-pig-and-cat delegation from Frankfurt."[22]

Jacob had by this time long since left the Assembly, having stayed in Frankfurt for only four months. His experience there only pushed him further away from public speaking and the political arena. His optimism that the year of revolution might produce a unified Germany with a constitutional government soon yielded to disillusionment—and this only compounded the bitterness he felt from his experience in Göttingen over a decade earlier. He continued to express his political views in letters to his friends and in prefaces to his works, and he took part in political events including a conference of the "Little German" party in Gotha and various election meetings. For the most part, however, he distanced himself from political matters and delved back into his scholarship.

Wilhelm, too, attended several election meetings. At one in March 1849, he found the noise and tobacco smoke not at all to his liking, but he felt duty-bound to attend and ended up feeling inspired by one of the speeches. For the first chamber, voters included only those who paid a certain level of taxes or had an income or land holdings of a particular minimum worth, whereas for the second chamber anyone could vote as long as they were not receiving poor relief. Wilhelm regarded the lack of voting restrictions for the second chamber as imprudent. Though his views were less moderate than Jacob's, Wilhelm was by no means as staunch a conservative as his brother-in-law Ludwig Hassenpflug, with whom the Grimms continued to have pronounced political disagreements; by 1849, their relationship with him was irreparably strained. After leaving Berlin in 1846, Hassenpflug had taken a position in Greifswald and then returned to Kassel in 1850 to serve as minister again until 1855. His reputation only continued to worsen during these years.[23]

The same year Jacob attended the Frankfurt National Assembly, he had completed his two-volume *History of the German Language*, which he later characterized as his best work. In the preface, he emphasized that he found linguistic research unsatisfying unless intertwined with other philological dimensions. That is, he wanted to study not just words themselves, but also what they signified for a people's culture and history. He had thus mined languages for etymologies and cognates to better understand how ancient peoples referred to agriculture, natural resources, numbers, months of the year, and festivals, customs, beliefs, and laws. As in his other works, at times his etymologies stretched too far; in probing the ancient migrations of peoples from Asia to Europe he established connections that have since been discredited. For example, he mistakenly linked the ancient Dacians to Danes and suggested that the people known as Getae were the ancestors of the Goths. Despite such errors, Jacob was right to point out the value of historical linguistics to archeology, even though his privileging of language over other extant sources might seem exaggerated. Reflecting on recent archeological finds, he declared that language supplies livelier evidence of ancient peoples than do bones, weapons, and graves.[24]

Jacob's publications around this time also included an essay on the origin of language as well as revised editions of *German Grammar*, *German Mythology*, and his study of German legal customs. His productivity, though impressive, was hampered by the never-ending dictionary work. He had taken on letters *A*, *B*, and *C* while Wilhelm attended to *D*. The Grimms received the first proofs for the dictionary on Jacob's sixty-seventh birthday in January 1852. Wilhelm branded the publishing schedule tyrannical. Correcting the proofs took three to four hours and had to be done at once; given his other dictionary work he rarely got to bed before midnight, found it difficult to fall asleep, and then was back at his desk by seven in the morning. Jacob, too,

worked on the dictionary for at least twelve hours a day and would have preferred exploring his other scholarly ideas. Aware of his publishers' investment
in the dictionary and the need to assure the public of its completion, he saw
the project as a contractual and moral obligation. This commitment would
overshadow the rest of their lives.[25]

CHAPTER 14

Final Years in Berlin, 1852–1863

"*A*, the noblest and most primordial of any sound, resounding with fullness from the chest and throat, the first and easiest sound that a child will learn to produce, and which the alphabets of most languages rightfully put at the beginning." So begins the first entry of the Grimms' *German Dictionary*. Volume 1 was published in installments, with the first appearing in 1852, fourteen years after the announcement of the dictionary project. The publication of the complete first volume, spanning the letter *A* to the word *Biermolke* (beer whey), followed two years later.[1] Facing its title page was a now-famous engraving based on a daguerreotype of the Brothers Grimm. To hide the brothers' height gap, the Hamburg daguerreotypist had seated Wilhelm with a book while Jacob stood beside him. Jacob, however, complained that the poses made it seem as if Wilhelm were a patient and Jacob his caretaker.[2]

From the loftiness of the letter *A* as primordial sound to the rusticity of beer-congealed whey, the first volume spanned over 1,800 densely packed columns of text. Each entry typically comprised the headword followed by the grammatical gender for nouns, the Latin equivalent of the word (sometimes accompanied by cognates in modern languages such as Dutch or French or in older Germanic languages), and examples of usage from German authors. Etymologies appeared occasionally, but there was no systematic approach to these and some were at best speculative. For example, in the entry for *arm*,

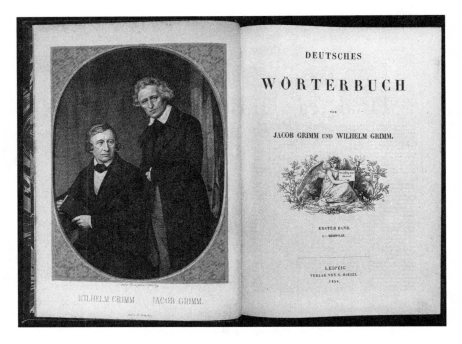

Frontispiece and title page of the Grimms' *German Dictionary*, vol. 1, 1854. Photo
courtesy of the Newberry Library.

which as a noun means "arm" and as an adjective "poor," Jacob suggested
there might be an ancient association between the two meanings, insofar as
we should take the poor into our arms and have compassion for them. Actual
definitions were sometimes given, but most often only the Latin equivalent
and examples of usage illustrated the word's meaning. Crucially, Jacob did not
intend for the Latin equivalent to cover the full range of meanings for a particular word; instead, he believed the examples of usage from German authors
would make an actual definition, whether in Latin or German, superfluous.[3]

In keeping with Jacob's insistence that the German capitalization of nouns
had crept into the language inorganically, nouns were lowercased. In a further
jolt to publishing conventions, the dictionary was published in the Antiqua
instead of Fraktur (or Gothic) typeface. Tucked away among the entries were
touching nods to the Grimms' family members. In addition to the tribute
to the Grimms' mother and father in the entry for *amtmännin* (wife of the
magistrate), the Grimms gave a subtle nod to Dortchen by including the

headword *bierlümmel* (beer lout), a nickname given to her because of her fondness for the beverage.

In the preface, Jacob situated the dictionary alongside the many national cultural monuments and memorials that had been erected in Germany since the end of the Napoleonic Wars. Most pertinent among these was Walhalla Hall, which the Bavarian king had commissioned near Regensburg and opened in 1842. Modeled after the Parthenon in Athens, it was intended as a temple to German heritage, with plaques and busts commemorating famous figures and events across centuries and regions. Similarly, Jacob described the dictionary as a lexicographical hall into which Germans of all faiths and regions were invited. He even hoped it would strengthen and sustain the nostalgia German immigrants in America felt for their native tongue.[4]

In the Grimms' eyes, the dictionary held pedagogical value as a vehicle for celebrating the German language and culture. Jacob suggested in the preface that a father might select a few words from the dictionary each evening to teach his boys; he added in typical gendered fashion that the mother—with her natural wit, untainted feeling for language, and ability to remember sayings and rhymes—would gladly listen along. Unlike an impoverished pocket lexicon retrieved a few times a year to settle an argument about spelling or to track down a fusty German equivalent for a popular foreign expression, he said, a true dictionary should enthrall its readers like an ever-replenishing cornucopia.[5]

The Grimms' goal was thus not a prescriptive dictate for the German language, but a tribute to its inexhaustible poetic power. Jacob had of course long rejected grammatical rigidity, arguing that it led too often to artificial formulations that impeded a language's natural development. His championing of the High German used by Luther and Goethe served as a counterweight to the pedantry of grammarians. Whereas the grammarians' strict rules yielded only forced imitations, Luther and Goethe had a natural feel for German's subtlety and range. Jacob averred that true command of a language was innocent and lacking in artifice, similar to how he and Wilhelm had glorified the naturalness of fairy tales emanating from the people and rejected the stylized revisions of modern writers.[6]

The Grimms' desire to eschew pedantry accounts for their approach to foreign words. In the preface, Jacob explained that while foreign words had generally not been included, some were so infused into German that it would be strange to leave them out. He dismissed the attempts of various grammarians to excise such words from the language and substitute manu-factured equivalents that could only ever sound stilted. This does not mean Jacob unequivocally endorsed further adoption of foreign words; on the con-trary, he hoped through the dictionary to strengthen Germans' regard for and usage of their native tongue so that loan words might not be as necessary.[7]

The *German Dictionary*, like the Grimms' fairy-tale collection, was never-theless indirectly prescriptive. By determining which tales or tale variants to publish in *Children's and Household Tales*, the Grimms had institutionalized notions of what constitutes a fairy tale; so, too, by choosing which words, examples, and dialects to include in the dictionary did the Grimms have a standardizing effect on the German language.

Some commentators enthusiastically endorsed Jacob's view of the diction-ary. In a passage reminiscent of myths of the Brothers Grimm venturing into the fields to obtain tales from the mouths of peasants, one reviewer con-structed an exaggerated image of Jacob and Wilhelm asking men young and old throughout Germany to peruse particular writers for word usage. He claimed that volunteers from all walks of life and political viewpoints had patriotically worked with "German industriousness" to write each word on a slip of paper with the source and sentence in which it appeared. Packages full of slips arrived from all over Germany, the reviewer went on, some even in old cigar boxes or cartons. In this glorified depiction of the compilation process, the reviewer conveniently glossed over the difficulties the Grimms had had with contributors who missed deadlines; he also made their pool of contribu-tors seem more representative and inclusive than was actually the case. Jacob called out eighty-three contributors by name in the preface and noted they were all professors and philologists, apart from a few preachers. When after the publication of the first installment the Grimms began to receive unsolic-ited contributions from well-meaning members of the public, they publicly requested that anyone sending in words and citations follow basic practices.[8]

Other critics doubted that the dictionary would serve as the cultural horn of plenty Jacob envisioned. They pointed out that the book's audience was unclear. While the work was obviously intellectual, it was so incomplete, uneven, and unsystematic that scholars would find it more of a collection than a dictionary. The strangeness of a dictionary that purported to capture German's poetic beauty but relied on Latin equivalents instead of German definitions was noted, and the erudition needed to understand the Latin and other explanations made it seem like caviar for the common people instead of hearty fare. Some words were missing, while words that did not exist but would have been predicted based on earlier Germanic languages were at times included as headwords and explained as such. The heavy reliance on Luther for examples of word usage was off-putting to Catholics, who also objected to the anti-Catholic sentiment in the entry for *Ablass* (indulgence), "principally the ecclesiastical remission of sin for money [. . .], against which the Reformation victoriously inveighed." Many entries were so old-fashioned in tone that they seemed to come straight out of a book of heraldry, one critic scoffed, yet the unconventional orthography and font were conversely too modern, even if in Jacob's mind they recaptured past practice that had been more recently corrupted. The Grimms' use of the lowercase for nouns inspired parodies in satirical periodicals, where the fruitlessness of publishing a German dictionary at a time when German rulers routinely censored their subjects' speech was also underscored. Outside of Germany, opinions regarding the Grimms' choices were rosier: for example, the London *Westminster Review* effusively predicted that the Grimms' lowercasing of nouns and use of roman type were innovations that would soon become universal in the German language (though the use of roman type did not become prevalent until the Nazis banned blackletter fonts such as Fraktur, and the capitalization of nouns remains to this day).⁹

Foremost among the Grimms' German critics were Christian Friedrich Wurm and Daniel Hendel Sanders. A Bavarian high school teacher, Wurm had offered his collection of entries to Jacob for a fee shortly after the first installment appeared; Jacob declined this offer both then and several years later when Wurm again approached him. Wurm subsequently embarked on his own dictionary project, but at the time of his death in 1861 he had published only the first volume, covering part of the letter *A*. Sanders had been a teacher and administrator at a Jewish school in Mecklenburg-Strelitz until its closure, whereupon he worked as an independent scholar. He embarked on his German dictionary project in 1854 and completed it in the 1860s. Whereas the Grimms sought to create a roadmap of national cultural heritage, Sanders focused on contemporary language usage. Wurm and Sanders had each harshly criticized the Grimms' first dictionary installment, which prompted Jacob to rail against them in the preface to the completed first volume. He did not mention them by name, but the targets of his attack were unmistakable. Two spiders had crawled onto plants in the garden of the German language, spread their venom, brutishly defamed a work vital to the fatherland, and in so doing revealed their deficient understanding, Jacob wrote. Critics found it undignified for a man of Jacob's stature to engage in such mean and tactless polemics, and they reminded him that every scholarly work was subject to criticism, as he should know from his own frequent critiques of others' work.

Jacob was unusually sensitive to attacks on the dictionary in part because he himself had become so thoroughly disillusioned with the project. Critics touched a nerve when they pointed out that the many years it had taken to publish just the entries for *A* and a portion of *B* meant that the dictionary might never be finished—at least not during the Grimms' lifetimes. True to his practice with other works, Jacob kept notes to be incorporated into later editions, but he acknowledged that doing so was a perverse joke since he could not possibly live long enough to see a second printing. He also knew that the unevenness in approach to the entries would only grow, since Jacob and Wilhelm had divided their work by letter. Jacob feared that Wilhelm's approach to *D* would be far different than his own execution of *A*, *B*, and *C*.[10]

For one thing, Wilhelm worked more slowly and methodically. It ended up taking him three years to finish the entries for *D*, which spanned around 750 columns; by contrast, in the same amount of time Jacob had produced almost 2,500 columns for *A*, *B*, and *C*. Jacob knew that even a modest assessment indicated that there were still around thirteen thousand columns of entries left to complete the entire alphabet. He had hoped to be able to turn even briefly to other projects; however, upon seeing how slowly Wilhelm worked, their publisher asked that Jacob begin at once to attend to the entries for *E*. To make matters worse, Jacob needed to devote considerable energy to cheering up and motivating Wilhelm, who continued to experience bouts of ill health and despondency.[11]

Jacob also considered the futility of writing a learned dictionary for a public that could not possibly appreciate it. He hoped that future generations would at least recognize its significance. It was not as if there was no appetite for dictionaries, however: by the late 1850s, seven major dictionary projects in addition to the Grimms' were underway. Some of these, such as Wurm's and Sanders's undertakings, were conceived in reaction to the Grimms' dictionary. Others were inspired by it or focused on a narrower scope, such as Low German or Middle High German.[12]

As Jacob and Wilhelm toiled away on entry after entry, they experienced other, more minor annoyances. The bulk of the Grimms' personal library was housed in bookcases flanking the walls of Jacob's study, which meant that Wilhelm had to go back and forth between his own and Jacob's study to fetch books pertinent to his work. If Wilhelm grabbed a title and then promptly brought it back, the doors to their studies seemed to be constantly opening and closing; if, however, he did not immediately return the book, Jacob might not be able to readily find it if he, too, needed it. Their daily approach to working also differed: Wilhelm preferred a measured pace without interruption, whereas Jacob interspersed intense periods of activity with short breaks.[13]

Dortchen, now in her sixties, fretted that Jacob and Wilhelm were straining themselves too much in their old age. But day after day they carried on out of a sense of duty. The rooms in which they worked were their world. In each brother's study there was a mahogany desk, positioned in the middle of the room and sandwiched to the left and right by low bookcases, so that Jacob and Wilhelm could easily reach for frequently used books as they worked. Piles of books and manuscripts topped their desks, tables, and bookcases; peeping out amid these piles were not only large inkwells, feather pen holders, paperweights, and containers of blotting sand, but also the various mementos that cheered them as they labored. Jacob's workspace featured shells, stones, fossils, a pine cone, a small bust of Dante Alighieri, a bear figurine, a sculpture of a lioness, a statuette depicting Briar Rose, and a child's doll seated on a doll's chair. Wilhelm's desk sported a petrified fish, a piece of feldspar, a female figurine from the second century BCE, a green statuette of an Egyptian king, and a centuries-old carved sandstone sculpture of a man's head. Numerous other busts and statuettes topped bookcases and cabinets in their workspaces. Among the many paintings and prints adorning their walls were works by their brother Ludwig as well as (in Jacob's study) portraits of their ancestors. Their scholarship was also quite literally a repository of their daily experiences and memories, as they lovingly tucked dried flowers, leaves, and feathers into their personal copies of the works they had published. These beautiful bookmarks served not only as testaments to the Grimms' daily walks and love of nature but also as fond mementos of a place, person, or event associated with the collecting of each item.[14]

As they toiled away, they at times reflected on how much time had elapsed since their dismissals from Göttingen in 1837 and the inception of the dictionary project. Jacob had returned to Göttingen in 1855 and found the experience uncanny. The town looked much as it did before, whereas Berlin continued to grow in population and commerce. The Grimms' neighborhood in Berlin had changed markedly with the construction of a new canal and many new buildings. In step with the technological innovations of the day, the Grimms often took the train and were fascinated by photographs.[15]

Wilhelm Grimm's study. Watercolor painting by Moritz Hoffmann, around 1860.
Germanisches Nationalmuseum, Nuremberg.

Jacob Grimm's study. Watercolor painting by Moritz Hoffmann, around 1860.
Germanisches Nationalmuseum, Nuremberg.

It was not only Berlin's physical contours that were changing, but also its political landscape. Prussian king Friedrich Wilhelm IV suffered a stroke in 1857; the following year his brother, the future kaiser Wilhelm I, became regent and in 1859 appointed Otto von Bismarck ambassador to Russia. In the 1850s, various European nations and alliances became ensnared in conflicts including the Crimean War and the Franco-Austrian War. In 1858, at the age of seventy-three, Jacob wrote Paul Wigand of his despair over what he viewed as Germany's lost chances for self-realization. In the middle of their lives, they had had reason to hope that better times were coming, but since then Germany's prospects had only darkened. Around the same time, he told another friend that he found himself becoming more democratically minded in his old age; if he were able to relive his experience at the Frankfurt National Assembly, he avowed, he would now sit with those who recognized the futility of trying to shoehorn a constitution into Germany's existing political structures without first ensuring other change. He also suggested, albeit cryptically, that only through force might Germany's situation improve.[16]

He and Wilhelm continued to attend meetings of the Academy, but they had ceased to give lectures at the university and increasingly withdrew from social events. Their circle of friends suffered a great loss with Lachmann's death in 1851, and other acquaintances, too, had passed. In Kassel, their brother Carl died in 1852. The deaths of many of their contemporaries made their immediate household that much more important to them. In Berlin, Wilhelm's son Herman had abandoned legal studies to write novellas and dramas and to study art history. In the years and decades to come, he would distinguish himself as a literary and art historian and a professor at the University of Berlin. He wrote a study of the *Iliad* and biographies of Michelangelo and Raphael, published the university lectures he gave on Goethe, and corresponded with Ralph Waldo Emerson. Herman's younger brother Rudolf had embarked on a military career and later became a jurist, while Auguste helped Dortchen run the household.

Scholars and dignitaries from around Germany and the world continued to visit the Grimms. Guests visiting the family found Dortchen loving and unpretentious, Wilhelm warmhearted, and Jacob, though intimidating, quick with a hearty laugh. Both brothers now had long gray hair, and Jacob was increasingly hard of hearing. They all retained their distinctive Hessian accents. Jacob would typically speak French with foreign visitors, but when a Japanese envoy visited they conversed in Dutch. Jacob delighted in showing visitors new books he had bought. He and Wilhelm had by now amassed a library of some eight thousand works amounting to twelve thousand volumes. Jacob enjoyed surveying their books, plucking one from the shelf, examining it, and then lovingly placing it back.

Dignitaries and scholars were not the only ones to visit. A young girl appeared at their residence one day bearing a copy of *Children's and Household Tales*. She proceeded to read aloud from a tale in which three tailors vie to win the hand of a princess by solving a riddle. After the successful suitor solves the riddle, confronts a bear, and wins the princess's hand, the tale teasingly concludes with the line "If you do not believe this, then you must pay a taler." Taking this playful challenge seriously, the girl confessed to the Grimms that she did not believe the tale but with her small allowance would not be able to pay them the taler at once. She took a coin from her little pink purse and handed it to Wilhelm in partial payment. When he replied that he wanted to make a gift of the coin back to her, she insisted that her mother had told her never to accept money as a gift. The girl's visit became a story in itself and made the rounds in the local papers. Some assumed the anecdote was fabricated, but Wilhelm assured friends that it had actually happened.[17]

The girl's visit to the Grimms is a testament to the impact of *Children's and Household Tales*, even though it never became a bestseller during their lifetimes. The sixth edition had appeared in 1850 and the seventh in 1857. By the sixth edition, the number of tales had swelled from the 155 in the first edition to 210.[18] While these later versions were not revised as dramatically as the second edition had been, Wilhelm nevertheless continued to substitute new tales or variants for others. The Grimms had also continued to publish the Small Edition of *Children's and Household Tales*, with the tenth edition appearing in 1858. Unfortunately, that same year Leipzig publisher Otto Wigand marketed a book of fairy tales, about two-thirds of which were plagiarized from the Grimms. Through legal action the Grimms ensured the book was pulled from the market in 1859, but their demand for damages dragged on in the courts for several years. By the time Wigand was ordered to compensate the Grimm family, Jacob and Wilhelm were both dead. One issue had pertained to whether Jacob and Wilhelm as editors and collectors, instead of authors, could claim *Children's and Household Tales* as their intellectual property or whether the tales were in the public domain.[19]

Between the sixth and seventh printings of the Large Edition, Wilhelm had republished the volume of notes to the tales, which had not been updated since 1822. He had long wished to return to the volume but found time to do so only when ill health forced him to take a spa holiday in summer 1855. In the updated edition, Wilhelm not only refreshed notes to individual fairy tales but also expanded his survey of European, Middle Eastern, and Asian tales to include Native American and African traditions. Although in *Children's and Household Tales* the Grimms had expunged tales deemed too foreign, Wilhelm's study of other fairy-tale collections reveals a fascination with the stories of other peoples and cultures. Nevertheless, it is not without stereotypes. His description of Native American tales follows eighteenth- and nineteenth-century constructions of the noble savage, for example. As for Africa, Wilhelm's eighteen-page overview of the tales brought back from Sierra Leone by the missionary S. W. Kölle is quite positive, and he describes one of these tales as superior to European variants because of its more meaningful ending. Wilhelm's further work on the fairy-tale collection and its scholarly apparatus served as a stark reminder to Jacob that his brother's talents and inclinations lay in his love of folk narratives and medieval literature. He regretted that Wilhelm had had to devote himself almost exclusively to the dictionary instead of pursuing these interests.[20]

Such regrets were never to be assuaged. On December 16, 1859, Wilhelm died at the age of seventy-three. His death followed a happy late summer and fall. Together with Dortchen and Auguste, he had taken a restful holiday to Pillnitz, on the Elbe near Dresden, and just weeks before his death his son Herman had married Bettina's daughter Gisela von Arnim. In the days before he died, a carbuncle developed on his back and required surgery. When he grew feverish, Jacob sat in a chair near his pillow and counted his breaths, as he had done so often over the decades when Wilhelm was ill. Wilhelm became so delirious before his death that he thought Jacob was a mere picture and not actually present. On the morning of December 20, his coffin was carried to the cemetery over snow-covered ground and through icy wind. Jacob, Herman, and Rudolf stood at Wilhelm's grave, and Jacob threw in a handful of earth.

Jacob now felt as if half of him were gone. From the time they were young, the two brothers had almost always been together. In a memorial speech to the Academy in July 1860, Jacob spoke of how they had shared a bed as schoolboys and had two beds and two desks in the same room as university students. Later in life, they had had two desks in the same study, and then two studies next to each other under one roof. Whenever Jacob now took

Children's and Household Tales into his hands, he said, he felt as if he could see Wilhelm on every page—an acknowledgment that Wilhelm had for several decades been the driving force behind the fairy tales. To protect the collection's integrity, Jacob and Herman registered a copyright for *Children's and Household Tales* after Wilhelm's death. Jacob left the door of Wilhelm's study open and his papers and books untouched, save for Wilhelm's personal copies of the Grimms' works, which Jacob now kept within reach as he worked. Eventually he moved much of their extensive library to Wilhelm's study, though he kept Wilhelm's desk in the middle of the room.[21]

With Auguste's help, the widowed Dortchen continued to manage the household while Jacob toiled on letters *E* and *F* for the dictionary. At the time of his death, Wilhelm had only just completed the letter *D*. In the preface to the second volume, published in 1860, Jacob wrote of how so much of the volume was his late brother's work. Wilhelm had worked slowly and at times missed deadlines, he conceded, but readers' patience was always rewarded. The vividness of Wilhelm's descriptions surpassed Jacob's own, and he hoped readers would excuse any unevenness resulting from their different writing styles. Although he himself had initially desired uniformity, he now was glad to see Wilhelm's voice pervading the second volume and compared their unique approaches to separate streams whose waters intermingle as they flow into the same river.[22]

Surrounded by books, papers, a vase of flowers, and mementos that now included photograph portraits, Jacob worked alone at his desk for much of the day. When the newspaper arrived, he put his pen down to read it through and keep abreast of political events. He continued his walks, too. The writer Berthold Auerbach recalled encountering Jacob on a street corner in 1863 and joining him for a stretch. He found Jacob gaunt, but his eyes were still bright and he walked with his left hand on his back, without a cane. He knew all the side paths in the Tiergarten where he could walk in the solitude he so craved.[23]

His family and social circle continued to shrink with Savigny's death in October 1861 and Ludwig's death in April 1863. Although Jacob had not been nearly as close to Savigny in Berlin as he had been decades ago in Marburg and Paris, he was at his former mentor's bedside when he died. During early adulthood Jacob had felt destined to die at a relatively early age; with Ludwig's death he became the sole surviving Grimm sibling.

Old age increasingly took its toll on him. Now in his late seventies, he awoke often during the night. Since he had always delighted in stargazing, he would go to his window and peer up at the sky when he could not fall back asleep. As his hearing declined further, he could not enjoy natural sounds such as birdsong or thunder, and he struggled to converse at social gatherings. Since he had never particularly enjoyed such gatherings anyway, he simply avoided them even more. Because of his hearing loss, Dortchen and Auguste no longer wanted him to travel alone, so Auguste accompanied him on a scholarly trip to Munich in 1862.

Jacob had conveyed his sentiments about sensory impairment and aging in a "Lecture on Old Age" presented to the Academy first in 1851 and again a month after Wilhelm's death. He set forth a compensatory view of aging, claiming that nature would not impair one's senses without bestowing a corresponding benefit. Blind storytellers had through the ages excelled at reciting oral folk literature, he insisted, because the absence of distracting eyesight enhanced their memory. Whereas blindness had earlier been less of a hindrance than deafness, he alleged, the inverse was true in an age of print. He nonetheless admired blind individuals' sense of touch, posited that deaf individuals often develop heightened senses of smell and taste, and asserted that some mobility limitations could boost intelligence. From a modern vantage point, many of his comments are pseudoscientific and insensitive, ignoring lived experiences and implying that disability is routinely offset by an extraordinary physical or mental gain. Nevertheless, the lecture can be read as commenting on Jacob's experience of hearing loss; he implied it did not affect him as much as blindness would have, given his unsocial nature and his scholarly engagement with the printed word. Most notably, the lecture continues the Grimms' lifelong tendency to find a silver lining in any deprivation: "Every misfortune and suffering leads gently and peacefully to a beneficial compensation," he wrote.[24]

But Jacob knew that silver linings were not so simple. Just as the fairy tales he and Wilhelm had issued often depicted extreme adversity on the road to a happy ending, the brothers had in their lifetimes coped with the loss of their father and the challenges that ensued as well as the fallout from the Göttingen Seven protest. With respect to their Göttingen dismissals, the dictionary project that had at first seemed like a silver lining had of course proved to be more of a millstone around their necks. After the publication in 1862 of the third volume, covering *E* and a portion of *F*, Jacob devoted himself to completing entries for *F*. As the end of his life neared, he had many other projects he still wished to realize. But apart from publishing the fourth part of his collection of historical legal guidance and customs and continuing to write smaller pieces such as reviews, he felt he had no choice but to continue with the dictionary.

Despite this focus, publisher Salomon Hirzel berated him for taking any precious time away from the dictionary to publish other pieces. Hirzel's impatience is understandable, given that half the dictionary portions published to date sat unsold and sales had waned. Jacob fired back that he was now at the age when most of his peers were twiddling their thumbs, while he continued to be a productive scholar. He refused to be so beholden to the dictionary that he could pursue no other scholarship, and in any case his work on German legal guidance and customs had provided additional expressions and examples to include in the dictionary. Such additions were not surprising, he added, given the interrelatedness of his work on grammar, mythology, legal customs, medieval literature, and folk culture. As for Hirzel's suggestion that Jacob enlist students to help with the dictionary, he curtly retorted that it was in his nature only to learn, not to teach. He gave Hirzel two options: he would continue to work on the dictionary at his own pace and accomplish as much as he could in his remaining lifetime, or he would give up on the dictionary altogether. He continued the work.[25]

Jacob took respite from his grueling scholarly schedule in late summer 1863 to travel with Dortchen and Auguste to the Harz Mountains in north-central Germany. Upon his return, he developed first a cold and then what was described as an inflamed liver. After being treated with leeches and calomel he appeared to convalesce, particularly during the day, when he would spend hours reading in bed and writing notes, but at night he battled fevers. On the day before he died, he got up from bed and, leaning on a wicker chair, made his way to the window. Auguste tried to talk with him, but he did not respond and fell against her. In that moment, she thought he had suddenly died, but then realized he was having a stroke. He grew feverish, his heart was racing, and he slept through the night and into the next day. Upon awakening, he felt the paralyzed right side of his body with his left hand. As he lay dying in the hours that followed, he was conscious and seemed to understand what was said to him, but he could no longer speak. At one point he reached for a picture of Wilhelm, drew it close to his eyes, and set it down on his coverlet. He died on the night of Sunday, September 20, 1863, at the age of seventy-eight.

It was strangely fitting that the childless and unmarried Jacob died surrounded by many of his beloved books, which Auguste compared to suddenly orphaned children. Jacob had feared that after his death the vast library he and Wilhelm had amassed would be dispersed; however, apart from a thousand works that were sold and a few hundred kept by Herman Grimm, the library went intact to the University of Berlin. It was rather fitting, too, that the last dictionary entry on which he had actively worked was for the word "fruit" (*Frucht*)—not only given the many organic metaphors the Grimms had employed in describing folk literature and culture, but especially in view of his description years earlier of the dictionary project as the "fruit of our banishment" from Göttingen. As a footnote in the published volume indicated, with that entry Jacob had unknowingly laid down his pen from working on the dictionary for the last time. The fifth and sixth parts of Jacob's collection of thousands of historical records on German legal guidance and customs were published posthumously in 1866 and 1869.[26]

In his speech given to the Academy in memory of Wilhelm, Jacob had noted that just as their beds had once stood next to each other as university students, they would soon find their final resting places next to each other, too. He was buried next to Wilhelm in Berlin. Among the flowers adorning Jacob's coffin was a wreath of white roses with ribbons that read "To the friend of the youth from thankful children," a testament to the impact of the Grimms' fairy tales. After his death, Dortchen and Auguste moved to a different apartment in Berlin. Dortchen died of a respiratory illness in 1867 while on a trip to Eisenach, where she had gone seeking to strengthen her fragile health. While alive, she had recoiled at the transportation of corpses, so she was buried in Eisenach, not Berlin. Neither Rudolf nor Auguste married, and Herman and his wife, Gisela, did not have children. Rudolf died in 1889, Herman in 1901, and Auguste in 1919.[27]

Conclusion

Less than a decade after Jacob's death, Prussian military victories and Bismarck's shrewd diplomatic maneuverings led to the unification of Germany in 1871 and the coronation of Prussian king Wilhelm I as emperor. The Grimms had regarded Wilhelm I as a learned and well-intentioned man with whom one could converse as freely as with a private citizen. Imperial iconography unsurprisingly portrayed the newly crowned kaiser in far grander terms, in part by drawing on the very tales and legends the Grimms explored in their works. Erected in the 1890s, the Kyffhäuser Monument honored both Wilhelm I and the legendary medieval emperor Barbarossa, prophesied to awaken from his slumber in Mount Kyffhäuser and bring about better times. The late nineteenth-century restoration of the medieval imperial palace in Goslar, a town in the Harz Mountains of north-central Germany, featured statues of Barbarossa and Kaiser Wilhelm I flanking the building's exterior. Inside, the emperor's hall showcased nineteenth-century frescoes of Barbarossa and Kaiser Wilhelm I along with Briar Rose (Sleeping Beauty), the fairy-tale heroine who, like Barbarossa, awakens from a long sleep. She, too, became a metaphor for German national awakening. In Bavaria, King Ludwig II's pseudo-medieval knight's castle Neuschwanstein served as an homage to Wagner's operas and to the medieval literature and legends that, partly through the Grimms' influence, had inspired the composer.[1]

Some late nineteenth- and early twentieth-century architectural imaginings of German culture drew on the Grimms' legacy in less palatial, more publicly accessible ways. In the Friedrichshain park in Berlin, a fountain featuring sculptures of Grimm fairy-tale characters was planned in the 1890s; upon its completion in 1913, it became the largest public fountain complex in the city. Unlike the grandiose depictions of Barbarossa and Briar Rose in Goslar, the statues in the park conveyed innocence and simplicity. They thus gestured toward the increasing association of the Grimms' fairy tales with children, which was bolstered by the growing popularity and reach of the collection at the time. An eighth edition of *Children's and Household Tales* appeared the year after Jacob died, and a further twenty-one editions were published between 1864 and 1886. In the decades after the Grimms' deaths, their collection finally began to achieve the success for which it is known today. At the beginning of the twentieth century, *Children's and Household Tales* was marketed broadly in Germany and the Austro-Hungarian Empire, and selected Grimm tales began to appear in schoolbooks in Europe and North America.[2]

Fatefully, the racialized nationalism and xenophobia of the early decades of the twentieth century further popularized the Grimms' work: influential commentators preferred the allegedly ethnic Germanic folksiness of the Grimms' tales to the witty, bourgeois tone of Ludwig Bechstein's. A case in point is the book of mostly Grimm fairy tales printed for a cigarette manufacturer, mentioned in the introduction to this book: it reached a staggering one hundred thousand copies sold by 1939. The popularity of the Grimms' collection during the Nazi years later led Allied occupation forces to ban the Grimms' fairy tales for a time after the war, believing that they had contributed to the Nazification of Germany. When the Large Edition reappeared on West German bookshelves, tales such as "The Jew in the Thornbush" were often omitted.[3] In East Germany, meanwhile, the Grimms' tales were viewed as an important part of German culture that the Nazis had exploited for their fascist aims. In keeping with socialist ideology, the live-action adaptations of Grimm fairy tales produced by the East German film studio DEFA emphasized poor characters' class struggles with a corrupt aristocracy. The DEFA adaptation of "Briar Rose," for example, includes scenes of angry peasant women protesting the kingdom's confiscation of their spindles, since the inability to spin yarn will impoverish them. Across the Atlantic, the so-called Disneyfication of the fairy tale was unleashed in 1937 with *Snow White and the Seven Dwarfs*. The animated film's opening credits announced that the story had been adapted from the Grimms' fairy tale. Since then, heavily commercialized Disney princess films have become almost synonymous with the fairy-tale genre and have in turn contributed to the permeation of fairy tales throughout popular culture, with treatments that range from serious to spoofing. Whether directly or indirectly, the popularity of *Children's and Household Tales* has contributed to what the Grimms themselves frowned on: radical artistic reshapings.

Some of these are saturated with fairy-tale kitsch, including predictable plots and clichéd punning of the Grimms' names. Others, however, are strikingly clever and provocative, such as Jane Yolen's use of the Grimms' "Briar Rose" to address the Holocaust in her award-winning novel *Briar Rose*. From the late nineteenth century to the present, prominent artists have also been drawn to the tales, including Walter Crane, Arthur Rackham, Kay Nielsen, Wanda Gág, Maurice Sendak, and David Hockney. Beyond popular adaptations of their stories, the Brothers Grimm have even become characters themselves, as for example in the syrupy film *The Wonderful World of the Brothers Grimm* (1962) or the less-than-memorable action movie *The Brothers Grimm* (2005), which depicts the characters Will and Jake Grimm as con men who perform bogus exorcisms.[4] Fairy tales' power to spark imagination and make sense of individual and human experience shines in Polish poet Wisława Szymborska's provocative declaration "I prefer Grimms' fairy tales to the newspapers' front pages" and Albert Einstein's reputed advice that parents who wish their children to be intelligent should read them fairy tales.[5]

Not surprisingly in view of fairy tales' imaginative power, in the twentieth century the Grimms' fairy tales also featured prominently on the therapist's couch. Psychoanalysts such as Sigmund Freud, Carl Jung, and Bruno Bettelheim explored their rich psychological, archetypal, and symbolic dimensions, often arriving at interpretations far different from the narratives' surface-level content. Bettelheim asserted that the stepmother's wickedness in "Snow White" is in part a psychological projection of Snow White's jealousy of the stepmother's power and station. He also saw in the depiction of child abandonment, the gingerbread house, and threatened cannibalism in "Hansel and Gretel" the child's oral regression: to Bettelheim, the gingerbread house represents the mother's body from which the child has nursed and wishes to continue being nourished, and the witch is the child's projection of the mother who no longer gratifies all the child's wants. These and other twentieth-century analyses yielded new ways of deriving meaning from particular tales, but it is disturbing that they so often blamed the abused child and exonerated the abusive power figure. Such blame has frequently revealed Freudian theory's misogynistic underpinnings, as when Alan Dundes ignored the strong likelihood that the Grimm tale "The Maiden without Hands" is about a father's sexual abuse of his daughter and instead read it as projected inversion. Failing to take into account the history and multiple variants of the tale, Dundes claimed that it is the daughter who actually has sexual desires for her father; he in effect suggested that the girl "asked for" the violence done to her when he interpreted the cutting off of her hands as her wished-for punishment for her sinful desires.[6]

Nevertheless, if psychologists have at times succumbed to reading tales too ahistorically, other interpreters have perhaps been too rigidly anti-psychological. Dundes rightly called out "literal-minded folklorists" whose approaches might preposterously lead them to see in depictions of giants in fairy tales evidence that "there must have been once a race of giant people who dwelled on earth."[7] But folkloric and psychological interpretations are not always at odds, and indeed often converge or inform each other. For example, it is impossible to prove what, if any, particular meaning the name "Rumpelstilzchen" (Rumpelstiltskin) bears, especially since tales in which the name of the spinning helper must be guessed were originally riddles and the names themselves could differ from one telling to the next. Nevertheless, "Rummel" (or "Rumpel," commotion, hubbub) could be used to refer to coitus or to labor during childbirth, and such folkloric connotations are significant considering the many twentieth-century critics (Freud among them) who equate Rumpelstiltskin with the phallus. And in "Hans My Hedgehog," the half-human, half-hedgehog hero's riding of a rooster recalls folkloric associations of roosters with male virility—what Dundes cleverly dubbed "the gallus as phallus"—and suggests the hero's oedipal conflict with his father.[8]

The multivalent interpretive horizons that any one tale might offer are manifested in recent scholarship, which has examined the Grimms' tales through lenses such as disability studies theory, feminist theory, queer theory, and a variety of psychological frameworks. Scholars have explored the vast international reception of the tales and the way various modern media and genres have adapted them.[9] As different as many of these interpretive frameworks are from the Grimms' scholarly orientation, the brothers' own published notes routinely suggested multiple interpretive avenues. With their copious references to German and European tale variants, Nordic and classical mythology, and regional customs and folk texts, the Grimms' notes pointed to the many layers of meaning any one tale might bear.

The accretion of such layers continues today as the Grimms' fairy tales are told and retold with astounding frequency and reach. Jacob and Wilhelm Grimm are not only the two most frequently translated German authors of all time, but also in tenth and eleventh place, respectively, on UNESCO's list of the top fifty translated authors in the world. One wonders how the scholarly Grimms would have regarded their places just behind horror, fantasy, and crime writer Stephen King and ahead of romance novelist Nora Roberts—or for that matter how they would have felt about Hans Christian Andersen's standing above them in eighth place.[10] They would presumably be saddened that their standings on such lists result almost exclusively from *Children's and Household Tales* and not also from works like the *German Dictionary* (which Jacob had hoped would be properly appreciated fifty or a hundred years after its publication).

Reception of the dictionary has ranged from enthusiastic to disparaging. Even though volumes produced during the Grimms' lifetimes sold only half their print run, the dictionary project did not die with them. In the immediate years after Jacob's death, scholars Rudolf Hildebrand and Karl Weigand continued the work, which then endured through two world wars and the division of Germany into east and west. It was eventually completed through a collaboration of West and East German scholars in 1961—the year the Berlin Wall was erected, a century after the Grimms' deaths, and 123 years from the inception of the project. Originally projected by the Grimms to comprise six or seven volumes, the finished work spanned thirty-two volumes plus a full book of sources published in 1971 and numbered over thirty-one thousand pages. A revision of the volumes compiled by the Grimms was also undertaken.

Because Jacob and Wilhelm had feared the dictionary might never be finished, they almost certainly would have been pleasantly surprised by its completion and astounded that work on it continued for over a hundred years after Jacob's death. It is a further irony that the dictionary project began when Germany was not yet politically united, continued in the decades after unification, and was completed when Germany was again divided. The prominent German literary critic Marcel Reich-Ranicki pronounced the *German Dictionary* "the most interesting novel and single most important book in the German language"—an apt judgment in light of the dictionary's cultural aims, the breadth of its sources, and its genesis over more than a century of historical upheavals.[11] The Grimms had aimed for the dictionary to convey the history of modern German by presenting word usage from

Luther to Goethe; however, its lengthy compilation and publication history makes it a historical timepiece in ways that Jacob could not possibly have imagined. Despite widespread recognition that the dictionary's completion represented a stunning accomplishment, many scholars and critics still regarded the project as ill-conceived and pointed to the unevenness of its entries, the length of its execution, and even what some saw as suspect political motivations.[12]

Indeed, for the last several decades the Grimms have been widely viewed in intellectual circles as quaint, old-fashioned, and even dangerous, largely because their constructions of Germany and Germanness were too easily appropriated by Nazi ideology. The "love of the word" that lay at the foundation of nineteenth-century linguistic and literary scholarship had been twinned with a love of the fatherland whose proponents, including the Grimms, at times voiced patriarchal and anti-Semitic sentiments. Critics of the *German Dictionary* thus saw it as symptomatic of a larger issue facing *Germanistik*, the study of German language and literature of which Jacob Grimm is often viewed as the de facto founder through his groundbreaking philological accomplishments. In the postwar reckoning over why *Germanistik* as a discipline had so readily been yoked to Nazi ideology, the Grimms and their fellow nineteenth-century philologists were easy to blame.[13]

It is in this vein that German critic and journalist Walter Boehlich attacked the completion of the dictionary as a Pyrrhic victory, suggesting that the work's national character had in fact been too nationalistic. The scholarly approach that the Grimms and their contemporaries saw as an escape from French cultural dominance and military occupation was viewed by Boehlich as a one-way street to National Socialism and its horrors. In rebuttal, Theodor Kochs and Hans Neumann, two twentieth-century scholars who had worked on the dictionary, argued that Boehlich failed to consider the changing connotations of political vocabulary such as "nationalism," "patriotism," "culture," "nation," and "folk" or "people" (*Volk*). Whereas Jacob declared at the 1846 meeting of Germanists in Frankfurt that a people is the embodiment of human beings who speak the same language, later figures took this a step further to mean ancestry, such that *Volk* became a biological category with racial overtones, instead of principally a cultural and political entity bound by language.[14] The National Socialists in any case readily appropriated nineteenth-century philology's emphasis on language, history, and nation to the Nazi focus on race and blood. But Kochs and Neumann argued that Boehlich seemed to expect that mid-nineteenth-century scholars such as the Grimms could have somehow foreseen the events of the twentieth century. To Kochs and Neumann, such an expectation was ahistorical, in part because it failed to acknowledge that the post-Napoleonic fervor for celebrating a people's history, language, and cultural expressions extended beyond the German-speaking lands to much of Europe. Indeed, the Grimms helped to catalyze an international network of scholars who sought to trace the evolution of language, literature, and customs and thus to probe the similarities and divergences between and across peoples. To Boehlich, however, Kochs and Neumann themselves were ahistorical in their failure to grasp the seeds of Nazi ideology in nineteenth-century philology.[15]

Among the many ironies here is the fact that the Grimms spent so much of their scholarly lives trying to convince rulers and the reading public of Germany's place in history—one that for so long had been dismissively regarded as barbaric and inferior compared to classical antiquity and to modern nations such as France. At the same time, in their efforts to remind others of this history the Grimms occasionally failed to adequately acknowledge their own role in shaping it. That is, they themselves often acted ahistorically, as when they failed to see themselves as participating in, rather than merely stewarding, the storytelling tradition with their extensive fairy-tale edits or when they recast the courtly medieval narrative poem *Poor Heinrich* as folk inspiration for Hessian soldiers fighting the French in the Wars of Liberation. Boehlich on one side and Kochs and Neumann on the other accused each other of essentially this—a false sense of objectivity that neglects how the present affects our view of the past and the future.

Considering such historical and interpretive complexities, Günter Grass's *Grimms' Words: A Declaration of Love* (2010) stands out as a playful and probing love letter to the German language and to the Grimms' reverence for it. Published just four years after the Nobel Prize winner's admission of having served in the Waffen-SS and five years before his death, *Grimms' Words* forms the third book in Grass's memoir trilogy. Grass had previously engaged with the Grimms' legacy not only through his design of the metal sculpture commemorating the Göttingen Seven, but also through his magical realist literary style, grounded in reality but including magical elements drawn from fairy tales and related genres. For example, Oskar Matzerath, the protagonist of Grass's novel *The Tin Drum*, is in part inspired by the Thumbling character in the Grimms' tales. *Grimms' Words* oscillates between biographical sketches of the Grimms' lives and autobiographical passages in which Grass reflects on his own life. It includes occasional lyrical passages and fictional dialogues in which Grass imagines meeting Jacob and Wilhelm in Berlin's Tiergarten park. Grass devotes each of the chapters to a letter of the alphabet, with a particular focus on *A* through *F*—the letters in the *German Dictionary* the Grimms worked on during their lifetimes. The first chapter, on *A*, for example, focuses on the Grimms' asylum (*Asyl*) in Hessen after their firing from the University of Göttingen; Grass muses on various connotations of words such as *ach*, the German interjection typically used to intensify an expression of lament, pity, regret, or surprise.

Throughout the memoir, Grass uses the Grimms' lives to shed light on his own experiences. At times, the equivalencies Grass draws are quite strained, and his legacy is in any case more immediately and palpably contested than that of the Grimms. His late-in-life admission of serving in the Waffen-SS was seen by critics as proof of his hypocrisy, given his years of moralistic political activism. Albeit in different ways, both Grass and the Grimms have thus figured into Germany's moral self-reckoning over the Nazi period that is expressed in the term *Vergangenheitsbewältigung* (coming to terms with the past). But the implied synecdoche of the title *Grimms' Words: A Declaration of Love* is more significant perhaps than any insights or misappropriations that Grass's juxtaposition of his own and the Grimms' lives might yield. As recent scholarship has pointed out, Grass suggests that Grimms' words are German words and German words are Grimms' words.[16] The subtitle not only captures Grass's "declaration of love" for the Grimms' words, but also evokes the Grimms' own love of the German language as well as the overarching "love of the word" that informs philology. The title of Grass's memoir thus subtly conveys the capaciousness of the Grimms' contributions to the study of language and literary and cultural expression, both in Germany and abroad.

A far different testament to the capaciousness of the Grimms' contributions is the Grimmwelt (Grimm world) in Kassel. Opened in 2015 as a successor to the previous Brothers Grimm Museum in Kassel, Grimmwelt bills itself not as a museum but as an *Erlebnisraum*—an "experience space" where one can grow acquainted with the Brothers Grimm through interactive displays, modern art, and historical objects that include the Grimms' personal copies of various editions of *Children's and Household Tales*. The modern art installations align with Kassel's international reputation as the site of Documenta, an exhibit of contemporary art that takes place every five years. Like the lettered chapters in Grass's memoir, museum exhibits are organized around the alphabet and thus celebrate the Grimms' dictionary. The exhibit for the letter *Z*, for example, focuses on the slips of paper (*Zettel*) on which the Grimms took notes for their various scholarly works. Other exhibits pay homage to the Grimms' vast network of correspondents, the artwork of their brother Ludwig, and individual fairy tales such as "Little Red Cap," "Hansel and Gretel," "Snow White," "Rumpelstiltskin," and "Briar Rose." Although the museum has won several architectural, marketing, and exhibit awards since its opening, reviews on popular online tourist forums are mixed. Parents expecting a Disneyesque children's museum are disappointed to find text-heavy displays, an emphasis on not just the Grimms' fairy tales but also their dictionary and other works, and an approach that some have regarded as too arty. Nevertheless, Grimmwelt's curators deserve credit for seeking to balance child-friendly displays with intellectual content. The museum evokes the imagination for which fairy tales and folklore are known while also spurring appreciation of the scientific and scholarly rigor with which the Grimms approached their work. Moreover, it goes beyond *Children's and Household Tales* to also capture the Grimms' other accomplishments.[17]

Indeed, through tens of thousands of painstakingly researched pages of published scholarship and collected texts, the Grimms were among the foremost contributors to the post-Napoleonic German national awakening. Together or individually, they had collected folk songs, fairy tales, legends, myths, customs, legal texts, and related documents attesting to the cultural production of the German-speaking lands. Their work on medieval literature would alone have assured them a place among the pathbreakers of German literary scholarship. They drew attention to the earliest origins of German literature through their deciphering of the ninth-century *Lay of Hildebrand*, showing that it is not a prose fragment about two cousins but an epic poem about a father and son who meet on the battlefield. They had helped revive the long-forgotten *Nibelungenlied* and spurred renewed interest in texts such as Hartmann von Aue's *Poor Heinrich* as well as in medieval literary forms and genres ranging from the beast epic to medieval lyric poetry to runic alphabets. As for linguistics, Jacob's decades of study of Germanic languages and dialects yielded his monumental *German Grammar*, "Grimm's Law," and his history of the German language. To him and his contemporaries, the reconstruction of past languages and grammars was a scientific undertaking analogous to the comparative analysis of various organisms' anatomies. Through this undertaking, Jacob sought to dispel notions of ancient Germanic tribes as uncultured barbarians. But he was also motivated by his belief that comparative philology would reveal similarities across peoples in addition to cultural uniquenesses.[18]

Some modern critics mock the nineteenth-century attempt to scientize the humanities, but they often fail to consider the challenges scholars faced and the aspirations they held.[19] Instead of just deriding the Grimms' scientization of the humanities and constructions of Germanness, recent scholarship has submitted the origins, premises, inconsistencies, and impacts of the Grimms' national tendencies to a long overdue examination, probing how the Grimms viewed comparative philology as a way out of the political instability and fragmentation of their time.[20] As young scholars, they had persevered through the French occupation of Hessen and surrounding regions. Despair over dreary library routines and mundane civil service work drove the Grimms to seek meaning and fulfillment in academic pursuits. Jacob and Wilhelm benefited from the kindness of the Hessian electresses but clashed with electors who could not understand the significance of the Grimms' scholarly accomplishments. The principled stand that Jacob, Wilhelm, and their colleagues took against King Ernst August of Hanover initially derailed their careers but eventually led to widespread acclamation. They were repeatedly disappointed by political realities and propelled by the hope that their work might help bring about a unification of Germany.

The Grimms' sense of the instability of their time was intensified by personal losses such as the premature death of their father and the deaths of their mother, their aunt Henriette Zimmer, Wilhelm's firstborn son, their sister Lotte, and others in their family. Wilhelm's many episodes of ill health further heightened their appreciation of life's fragility. They endured both despite and because of the personal and social challenges that confronted them. In view of such challenges and the protracted publication history of the *German Dictionary*, recent scholars have correctly recast the dictionary project as Sisyphean, rather than the Pyrrhic victory that Walter Boehlich had dubbed it.[21]

To the Grimms, however, their scholarly endeavors were not so much a matter of pushing a boulder up a mountain, but of needing first of all to mine the ore. Inspired in part by the image of the Nibelungs' treasure submerged in the Rhine, Wilhelm used the excavation of gold as a metaphor for the Grimms' reclamation of tales and other texts. The frog's retrieval of the golden ball in "The Frog King or Iron Heinrich" and the finding of the key in "The Golden Key" stand as testaments to this recovery at the beginning and end of *Children's and Household Tales*. At a time when expected liberties were repeatedly denied, the Grimms believed that an understanding of the past could help build a better future. Indeed, they viewed the literary and linguistic treasures yet to be unearthed by scholarship as an inexhaustible hoard: not only does their placement of "The Golden Key" at the end of *Children's and Household Tales* suggest more fairy tales to be discovered, but their habit of publishing revised editions of works such as Jacob's *German Grammar* also points to their view of the unending nature of scholarly discovery.[22]

Yet it was not simply a matter of excavating such fairy tales and folk texts, but also of determining how much to conserve or restore them. While gold served as a metaphor for the value of the Germanic past, it also represented an overzealous stylizing of *Naturpoesie* which, akin to Midas's touch, deadened rather than enlivened it. The Grimms' own edits, however, were often more radical than the simple shaping and nurturing they espoused. They selectively chose texts that best corresponded to their idealized notions of folklore and further edited texts with these parameters in mind. Nevertheless, it is this editing—including smoothing the narration, adding images and sayings, and making the tales more suitable, in the eyes of parents, for children—that with time launched *Children's and Household Tales* into international renown.

Seen in the context from which their work emerged, the Grimms themselves appear as hidden treasures to be reclaimed but not subjected to Midas-like restyling. Any presentation of their lives and scholarship is itself a collection of interrelated parts. In the year of his death, Jacob had curtly defended his publication of the fourth part of his collection of historical legal customs to Salomon Hirzel, the publisher who exhorted him to focus solely on the *German Dictionary*. Jacob's defense that all his scholarly pursuits were so intertwined that the success of one enabled the success of another deserves pause, since their other works have been overshadowed by the almost exclusive celebration today of the Grimms' fairy tales. Years earlier, in his inaugural lecture in Berlin, Jacob had spoken of the interrelatedness of language and law; he characterized each as both young and old, grounded in history and yet always evolving and thus ever-renewing. Acknowledging scholarly dilemmas of whether one should proceed from the general to the particular or vice versa, emphasize the real or the ideal, or hew more to philosophy or history, Jacob characteristically confessed to seeing merit in each side. Above all, he valued studying the past while staying connected to the present. "Anyone who tries to quench the demands of the present without listening to the past," he argued, "actually just deprives the present of its due, insofar as he empowers the future to someday do the same to him." Conversely, anyone who sought to hold stiffly on to the past deprives himself of the uniqueness of the present, and "foolishly cuts off the very branch on which his foot rests." Jacob aimed for his scholarship to unlock the doors of law, language, and other cultural expression for his audience. To this end, just as he and Wilhelm had closed *Children's and Household Tales* with the image of a key opening a chest, in concluding his lecture he noted his hope of "putting into your hands lost or misplaced keys"—which, he noted, "I myself still do not possess all."[23]

Note on Orthography and Translations

Writing in English about nineteenth-century Germany presents many orthographical considerations for which there is no standard approach. In this book, I have generally kept German spellings of individuals' names, referring, for example, to "Friedrich Wilhelm IV" of Prussia instead of "Frederick William IV." German orthography in the nineteenth century was less consistent than it is today, and even within families the spellings of members' names and nicknames might vary. For example, Jacob and Wilhelm Grimm referred to their brother Ludwig also as "Louis" and "Lui," and they spelled another brother's name as "Carl" or "Karl." Similarly, Bettina von Arnim's name sometimes appears as "Bettine." In these and other cases, I have used the form that tends to be the most prevalent. In agreement with Jacob Grimm's disdain for the "pointless accumulation of our forenames," for individuals who went by their middle name or another moniker I use this name in the text and, as relevant, provide the full given name upon initial usage.[1] A notable exception is the Grimms' father, Philipp Wilhelm Grimm, who was called "Wilhelm" by family members but to whom I refer using his first and middle name—both to avoid confusion with his son Wilhelm and because he is generally known in scholarship as Philipp Wilhelm Grimm. I have transliterated the German *Eszett* (ß) in names as "ss" (thus "Voss," not "Voß") but have retained umlauts. Titles of German works, including those of individual tales and legends, are generally given in English in the text, following the translation most typically used. For works by the Grimms, I provide both the English translation and the original German title in the index.

I have used German geographical names for places in the German-speaking lands, except where the English designation is so prevalent that the German place name might be incomprehensible. I therefore refer to "Cologne" and not "Köln," "Vienna" and not "Wien," and the "Rhine" instead of the "Rhein." In cases where an English designation has become increasingly obsolete, I prefer the German (thus "Braunschweig," not "Brunswick"). And in cases where the English and German spellings are in fairly even circulation, I use the German, unless doing so would lead to inconsistencies (thus "Hanover" instead of "Hannover," due to the "Hanoverian" dynasty). For cities that were part of the German lands in the nineteenth century but are no longer, I use the German place name (thus "Breslau," not "Wrocław"; "Königsberg," not "Kaliningrad").

Deciding whether to adopt an English designation, a German designation, an older German spelling, or a modern German spelling can result in a plethora of options, each of which might have advantages and disadvantages in terms of comprehension and currency. The principality in which the Grimms were born and spent much of their lives provides a vivid example of this: faced with choices that include "Hesse-Cassel," "Hesse-Kassel," "Hessen-Cassel," and "Hessen-Kassel," I have chosen the last of these. I use modern German spellings except in cases where there is a terminological reason to use either the English spelling or an older German spelling (e.g., the "Carlsbad Decrees," not the "Karlsbad Decrees").

There is often no elegant or consistent solution for these and related challenges. It is in this regard a consolation that the Grimms themselves delighted in orthographical variants and were not wedded to systematization. Jacob Grimm's defiance of the convention of capitalizing German nouns is perhaps the best-known example of this, but his admission that he preferred the alternate spelling *Getraide* (grain) to the more common *Getreide* out of sheer pity for the lack of words with "ai" stands out as well.[2] Although I have tried to make orthographical decisions on the basis of comprehension and consistency, not compassion, I take heart that the Grimms themselves eschewed prescriptiveness and welcomed exceptions.

Unless otherwise noted, all translations are my own.

Chronology

1785	Jacob Ludwig Carl Grimm is born to Philipp Wilhelm and Dorothea Grimm on January 4 in Hanau. In October, Landgrave Friedrich II of Hessen-Kassel dies and is succeeded by Landgrave Wilhelm IX of Hessen-Kassel (later Wilhelm I, Elector of Hessen).
1786	Wilhelm Carl Grimm is born on February 24 in Hanau.
1787	The Grimms' brother Carl Friedrich Grimm is born on April 24 in Hanau.
1788	The Grimms' brother Ferdinand Philipp Grimm is born on December 18 in Hanau.
1789	The French Revolution begins.
1790	The Grimms' brother Ludwig Emil Grimm is born on March 14 in Hanau.
1791	In January, the Grimm family moves to Steinau, where the Grimms' father serves as district magistrate.
1792	The French Revolutionary Wars begin and last until 1802.
1793	The Grimms' sister Charlotte (Lotte) Amalie Grimm is born on May 10 in Steinau.
1796	Philipp Wilhelm Grimm dies of pneumonia on January 10. The Grimms' aunt Juliane Charlotte Friederike Schlemmer dies on December 18.

1798   In the fall, Jacob and Wilhelm begin their studies at the Lyceum
        Fridericianum in Kassel. The Grimms' grandfather Johann Hermann
        Zimmer dies on November 22.
1799   Napoleon becomes First Consul of France.
1802   In April, Jacob enters the University of Marburg to study law. Wil-
        helm grows ill and is unable to attend school in Kassel for six months.
1803   Wilhelm enters the University of Marburg to study law. The landgravi-
        ate of Hessen-Kassel is elevated to an electorate. Landgrave Wilhelm
        IX becomes Elector Wilhelm I. The Napoleonic Wars begin and last
        until 1815.
1804   Napoleon declares himself Emperor of the French.
1805   In January, Jacob travels to Paris to help Friedrich Carl von Savigny
        with his research and remains there until September. Dorothea Grimm
        moves with Lotte to Kassel. Clemens Brentano and Achim von Arnim
        publish the first volume (of three) of *The Boy's Magic Horn*. Over the
        next few years, the Grimms assist Brentano and Arnim with the col-
        lecting of folk songs and begin to collect fairy tales.
1806   Jacob begins serving as secretary at the War Board in Kassel. In May,
        Wilhelm takes his university exams in Marburg. In summer, Napoleon
        creates the Confederation of the Rhine and the Holy Roman Empire
        is dissolved. The French invade Electoral Hessen in October and begin
        their occupation of Kassel on November 1. The Hessian elector flees.
        Jacob serves on the commission responsible for overseeing provisions
        for French troops.
1807   Jacob publishes his essay "On the *Nibelungenlied*." France annexes
        Electoral Hessen into the Kingdom of Westphalia. Napoleon declares
        his brother Jérôme King of Westphalia. Jacob resigns from his position
        at the commission.
1808   In spring, Jacob sends several tales he had collected to Savigny for his
        daughter. The Grimms' mother dies on May 27. In July, Jacob is ap-
        pointed librarian to King Jérôme.
1809   Jacob becomes auditor of the state council in February. In April,
        Wilhelm travels to Halle, where he receives treatment for his heart ail-
        ment. In September, he travels with Clemens Brentano from Halle to
        Berlin, where they stay with Achim von Arnim. En route to Kassel, he
        meets Goethe in Weimar.
1810   In October, the Grimms send Clemens Brentano a packet of fairy
        tales, later known as the Ölenberg manuscript.
1811   Wilhelm publishes *Old Danish Heroic Songs, Ballads, and Tales*. Jacob
        publishes *On the Old German Meistergesang*. In winter, the Grimms
        begin hosting a weekly evening reading group in their apartment in

Kassel (which lasts until the end of 1813). Several of the reading group members share fairy tales with Jacob and Wilhelm. In summer, Wilhelm makes his first visit to Bökerhof, the Haxthausen family estate.

1812   The Grimms publish volume 1 of the first edition of *Children's and Household Tales* as well as their editions of the *Lay of Hildebrand* and the *Wessobrunn Prayer*.

1813   The Grimms are introduced to storyteller Dorothea Viehmann. They publish the first volume (of three) of *Old German Forests*. In summer, Wilhelm travels to the Haxthausen estate Bökerhof, where he meets Jenny and Annette von Droste-Hülshoff. Like her relatives the Haxthausens, Jenny helps the Grimms collect tales. The Wars of Liberation begin. In the aftermath of the Battle of Leipzig in October, the French are driven out of Hessen and in November the Hessian elector returns from exile. In December, Jacob successfully petitions the elector for an appointment as secretary to a diplomatic legation and leaves days later for France.

1814   In February, Wilhelm receives a secretarial position at the library in Kassel. In summer, Jacob returns home from France but spends only a few months in Kassel before departing to Vienna, where he is part of the Hessian legation at the Congress of Vienna (1814–15).

1815   At the end of February, Napoleon escapes from his exile in Elba. He enters Paris on March 20. The Grimms' aunt Henriette Zimmer dies on April 15. In June, Napoleon is defeated at Waterloo and the Napoleonic Wars end; at the Congress of Vienna, the German Confederation is founded. Jacob leaves Vienna to return to Kassel, but just months later must travel once again to Paris. The Grimms publish their editions of the *Poetic Edda* and *Poor Heinrich* as well as volume 2 of the first edition of *Children's and Household Tales*.

1816   Jacob receives the position of second librarian in Kassel. The first volume of the Grimms' *German Legends* is published. In Europe, weather changes lead to widespread crop failure and famine.

1818   The second volume of the Grimms' *German Legends* is published.

1819   In January, the Grimms receive honorary doctorates from the University of Marburg. The second edition of the Grimms' *Children's and Household Tales* and the first volume of Jacob's *German Grammar* are published. The Carlsbad Decrees curtail press freedoms, dissolve student organizations, and clamp down on reformers' constitutional goals.

1820   Between late 1820 and the end of 1822, Wilhelm spends around three hours a week tutoring the teenaged Hessian crown prince Friedrich Wilhelm, who will later reign as the last elector of Hessen.

1821   Wilhelm publishes *On German Runes*. Hessian Elector Wilhelm I dies and is succeeded by Wilhelm II.

1822   A revised edition of Jacob's *German Grammar* is published. It contains the description of sound shift that later comes to be known as "Grimm's Law." The third volume of the second edition of *Children's and Household Tales* appears. Lotte marries Ludwig Hassenpflug.

1823   In London, Edgar Taylor publishes the first volume (of two) of *German Popular Stories*, a freely translated edition of a subset of tales from the Grimms' *Children's and Household Tales*. The Grimms suggest to their publisher that a similar abridged edition be published in Germany.

1825   Wilhelm marries Henriette Dorothea ("Dortchen") Wild on May 15. The first Small Edition of *Children's and Household Tales* is published in December. In total, ten Small Editions appear over the course of the Grimms' lifetimes.

1826   Wilhelm and Dortchen's son Jacob is born on April 3 and dies on December 15. The Grimms publish *Irish Elf Tales*, a German translation of the first volume of a collection by Thomas Crofton Croker. Jacob publishes the second part of *German Grammar*.

1828   Wilhelm and Dortchen's son Herman is born on January 6. Jacob publishes a study of Germanic law.

1829   Passed over for promotions at the library in Kassel, the Grimms accept positions at the University of Göttingen in the Kingdom of Hanover. Wilhelm publishes his study of the German heroic saga.

1830   Wilhelm and Dortchen's son Rudolf is born on March 31. Wilhelm publishes a facsimile of the *Lay of Hildebrand*. The July Revolution occurs in Paris and reverberates throughout the German-speaking lands.

1831   In January, rioters take over the Göttingen city hall and sentry points. Achim von Arnim dies on January 21. A cholera pandemic that had begun in 1827 reaches Germany. Jacob publishes the third part of *German Grammar*.

1832   Wilhelm and Dortchen's daughter Auguste is born on August 21. Ludwig becomes a professor at the art academy in Kassel and marries Marie Böttner. Otto von Bismarck studies law at Göttingen (until 1833).

1833   The Grimms' sister Lotte dies on June 15. In Göttingen, Wilhelm Weber and Carl Friedrich Gauss develop the first electromagnetic telegraph.

1834   Jacob publishes his comparative study of versions of the medieval beast epic *Reynard the Fox*.

1835   Jacob publishes the first edition of *German Mythology*.

1837	Ernst August, Duke of Cumberland, becomes King of Hanover. The third edition of *Children's and Household Tales* is published and the fourth part of *German Grammar*. In September, the University of Göttingen celebrates the centenary of its opening. In November, Ernst August annuls the 1833 constitution. Together with five other professors, Jacob and Wilhelm Grimm protest the king's actions and are dismissed from their positions on December 14. Jacob and two other professors are forced to leave the Kingdom of Hanover within three days. Jacob flees to Kassel, while Wilhelm and his family temporarily remain in Göttingen.
1838	In January, Jacob writes "Jacob Grimm on His Dismissal." It is published in Basel in April. The Grimms embark on work for the *German Dictionary*. In October, Wilhelm and his family leave Göttingen to join Jacob in Kassel.
1840	Jacob publishes a third, revised edition of the first volume of *German Grammar* and parts 1 and 2 of his collection of historical texts related to German legal customs and guidance. The Grimms publish the fourth edition of *Children's and Household Tales*. In Prussia, Friedrich Wilhelm IV ascends the throne. Toward the end of the year, the Grimms accept an offer to move to Berlin to pursue their scholarship and work on the dictionary with an annual salary.
1841	In March, the Grimms move to Berlin. In the coming years, they periodically lecture at the University of Berlin.
1842	Clemens Brentano dies on July 28. Jacob publishes part 3 of his collection of legal customs.
1843	The Grimms publish the fifth edition of *Children's and Household Tales*. Jacob travels to Italy.
1844	Ferdinand Grimm dies on January 6. The Grimms have a falling out with the poet August Heinrich Hoffmann von Fallersleben in what becomes known as the "Hoffmann Affair." Jacob travels to Denmark and Sweden and publishes a revised edition of *German Mythology*.
1846	In September, the Grimms attend the conference of Germanists in Frankfurt. Jacob is elected chair.
1847	Germanists gather in Lübeck for a second conference. Jacob is again elected chair.
1848	The February Revolution in Paris sparks the March Revolution in Prussia and elsewhere. In May, Jacob begins serving as a representative at the National Assembly, held in Frankfurt at St. Paul's Church. He returns to Kassel after only four months. Jacob publishes his two-volume *History of the German Language*.
1850	The sixth edition of *Children's and Household Tales* is published.

1851   Karl Lachmann dies on March 13.

1852   The first installment of volume 1 of the Grimms' *German Dictionary* is published. Carl Grimm dies on May 25.

1854   The first volume of the Grimms' *German Dictionary* is published in full. Jacob publishes a revised edition of his study of Germanic law.

1856   The Grimms publish a revised edition of the third volume (containing notes and related scholarly material) of *Children's and Household Tales.*

1857   The seventh edition of *Children's and Household Tales* is published.

1859   Wilhelm Grimm dies in Berlin on December 16.

1860   The second volume of the *German Dictionary* is published.

1861   Jacob is at Savigny's bedside when he dies on October 25.

1862   The third volume of the *German Dictionary* is published.

1863   Jacob publishes part 4 of his collection of legal customs. (Parts 5 and 6 are published posthumously in 1866 and 1869.) Ludwig Emil Grimm dies on April 4. Jacob Grimm dies in Berlin on September 20.

1867   Dortchen Grimm dies on August 22.

1871   The unification of Germany takes place. Prussian King Wilhelm I is crowned German Emperor and Otto von Bismarck becomes chancellor.

1961   The final volume of the *German Dictionary* is published. A volume of sources is published in 1971.

1985–1986   The bicentennial years of the Grimms' births are celebrated with academic events, publications, and media coverage.

2005   *Children's and Household Tales* is designated a UNESCO "Memory of the World" heritage document.

2012   The bicentennial of the publication of the first volume of the Grimms' *Children's and Household Tales* is celebrated.

Genealogy

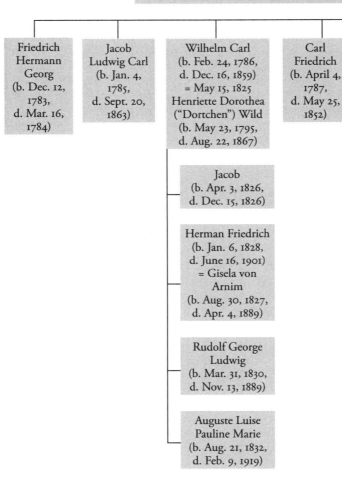

Philipp Wilhelm Grimm (b. Sept. 19, 1751, d. Jan. 10, 1796) =

Friedrich Hermann Georg (b. Dec. 12, 1783, d. Mar. 16, 1784)

Jacob Ludwig Carl (b. Jan. 4, 1785, d. Sept. 20, 1863)

Wilhelm Carl (b. Feb. 24, 1786, d. Dec. 16, 1859) = May 15, 1825 Henriette Dorothea ("Dortchen") Wild (b. May 23, 1795, d. Aug. 22, 1867)

Carl Friedrich (b. April 4, 1787, d. May 25, 1852)

Ferdinand Philipp (b. Dec. 18, 1788, d. Jan. 6, 1844)

Jacob (b. Apr. 3, 1826, d. Dec. 15, 1826)

Herman Friedrich (b. Jan. 6, 1828, d. June 16, 1901) = Gisela von Arnim (b. Aug. 30, 1827, d. Apr. 4, 1889)

Rudolf George Ludwig (b. Mar. 31, 1830, d. Nov. 13, 1889)

Auguste Luise Pauline Marie (b. Aug. 21, 1832, d. Feb. 9, 1919)

Feb. 23, 1783 Dorothea Zimmer (b. Nov. 20, 1755, d. May 27, 1808)

Ludwig Emil
(b. Mar. 14, 1790,
d. April 4, 1863)
= May 25, 1832
Marie Elisabeth
Böttner
(b. Aug. 9, 1803,
d. Aug. 15, 1842)

= Apr. 14, 1845
Friederike Ernst
(b. Dec. 24, 1806,
d. 1894)

(with M. E.
Böttner)
Friederike
("Ideke") Lotte
Amalia Maria
(b. July 23, 1833,
d. Dec. 17, 1914)
= Rudolf von
Eschwege
(b. Jan. 22, 1821,
d. Nov. 24, 1875)

(with M. E.
Böttner)
Unnamed son
(b. 1836, d. 1836
at four
weeks old)

Friedrich
(b. June 15,
1791, d. Aug.
20, 1792)

Charlotte Amalie
("Lotte") (b. May 10,
1793, d. June 15, 1833)
= July 2, 1822 Hans
Daniel Ludwig Friedrich
("Ludwig") Hassenpflug
(b. Feb. 26, 1794, d. Oct.
10, 1862)

Carl
(b. Jan. 5, 1824,
d. Feb. 18, 1890)

Agnes
(b. Dec. 11, 1825,
d. Oct. 29, 1826)

Friedrich
(b. Sept. 10, 1827,
d. Jan. 23, 1892)

Bertha
(b. Apr. 27, 1829,
d. June 9, 1830)

Ludwig
(b. Dec. 1, 1831,
d. Oct. 11, 1878)

Dorothea
(b. May 23, 1833,
d. Jan. 24, 1898)

Georg Eduard
(b. July 26,
1794,
d. April 19,
1795)

Notes

ABBREVIATIONS

AANS   Reinhold Steig and Herman Grimm, eds. *Achim von Arnim und die ihm nahe standen.* 3 vols. Stuttgart/Frankfurt: Cotta, 1894–1913.

ATBG   Jacob Grimm and Wilhelm Grimm. *Actenstücke über die Thätigkeit der Brüder Grimm im hessischen Staatsdienste.* Vol. 2 of Jacob and Wilhelm Grimm, *Private und amtliche Beziehungen der Brüder Grimm zu Hessen: Eine Sammlung von Briefen und Actenstücken, als Festschrift zum hundertsten Geburtstag Wilhelm Grimms den 24. Februar 1886.* Ed. E. Stengel. 3 vols. Marburg: N. G. Elwertsche Verlagsbuchhandlung, 1886.

BABG   Bettina von Arnim, Jacob Grimm, and Wilhelm Grimm. *Der Briefwechsel Bettina von Arnims mit den Brüdern Grimm, 1838–1841.* Ed. Hartwig Schultz. Frankfurt: Insel, 1985.

BBG   Jacob Grimm and Wilhelm Grimm. *Briefe der Brüder Grimm.* Ed. Hans Gürtler and Albert Leitzmann. Jena: Verlag der Frommannschen Buchhandlung, 1923.

BBGB   Jacob Grimm and Wilhelm Grimm. *Briefe der Brüder Jacob und Wilhelm Grimm an Georg Friedrich Benecke aus den Jahren 1808–1829.* Ed. Wilhelm Müller. Göttingen: Vandenhoeck & Ruprecht, 1889.

BBGS   Jacob Grimm and Wilhelm Grimm. *Briefe der Brüder Grimm an Savigny.* Ed. Ingeborg Schnack and Wilhelm Schoof. Berlin: Erich Schmidt Verlag, 1953.

BGDG   Eduard Ippel, ed. *Briefwechsel zwischen Jacob und Wilhelm Grimm, Dahlmann und Gervinus.* 2 vols. Berlin: Dümmlers, 1885.

BGHF   Jacob Grimm and Wilhelm Grimm. *Briefe der Brüder Grimm an hessische Freunde*. Vol. 1 of Jacob and Wilhelm Grimm, *Private und amtliche Beziehungen der Brüder Grimm zu Hessen: Eine Sammlung von Briefen und Actenstücken, als Festschrift zum hundertsten Geburtstag Wilhelm Grimms den 24. Februar 1886*. Ed. E. Stengel. 3 vols. Marburg: N. G. Elwert'sche Verlagsbuchhandlung, 1886–1910.

BGJ   Jacob Grimm and Wilhelm Grimm. *Briefwechsel zwischen Jacob und Wilhelm Grimm aus der Jugendzeit*. 2nd ed. Ed. Wilhelm Schoof. Weimar: Hermann Böhlaus Nachfolger, 1963.

BGKL   Albert Leitzmann, ed. *Briefwechsel der Brüder Jacob und Wilhelm Grimm mit Karl Lachmann*. 2 vols. Jena: Verlag der Frommannschen Buchhandlung, 1927.

BGPW   Jacob Grimm and Wilhelm Grimm. *Briefe der Brüder Grimm an Paul Wigand*. Vol. 3 of Jacob and Wilhelm Grimm, *Private und amtliche Beziehungen der Brüder Grimm zu Hessen*. Ed. E. Stengel. 3 vols. Marburg: N. G. Elwert'sche Verlagsbuchhandlung, 1886–1910.

BJWG   Jacob Grimm and Wilhelm Grimm. *Briefwechsel zwischen Jacob und Wilhelm Grimm*. Ed. Heinz Rölleke. Vol. 1.1 of *Jacob und Wilhelm Grimm: Briefwechsel: Kritische Ausgabe*. Stuttgart: S. Hirzel Verlag, 2001.

BLH   Jacob Grimm and Wilhelm Grimm. *Briefwechsel mit Ludwig Hassenpflug*. Ed. Ewald Grothe. Vol. 2 of *Werke und Briefwechsel der Brüder Grimm*. Kassel: Verlag der Brüder Grimm-Gesellschaft, 2000.

BMG   Camillus Wendeler, ed. *Briefwechsel des Freiherrn Karl Hartwig Gregor von Meusebach mit Jacob und Wilhelm Grimm*. Heilbronn: Verlag von Gebr. Henninger, 1880.

CBBG   Reinhold Steig, ed. *Clemens Brentano und die Brüder Grimm*. Bern: Herbert Lang, 1969. Reprint of the edition first published 1914 by J. G. Cotta in Stuttgart and Berlin.

FWJG   Jacob Grimm and Wilhelm Grimm. *Freundesbriefe von Wilhelm und Jacob Grimm*. Ed. Alexander Reifferscheid. Heilbronn: Verlag von Gebr. Henninger, 1878.

JGKS   Jacob Grimm. *Kleinere Schriften*. Ed. K. Müllerhoff and Eduard Ippel. 8 vols. Hildesheim: Olms, 1965. Reprint of the edition first published 1864–90 by F. Dümmler in Berlin (vols. 1–7) and C. Bertelsmann in Gütersloh (vol. 8).

KHM1   Jacob Grimm and Wilhelm Grimm. *Kinder- und Hausmärchen der Brüder Grimm: Vollständige Ausgabe in der Urfassung*. Ed. Friedrich Panzer. Wiesbaden: Vollmer, 1956.

KHM2   Jacob Grimm and Wilhelm Grimm. *Kinder- und Hausmärchen: Nach der zweiten vermehrten und verbesserten Auflage von 1819, textkritisch revidiert und mit einer Biographie der Grimmschen Märchen versehen.* Ed. Heinz Rölleke. 2 vols. Cologne: Diederichs, 1982.

KHM3 Jacob Grimm and Wilhelm Grimm. *Kinder- und Hausmärchen gesammelt durch die Brüder Grimm: Vollständige Ausgabe auf der Grundlage der dritten Auflage (1837).* Ed. Heinz Rölleke. Frankfurt: Deutscher Klassiker Verlag, 1985.

KHM4 Jacob Grimm and Wilhelm Grimm. *Kinder- und Hausmärchen gesammelt durch die Brüder Grimm.* 4th ed. 2 vols. Göttingen: Druck und Verlag der Dieterichischen Buchhandlung, 1840.

KHM7 Jacob Grimm and Wilhelm Grimm. *Kinder- und Hausmärchen: Ausgabe letzter Hand mit den Originalanmerkungen der Brüder Grimm.* Ed. Heinz Rölleke. 3 vols. Stuttgart: Reclam, 2001.

WGKS Wilhelm Grimm. *Kleinere Schriften.* Ed. Gustav Hinrichs. 4 vols. Berlin: F. Dümmlers Verlagsbuchhandlung, 1881–87.

Introduction

1. The book was presumably *Deutsche Märchen* (German fairy tales), first published in 1939 for the Reemtsma tobacco company and sold at cigarette stands around Germany. See Hiram Kümper, "Nichts als blauer Dunst? Zigarettensammelbilder als Medien historischer Sinnbildung," *Geschichte in Wissenschaft und Unterricht* 59 (2008): 492–508; Carolin Raffelsbauer, *Paul Hey—Der Maler heiler Welten,* vol. 1 (Munich: Herbert Utz Verlag, 2007); Erik Lindner, *Die Reemtsmas: Geschichte einer deutschen Unternehmerfamilie* (Hamburg: Hoffmann und Campe, 2007), esp. 110–13; and Heinz-Peter Mielke, *Vom Bilderbuch des Kleinen Mannes: Über Sammelmarken, Sammelbilder und Sammelalben* (Cologne: Rheinland-Verlag, 1982).

2. Ann Schmiesing, "A Bicentennial Trio: Reading the *Kinder- und Hausmärchen* in the Context of the Grimms' *Deutsche Sagen* and Edition of *Der arme Heinrich,*" *Colloquia Germanica* 45 (2012): 354–68 (354).

3. In German: "Und wenn sie nicht gestorben sind, dann leben sie noch heute." Unless otherwise noted, all translations are my own.

4. The tale is "Foundling," and it is not particularly well-known even in Germany. Most Grimm tales do not end with direct statements of enduring happiness; instead, the final sentence might specify the punishment meted out to the evildoers (as in "Cinderella"), consist of a short rhyme only indirectly related to the plot (as in "Hansel and Gretel"), or simply state that the hero or heroine married or acquired a kingdom.

5. Hessen is also known in English as "Hesse." See the Note on Orthography and Translations.

6. Ambrose Merton [William John Thoms], "Folk-Lore," *Athenaeum: Journal of Literature, Science, and the Fine Arts,* no. 982 (August 22, 1846): 862–63 (863). As Thoms observed, before his coining of "folklore" terms such as "popular antiquities" or "popular literature" tended to be used in English. He appears to have been unaware of the rare Old English compound "folc-lār," which meant "homily" or "sermon"; see

OED Online, s.v. "folklore, n.," accessed November 13, 2023, https://doi.org/10.1093/
OED/1811933811. Regarding inconsistencies in definitions of "folklore" from Thoms
to the twenty-first century, see Linda Dégh, *Legend and Belief: Dialectics of a Folklore
Genre* (Bloomington: Indiana University Press, 2001), 29–34. For a discussion of the
relationship of "folklore" to the German term *Volkskunde*, see Peter Tokofsky, "Folk-
Lore and Volks-Kunde: Compounding Compounds," *Journal of Folklore Research* 33,
no. 3 (1996): 207–11.

7. Letter from Jacob to Achim von Arnim, December 31, 1812, *AANS* 3:255.
8. Heinz Rölleke, *"Nebeninschriften": Brüder Grimm—Arnim und Brentano—
   Droste-Hülshoff: Literarische Studien* (Bonn: Bouvier, 1980), 1–15.
9. Jack Zipes, *The Brothers Grimm: From Enchanted Forests to the Modern World*, 2nd ed.
   (New York: Palgrave Macmillan, 2002); Donald R. Hettinga, *The Brothers Grimm: Two
   Lives, One Legacy* (New York: Clarion, 2001); Ruth Michaelis-Jena, *The Brothers Grimm*
   (New York: Praeger, 1970); Murray B. Peppard, *Paths through the Forest: A Biography of
   the Brothers Grimm* (New York: Holt, Rinehart, and Winston, 1971); Steffen Martus, *Die
   Brüder Grimm: Eine Biographie* (1st ed., Berlin: Rowohlt, 2009; 3rd ed., Reinbek: Ro-
   wohlt Taschenbuch, 2017). See also Hans-Georg Schede, *Die Brüder Grimm* (Munich:
   dtv, 2004). Recent Grimm scholarship includes Axel Winzer, *Permanente Metamorphosen: Neues zur Verlags- und Editionsgeschichte der Kinder- und Hausmärchen der Brüder
   Grimm* (Marburg: Büchner-Verlag, 2021); Philip Kraut, *Die Arbeitsweise der Brüder
   Grimm* (Stuttgart: S. Hirzel Verlag, 2023); and Jakob Norberg, *The Brothers Grimm and
   the Making of German Nationalism* (Cambridge: Cambridge University Press, 2022).
10. Ludwig Denecke, *Jacob Grimm und sein Bruder Wilhelm* (Stuttgart: J. B. Metzler,
    1971).
11. Adolf Stoll, *Der junge Savigny: Kinderjahre, Marburger und Landshuter Zeit Friedrich
    Karl von Savignys* (Berlin: Carl Heymanns Verlag, 1927), 49; letter from Brentano to
    Jacob and Wilhelm, January 1811, *CBBG* 155; letter from Achim von Arnim to Jacob
    and Wilhelm, December 24, 1812, *AANS* 3:252.
12. Jacob Grimm, *Deutsche Grammatik*, pt. 1 (Göttingen: In der Dieterichschen Buch-
    handlung, 1819), xii.

Chapter 1. Childhood Memories, 1785–1796

1. KHM7 1:20. This description first appeared in the preface to the second edition of
   Children's and Household Tales, published in 1819.
2. See the 2012 inventory of German forests (*Bundeswaldinventur*) available at https://
   www.bundeswaldinventur.de/fileadmin/SITE_MASTER/content/Diagramme/Die
   _Waldverteilung_in_Deutschland.jpg (accessed June 16, 2023); Tacitus, *"Agricola" and
   "Germany,"* ed. and trans. Anthony R. Birley (Oxford: Oxford University Press, 1999),
   53; KHM7 1:20.
3. William Jacob, *A View of the Agriculture, Manufactures, Statistics, and State of Society,
   of Germany, and Parts of Holland and France: Taken during a Journey through Those
   Countries in 1819* (London: John Murray, 1820), 379, 383, 377.
4. James Boswell, *The Journal of His German and Swiss Travels, 1764*, ed. Marlies K.
   Danziger (New Haven, CT: Yale University Press, 2008), 191–92; Fynes Moryson, *An*

Itinerary Concerning His Ten Yeeres Travell through the Twelve Dominions of Germany, Bohmerland, Sweitzerland, Netherland, Denmarke, Poland, Italy, Turky, France, England, Scotland, and Ireland, 4 vols. (Glasgow: James MacLehose and Sons, 1907–8), 3:454–55.

5. Jacob described himself in 1826 as a "quintessential Hessian, who gladly appreciates the advantages of other regions over my fatherland, and yet stubbornly adheres to it"; Jacob Grimm et al., "Briefe von Jacob und Wilhelm Grimm, Karl Lachmann, Creuzer und Joseph von Lassberg an F. J. Mone, I," ed. Max Freiherr von Waldberg, *Neue Heidelberger Jahrbücher* 7 (1897): 68–94 (89).

6. *Landgraf* literally means "land count," but this German noble rank was equivalent not so much to a count as to the higher rank of duke (*Herzog*), insofar as landgraves, like dukes, exercised sovereign rights and were not subject to intermediate powers.

7. Voltaire, *Essai sur les mœurs et l'esprit des nations*, vol. 24 of *Les Œuvres completes de Voltaire*, ed. Bruno Bernard, John Renwick, Nicholas Cronk, and Janet Godden (Oxford: Voltaire Foundation, 2011), 41; Mark Jarrett, *The Congress of Vienna and Its Legacy: War and Great Power Diplomacy after Napoleon* (London: I. B. Tauris, 2013), 10.

8. Bodo Nischan, *Lutherans and Calvinists in the Age of Confessionalism* (Aldershot, UK: Ashgate, 1999), ix; Philip Benedict, *Christ's Churches Purely Reformed: A Social History of Calvinism* (New Haven, CT: Yale University Press, 2002), xxiii.

9. Letter from Jacob to Karl Hartwig Gregor von Meusebach, December 24, 1822, *BMG* 6. For a genealogy of the Grimm family, see Heinrich Bott, "Die Vorfahren der Brüder Grimm im Hanauer Land," in *Brüder Grimm Gedenken 1963*, ed. Ludwig Denecke and Ina-Maria Greverus (Marburg: Elwert, 1963), 23–47.

10. *Memoirs of the Court of Westphalia under Jerome Bonaparte; with Anecdotes of His Favourites, Ministers, etc.* (London: Henry Colborn & Co., 1820), 3; William VIII, letter of April 7, 1745, qtd. by Moriz von Rauch, "Politik Hessen-Kassels im österreichischen Erbfolgekrieg bis zum Dresdener Frieden" (PhD diss., University of Marburg, 1897), 122.

11. Winfried Speitkamp, "Die Landgrafschaft Hessen-Kassel und die Französische Revolution," *Hessisches Jahrbuch für Landesgeschichte* 40 (1990): 145–67 (148); Fritz Wolff, "Absolutismus und Aufklärung in Hessen-Kassel 1730–1806," in *Die Geschichte Hessens*, ed. Uwe Schultz (Stuttgart: Konrad Theiss, 1983), 133–44 (143).

12. Frederik Ohles, *Germany's Rude Awakening: Censorship in the Land of the Brothers Grimm* (Kent, OH: Kent State University Press, 1992), 13; Jacob, *View of the Agriculture*, 383–85. For centuries, Hanau had served as the capital of the County of Hanau. Twice in its history, the county had been divided into the County of Hanau-Münzenberg (in which the town of Hanau lay) and the County of Hanau-Lichtenberg. In 1736 the Landgraviate of Hessen-Kassel inherited Hanau-Münzenberg. It became a secundogeniture for younger princes of Hessen-Kassel such as Friedrich II's son Wilhelm.

13. A. Winkler and J. Mittelsdorf, *Die Bau- und Kunstdenkmäler der Stadt Hanau* (Hanau: Kommissionsverlag von G. M. Alberti, 1897), 18.

14. Erich Kleeberg, "Stadtschreiber und Stadtbücher in Mühlhausen i. Th. vom 14.–16. Jahrhundert nebst einer Übersicht über die Editionen mittelalterlicher Stadtbücher; Erstes Kapitel" (PhD diss., University of Göttingen, 1909), 33.

15. The area where Parade Square (Paradeplatz) lay is today known as Freedom Square (Freiheitsplatz).

16. Jacob conveyed many of his memories of Hanau in an autobiographical essay he wrote in Dijon in 1814, reproduced in *200 Jahre Brüder Grimm: Dokumente ihres Lebens und Wirkens*, ed. Dieter Hennig and Bernhard Lauer (Kassel: Verlag Weber & Weidemeyer, 1985), 141–42, 157–60. He also imparted memories of Hanau in a letter of December 20, 1858, to Luise Gies; *BGHF* 16–18.

17. Their grandparents lived in a house owned by Martin Dienald, the city wall master, at Johanneskirchgasse 9, not far from the Lutheran church; Heinrich Bott, *Die Altstadt Hanau: Baugeschichte, Häuserverzeichnis, Bilder: Ein Gedenkbuch zur 650-Jahrfeier der Altstadt Hanau* (Hanau: Verlag des Hanauer Geschichtsvereins, 1953), 138.

18. Wilhelm Praesent, *Märchenhaus des deutschen Volkes* (Kassel: Bärenreiter-Verlag Kassel, 1957), 11; Landesgeschichtliches Informationssystem Hessen (State Historical Information System of Hessen), http://www.lagis-hessen.de/de/subjects/xsrec/id/12557/current/3/sn/ol?q=YTozOntzOjM6Im9ydCI7czo3OiJTdGGVpbmF1IjtzOjEwOiJocnVuazllcmVuVuIjtzOjE6IjEiO3M6NTToib3JkZXIiO3M6Mzoib3J0Ijt9 (accessed June 16, 2023); *Neueste Kunde von Meklenburg, Kur-Hessen, Hessen-Darmstadt und den freien Städten, aus den besten Quellen bearbeitet* (Weimar, 1823), 344; Irma Hildebrandt, *Es waren ihrer Fünf: Die Brüder Grimm und ihre Familie* (Cologne: Eugen Dietrichs Verlag, 1984), 24.

19. Ludwig Emil Grimm recalled these and other memories of the Grimms' home and upbringing in Steinau in his memoir *Erinnerungen aus meinem Leben,* ed. Adolf Stoll (Leipzig: Hesse & Becker Verlag, 1913), esp. 30–33.

20. Friedrich Wilhelm Haberland, *Der Amtmann zu Reinhausen oder Franks Geheimnisse* (Leipzig: Karl Franz Köhler, 1818), 133–34. Similar portrayals can be found in Gustav von Heeringen's historical novella *Des Amtmanns Pflegling: Historische Novelle aus den Zeiten des ersten schlesischen Krieges*, 2 vols. (Leipzig: Gustav Mayer, 1846); and Friedrich Kaiser's play *Wer wird Amtmann? oder, Des Vaters Grab: Lokales Lebensbild mit Gesang in 2 Acten* (Vienna: A. Pichler, 1842), 9.

21. Grimm, *Erinnerungen aus meinem Leben*, 32.

22. Jacob and Wilhelm Grimm, *Deutsches Wörterbuch*, vol. 1 (Leipzig: S. Hirzel, 1854), 282; qtd. in Praesent, *Märchenhaus des deutschen Volkes*, 17; Samuel Richardson, *The History of Sir Charles Grandison* (London: G. Routledge and Sons, 1924), v. Dorothea was also known to recite passages from a drama by Christian Fürchtegott Gellert in which she had played a role in a childhood production.

23. Grimm, *Erinnerungen aus meinem Leben*, 32, 37; Hennig and Lauer, *200 Jahre Brüder Grimm*, 158.

24. Hennig and Lauer, *200 Jahre Brüder Grimm*, 159–60.

25. Grimm, *Erinnerungen aus meinem Leben*, 38–39; "Selbstbiographie," JGKS 1:1–24 (2).

26. Ernst Hartmann, *Geschichte der Stadt und des Amtes Steinau a. d. Straße*, 3 vols. (Steinau: Stadt Steinau, 1975), 3:208; Ludwig Emil Grimm, *Briefe*, ed. Egbert Koolman, 2 vols. (Marburg: N. G. Elwert Verlag, 1985), 1:9, 1:19, 2:831. Jochil Strauss was also referred to as Jochil Kiefe.

27. Gerd Bockwoldt, "Das Bild des Juden in den Märchen der Brüder Grimm," *Zeitschrift für Religions- und Geistesgeschichte* 63, no. 3 (2011): 234–49 (238–39); Gerhard Henschel, "'etwas vorlautes widriges': Das Judenbild der Brüder Grimm," *Merkur* 846 (2019): 79–87.

28. "Selbstbiographie," JGKS 1:1–2; Bodo Nischan, "Ritual and Protestant Identity in Late Reformation Germany," in *Protestant History and Identity in Sixteenth-Century Europe*, ed. Bruce Gordon (Brookfield, VT: Scolar Press, 1996), 142–58 (151); Bridget Heal, "'Better Papist Than Calvinist': Art and Identity in Later Lutheran Germany," *German History* 29, no. 4 (2011): 584–609. Lutherans in Hessen had nevertheless not practiced the exorcism rite in baptism; Bodo Nischan, "The Exorcism Controversy and Baptism in the Late Reformation," *The Sixteenth Century Journal* 18, no. 1 (1987): 31–52 (33).

29. "Selbstbiographie," JGKS 1:2.

30. Hartmann, *Geschichte der Stadt und des Amtes Steinau a. d. Straße*, 3:76.

31. Grimm, *Erinnerungen aus meinem Leben*, 51–53.

32. Grimm, 33–34; "Selbstbiographie," JGKS 1:1.

33. See, for example, the descriptions of Wilhelm's dreams in November 1811 and March 1813 in Praesent, *Märchenhaus des deutschen Volkes*, 21–23; and *BBGS* 266.

Chapter 2. Transition to Adulthood, 1796–1805

1. Hartmann, *Geschichte der Stadt und des Amtes Steinau a. d. Straße*, 2:260; Hildebrandt, *Es waren ihrer Fünf*, 35–37; Martus, *Die Brüder Grimm*, 34. The *Reichstaler*, or simply *Taler*, was the primary monetary unit of Hessen-Kassel; however, in Hanau and the region known as Upper Hessen the currency of Frankfurt (the guilder, or florin) was also used. See Gregory W. Pedlow, *The Survival of the Hessian Nobility, 1770–1870* (Princeton, NJ: Princeton University Press, 1988), 270.

2. Letter from Johann Hermann Zimmer to Jacob, May 11, 1796, in Hennig and Lauer, *200 Jahre Brüder Grimm*, 164.

3. Ohles, *Germany's Rude Awakening*, 17.

4. Friedrich Lometsch, *Wilhelmshöhe: Natur und Formgeist in dem schönsten Bergpark Europas: Alte Ansichten und Pläne nebst einer Beschreibung von W. Döring aus dem Jahre 1804* (Kassel: Friedrich Lometsch Verlag, 1961), 82.

5. Letter from Johann Hermann Zimmer to Jacob and Wilhelm, October 6, 1798, and letter from Johann Hermann Zimmer to Henriette Zimmer, October 12, 1798, both in Hennig and Lauer, *200 Jahre Brüder Grimm*, 171; letter from Dorothea Grimm to Wilhelm, October 27, 1798, in *Die Brüder Grimm: Ihr Leben und Werk*, ed. Hermann Gerstner (Ebenhausen bei München: Wilhelm Langewiesche-Brandt, 1952), 23.

6. Letter from Jacob to Dorothea Grimm, September 30, 1798, in Gerstner, *Die Brüder Grimm*, 22.

7. Nadine Akkerman and Birgit Houben, introduction to *The Politics of Female Households: Ladies-in-Waiting across Early Modern Europe*, ed. Akkerman and Houben (Leiden: Brill, 2014), 5; Jeroen Duindam, "The Politics of Female Households: Afterthoughts," in Akkerman and Houben, *Politics of Female Households*, 365–70 (366).

8. Qtd. in Annette von Stieglitz, "Hof und Hofgesellschaft der Residenz Kassel in der zweiten Hälfte des 18. Jahrhunderts," in *Kassel im 18. Jahrhundert: Residenz und Stadt*, ed. Heide Wunder, Christina Vanja, and Karl-Hermann Wegner (Kassel: Euregio, 2000), 321–49 (341–42). See also Wolff, "Absolutismus und Aufklärung in Hessen-Kassel," 144; and F. Piderit, *Geschichte der Haupt- und Residenzstadt Kassel* (Kassel: Wilhelm Appel, 1844), 365.

9. "Selbstbiographie," JGKS 1:3–4; Johann Christian Krieger, *Cassel in historisch-topographischer Hinsicht: Nebst einer Geschichte und Beschreibung von Wilhelmshöhe und seinen Anlagen* (Marburg, 1805), 325–26; George J. Metcalf, *Forms of Address in German (1500–1800)* (St. Louis: Washington University Studies, 1938), 147–53.

10. See Jacob's letter of October 10, 1802, to Paul Wigand, and editor's note, *BGPW* 19–20, 333–34.

11. Letter from Wilhelm to Otto von der Malsburg, May 18, 1802, *Wilhelm Grimm: Aus seinem Leben*, ed. Wilhelm Schoof (Bonn: Ferd. Dümmlers Verlag, 1960), 28; letters from Jacob to Paul Wigand, September 7, May 15, November 13, 1802, *BGPW* 17, 1, 22.

12. Letters from Jacob Grimm to Paul Wigand, May 15, August 12, 1802, *BGHF* 1–2.

13. H. Hermelink and S. A. Kaehler, *Die Philipps-Universität zu Marburg, 1527–1927: Fünf Kapitel aus ihrer Geschichte (1527–1866)* (Marburg: Elwert, 1927), 416–17, 462; Charles E. McClelland, *State, Society, and University in Germany, 1700–1914* (Cambridge: Cambridge University Press, 1980), 63–64, 70; Alfred Höck, "Die Brüder Grimm als Studenten in Marburg," in Denecke and Greverus, *Brüder Grimm Gedenken 1963*, 67–96 (84). Instead of moving the University of Marburg to Kassel, the government relocated professors at the Collegium Carolinum in Kassel to Marburg.

14. Schoof, *Wilhelm Grimm*, 43.

15. "Selbstbiographie," JGKS 1:5. The exact circumstances under which Malsburg received the scholarship are unknown, due to a lack of records; see Adolf Stoll's comments in Grimm, *Erinnerungen aus meinem Leben*, 584.

16. Schoof, *Wilhelm Grimm*, 25, 29–30; Höck, "Die Brüder Grimm als Studenten in Marburg," 70.

17. "Selbstbiographie," JGKS 1:4–5; James Q. Whitman, *The Legacy of Roman Law in the German Romantic Era: Historical Vision and Legal Change* (Princeton, NJ: Princeton University Press, 1990), xiii, 80; McClelland, *State, Society, and University in Germany*, 117.

18. Whitman, *Legacy of Roman Law in the German Romantic Era*, xiv, 3.

19. Stoll, *Der junge Savigny*, 171–73.

20. Friedrich Carl von Savigny, "Ueber den Zweck dieser Zeitschrift," in *Zeitschrift für geschichtliche Rechtswissenschaft*, ed. Friedrich Carl von Savigny, C. F. Eichhorn, and J. F. L. Göschen (Berlin, 1815), 1–12 (6). In the late 1700s, Gustav Hugo, a professor at the University of Göttingen, developed a method for analyzing law historically, which was contrary to the prevailing natural law paradigm. However, Savigny's *Law of Possession* was the first text to present a systematic framework for historical analysis; Antonio Padoa-Schioppa, *A History of Law in Europe from the Early Middle Ages to the Twentieth Century* (Cambridge: Cambridge University Press, 2017), 521–22.

21. "Das Wort des Besitzes," JGKS 1:113–44 (115). Jacob also wrote of his intellectual debt to Savigny in his dedication of *German Grammar*.

22. Although written in Zurich, the manuscript was later housed in Heidelberg and then, from the second half of the seventeenth century, at the Royal Library in Paris. Today it is back in Heidelberg and often referred to as the Great Heidelberg Book of Songs (Große Heidelberger Liederhandschrift). *Minnelieder* typically portray unfulfilled physical and spiritual passion, and in so doing exalt the nobility of suffering; Barbara

Garvey Seagrave and Wesley Thomas, *The Songs of the Minnesingers* (Urbana: University of Illinois Press, 1966), 11.

23. Johann Jakob Bodmer and Johann Jakob Breitinger, eds., *Sammlung von Minnesingern aus dem schwaebischen Zeitpuncte*, 2 vols. (Zurich: Conrad Orell und Comp., 1758–59), 1:iv–v.

24. Letter from Friedrich II of Prussia to Christoph Heinrich Müller, February 22, 1784, in *Briefe Friedrichs des Großen*, 2 vols., ed. Max Hein (Berlin: Verlag von Reimar Hobbing, 1914), 2:257.

25. John A. McCarthy, "The 'Great Shapesphere': An Introduction," in *Shakespeare as German Author: Reception, Translation Theory, and Cultural Transfer*, ed. McCarthy (Leiden and Boston: Brill Rodopi, 2018), 1–74; "Über Ossian," 7:536–43, and "Zur Rede auf Wilhelm Grimm," 1:178–87 (186), both in JGKS. As Fiona J. Stafford has pointed out, throughout the reception of Macpherson's work the question of whether he was a forger for blending genuine material with passages of his own creation has depended on critics' definitions of forgery; *The Sublime Savage: A Study of James Macpherson and the Poems of Ossian* (Edinburgh: Edinburgh University Press, 1988), 170–71. Published in 1778 and 1779, Herder's two-volume collection of folk songs consisted mostly of translations of foreign songs; however, a few years later, in 1784, Anselm Elwert published a collection of songs that were largely German in origin. Herder and Elwert were influenced by not only Macpherson but also English bishop Thomas Percy, who published a three-volume collection of ballads and folk songs.

26. "Selbstbiographie," JGKS 1:6. On the face of it, Tieck's *Minnelieder from the Swabian Age* (1803), although published decades after Bodmer's and presented in modernized German, appeared "older"—printed as it was not in the roman type of Bodmer's collection but in Gothic typeface (Fraktur) and with a title page that archaicized Tieck's forename from "Ludwig" to "Ludewig"; Roger Paulin, "The Romantic Book as 'Gesamtkunstwerk,'" *Bulletin of the John Rylands University Library of Manchester* 71, no. 3 (1989): 47–62 (55, 60); Petra McGillen, "The Romantic Editor as Modern Media Practitioner: The Poetics of Reading in Ludwig Tieck's *Minnelieder* Anthology," *German Life and Letters* 70, no. 1 (2017): 57–78.

27. Friedrich Karl von Savigny, *The History of the Roman Law during the Middle Ages*, trans. E. Cathcart (1829; repr., Westport, CT: Hyperion, 1979), xii.

28. Letter from Achim von Arnim to Brentano, July 9, 1802, 1:38–39, and letter from Brentano to Achim von Arnim, September 6, 1802, 1:42, both in *AANS*. See also Roland Hoermann, *Achim von Arnim* (Boston: Twayne, 1984), 19–21.

29. Letter from Jacob to Brentano, December 15, 1810, *CBBG* 152.

30. Letter from Friedrich Carl von Savigny to Hans von Bostel, February 4, 1805, in Stoll, *Der junge Savigny*, 244; McClelland, *State, Society, and University in Germany*, 55.

31. Letter from Wilhelm to Jacob, February 2–13, 1805, *BJWG* 30.

Chapter 3. Contributions to Scholarship, 1805–1808

1. Letter from Dorothea Grimm to Jacob, February 24, 1805, in Gerstner, *Die Brüder Grimm*, 35.

2. Grimm, *Erinnerungen aus meinem Leben*, 582–83.

3. Letter from Jacob to Wilhelm, March 1, 1805, *BJWG* 39; Padoa-Schioppa, *History of Law in Europe*, 82.

4. Friedrich Karl von Savigny, *Geschichte des römischen Rechts im Mittelalter*, 2nd ed., 7 vols. (Heidelberg: J. C. B. Mohr, 1851), 1:xvi, 5:224.

5. Letter from Savigny to Hans von Bostel, February 4, 1805, 244 (see also 198–99), and letter from Savigny to Friedrich Creuzer, February 20, 1805, 244–45, both in Stoll, *Der junge Savigny*; letter from Jacob to Wilhelm, March 1, 1805, *BJWG* 39.

6. Letter from Wilhelm to Otto von der Malsburg, February 21, 1805, in Schoof, *Wilhelm Grimm*, 31; letters from Jacob to Wilhelm, July 12, 1805, August 4, 1805, *BGJ* 67, 69; letter from Wilhelm to Jacob, March 24, 1805, *BJWG* 52.

7. Jarrett, *Congress of Vienna and Its Legacy*, 28–30.

8. Qtd. in Sam A. Mustafa, *Napoleon's Paper Kingdom: The Life and Death of Westphalia, 1807–1813* (Lanham, MD: Rowman and Littlefield, 2017), 11.

9. Piderit, *Geschichte der Haupt- und Residenzstadt Kassel*, 373; Jarrett, *Congress of Vienna and Its Legacy*, 31.

10. "Selbstbiographie," WGKS 1:3–26 (11); "Das Wort des Besitzes," JGKS 1:114.

11. The northern Hessian town of Melsungen, for example, was made to pay wages and provide room and board for almost 2,500 French soldiers, which nearly equaled the town's number of Hessian inhabitants; L. Armbrust, "Melsungen zur westfälischen Zeit," *Zeitschrift des Vereins für hessische Geschichte und Landeskunde* 35 (1901): 1–30 (9); Mustafa, *Napoleon's Paper Kingdom*, 13, 15, 19; Piderit, *Geschichte der Haupt- und Residenzstadt Kassel*, 375.

12. Letter from Jacob to Savigny, November 16, 1806, *BBGS* 26.

13. "Über meine Entlassung," 1:25–56 (27), and "Das Wort des Besitzes," 1:114, both in JGKS; P. A. Winkopp, "Konstitution des Königreichs Westphalen," in *Der Rheinische Bund: Eine Zeitschrift historisch-politisch-statistisch-geographischen Inhalts*, ed. Winkopp, vol. 4 (Frankfurt am Main: Mohr, 1807), 472–501 (473).

14. Piderit, *Geschichte der Haupt- und Residenzstadt Kassel*, 383; Mustafa, *Napoleon's Paper Kingdom*, 53–64.

15. P. A. Winkopp, "Rede des Königs von Westphalen, als die gesammten Repräsentanten des Landes für sich und das Land, welches sie repräsentirten, dem Könige Gehorsam, der Konstitution Treue schwuren," in *Der Rheinische Bund: Eine Zeitschrift historisch-politisch-statistisch-geographischen Inhalts*, ed. Winkopp, vol. 5 (Frankfurt am Main: Mohr, 1808), 329–333 (330).

16. Ewald Grothe, "Model or Myth? The Constitution of Westphalia of 1807 and Early German Constitutionalism," *German Studies Review* 28, no. 1 (2005): 1–19 (4–5). The text of the constitution in French and German can be found in Winkopp, "Konstitution des Königreichs Westphalen," 474–501.

17. *Memoirs of the Court of Westphalia*, 6, 81.

18. Letters from Jacob to Savigny, January 26, March 9, 1807, *BBGS* 27, 30; "Selbstbiographie," 1:9, and "Das Wort des Besitzes," 1:114, both in JGKS. Because the Code Napoléon disrupted long-standing German interpretations and applications of Roman law, its implementation proved thorny. See Whitman, *Legacy of Roman Law*

in the German Romantic Era, 103; and Charles M. Radding and Antonio Ciaralli, *The Corpus Iuris Civilis in the Middle Ages: Manuscripts and Transmission from the Sixth Century to the Juristic Revival* (Leiden: Brill, 2014), 1.

19. Henriette Herz, *Henriette Herz: Ihr Leben und ihre Erinnerungen*, ed. J. Fürst, 2nd ed. (Berlin: Wilhelm Herz, 1858), 310–11.

20. Johann Jakob Bodmer published parts of the *Nibelungenlied* in 1757. In 1784 Bodmer's friend Christoph Heinrich Müller published the first complete edition, based on two separate manuscripts, in an anthology of German literature from the twelfth to the fourteenth centuries. In his lectures on the *Nibelungenlied* in Berlin in 1802 and 1803, the Romantic August Wilhelm Schlegel described it as the product of the collective genius of an entire epoch and too momentous to have issued from a single author.

21. Hans-Bernd Harder and Ekkehard Kaufmann, eds., *Ausstellungskatalog*, vol. 1 of *Die Brüder Grimm in ihrer amtlichen und politischen Tätigkeit* (Kassel: Verlag Weber & Weidemeyer, 1985), 29–30; "Selbstbiographie," WGKS 1:11.

22. Letter from Brentano to Achim von Arnim, October 19, 1807, *AANS* 1:224; Gunhild Ginschel, *Der junge Jacob Grimm, 1805–1819* (Berlin: Akademie-Verlag, 1967), 28.

23. Letter from Achim von Arnim to Ludwig Tieck, December 3, 1807, in *Briefe an Ludwig Tieck*, ed. Karl von Holtei, 4 vols. (Breslau: Eduard Trewendt, 1864), 1:11. For a detailed account of the Grimms' practice of collecting, copying, excerpting, and ordering books and manuscripts throughout their scholarly projects, see Kraut, *Die Arbeitsweise der Brüder Grimm*.

24. Letters from Brentano to Achim von Arnim, October 19, 1807, *AANS* 1:224; and from Jacob Grimm to Brentano, February 10, 1807, *CBBG* 6; Heinz Rölleke, "Die Beiträge der Brüder Grimm zu 'Des Knaben Wunderhorn,'" *Hessische Blätter für Volkskunde* 64–65, no. 1 (1974): 28–42; Heinz Rölleke, "Die Titelkupfer zu des Knaben Wunderhorn: Richtigstellungen und neue Funde," *Jahrbuch des Freien Deutschen Hochstifts*, 1971, 123–30.

25. Charlotte Brontë, *Jane Eyre*, ed. Margaret Smith (Oxford: Oxford University Press, 1980), 120; letter from Achim von Arnim to Ludwig Tieck, November 1808, von Holtei, *Briefe an Ludwig Tieck*, 1:15.

26. Josef Körner, *Nibelungenforschungen der deutschen Romantik* (Leipzig: H. Haessel, 1911), 80; Jon Vanden Heuvel, *A German Life in the Age of Revolution: Joseph Görres, 1776–1848* (Washington, DC: Catholic University of America Press, 2001), 127.

27. Tales involving magic and enchantment are sometimes referred to in German as *Zaubermärchen* (magic tales). Two main subtypes of *Märchen* are *Volksmärchen* (folk tale), a term that generally implies the text has its roots in oral transmission and is the collective product of telling and retelling through time by multiple storytellers; and *Kunstmärchen* (artistic or literary fairy tale), which typically indicates a single-authored story.

28. Jack Zipes, *Fairy Tale as Myth / Myth as Fairy Tale* (Lexington: University Press of Kentucky, 1994), 57–58; KHM1, 312.

29. Letter from Jacob to Savigny, April 10, 1808, *BBGS* 42; Christa Kamenetsky, *The Brothers Grimm and Their Critics: Folktales and the Quest for Meaning* (Athens: Ohio University Press, 1992), 43.

Chapter 4. Wilhelm's Journey, 1809

1. Letter from Jacob to Henriette Zimmer, May 27, 1808, and letter from Wilhelm Grimm to Henriette Zimmer, June 10, 1808, both in Schoof, *Wilhelm Grimm*, 67–70; "Selbstbiographie," JGKS 1:22.

2. Letter from Henriette Zimmer to Lotte Grimm, June 20, 1808, in Denecke and Greverus, *Brüder Grimm Gedenken 1963*, 97–113 (99–100).

3. "Selbstbiographie," WGKS 1:8; "Selbstbiographie," JGKS 1:10; letter from Jacob to Savigny, May 21, 1808, BBGS 48–49.

4. "Gedanken, wie sich die Sagen zur Poesie und Geschichte verhalten," *Zeitung für Einsiedler*, no. 19 (June 4, 1808), JGKS 1:399–403 (399).

5. Like Jacob, Wilhelm grounded the *Nibelungenlied* in history, arguing that the main characters must have lived and that, strictly speaking, nothing can be completely imagined since everything must have some roots in experience. He also countered views that the *Nibelungenlied* was originally influenced by Greek and Asian sources; according to him, it had been formed from shorter songs, multiple versions had existed in the oral tradition, and these became more fixed through transcriptions in the twelfth and thirteenth centuries. See "Über die Entstehung der altdeutschen Poesie und ihr Verhältnis zu der Nordischen," WGKS 1:92–170. For analysis of the similarities and differences in Jacob's and Wilhelm's views of the *Nibelungenlied*, see Mary Thorp, *The Study of the "Nibelungenlied": Being the History of the Study of the Epic and Legend from 1755 to 1937* (Oxford: Clarendon, 1940), 16–19, 34–35.

6. "Selbstbiographie," WGKS 1:12; letter from Wilhelm to Brentano, August 2, 1809, CBBG 56; letter from Jacob to Achim von Arnim, April 26, 1809, AANS 3:31.

7. Letters from Jacob to Savigny, June 1, 1809, August 31, 1809, BBGS 72, 73; letter from Jacob to Wilhelm, August 16–17, 1809, BJWG 1:164.

8. Martus, *Die Brüder Grimm*, 141–43; "Selbstbiographie," WGKS 1:15; letter from Wilhelm to Savigny, March 15, 1809, BBGS 66.

9. Letter from Wilhelm to Jacob, May 24–28, 1809, BGJ 103. See also Ann Schmiesing, "Folklore and Physiology: The Vitality of Blood in the Works of the Brothers Grimm," in *The Early History of Embodied Cognition, 1740–1921: The "Lebenskraft"-Debate and Radical Reality in German Science, Music, and Literature*, ed. John A. McCarthy, Stephanie M. Hilger, Heather I. Sullivan, and Nicholas Saul (Leiden: Brill Rodopi, 2016), 185–207 (188); and Schmiesing, *Disability, Deformity, and Disease in the Grimms' Fairy Tales* (Detroit: Wayne State University Press, 2014), 47–48.

10. Letter from Wilhelm to Jacob, [July 15, 1809?], BJWG 145; see also Wilhelm's letters to Jacob of June 18, July 1, July 20, 1809, BJWG 135, 139, 149–50; and Wilhelm's letter to Brentano, August 2, 1809, CBBG 52–52.

11. Devin K. Binder, Karl Schaller, and Hans Clusmann, "The Seminal Contributions of Johann-Christian Reil to Anatomy, Physiology, and Psychiatry," *Neurosurgery* 61, no. 5 (2007): 1091–96. Reil originated the word *Psychiaterie*, which he later shortened to *Psychiatrie*. See also Martus, *Die Brüder Grimm*, 146; and Schmiesing, "Folklore and Physiology," 187–91.

12. Letter from Wilhelm to Jacob, April 14, 1809, *BJWG* 107; see also letter from Wilhelm to Brentano, August 2, 1809, *CBBG* 52; and letter from Wilhelm to Jacob, [July 15, 1809?], *BJWG* 145.

13. Letter from Wilhelm to Jacob, June 18, 1809, *BJWG* 135; letter from Wilhelm to Savigny, August 1809, *BBGS* 81; letter from Wilhelm to Brentano, August 2, 1809, *CBBG* 53; Schmiesing, "Folklore and Physiology," 190–91.

14. Letter from Wilhelm to Jacob, May 28, 1809, *BJWG* 127–28.

15. Letters from Wilhelm to Henriette Zimmer, March 3, 1810, May 11, 1812, in Schoof, *Wilhelm Grimm*, 73–74; letter from Jacob to Savigny, July 31, 1808, *BBGS* 55.

16. Letter from Wilhelm to Brentano, August 2, 1809, *CBBG* 53; letter from Wilhelm to Jacob, July 1, 1809, *BJWG* 140–41; letters from Jacob to Wilhelm, June 16, June 25, 1809, *BJWG* 133, 137. Wilhelm countered that a community of that size would have all the disadvantages of town life without any of the advantages of a truly rural village existence, and he suggested they live either out in the countryside or near a larger city; see his letter of mid-July 1809 to Jacob, *BJWG* 147.

17. Letter from Jacob to Wilhelm, July 19, 1809, *BGJ* 127; letter from Wilhelm to Jacob, July 26, 1809 (postscript to letter of July 20, 1809), *BJWG* 150.

18. Letter from Jacob to Achim von Arnim, September 26, 1812, *AANS* 3:218; see also Wilhelm's letter to Brentano, August 2, 1809, *CBBG* 57.

19. Letter from Wilhelm to Brentano, August 2, 1809, *CBBG* 55. Wilhelm did, however, describe Reichardt in positive terms in the autobiographical essay he wrote years later; see "Selbstbiographie," WGKS 1:17.

20. Letter from Wilhelm to Brentano, August 2, 1809, *CBBG* 55; Heinrich Steffens, *Was ich erlebte: Aus der Erinnerung niedergeschrieben*, vol. 6 (Breslau: Josef Max, 1842), 116–17.

21. Letter from Wilhelm to Savigny, March 15, 1809, *BBGS* 68.

22. Letter from Brentano to Achim von Arnim, February 15, 1805, *AANS* 1:132. The majority of the songs in *The Boy's Magic Horn* were taken from printed sources whose authors had themselves substantially revised songs from the oral tradition; Heinz Rölleke, "*Des Knaben Wunderhorn* und seine Stellung zu Volks- und Kirchenlied," *Jahrbuch für Liturgik und Hymnologie* 28 (1984): 29–38 (30); Hoermann, *Achim von Arnim*, 24.

23. Letter from Jacob to Wilhelm, May 17, 1809, *BJWG* 123.

24. Johann Heinrich Voss, "Beitrag zum Wunderhorn," *Morgenblatt für gebildete Stände* 283 (November 25, 1808): 1129–30 (1129); letter from Brentano to Jacob and Wilhelm, January 20, 1809, *CBBG* 33–34. The acerbity of Voss's criticism is intensified by the repetition of the harsh consonant cluster *tz* (pronounced like the *ts* in the English word *cats*) in the German phrase "butzigen, trutzigen, schmutzigen und nichtsnutzigen" (lumpy, sulky, dirty, and useless).

25. Letter from Jacob to Wilhelm, July 28, 1809, *BJWG* 152.

26. Letter from Wilhelm to Jacob, [August 4, 1809?], *BJWG* 155; letter from Wilhelm to Savigny, August 1809, *BBGS* 81; "Selbstbiographie," WGKS 1:17; letter from Achim von Arnim to Bettina Brentano, November 25, 1809, *CBBG* 74.

27. Letter from Wilhelm to Henriette Zimmer, October 10, 1809, *CBBG* 70; letter from Wilhelm to Louise Reichardt, excerpted in *CBBG* 78–79; Bockwoldt, "Das Bild des Juden in den Märchen der Brüder Grimm," 238–39; Henschel, "'etwas vorlautes widriges,'" 81–82.

28. Letter from Jacob to Wilhelm, October 18, 1809, *BJWG* 182; letters from Jacob to Achim von Arnim, January 22, 1811, September 26, 1812, *AANS* 3:97, 3:221; letter from Wilhelm to Brentano, April 12, 1810, *CBBG* 94.

29. Nachlass Grimm o.Nr. B. 1,1, Staatsbibliothek zu Berlin.

30. Letter from Wilhelm to Lotte, August 19, 1809, in Denecke and Greverus, *Brüder Grimm Gedenken 1963*, 102; letter from Jacob to Wilhelm, September 3, 1809, 170, and letter from Wilhelm to Jacob, [September 15–19, 1809?], 174, both in *BJWG*. See also Jacob's letter to Savigny of May 21, 1808, *BBGS* 48–49.

31. Letters from Wilhelm to Jacob, December 13, 1809, December 29, 1809, *BGJ* 185–89.

Chapter 5. Collecting Tales, 1810–1812

1. Heinz Rölleke, ed., *Die älteste Märchensammlung der Brüder Grimm: Synopse der handschriftlichen Urfassung von 1810 und der Erstdrucke von 1812* (Geneva: Fondation Martin Bodmer, 1975), 16.

2. Rölleke, 244–45.

3. Rölleke, 52.

4. Letter from Wilhelm to Brentano, October 25, 1810, *CBBG* 118.

5. Grimm, "Aufforderung an die gesammten Freunde deutscher Poesie und Geschichte erlassen," *CBBG* 165.

6. Grimm, 171.

7. Letter from Jacob to Georg Friedrich Benecke, December 22, 1811, *BBGB* 34.

8. Jacob found Herder's writings somewhat tedious and unoriginal, perhaps failing to recognize their innovativeness for their time. See Jacob's letter to Wilhelm of May 27, 1805, *BJWG* 73; Ernst Lichtenstein, "Die Idee der Naturpoesie bei den Brüdern Grimm und ihr Verhältnis zu Herder," *Vierteljahrsschrift für Literatur und Geistesgeschichte*, no. 6 (1928): 513–47; and Ginschel, *Der junge Jacob Grimm*, 33.

9. Letter from Jacob to Savigny, October 29, 1814, *BBGS* 172–73; "Zu den Altdänischen Heldenliedern," WGKS 1:176–203 (201). See also Lichtenstein, "Die Idee der Naturpoesie bei den Brüdern Grimm," 538.

10. Letter from Wilhelm to Achim von Arnim, May 28, 1811, *AANS* 3:123. See also Schmiesing, *Disability, Deformity, and Disease in the Grimms' Fairy Tales*, 24.

11. "Zu den altdänischen Heldenliedern," WGKS 1:203; Lichtenstein, "Die Idee der Naturpoesie bei den Brüdern Grimm," 522, 544.

12. Letter from Wilhelm to Savigny, May 5, 1811, 101, and letter from Jacob to Savigny, May 20, 1811, 102, 105, both in *BBGS*.

13. Ernst S. Dick, "The Grimms' *Hildebrandslied*," in *The Grimm Brothers and the Germanic Past*, ed. Elmer H. Antonsen (Amsterdam and Philadelphia: John Benjamins, 1990), 71–87 (74–75).

14. Jacob and Wilhelm Grimm, *Die beiden ältesten deutschen Gedichte aus dem achten Jahrhundert: Das Lied von Hildebrand und Hadubrand und das Weißenbrunner Gebet zum erstenmal in ihrem Metrum dargestellt und herausgegeben durch die Brüder Grimm* (Kassel: Thurneisen, 1812), 1, 3.

15. The translation is by Christopher Young and Thomas Gloning, *A History of the German Language through Texts* (London: Routledge, 2004), 44–45.

16. Dick, "Grimms' *Hildebrandslied*," 79.

17. Dick, 83; Cyril Edwards, *The Beginnings of German Literature: Comparative and Interdisciplinary Approaches to Old High German* (Rochester, NY: Camden House, 2002), 70–74.

18. For more on the *bibliothèque bleue* and its influence on the Grimms' informants, see Rudolf Schenda, *Von Mund zu Ohr: Bausteine zu einer Kulturgeschichte volkstümlichen Erzählens in Europa* (Göttingen: Vandenhoeck & Ruprecht, 1993), 224–26, 253–54.

19. Franz-Anton Kadell, *Die Hugenotten in Hessen-Kassel* (Darmstadt and Marburg: Selbstverlag der Hessischen Historischen Kommission Darmstadt und der Historischen Kommission für Hessen, 1980), vii, ix.

20. Heinz Rölleke, *Die Märchen der Brüder Grimm: Quellen und Studien: Gesammelte Aufsätze* (Trier: Wissenschaftlicher Verlag Trier, 2004), 34.

21. Rölleke, *"Nebeninschriften": Brüder Grimm—Arnim und Brentano—Droste-Hülshoff: Literarische Studien*, 1–15.

22. Letter from Wilhelm to Achim von Arnim, September 26, 1812, *AANS* 3:215. Krause titled his notebook "Aufnahme, der Gespräche, aus denen Spinstuben der Gemeinde Hohf Im Jahr 1811" (Record of the conversations from the spinning parlors of the Hoof township in the year 1811).

23. Heinz Rölleke and Albert Schindehütte, eds., *Es war einmal: Die wahren Märchen der Brüder Grimm und wer sie ihnen erzählte* (Frankfurt am Main: Eichborn, 2011), 95; *Orbis lumen et Atlantis iuga texta retecta* (Frankfurt, 1656), 1092; Hans Medick, "Village Spinning Bees: Sexual Culture and Free Time among Rural Youth in Early Modern Germany," in *Interest and Emotion: Essays on the Study of Family and Kinship*, ed. Hans Medick and David Warren Sabean (Cambridge: Cambridge University Press, 1984), 317–39. As Medick points out, church and government officials at times banned unmarried men from spinning parlors due to disapproval of their mingling with unmarried women.

24. *CBBG* 186–88; "An die Frau Bettina von Arnim," WGKS 1:317–19 (317).

25. Letter from Brentano to Jacob and Wilhelm, January 1811, *CBBG* 156.

26. Letter from Achim von Arnim to Jacob, October 22, 1812, *AANS* 3:223–25.

27. Letter from Jacob to Achim von Arnim, September 1812, 3:220, and letter from Jacob to Achim von Arnim, October 29, 1812, 3:234–35, both in *AANS*.

28. Letter from Jacob to Achim von Arnim, October 29, 1812, *AANS* 3:236.

29. Letter from Achim von Arnim to Jacob, December 24, 1812, 3:250, and letter from Jacob to Achim von Arnim, December 31, 1812, 3:254, both in *AANS*.

30. Letter from Wilhelm to Louise Reichardt, excerpted in *CBBG* 77.

Chapter 6. Reception of *Children's and Household Tales*, 1812–1814

1. Letter from Wilhelm to Georg Andreas Reimer, January 5, 1813, in Wilhelm Schoof, "Neue Beiträge zur Entstehungsgeschichte der Grimmschen Märchen," *Zeitschrift für Volkskunde* 52 (1955): 112–43 (121).
2. "Vorrede," WGKS 1:320–28 (320).
3. "Vorrede," WGKS 1:327–28. See also Schmiesing, *Disability, Deformity, and Disease in the Grimms' Fairy Tales*, 24–25.
4. See Jacques Barchilon, introduction to Charles Perrault, *Tales of Mother Goose: The Dedication Manuscript of 1695 Reproduced in Collotype Facsimile* (New York: Pierpont Morgan Library, 1956), 88.
5. Christoph Martin Wieland, *Dschinnistan, oder auserlesene Feen- und Geister-Mährchen*, 3 vols. (Winterthur, 1810), 1:xiv–xv.
6. Letter from Jacob to Achim von Arnim, October 29, 1812, *AANS* 3:236.
7. "Vorrede," WGKS 1:325.
8. "Vorrede," WGKS 1:325.
9. Jacob and Wilhelm Grimm, *Grimms' Goblins and Wonder Tales*, trans. H. B. Paull and L. A. Wheatley (London: Frederick Warne and Co., 1890), vii–viii; William Paton Ker, *Jacob Grimm: An Address Delivered at the Annual Meeting of the Philological Society on Friday, May 7, 1915* (London: Oxford University Press, 1915), 7; Louis L. Snyder, "Nationalistic Aspects of the Grimm Brothers' Fairy Tales," *Journal of Social Psychology* 33 (1951): 209–23 (213). See also Schenda, *Von Mund zu Ohr*, 224–26, 253–54.
10. See, for example, Alan Dundes, "Nationalistic Inferiority Complexes and the Fabrication of Fakelore: A Reconsideration of Ossian, the *Kinder- und Hausmärchen*, the *Kalevala*, and Paul Bunyan," *Journal of Folklore Research* 22, no. 1 (1985): 5–18 (8–9); John M. Ellis, *One Fairy Story Too Many: The Brothers Grimm and Their Tales* (Chicago: University of Chicago Press, 1983), 100.
11. Richard M. Dorson, "Fakelore," *Zeitschrift für Volkskunde* 65, no. 1 (1969): 56–64 (60).
12. Schenda, *Von Mund zu Ohr*, 101–2, 217–38.
13. Letter from Achim von Arnim to Jacob and Wilhelm, December 24, 1812, *AANS* 3:251–52.
14. Letter from Jacob to Achim von Arnim, December 31, 1812, 3:255, and letter from Wilhelm to Achim von Arnim, January 28, 1813, 3:267, both in *AANS*.
15. Unsent letter from Brentano to Achim von Arnim, early 1813, *AANS* 1:309.
16. Unsent letter from Brentano to Achim von Arnim, early 1813, *AANS* 1:309; letter from Jacob to Savigny, November 19, 1812, *BBGS* 141; Kamenetsky, *Brothers Grimm and Their Critics*, 45.
17. Letter from Achim von Arnim to Jacob and Wilhelm, December 24, 1812, *AANS* 3:252.
18. Letter from Achim von Arnim to Jacob and Wilhelm, January 1813, *AANS* 3:263.
19. Letter from Wilhelm to Achim von Arnim, January 28, 1813, 3:266, and letter from Jacob to Achim von Arnim, January 28, 1813, 3:269–71, both in *AANS*; Albert Ludwig Grimm, *Kindermärchen*, 3rd ed. (Frankfurt: Brönner, 1839), v.

20. Jacob wrote "just one year before the Battle of Leipzig" beneath the date "Kassel, October 18" in the Grimms' personal copy of the first edition; Herman Grimm, "Die Brüder Grimm und die Kinder- und Hausmärchen," in Herman Grimm, *Aufsätze zur Literatur*, ed. Reinhold Steig (Gütersloh: Bertelsmann, 1915), 174–75; "Vorrede," WGKS 1:328.

21. Letter from Wilhelm to Paul Wigand, May 29, 1813, *BGPW* 150–51.

22. Letter from Wilhelm to Ferdinand Grimm, July 17, 1813, qtd. in Rölleke and Schinde-hütte, *Es war einmal*, 117; Willem de Blécourt, "Fairy Grandmothers: Images of Story-telling Events in Nineteenth-Century Germany," *Relief* 4, no. 2 (2010): 174–97 (180).

23. De Blécourt, "Fairy Grandmothers," 180; Stefan Schweizer, *Geschichtsdeutung und Geschichtsbilder: Visuelle Erinnerungs- und Geschichtskultur in Kassel, 1866–1914* (Göttingen: Wallstein Verlag, 2004), 90–93. One of the portraits from which Katzenstein copied heads and stances had been used as the frontispiece to the *German Dictionary* (see chap. 14).

24. Karl Schulte Kemminghausen, "Dokumente zu Besuchen des westfälischen Freun-deskreises der Brüder Grimm in Kassel," in Denecke and Greverus, *Brüder Grimm Gedenken 1963*, 125–46 (126); letter from Wilhelm to Ludowine von Haxthausen, January 12, 1814, *FWJG* 19.

25. Nachlass Grimm o.Nr. B. 1,1, Staatsbibliothek zu Berlin. At the suggestion of Brentano, Wilhelm had also kept a dream diary in 1810. See Heinz Rölleke, "Wilhelm Grimms Traumtagebuch," *Brüder Grimm Gedenken* (1981): 15–37.

26. Wilhelm to August von Haxthausen, August 8, 1813, *FWJG* 13; letter from Ludowine von Haxthausen to Wilhelm, April 1818, in Wilhelm Schoof, ed., "Freundesbriefe der Familie von Haxthausen an die Brüder Grimm," *Westfälische Zeitschrift—Zeitschrift für vaterländische Geschichte und Altertumskunde* 94 (1938): 57–142 (131).

27. Jacob Grimm, "Commentar zu einer Stelle in Eschenbachs Parcifal," in *Altdeutsche Wälder*, vol. 1, ed. Jacob and Wilhelm Grimm (Kassel: Thurneissen, 1813), 1–30 (14), reproduced in Jacob Grimm, *Selbstbiographie: Ausgewählte Schriften, Reden und Ab-handlungen*, ed. Ulrich Wyss (Munich: Deutscher Taschenbuch Verlag, 1984), 106–24 (114); see also Jacob Grimm, *Deutsche Mythologie*, photomechanical reproduction of the fourth edition, ed. Elard Hugo Meyer, 3 vols. (Graz: Akademische Druck- und Verlagsanstalt, 1953), 2:752; Heinz Rölleke, "Weiß–Rot–Schwarz: 'Die drei Farben der Poesie': Zu Farbspielen in Grimms' 'Sneewittchen'-Märchen und anderwärts," *Fabula* 54 (2013): 214–34; and Schmiesing, "Folklore and Physiology," 198–99.

28. August Wilhelm Schlegel, review of *Altdeutsche Wälder*, vol. 1, ed. Jacob and Wilhelm Grimm, *Heidelbergische Jahrbücher der Litteratur*, no. 46 (1815): 721–36 (esp. 731).

29. Jacob and Wilhelm Grimm, "Aufruf: Pränumeration zum Besten der Hessischen Freiwilligen," WGKS 2:504; review of *Der arme Heinrich*, ed. Johann Gustav Büsching, JGKS 6:64–70 (esp. 64).

30. Grimm and Grimm, "Aufruf," 2:504; Jacob and Wilhelm Grimm, *Walthari-Lied, nacherzählt von Jacob Grimm; Der arme Heinrich, nacherzählt von Wilhelm Grimm*, ed. Reinhold Steig (Wiesbaden: Verlag des Volksbildungsvereins, 1904), 4–5.

31. Letter from Jacob to Achim von Arnim, November 16, 1813, *AANS* 3:281; Mustafa, *Napoleon's Paper Kingdom*, xiii–xxi.

32. Letter from Wilhelm to Wigand, February 9, 1814, *BGHF* 4.
33. Letters from Jacob to Wilhelm, January 8–9, February 2, 1814, *BJWG* 256–58, 273–74.
34. Letter from Jacob to Wilhelm, February 8, 1814, *BJWG* 286.
35. Letters from Jacob to Wilhelm, February 8, March 9, March 19, 1814, 283–85, 293, 299–300, and letters from Wilhelm to Jacob, February 9–13, March 8–9, March 22, 1814, 279, 290, 301–2, all in *BJWG*. See also Grimm, *Erinnerungen aus meinem Leben*, 137.
36. Letter from Wilhelm to Achim von Arnim, October 7, 1814, 3:312, and letter from Wilhelm to Achim von Arnim, June 21, 1814, 3:306, both in *AANS*.
37. Letter from Wilhelm to Elector Wilhelm I of Hessen-Kassel, *ATBG* 4.
38. Letters from Wilhelm to Jacob, April 15, May 5, 1814, *BJWG* 318, 334; letter from Wilhelm to Achim von Arnim, June 21, 1814, *AANS* 3:307.
39. Letters from Jacob to Wilhelm, March 9, March 19, 1814, *BJWG* 293, 299.
40. Letters from Jacob to Wilhelm, March 26, April 19, 1814, *BJWG* 306, 321.
41. Letter from Jacob to Wilhelm, June 21, 1814, *BJWG* 357.
42. Letter from Jacob to Wilhelm, May 1, 1814, *BJWG* 331; Jarrett, *Congress of Vienna and Its Legacy*, 63–65, 69–72.

Chapter 7. Unveiling the Second Volume of *Children's and Household Tales*, 1815

1. Letter from Jacob to Wilhelm, September 22, 1814, *BJWG* 359.
2. Ohles, *Germany's Rude Awakening*, 17; Jarrett, *Congress of Vienna and Its Legacy*, xiii, 95; *The Journal of a Nobleman: Being a Narrative of His Residence at Vienna during the Congress* (Philadelphia: Key and Biddle, 1833), 16; Hilde Spiel, ed., *The Congress of Vienna: An Eyewitness Account*, trans. Richard H. Weber (Philadelphia: Chilton Book Company, 1968), 86, 153–243.
3. Letters from Jacob to Wilhelm, September 23, October 8, 1814, *BJWG* 363, 365–66; Charles Edward Dodd, *An Autumn on the Rhine: Or, Sketches of Courts, Society, Scenery, etc. in Some of the German States* (London: Longman, Hurst, Rees, Orme, and Brown, 1818), 86–87; Ohles, *Germany's Rude Awakening*, 22; Jens Flemming, "Die Rückkehr des Kurfürsten: Verfassungsbewegungen und Verfassungspolitik (1813–1862)," in *Fremdherrschaft und Freiheit: Das Königreich Westphalen als Napoleonischer Modellstaat*, ed. Jens Flemming and Dietfrid Krause-Vilmar (Kassel: Kassel University Press, 2009), 237–53 (242).
4. Letter from Jacob to Wigand, August 1814, *BGHF*; Karl Julius Weber, *Deutschland: Oder, Briefe eines in Deutschland Reisenden Deutschen*, 4 vols., 2nd ed. (Stuttgart: Hallberger, 1834), 3:280; Gabriel Gottfried Bredow and Carl Venturini, *Chronik des Neunzehnten Jahrhunderts*, vol. 13 (1816) (Altona: J. F. Hammerich, 1819), 412; Josephine Clifford, "The Imperial Prison," *Overland Monthly* 5 (1870): 449–55 (452).
5. Letters from Jacob to Wilhelm, October 2, October 8, 1814, *BJWG* 363, 366; Spiel, *Congress of Vienna*, 93.
6. Letter from Jacob to Wilhelm, November 23, 1814, *BJWG* 388; Jarrett, *Congress of Vienna and Its Legacy*, 94–96; letter from Jacob to Joseph Görres, December 3, 1814, in Görres, *Gesammelte Schriften*, ed. Marie Görres and Franz Binder, 9 vols. (Munich: In

Commission der literarisch-artistischen Anstalt, 1854–74), 8:444; letter from Wilhelm to Jacob, November 3, 1814, *BJWG* 380; Spiel, *Congress of Vienna*, xii, 102–108, 138–40; Brian Vick, *The Congress of Vienna: Power and Politics after Napoleon* (Cambridge, MA: Harvard University Press, 2014), 11, 53.

7. Letter from Jacob to Wilhelm, October 21, 1814, 372, and letter from Jacob to Wilhelm, November 23, 1814, 390, both in *BJWG*.

8. Letter from Jacob to Wilhelm, October 8, 1814, *BJWG* 368.

9. Letter from Jacob to Brentano, December 18, 1814, 199, and letter from Brentano to Wilhelm, February 15, 1815, 201, both in *CBBG*.

10. Letters from Jacob to Wilhelm, November 23, December 31, 1814, 388, 399, and letter from Wilhelm to Jacob, November 12, 1814, 386–87, all in *BJWG*.

11. Letter from Jacob to Wilhelm, December 16, 1814, *BJWG* 394–95. See also Jacob's essays "Die Elsasser," "Über Sachsen," "Vom Kongreß," "Über die Bundesverfassung," "Über Ländertausch in Deutschland," "Sachsen, Spielerei und Schwierigkeit," and "Großtun," in JGKS 8:397–415.

12. Letters from Jacob to Wilhelm, December 16, December 31, 1814, *BJWG* 396, 399–400.

13. Letter from Wilhelm to Elector Wilhelm I of Hessen-Kassel, November 4, 1814, *ATBG* 6; letter from Wilhelm to Jacob, December 5, 1814, *BJWG* 393.

14. Letter from Wilhelm to Ludowine von Haxthausen, January 21, 1813, *FWJG* 1–2; Gerstner, *Die Brüder Grimm*, 63.

15. Letter from Wilhelm to Savigny, December 12, 1814, *BBGS* 183, 187.

16. Ines Köhler, "Hans mein Igel," in *Enzyklopädie des Märchens: Handwörterbuch zur historischen und vergleichenden Erzählforschung*, ed. Kurt Ranke et al., 6 vols. (Berlin: de Gruyter, 1999), 6:494–98 (497); Lutz Röhrich, *Folktales and Reality*, trans. Peter Tokofsky (1979; repr., Bloomington: Indiana University Press, 1991), 87; KHM7 3:240.

17. Jan M. Ziolkowski, *Fairy Tales from Before Fairy Tales: The Medieval Latin Past of Wonderful Lies* (Ann Arbor: University of Michigan Press, 2007), 202–29, esp. 206, 226–28.

18. Ziolkowski, 202–29, esp. 227–29; Schmiesing, *Disability, Deformity, and Disease in the Grimms' Fairy Tales*, 128–40.

19. Letter from Jacob to Wilhelm, March 18, 1815, *BJWG* 431; KHM1, 552.

20. KHM1, 341–42.

21. Ellis, *One Fairy Story Too Many*, 32; Dundes, "Nationalistic Inferiority Complexes and the Fabrication of Fakelore," 159; Donald Ward, "New Misconceptions about Old Folktales: The Brothers Grimm," in *The Brothers Grimm and Folktale*, ed. James M. McGlathery with Larry W. Danielson, Ruth E. Lorbe, and Selma K. Richardson (Urbana: University of Illinois Press, 1988), 91–100 (91–92).

22. Heinz Rölleke, "Die Beiträge der Dorothea Viehmann zu Grimms 'Kinder- und Hausmärchen,'" in *Dorothea Viehmann*, ed. Holger Ehrhardt (Kassel: Euregioverlag, 2012), 30–45 (35–37); Rölleke, "New Results of Research on *Grimms' Fairy Tales*," in McGlathery, *Brothers Grimm and Folktale*, 101–11 (105).

23. Schmiesing, *Disability, Deformity, and Disease in the Grimms' Fairy Tales*, 27–41.

24. Rölleke and Schindehütte, *Es war einmal*, 14; Schmiesing, *Disability, Deformity, and Disease in the Grimms' Fairy Tales*, 32–34.

25. Letter from Jacob and Wilhelm to Ferdinand Grimm, July 17, 1813, qtd. in Rölleke and Schindehütte, *Es war einmal*, 44. The note incorrectly gives the year of her death as 1816; KHM7 1:19.

26. Letters from Wilhelm to Achim von Arnim, January 26, 1815, November 16, 1813, 3:123, 3:286, *AANS*; letter from August von Haxthausen to Wilhelm, December 20, 1813, in Schoof, "Freundesbriefe der Familie von Haxthausen an die Brüder Grimm," 84; letter from Wilhelm to Savigny, December 12, 1814, *BBGS* 187; letter from Wilhelm to Joseph Görres, in Görres, *Gesammelte Schriften*, 8:451; "An die Frau Bettina von Arnim," WGKS 317–19 (319); KHM7 1:19.

27. Volker Schupp, *"Wollzeilergesellschaft" und "Kette": Impulse der frühen Volkskunde und Germanistik* (Marburg: N. G. Elwert Verlag, 1983), 10–15, 33–39. See also Jacob's letters to Wilhelm, December 10, December 31, 1814, 1815, *BJWG* 393, 400.

28. "Circular, die Sammlung der Volkspoesie betreffend," JGKS 7:593–95; letters from Jacob to Wilhelm, January 18, February 10, 1815, 410, 418–19, and letter from Wilhelm to Jacob, March 19, 1815, 433, all in *BJWG*; Susan A. Crane, *Collecting and Historical Consciousness in Early Nineteenth-Century Germany* (Ithaca, NY: Cornell University Press, 2000), 60–74.

29. Letter from Jacob to Wilhelm, May 11, 1815, *BJWG* 441; Vick, *Congress of Vienna*, 4–5; Schupp, *"Wollzeilergesellschaft" und "Kette,"* 16. In a letter of August 1, 1816, to Goethe, Wilhelm described the *Songs of the Elder Edda* as so interconnected with German heritage as to hardly be foreign; Gerstner, *Die Brüder Grimm*, 105.

30. Letters from Jacob to Wilhelm, January 18, January 27, 1815, *BJWG* 409, 412–14.

31. Letters from Jacob to Wilhelm, April 24, May 2, 1815, 436–37, and letter from Wilhelm to Jacob, May 4, 1815, 439, all in *BJWG*.

32. Letter from Jacob to Wilhelm, March 6, 1815 (postscript dated March 7), *BJWG* 429.

33. Letters from Jacob to Wilhelm, January 27, May 11, 1815, *BJWG* 414, 442.

Chapter 8. Exploring German Legends, 1816–1818

1. Jacob and Wilhelm Grimm, "Vorrede," WGKS 2:505.

2. Jacob and Wilhelm Grimm, eds., *Hartmann von Aue: Der arme Heinrich: Aus der Straßburgischen und vatikanischen Handschrift herausgegeben und erklärt durch die Brüder Grimm* (Berlin: Realschulbuch, 1815; Nachlass Grimm 105, Staatsbibliothek zu Berlin), 215–16; Ursula Rautenberg, *Das "Volksbuch vom armen Heinrich": Studien zur Rezeption Hartmanns von Aue im 19. Jahrhundert und zur Wirkungsgeschichte der Übersetzung Wilhelm Grimms* (Berlin: Erich Schmidt, 1985), 122–28; Rüdiger Krohn, "A Tale of Sacrifice and Love: Literary Way Stations of the *Arme Heinrich* from the Brothers Grimm to Tankred Dorst," in *A Companion to the Works of Hartmann von Aue*, ed. Francis G. Gentry (Rochester, NY: Camden House, 2005), 223–53 (224); Schmiesing, "Bicentennial Trio," 361–63.

3. Schmiesing, "Bicentennial Trio," 362–63, 365; Krohn, "Tale of Sacrifice and Love," 226–27.

4. Whitman, *Legacy of Roman Law in the German Romantic Era*, 93; H. A. Korff, *Geist der Goethezeit*, vol. 4 (Leipzig: Koehler & Amelang, 1962), 165.

5. Martus, *Die Brüder Grimm*, 208; Steffen Martus, "Moderne Traditionalisten: Die Brüder Grimm und ihre Zeit," in *Expedition Grimm: Hessische Landesausstellung Kassel 2013*, ed. Thorsten Smidt (Dresden: Sandstein Verlag, 2013), 17–27.

6. Whitman, *Legacy of Roman Law in the German Romantic Era*, 94–98; Vick, *Congress of Vienna*, 235–40.

7. Letter from Wilhelm to Bang, August 28, 1815, *BGHF* 26–27; Jarrett, *Congress of Vienna and Its Legacy*, xiii.

8. Letter from Wilhelm to David Theodor August Suabedissen, December 15, 1815, 144–45, and letter from Jacob to Elector Wilhelm I of Hessen-Kassel, August 10, 1815, 5–6, both in *BGHF*; letter from Jacob to Wilhelm, November 23, 1814, *BJWG* 389.

9. "Selbstbiographie," *WGKS* 1:20.

10. Letter from Wilhelm to Ludowine von Haxthausen, March 15, 1816, *FWJG* 36; Grimm, *Erinnerungen aus meinem Leben*, 213.

11. Grimm, *Erinnerungen aus meinem Leben*, 213; Reinhold Steig, *Goethe und die Brüder Grimm*, foreword by Ludwig Denecke (1892; repr., Kassel: Horst Hamecher, 1972), 96.

12. Letter from Jacob to Wilhelm and Ludwig, September 13, 1815, 454, and letter from Jacob to Wilhelm, October 21, 1815, 460–61, both in *BJWG*.

13. Letter from Jacob to Ludowine von Haxthausen, May 15, 1818, *FWJG* 64–65. Later in life, Jacob espoused a similar view of artwork in galleries in his account of his travel to Italy; "Italienische und Scandinavische Eindrücke," *JGKS* 1:56–82 (72).

14. Jacob Grimm, report of November 7, 1815, *ATBG* 83.

15. Letter from Jacob to August von Haxthausen, September 4, 1815, *FWJG* 29.

16. Letter from Jacob to Elector Wilhelm I of Hessen-Kassel, October 28, 1815, *BGHF* 7; letter from Wilhelm to Jacob, November 5, 1815, *BJWG* 464–65.

17. Letter from Wilhelm to Jacob, October 14, 1815, *BJWG* 459.

18. "Selbstbiographie," *JGKS* 1:14; letter from Wilhelm to Ludowine von Haxthausen, March 15, 1816, *FWJG* 35–36.

19. Jacob and Wilhelm Grimm, *Deutsche Sagen* (Munich: Winkler Verlag, 1956), 436n1. The Haxthausens also visited the Grimms in Kassel in 1818.

20. Letter from Jacob to Joseph Görres, June 10, 1816, in Görres, *Gesammelte Schriften*, 8:500.

21. Letter from Wilhelm to Suabedissen, March 23, 1816, *BGHF* 146.

22. Letter from Jacob to F. J. Mone, August 12, 1819, in Grimm et al., "Briefe von Jacob und Wilhelm Grimm," 78–79; letter from Wilhelm to Bang, January 7, 1817, *BGHF* 30.

23. Letter from Wilhelm to Suabedissen, March 23, 1816, *BGHF* 148–49; Lutz Röhrich, afterword to Grimm and Grimm, *Deutsche Sagen*, 635–36.

24. Letter from Jacob to Wilhelm, October 29, 1815, *BJWG* 462; Lutz Röhrich, *Sage und Märchen: Erzählforschung heute* (Freiburg: Herder, 1976), 44–45; Jack Zipes, "The Grimm *German Legends* in English," *Children's Literature* 12 (1984): 162–66; Schmiesing, "Bicentennial Trio," 357–59.

25. Tom Shippey, "A Revolution Reconsidered: Mythography and Mythology in the Nineteenth Century," in *The Shadow-Walkers: Jacob Grimm's Mythology of the Monstrous*, ed. Shippey (Tempe: Arizona Center for Medieval and Renaissance Studies,

2005), 1–28 (24); Schmiesing, "Bicentennial Trio," 356–59; letter from Jacob to Savigny, February 5, 1815, *BBGS* 192.

26. The English translation is by Donald Ward; Jacob and Wilhelm Grimm, *The German Legends of the Brothers Grimm*, ed. and trans. Donald Ward, 2 vols. (Philadelphia: Institute for the Study of Human Issues, 1981), 1:1.

27. Grimm and Grimm, *Deutsche Sagen*, 17.

28. The Grimms portray the Jewish characters in "The Jew in the Thornbush" and "The Good Bargain" as dishonest and deceptive. In "The Bright Sun Will Bring It to Light," a tailor tells a Jew to give him money; the Jew protests that he has only eight farthings. The tailor assumes that the Jew is lying and murders him. Although the Jew in that tale is depicted as telling the truth, he still loses his life; the tailor is later brought to justice. For analysis of the tales, see Bockwoldt, "Das Bild des Juden in den Märchen der Brüder Grimm."

29. Röhrich, *Sage und Märchen*, 44. The Grimms' *Old German Forests*, the second and third volumes of which were published in 1815 and 1816, was not a commercial success either.

30. Taylor Starck, "Die *Deutschen Sagen* der Brüder Grimm als Balladenquelle," *Modern Language Notes* 31, no. 8 (1916): 449–65; Ward, epilogue to Grimm and Grimm, *German Legends*, 2:379–80: Schmiesing, "Bicentennial Trio," 354–55, 365.

31. Hans-Jörg Uther, "Die 'Deutschen Sagen' der Brüder Grimm im Spiegel ihrer Kritiker: Ein Beitrag zur frühen Sagenrezeption," in *Hören–Sagen–Lesen–Lernen: Bausteine zu einer Geschichte der kommunikativen Kultur*, ed. Ursula Brunold-Bigler and Hermann Bausinger (Bern: Peter Lang, 1995), 721–39; Schmiesing, "Bicentennial Trio," 363–64.

Chapter 9. Revising *Children's and Household Tales*, 1819

1. Letter from Jacob to Wilhelm, May 11, 1815, *BJWG* 442; Heinz Rölleke, afterword to KHM2 2:521–78.

2. Letter from Wilhelm to Georg Andreas Reimer, September 25, 1818, 125, and letter from Reimer to Wilhelm, October 1, 1818, 126–27, both in Schoof, *Neue Beiträge*. See also Winzer, *Permanente Metamorphosen*, 69–70.

3. Letter from Wilhelm to Jenny von Droste-Hülshoff, December 7, 1819, in *Briefwechsel zwischen Jenny von Droste-Hülshoff und Wilhelm Grimm*, ed. Karl Schulte Kemminghausen (Münster: Aschendorff, 1929), 30; Winzer, *Permanente Metamorphosen*, 79.

4. Letter from Ludowine von Haxthausen to Wilhelm, June 1, 1818, in Schoof, "Freundesbriefe der Familie von Haxthausen an die Brüder Grimm," 133; letter from Wilhelm to Ludowine von Haxthausen, December 7, 1819, *FWJG* 78; Wilhelm Schoof, *Zur Entstehungsgeschichte der Grimmschen Märchen* (Hamburg: Dr. Ernst Hauswedell und Co., 1959), 103–4. Although the Haxthausens are not mentioned by name in the preface, beginning with the 1822 edition of notes the Grimms credited them with providing seven of the children's legends and thanked them for other contributions to *Children's and Household Tales*. See Jacob Grimm and Wilhelm Grimm, *Kinder- und Hausmärchen gesammelt durch die Brüder Grimm: Zweite vermehrte und verbesserte Auflage*, vol. 3 (Berlin: G. Reimer, 1822), 253. Regarding the silence of the Grimms'

informants and August von Haxthausen's contribution of "The Bremen Town Musicians," see Rölleke and Schindehütte, *Es war einmal*, 34, 337–39.

5. Grimm, *Erinnerungen aus meinem Leben*, 205; "Aus Hessen," April 17, 1815, 1:544, and "Aus Hessen," April 23, 1815, 1:548, both in WGKS.

6. KHM7 1:23.

7. A tenth legend was added from 1850 on.

8. KHM2 1:91; Maria Tatar, *The Hard Facts of the Grimms' Fairy Tales* (Princeton, NJ: Princeton University Press, 1987), 5, 181.

9. KHM2 1:85.

10. Ruth B. Bottigheimer, *Grimms' Bad Girls and Bold Boys: The Moral and Social Vision of the Tales* (New Haven, CT: Yale University Press, 1987), 59.

11. KHM7 1:32; KHM2 1:50–51; Schmiesing, *Disability, Deformity, and Disease in the Grimms' Fairy Tales*, 31–32.

12. Schmiesing, *Disability, Deformity, and Disease in the Grimms' Fairy Tales*, 67–68.

13. Jack Zipes, *The Brothers Grimm: From Enchanted Forests to the Modern World* (New York: Palgrave Macmillan, 2002), 31.

14. KHM7 1:22.

15. Schmiesing, *Disability, Deformity, and Disease in the Grimms' Fairy Tales*, 69–70.

16. KHM7 3:70.

17. KHM7 3:69; Tatar, *Hard Facts of the Grimms' Fairy Tales*, 10; Zipes, *Brothers Grimm*, 172–73; Schmiesing, *Disability, Deformity, and Disease in the Grimms' Fairy Tales*, 80–98.

18. The translation is by Jack Zipes, *The Complete Fairy Tales of the Brothers Grimm*, 3rd ed. (New York: Bantam, 2003), 582.

19. Letter from Wilhelm to Brentano, October 25, 1810, *CBBG* 118. It is striking, too, that the pharmacy run by Rudolf Wild—whose wife and daughters (including Wilhelm's future wife Dortchen) told tales to the Grimms—was named the Golden Sun (Zur güldenen Sonne). Some modern editions place "The Golden Key" first; see, for example, *Zur Zeit, wo das Wünschen noch geholfen hat: Die schönsten Märchen der Brüder Grimm* (Hildesheim: Gerstenberg Verlag, 2021).

20. Ellis, *One Fairy Story Too Many*, 100; Dundes, "Nationalistic Inferiority Complexes," 159–60.

21. Zipes, *Brothers Grimm*, 32, 76.

22. Letter from Wilhelm to Bang, December 7, 1819, *BGHF* 53; Rölleke, *Die Märchen der Brüder Grimm*, 57–66.

23. Letter from Jacob to Savigny, December 30, 1819, *BBGS* 273.

Chapter 10. Grimm's Law and the Small Edition of the *Tales*, 1820s

1. Letter from Jacob to Karl Lachmann, April 1, 1821, *BGKL* 1:293.

2. Fritz Lochner von Huttenbach, "Jacob Grimm und die Wurzeln der historisch-vergleichenden Sprachwissenschaft," *Grazer linguistische Monographien* 11 (1994): 115–27 (119); Konrad Koerner, "Jacob Grimm's Position in the Development of Linguistics as a Science," in Antonsen, *Grimm Brothers and the Germanic Past*, 7–23 (22); Margaret

Thomas, *Fifty Key Thinkers on Language and Linguistics* (New York: Routledge, 2011), 97–103 (99). Regarding views that the designation "Grimm's Law" obscured Rask's achievements, see, for example, T. Le Marchant Douse, *Grimm's Law: A Study, or Hints towards an Explanation of the So-Called "Lautverschiebung" to Which Are Added Some Remarks on the Primitive Indo-European "K" and Several Appendices* (London: Trübner & Company, 1876), x.

3. Huttenbach, "Jacob Grimm und die Wurzeln der historisch-vergleichenden Sprachwissenschaft," 119; Winfred P. Lehmann, ed. and trans., *A Reader in Nineteenth-Century Historical Indo-European Linguistics* (Bloomington: Indiana University Press, 1967), 29–30; Holger Pedersen, *Linguistic Science in the Nineteenth Century: Methods and Results* (Cambridge, MA: Harvard University Press, 1931), 37–38, 42, 258–62; Thomas, *Fifty Key Thinkers on Language and Linguistics*, 100. The description of sound changes and French and English examples rely in particular on Lyle Campbell and Mauricio J. Mixco, *A Glossary of Historical Linguistics* (Edinburgh: Edinburgh University Press, 2007), 75.

4. Chauncey Jeffries Mellor, "Scholarly Purpose and National Purpose in Jacob Grimm's Work on the *Deutsches Wörterbuch*" (PhD diss., University of Chicago, 1972), 21; Thomas, *Fifty Key Thinkers on Language and Linguistics*, 100–101.

5. James Turner, *Philology: The Forgotten Origins of the Modern Humanities* (Princeton, NJ: Princeton University Press, 2014), 91–99, 127–28; Johann Gottfried Herder, *Essay on the Origin of Language*, trans. Alexander Gode, in Jean-Jacques Rousseau and Johann Gottfried Herder, *On the Origin of Language* (Chicago: University of Chicago Press, 1986), 154–55; Brian Vick, *Defining Germany: The 1848 Frankfurt Parliamentarians and National Identity* (Cambridge, MA: Harvard University Press, 2002), 24–27.

6. Hans Frede Nielsen, "Jacob Grimm and the 'German' Dialects," in Antonsen, *Brothers Grimm and the Germanic Past*, 25–32 (25–26); letter from Jacob to Rasmus Rask, November 25, 1825, in Jacob and Wilhelm Grimm, *Briefwechsel der Gebrüder Grimm mit Nordischen Gelehrten*, ed. Ernst Schmidt (1885; repr., Walluf: Dr. Martin Sändig Verlag, 1974), 125.

7. Jacob Grimm, *Deutsche Grammatik*, part 1 (Göttingen: In der Dieterichschen Buchhandlung, 1819), x.

8. Robert A. Fowkes, "The Linguistic Modernity of Jakob Grimm," *Linguistics* 8 (1964): 56–61; "Deutsche Grammatik," JGKS 8:49–50.

9. Grimm, *Deutsche Grammatik*, xviii; letter from Jacob to Lachmann, November 25, 1820, *BGKL* 1:234.

10. Letter from Jacob to Ludowine and August von Haxthausen, September 10, 1822, *FWJG* 88.

11. Letters from Jacob to Lachmann, April 1–8, October 24, 1820, December 11, 1821, *BGKL* 1:81, 208, 335.

12. Letters from Jacob to Lachmann, November 25, 1820, February 18, April 1, May 29, 1821, *BGKL* 1:234, 273, 293, 297.

13. Thorp, *Study of the "Nibelungenlied,"* 23–37; letters from Jacob to Lachmann, April 1–8, 1820, April 1, 1821, *BGKL* 1:89, 294.

14. Letters from Lachmann to Jacob, December 1820, January 21–24, September 2, 1821, *BGKL* 1:249, 273, 304.

15. Letter from Jacob to Lachmann, April 10, 1822; *BGKL* 1:347; Nielsen, "Jacob Grimm and the 'German' Dialects," 31; Fowkes, "Linguistic Modernity of Jakob Grimm," 56–57.

16. Tom Shippey, *The Road to Middle-Earth: How J. R. R. Tolkien Created a New Mythology* (Boston and New York: Houghton Mifflin Company, 2003), 16; Tom Shippey, "Grimm's Law: How One Man Revolutionized the Humanities," *Times Literary Supplement*, November 7, 2003, 16–17 (17); Günter Grass, *Grimms Wörter: Eine Liebeserklärung* (Göttingen: Steidl Verlag, 2010), 48; Heinrich Heine, *Elementargeister*, in Manfred Windfuhr, ed., *Heinrich Heine: Historisch-kritische Gesamtausgabe der Werke*, vol. 9, ed. Ariane Neuhaus-Koch (Hamburg: Hoffmann und Campe Verlag, 1987), 9–64 (11–12).

17. Norberg, *Brothers Grimm and the Making of German Nationalism*, 2–3.

18. Clifford, "Imperial Prison," 450–51.

19. Letter from Jacob to Lachmann, April 1, 1821, *BGKL* 1:292; Dodd, *An Autumn on the Rhine*, 95.

20. Letters from Jacob to Lachmann, March 2, May 12, 1823, *BGKL* 1:380, 390.

21. Letter from Jacob to Lachmann, May 27, 1820, *BGKL* 1:142; "Acten über Jacob Grimm als Mitglied der Censur-Commission," *ATBG* 128–33; Ohles, *Germany's Rude Awakening*, 51–52, 70–73.

22. Vick, *Congress of Vienna*, 110; Rudolf Schenda, *Volk ohne Buch: Studien zur Sozialgeschichte der populären Lesestoffe, 1770–1910* (Frankfurt am Main: Vittorio Klostermann, 1970), 444.

23. Letter from Jacob to Lachmann, March 2, 1823, *BGKL* 1:380.

24. Philipp Losch, *Der letzte deutsche Kurfürst Friedrich Wilhelm I. von Hessen* (Marburg: N. G. Elwertsche Verlagsbuchhandlung, 1937), 16–18; Klaus Düwel, introduction to Wilhelm Grimm, *Ueber deutsche Runen und Zur Literatur der Runen* (Hildesheim: Olms-Weidmann, 2009), 7–68.

25. Letter from Jacob to Georg Friedrich Benecke, June 27, 1822, *BBGB* 151.

26. Letter from Wilhelm to Suabedissen, second Easter Day, 1817, *BGHF* 162; letters from Jacob to Lachmann, December 11, 1821, April 10, 1822, May 1, 1822, May 12, 1823, *BGKL* 1:335, 347, 349, 391.

27. Letter from Jacob to Lachmann, June 10, 1823, *BGKL* 1:399–400.

28. Letter from Jacob to Ludowine and August von Haxthausen, March 28, 1824, *FWJG* 91; letter from Wilhelm to Jenny von Droste-Hülshoff, May 8, 1825, in Kemminghausen, *Briefwechsel zwischen Jenny von Droste-Hülshoff und Wilhelm Grimm*, 69–72. Bellevue is known today not by its French name, but by the German equivalent "Schöne Aussicht."

29. Letter from Wilhelm to Suabedissen, July 17, 1822, *BGHF* 212; Josef Ehmer, *Heiratsverhalten* (Göttingen: Vandenhoeck und Ruprecht, 1991), 292.

30. Jacob Grimm, "Hausbüchel für unser Lebenlang," *JGKS* 8:462; letter from Wilhelm to Bang, March 10, 1825, *BGHF* 90; Rölleke and Schindehütte, *Es war einmal*, 349.

31. Letter from Wilhelm to Suabedissen, May 23, 1825, *BGHF* 238; letter from Wilhelm to Lachmann, May 20, 1825, *BGKL* 2:824; letter from Wilhelm to Bang, March 10, 1825, *BGHF* 90; letter from Wilhelm to Wigand, May 20, 1825, *BGPW* 244; letter from Jacob to Lachmann, January 15, 1825, *BGKL* 1:452.

32. The German title of Wilhelmi's play is *Einer muß heiraten!* It was first performed in 1850 and published in 1853.

33. Letter from Jacob to Benecke, September 25, 1822, *BBGB* 155; letter from Jacob to Lachmann, March 8, 1824, *BGKL* 1:441.

34. Friedrich Neumann, "Ein 'Heiratsplan' Jacob Grimms?," *Zeitschrift des Vereins für Hessische Geschichte und Landeskunde* 72 (1961): 143–59; letter from Jacob to Charlotte Ramus, December 5, 1817, *BGHF* 9; Rölleke and Schindehütte, *Es war einmal*, 329.

35. Ulrich Wyss, *Die wilde Philologie: Jacob Grimm und der Historismus* (Munich: C. H. Beck, 1979), 288.

36. Letter from Wilhelm to Achim von Arnim, December 26, 1826, *AANS* 3:556; see also letter from Jacob to Wigand, November 8, 1826, *BGPW* 253; and letter from Wilhelm to Lachmann, April 21, 1827, *BGKL* 2:827.

37. Letter from Jacob to Lachmann, April 20, 1825, *BGKL* 1:455; letter from Wilhelm to Suabedissen, January 3, 1827, *BGHF* 244–45.

38. Letter from Wilhelm to Meusebach, March 22, 1828, *BMG* 87.

39. Letter from Jacob to Meusebach, October 7, 1828, 100, and letter from Wilhelm to Meusebach, December 19, 1830, 136, both in *BMG*. See also E. Stengel's note to Jacob's letter to Bang, January 19, 1829, *ATBG* 181.

40. John Bowring and Harry S. Van Dyk, *Batavian Anthology, or, Specimens of the Dutch Poets* (London: Taylor and Hessey, 1824), 32; review of *The Italian Novelists, Selected from the Most Approved Authors in That Language,* by Thomas Roscoe, *Edinburgh Review* 83 (1825): 174–206; David Carey, *A Legend of Argyle, or 'Tis a Hundred Years Since* (London: G. & W. B. Whitaker, 1821), n.p.; Kamenetsky, *Brothers Grimm and Their Critics*, 48; letter from Jacob to Lachmann, May 12, 1823, *BGKL* 1:390. Taylor later published a second volume of Grimm tales, plus a couple tales from other sources, in 1826. Literacy rates in Britain and Germany were roughly equal during this period; see Vick, *Congress of Vienna*, 110.

41. Letter from Wilhelm to Reimer, August 16, 1823, *BBG* 285–86; Winzer, *Permanente Metamorphosen*, 92, 116; Ruth B. Bottigheimer, "The Publishing History of Grimms' Tales: Reception at the Cash Register," in *The Reception of the Grimms' Fairy Tales: Responses, Reactions, Revisions*, ed. Donald Haase (Detroit: Wayne State University Press, 1993): 78–101 (84).

42. Edgar Taylor, *German Popular Stories, Translated from the "Kinder- und Hausmärchen" Collected by M. M. Grimm from Oral Tradition*, vol. 1 (London: C. Baldwyn, 1823), vi–viii. See also the review of *Fairy Tales, or the Lilliputian Cabinet, Containing Twenty-Four Choice Pieces of Fancy and Fiction, Collected by Benjamin Tabart*, in *Quarterly Review* 21 (1819): 91–112 (esp. 97).

43. Letter from Jacob to Lachmann, February 22, 1829, *BGKL* 2:522–23; Ohles, *Germany's Rude Awakening*, 52–53; letter from Jacob and Wilhelm to Elector Wilhelm II, *ATBG*

102–3; letter from Jacob to Meusebach, November 15, 1829, *BMG* 116–19; letter from Jacob to Ludwig Hassenpflug, January 15, 1835, *BLH* 252.

44. Letter from Jacob to Meusebach, November 15, 1829, *BMG* 116; letter from Jacob to Johann Smidt, October 27, 1829, *BBG* 143.

45. Wilhelm Grimm, diary entry of November 4, 1829, Nachlass Grimm o.Nr. B. 1,1, Staatsbibliothek zu Berlin; letter from Wilhelm to Electress Auguste of Hessen-Kassel, November 2, 1829, *BGHF* 404–5; see also letter from Jacob to Lachmann, October 28, 1829, *BGKL* 2:541; and letter from Wilhelm to Suabedissen, January 11, 1829, *BGHF* 266.

46. Letters from Jacob to Lachmann, May 27, 1820, October 18, 1821, *BGKL* 1:138, 314.

47. Letter from Jacob to Meusebach, November 15, 1829, *BMG* 119.

48. Letter from Jacob to Benecke, December 6, 1829, *BBGB* 168–69.

Chapter 11. The Göttingen Era, 1829–1838

1. Letter from Wilhelm to Achim von Arnim, March 4, 1830, *AANS* 3:592–93.

2. Letter from Jacob to Lachmann, February 8, 1830, *BGKL* 2:545–46; letter from Wilhelm to Bang, March 15, 1830, *BGHF* 112–13.

3. Ralf Roth, "Bevölkerungsentwicklung, Konfessionsgliederung und Haushaltsanteile," in *Stadt und Bürgertum im Übergang von der traditionalen zur modernen Gesellschaft*, ed. Lothar Gall (Berlin: Oldenbourg Wissenschaftsverlag, 2015), 17–50 (26); Frances Milton Trollope, *Belgium and Western Germany in 1833; Including Visits to Baden-Baden, Wiesbaden, Cassel, Hanover, the Harz Mountains, etc. etc.*, vol. 2 (London: J. Murray, 1835), 223–25; James Morgan Hart, *German Universities: A Narrative of Personal Experience, Together with Recent Statistical Information, Practical Suggestions, and a Comparison of the German, English, and American Systems of Higher Education* (New York: Putnam, 1874), 1–2, 9, 12, 16.

4. McClelland, *State, Society, and University in Germany*, 38–39.

5. Letters from Jacob to Lachmann, February 8, July 21, 1830, *BGKL* 2:545, 550. Nikolaus Heinrich Julius, *Vorlesungen über die Gefängniß-Kunde, oder über die Verbesserung der Gefängnisse und sittliche Verbesserung der Gefangenen, entlassenen Sträflinge, u.s.w., gehalten im Frühlinge 1827 zu Berlin* (Berlin: In der Stuhrschen Buchhandlung, 1828), 156, 193–213.

6. Letter from Jacob to Lachmann, July 21, 1830, *BGKL* 2:549–51; "Selbstbiographie," *JGKS* 1:14.

7. Letter from Wilhelm to Lachmann, March 8, 1830, *BGKL* 2:854–55; letter from Wilhelm to Jenny von Droste-Hülshoff, July 18, 1830, in Kemminghausen, *Briefwechsel zwischen Jenny von Droste-Hülshoff und Wilhelm Grimm*, 125; Wilhelm Bleek, "Die Brüder Grimm und Friedrich Dahlmann—Freundschaft zwischen drei Gelehrten," in *Die Grimms: Kultur und Politik*, ed. Bernd Heidenreich and Ewald Grothe, 2nd ed. (Frankfurt: Societäts-Verlag, 2008), 259–89 (esp. 259–65).

8. August Heinrich Hoffmann von Fallersleben, *Mein Leben: Aufzeichnungen und Erinnerungen*, 4 vols. (Hannover: Carl Rümpler, 1868), 2:347.

9. Letter from Wilhelm to Bang, March 15, 1830, *BGHF* 114; letter from Jacob to Meusebach, November 26, 1831, *BMG* 143.

10. Letter from Jacob to Lachmann, February 2, 1831, *BGKL* 558–59; see also Jacob's letter to Bang of February 22, 1831, *BGHF* 116; and his letter to Lachmann of November 15, 1830, *BGKL* 2:552–53.

11. Letter from Jacob to Lachmann, February 2, 1831, *BGKL* 558–59.

12. Letter from Jacob to Bang, February 22, 1831, 116–17, and letter from Wilhelm to Suabedissen, October 18, 1832, 271–73, both in *BGHF*.

13. Letter from Wilhelm to Hassenpflug, September 7, 1832, 208–9, and letter from Jacob to Hassenpflug, February 22, 1837, 277, both in *BLH*; Ohles, *Germany's Rude Awakening*, 38–39.

14. Ohles, *Germany's Rude Awakening*, 34–35; Dieter Langewiesche, *Europa zwischen Restauration und Revolution, 1815–1849*, 5th ed. (Munich: Oldenbourg Wissenschaftsverlag, 2007), 63.

15. Letter from Jacob to Dahlmann, March 2, 1833, *BGDG* 1:57; letter from Jacob to Bang, February 22, 1831, *BGHF* 116–17; letter from Wilhelm to Lachmann, May 27, 1832, 2:861, and letter from Jacob to Lachmann, January 6, 1835, 2:646, both in *BGKL*; Karl Goedeke, "Jacob Grimm," in *Göttinger Professoren: Ein Beitrag zur deutschen Cultur und Literärgeschichte in acht Vorträgen*, ed. Friedrich Ehrenfeuchter (Gotha: Friedrich Andreas Perthes, 1872), 167–203 (187–88); letter from Jacob to Friedrich Blume, January 28, 1834, *BBG* 16.

16. Letter from Wilhelm to Suabedissen, October 18, 1832, *BGHF*; letter from Wilhelm to Lachmann, May 27, 1832, *BGKL* 2:861.

17. Letter from Wilhelm to Suabedissen, October 18, 1832, *BGHF* 273; Herman Grimm, "Die Brüder Grimm: Erinnerungen von Herman Grimm," in Jacob and Wilhelm Grimm, *Kinder- und Hausmärchen*, 31st ed. (Berlin: W. Hertz, 1901), iii–xxv (vi).

18. Letter from Wilhelm to Lachmann, October 17, 1833, 2:866, and letter from Jacob to Lachmann, June 13, 1833, 2:614, both in *BGKL*; letter from Jacob to Blume, June 19, 1833, *BBG* 12–15; letter from Jacob to Bang, June 9, 1833, *BGHF* 118–20.

19. Letter from Jacob to Lachmann, July 3, 1836, *BGKL* 2:671; Grimm, *Erinnerungen aus meinem Leben*, 551.

20. Letter from Jacob to Lachmann, December 12, 1834, *BGKL* 2:643; letter from Jacob to Wigand, April 28, 1835, *BGPW* 297; letter from Jacob to Blume, June 28, 1835, *BBG* 16–17; letter from Jacob to Lachmann, October 20, 1835, 2:653–54, and letter from Jacob to Lachmann, mid-February 1836, 2:661–62, both in *BGKL*. Wilhelm had been promoted to the rank of "ordentlicher Professor," roughly equivalent to full professor.

21. Letter from Jacob to Lachmann, June 4, 1820, *BGKL* 1:144; "Selbstbiographie," *JGKS* 1:18; Vick, *Defining Germany*, 24–27; Jacob Grimm, announcement of *Deutsche Mythologie* in *Göttingische Gelehrte Anzeigen*, October 24, 1835, 1665–72 (1666); Kamenetsky, *Brothers Grimm and Their Critics*, 26.

22. Jacob Grimm, *Teutonic Mythology*, trans. James Steven Stallybrass, 4 vols. (London: Bell, 1882–88; New York: Dover, 1966), 1:103.

23. Jacob Grimm, review of *Untersuchungen über die geschichte der Harzburg und den vermeinten götzen Krodo, vom regierungsrath Delius zu Wernigerode*, *JGKS* 5:18–23 (21). See also Ann Schmiesing, "Blackness in the Grimms' Fairy Tales," *Marvels and Tales* 30, no. 2 (2016): 210–33 (213).

24. Jacob Grimm, *Deutsche Mythologie* (Göttingen: In der Dieterichschen Buchhandlung, 1835), 122.

25. Richard Wagner, *Mein Leben*, vol. 1 (Munich: F. Bruckmann, 1911), 310–11. Wagner was influenced by several of the Grimms' other works, and for a couple years he also imitated Jacob's practice of not capitalizing German nouns; see Eckart Kröplin, *Richard Wagner-Chronik* (Stuttgart: J. B. Metzler Verlag, 2016), 150.

26. Merton [Thoms], "Folk-Lore," 862–63.

27. Sophie Salvo, "The Sex of Language: Jacob Grimm on Grammatical Gender," *MLN* 136 (2021): 770–93 (775–78).

28. Salvo, 780–81.

29. Salvo, 780–82, 784–85; Neumann, "Ein 'Heiratsplan' Jacob Grimms?," 155.

30. Winzer, *Permanente Metamorphosen*, 166–68.

31. Heinz Rölleke, "Schneeweisschen und Rosenroth: KHM 161 in der Grimmschen 'Urfassung,'" *Fabula* 27, nos. 3–4 (1986): 265–87.

32. KHM7 2:278; letter from Jacob to Wilhelm, July 12, 1805, *BJWG* 86.

33. KHM7 2:123; Lothar Bluhm and Heinz Rölleke, *"Redensarten des Volks, auf die ich immer horche": Märchen–Sprichwort–Redensart: Zur volkspoetischen Ausgestaltung der "Kinder- und Hausmärchen" durch die Brüder Grimm*, 2nd ed. (Stuttgart: Hirzel, 1997), 23–24, 123.

34. KHM2 1:9; KHM3 1:2. The wording of the opening line is slightly different in later editions.

35. Letters from Ernst August to George III, October 2, 1788, January 11, 1791, in *The Later Correspondence of George III*, vol. 1, ed. A. Aspinall (Cambridge: Cambridge University Press, 1966), 395, 514; John van der Kiste, *George III's Children* (Stroud: Sutton, 2004), 35–36.

36. Percy Fitzgerald, *The Royal Dukes and Princesses of the Family of George III*, 2 vols. (London: Tinsley, 1882), 2:247, 251–52; van der Kiste, *George III's Children*, 98, 114.

37. Anthony Bird, *The Damnable Duke of Cumberland: A Character Study and Vindication of Ernest Augustus Duke of Cumberland and King of Hanover* (London: Barrie and Rockliff, 1966), 258–59.

38. T. Witten Davies, *Heinrich Ewald: Orientalist and Theologian, 1803–1903* (London: T. Fisher Unwin, 1903), 16–17; Guy Waldo Dunnington, *Carl Friedrich Gauss, Titan of Science: A Study of His Life and Work* (New York: Exposition Press, 1955), 195–96; Bird, *Damnable Duke of Cumberland*, 221.

39. Jonathan F. Wagner, "Gervinus und der Protest der Göttinger Sieben: Acht Briefe aus den Jahren 1837–1848," *Archiv für Kulturgeschichte* 58 (1976): 178–203 (179–80).

40. Anton Springer, *Friedrich Christoph Dahlmann*, 2 vols. (Leipzig: S. Hirzel, 1870–72), 1:427–29. Although Dahlmann had no reason to suspect the communication was wrong, Anthony Bird notes that Ernst August had in fact conveyed his concerns in a letter to William IV and subsequently avoided any action that might be seen as tacit approval of the constitution; *Damnable Duke of Cumberland*, 261. However, a letter Ernst August sent to his brother around the time the constitution was being drafted appears to suggest his overall consent; *Die Göttinger Sieben: Eine Ausstellung*

der Georg-August-Universität Göttingen (Göttingen: Georg-August-Universität Göttingen, 1987), 32–34.

41. Wagner, "Gervinus und der Protest der Göttinger Sieben," 188, 193–94; Grimm, *Erinnerungen aus meinem Leben*, 507–8.

42. "Über meine Entlassung," JGKS 1:52.

43. Schultz, introduction to *BABG* 10; letters from Dahlmann to Jacob, February 17, March 3, 1838, 1:85, 112, and letters from Jacob to Dahlmann, February 24, March 6, May 7, 1838, 1:98, 123, 169, all in *BGDG*.

44. Wagner, "Gervinus und der Protest der Göttinger Sieben," 195–96; "Über meine Entlassung," JGKS 1:38–39; Schoof, introduction to *BBGS* 7.

45. Letter from Wilhelm to A. v. Arnswaldt (née Haxthausen), December 24, 1837, *FWJG* 149–50; letters from Wilhelm to Blume, January 1, 1838, *BBG* 189; letter from Wilhelm to Wigand, January 11, June 3, 1838, *BGPW* 300; letter from Wilhelm to Julius Müller, December 30, 1837, *BGHF* 290–91.

46. Letter from Wilhelm to Lachmann, January 18, 1838, *BGKL* 2:886–87; letter from Dahlmann to Jacob, February 14, 1838, 1:279, and letter from Dahlmann to Wilhelm, February 26, 1838, 1:99–100, both in *BGDG*. The king's response to Humboldt is quoted in Dunnington, *Carl Friedrich Gauss*, 200. Wilhelm also recounted this anecdote in a letter to Hugo of April 23, 1842; see Wilhelm Schoof, ed., *Unbekannte Briefe der Brüder Grimm* (Bonn: Athenäum, 1960), 322.

47. Davies, *Heinrich Ewald*, 19; Dunnington, *Carl Friedrich Gauss*, 199.

48. Grimm, *Erinnerungen aus meinem Leben*, 505–7; Friedrich Wilhelm Rettberg, *Die Säcular-Feier der Georgia Augusta im September 1837* (Göttingen: In Commission bei Vandenhoeck und Ruprecht, 1838); Sonja Schreiner, *100 Jahre Georgia Augusta Gottingensis—(K)ein Grund zum Feiern: Prosa und Dichtung über die Säkularfeier 1837* (Göttingen: Universitätsverlag Göttingen, 2010); "Zur Beschreibung der Göttinger Säcularfeier," JGKS 8:424–28 (425).

49. Qtd. in Roger Fulford, *Royal Dukes: The Fathers and Uncles of Queen Victoria*, rev. ed. (London: Collins, 1973), 247; see also Fitzgerald, *Royal Dukes and Princesses of the Family of George III*, 2:282.

50. John Mitchell Kemble, "The Hanoverian Coup d'Etat," *British and Foreign Review; or, European Quarterly Journal* 6 (1838): 269–338 (esp. 276–77, 335). Kemble's essay also includes English translations of Ernst August's edicts and the Göttingen Seven's protest letter.

51. Letter from Jacob to Otfried Müller, March 13, 1838, *BGDG* 131–32.

52. Bird, *Damnable Duke of Cumberland*, 272–73; van der Kiste, *George III's Children*, 190; Miriam Saage-Maaß, *Die Göttinger Sieben—demokratische Vorkämpfer oder nationale Helden? Zum Verhältnis von Geschichtsschreibung und Erinnerungskultur in der Rezeption des Hannoverschen Verfassungskonfliktes* (Göttingen: V&R Unipress, 2007), 150–55; "Die Göttinger Sieben," *Statues: Hither and Thither*, René and Peter van der Krogt, https://statues.vanderkrogt.net/object.php?webpage=ST&record=dens139. A group of sculptures in Berlin by Sabina Grzimek was also inspired by the Göttingen Seven protests.

53. Heinrich Detering, "Günter Grass und *Grimms Wörter*: Zum Abschluss der Neubearbei-
    tung des *Deutschen Wörterbuchs*," in *Historische Lexikographie des Deutschen: Perspektiven
    eines Forschungsfeldes im digitalen Zeitalter*, ed. Gerhard Diehl and Volker Harm (Berlin:
    De Gruyter, 2022), 11–27 (26–27).

54. Heidi Niemann, "Verstehen Sie dieses Denkmal? Göttingen enthüllt umstrit-
    tenes Denkmal," *Hannoversche Allgemeine*, November 19, 2015, https://www.haz.de/
    Nachrichten/Der-Norden/Uebersicht/Goettingen-enthuellt-umstrittenes-Denkmal;
    Stefan Christmann, "A Controversial Monument," *The Passenger*, November 21, 2015,
    https://the-passenger.de/2015/11/21/a-controversial-monument/.

55. KHM4 2:164.

56. Achim Hölter, *Die Invaliden: Die vergessene Geschichte der Kriegskrüppel in der eu-
    ropäischen Literatur bis zum 19. Jahrhundert* (Stuttgart: Metzler, 1995), 241–43; Zipes,
    Brothers Grimm, 65–67. Without reference to Wilhelm's alteration of "The Blue Light,"
    Anthony Bird paints English sympathy for the Grimms as the misguided product of
    the Victorian fascination with their fairy tales, which led to "the pathetic picture of
    two gentle, silver-haired, apple-cheeked old scholars [. . .] turned out to starve like
    orphans of the storm by the wicked old King of Hanover" (*Damnable Duke of Cum-
    berland*, 272).

Chapter 12. Aftermath of the Göttingen Seven Protest, 1838–1841

1. Grimm, *Erinnerungen aus meinem Leben*, 508–9.

2. Bettina von Arnim, *Ilius Pamphilius und die Ambrosia*, 2 vols., 2nd ed. (Leipzig: Friedrich Volckmar, 1848), 1:282.

3. Letter from Jacob to Lachmann, August 24, 1838, *BGKL* 2:685; letter from Jacob to
   Dahlmann, October 27, 1838, *BGDG* 1:261; letter from Jacob to Blume, November 4,
   1838, *BBG* 23–24.

4. Jacob and Wilhelm Grimm, announcement of the *German Dictionary* in the *Leipziger
   Allgemeine Zeitung*, August 29, 1838, *JGKS* 8:542–43; letters from Jacob to Lachmann,
   March 12, August 24, 1838, 2:680, 688–90, and letter from Lachmann to Jacob, March 18,
   1838, 2:683, both in *BGKL*; letter from Gervinus to Jacob, January 30, 1839, *BGDG* 2:11.

5. Lynda Mugglestone, *Dictionaries: A Very Short Introduction* (Oxford: Oxford University Press, 2011), 20–38.

6. Letter from Jacob to Dorothee Dahlmann, [183?], *BGHF* 22; Grimm, *Teutonic Mythology*, trans. Stallybrass, 1:v.

7. Letter from Wilhelm to Dahlmann, August 31, 1839, *BGDG* 1:339; letter from Jacob
   to Hans Ferdinand Massmann, September 15, 1839, *BBG* 104; letter from Jacob to
   Kemble, December 1, 1838, in *John Mitchell Kemble and Jakob Grimm: A Correspondence, 1832–1852*, ed. and trans. Raymond A. Wiley (Leiden: E. J. Brill, 1971), 175; letter
   from Jacob to Dahlmann, October 13, 1839, *BGDG* 1:349; preface to *Deutsches Wörterbuch*, *JGKS* 8:304; Kelly Kistner, "A Dictionary without Definitions: Romanticist Science in the Production and Presentation of the Grimm Brothers' German Dictionary,
   1838–1863," *Science in Context* 27, no. 4 (2014): 683–707 (689–90).

8. Letter from Wilhelm to Dahlmann, March 16, 1839, *BGDG* 1:315; Samuel Johnson, *A Dictionary of the English Language*, 2 vols. (London: W. Strahan, 1755), 1:n.p. and 2:n.p.; letter from Jacob to Kemble, December 1, 1838, in Wiley, *John Mitchell Kemble*, 169; letter from Jacob to Blume, November 4, 1838, 25, and letter from Wilhelm to Blume, February 20, 1839, 194, both in *BBG*.

9. Letter from Jacob to Dahlmann, August 19, 1838, *BGDG* 1:220; letter from Bettina von Arnim to Savigny, November 4, 1839, *BABG* 242.

10. Letter from Wilhelm to Gervinus, July 29, 1840, *BGDG* 2:33; letter from Jacob to Lachmann, May 13, 1840, *BGKL* 2:710–11.

11. Bottigheimer, "Publishing History of Grimms' Tales," 85–89.

12. "An die Frau Bettina von Arnim," *WGKS* 1:318–19.

13. Letter from Jacob to Dahlmann, August 19, 1838, *BGDG* 1:220; see also letter from Jacob to Lachmann, June 27, 1839, *BGKL* 2:705.

14. Letter from Wilhelm to Suabedissen, October 2, 1824, *BGHF* 233; letter from Wilhelm to Lachmann, May 27, 1832, *BGKL* 2:863; letter from Jacob to Dahlmann, October 13, 1839, *BGDG* 1:349.

15. Letter from Achim von Arnim to Wilhelm, April 22, 1822, *AANS* 3:508.

16. Letter from Bettina von Arnim to Wilhelm, February/March 1839, *BABG* 68.

17. Letter from Wilhelm and Jacob to Bettina von Arnim, November 24, 1839, *BABG* 122–23.

18. Letters from Bettina von Arnim to Wilhelm, July 1, 18, 20, November 11, 1839, 109, 107, 116, and letter from Savigny to Bettina von Arnim, December 2, 1839, 273, all in *BABG*.

19. Letter from Prussian crown prince Friedrich Wilhelm to Bettina von Arnim, April 20, 1840, *BABG* 204. To convey the pun here, I have translated "Grimm" as "grim" instead of as "fierce" or "wrathful." See also Friedrich Wilhelm's letter of December 2, 1840, to Grand Duke Georg of Mecklenburg-Strelitz, *BABG* 212–13.

20. Letter from Alexander von Humboldt to August Varnhagen von Ense, October 27, 1840, *BABG* 185.

21. August Varnhagen von Ense, diary entry of October 28, 1840, *BABG* 186.

22. Wilhelm Grimm, diary entries of February 4, 15, 19, March 17; Nachlass Grimm 151.1, Staatsbibliothek zu Berlin.

Chapter 13. Berlin Beginnings, 1841–1852

1. *A Hand-Book for Travellers on the Continent: Being a Guide through Holland, Belgium, Prussia, and Northern Germany, and along the Rhine, from Holland through Switzerland* (London: John Murray and Son, 1840), 326.

2. Samuel Laing, *Notes of a Traveller, on the Social and Political State of France, Prussia, Switzerland, Italy, and Other Parts of Europe, during the Present Century*, 2nd London ed. (Philadelphia: Cary and Hart, 1846), 240. See also Friedrich Sass, *Berlin in seiner neuesten Zeit und Entwicklung* (Leipzig: Julius Koffka, 1846), 247; and *Hand-Book for Travellers on the Continent*, 325.

3. Letter from Jacob to Dahlmann, June 11, 1841, *BGDG* 1:458.

4. Wilhelm Grimm, diary entry for August 31, 1842, Nachlass Grimm 151.1, Staatsbibliothek zu Berlin.

5. Letter from Jacob to Dahlmann, June 11, 1841, *BGDG* 1:453.

6. Wilhelm Schoof, *Die Brüder Grimm in Berlin* (Berlin: Haude & Spenersche Verlagsbuchhandlung, 1964), 37.

7. Letter from Wilhelm to Dahlmann, October 8, 1842, *BGDG* 1:470; Schoof, *Die Brüder Grimm in Berlin*, 32, 91.

8. Hoffmann, *Mein Leben*, 4:118–22.

9. Schoof, *Die Brüder Grimm in Berlin*, 45–46.

10. Schoof, 49–52.

11. Alice Arnold-Becker, *Schloss Hohenschwangau: Die Wandbilder eines Gebirgspalasts* (Stuttgart, 2011), 19. Hohenschwangau Castle lies just down the mountain from the more famous Neuschwanstein Castle, which was begun under Maximilian's son King Ludwig II but not finished during Ludwig's lifetime.

12. Wilhelm Hansen, "Die Brüder Grimm in Berlin," in Denecke and Greverus, *Brüder Grimm Gedenken 1963*, 227–307 (290–91).

13. "Italienische und Scandinavische Eindrücke," JGKS 1:57–82.

14. Letter from Jacob to Wilhelm and Dortchen, September 18, 1841, JGKS 8:464; letter from Jacob to Hoffmann, November 8, 1841, in Hoffmann, *Mein Leben*, 2:240.

15. Schoof, *Die Brüder Grimm in Berlin*, 54.

16. Letter from Jacob to Dahlmann, April 14, 1847, *BGDG* 1:519.

17. Schoof, *Die Brüder Grimm in Berlin*, 55.

18. Vick, *Defining Germany*, 80.

19. G. G. Gervinus, *G. G. Gervinus Leben: Von ihm selbst* (Leipzig: Verlag von Wilhelm Engelmann, 1893), 257.

20. Franz Wigard, *Stenographischer Bericht über die Verhandlungen der deutschen constituirenden Nationalversammlung zu Frankfurt am Main*, vol. 1 (Frankfurt: Johann David Sauerländer, 1848), 737, and vol. 2 (Leipzig: Breitkopf und Härtel und B.G. Teubner, 1848), 1063; Steffen Seybold, "Freiheit statt Knechtschaft: Jacob Grimms Antrag zur Paulskirchenverfassung," *Der Staat* 51, no. 2 (2012): 215–31 (216–17, 222–23, 226); Ulrich Hussong, *Jacob Grimm und der Wiener Kongreß: Mit einem Anhang größtenteils unveröffentlicher Dokumente* (Kassel: Brüder Grimm-Gesellschaft, 2002), 97–100, 148–49.

21. W. Carr, *Schleswig-Holstein, 1815–1848: A Study in National Conflict* (Manchester: Manchester University Press, 1963), 39–60, 63–73; Norberg, *Brothers Grimm and the Making of German Nationalism*, 31–37.

22. Qtd. in Christopher Clark, *Iron Kingdom: The Rise and Downfall of Prussia, 1600–1947* (Cambridge, MA: Harvard University Press, 2006), 494.

23. Letter from Wilhelm to Amalie Hassenpflug, March 4, 1849, *BLH* 299.

24. "Ein Lebensabriss," JGKS 8:459–61 (461).

25. Letter from Wilhelm to Ludwig, June 26, 1852, and letter from Jacob to August Stöber, October 20, 1852, both in Gerstner, *Die Brüder Grimm*, 277.

Chapter 14. Final Years in Berlin, 1852–1863

1. Jacob and Wilhelm Grimm, *Deutsches Wörterbuch*, vol. 1 (Leipzig: S. Hirzel, 1854), 1, 1824.

2. Grimm and Grimm, 1; letter from S. Hirzel to Jacob, August 14, 1852, in "Zur Geschichte des deutschen Wörterbuches: Mitteilungen aus dem Briefwechsel zwischen den Brüdern Grimm und Salomon Hirzel," ed. M. Lexer, *Anzeiger für deutsches Alterthum und deutsche Litteratur* 36 (1890): 220–64 (225).

3. Ulrike Haß-Zumkehr, *"Deutsche Wörterbücher": Brennpunkt von Sprach- und Kulturgeschichte* (Berlin: Walter de Gruyter, 2001), 125; Mellor, *Scholarly Purpose and National Purpose in Jacob Grimm's Work on the "Deutsches Wörterbuch,"* 246–48.

4. Haß-Zumkehr, *"Deutsche Wörterbücher,"* 121–22.

5. Preface to *Deutsches Wörterbuch*, JGKS 8:315.

6. "Über das Pedantische," JGKS 1:327–73 (328).

7. The Grimms used similar discretion regarding dialects. In general, they included a dialect only if they believed it to be an offshoot or enrichment of High German, for which reason Low German dialects were not covered. Their approach meant that some dialects prevalent in regions within the German Confederation were not included while others outside the Confederation (such as in Switzerland) were. Regarding their approach to dialects and foreign words, see Mellor, *Scholarly Purpose and National Purpose in Jacob Grimm's Work on the "Deutsches Wörterbuch,"* 13–21, 120–21, 129, 154.

8. Review of the *German Dictionary* in *Die Grenzboten: Zeitschrift für Politik und Literatur*, March 26, 1852, reproduced in *Das Grimmsche "Deutsche Wörterbuch" in der öffentlichen Diskussion, 1838–1863*, ed. Alan Kirkness (Stuttgart: S. Hirzel Verlag, 2021), 124–35; see also Alan Kirkness, ed., *Geschichte des deutschen Wörterbuchs, 1838–1863* (Stuttgart: S. Hirzel Verlag, 1980), 141–42.

9. Reviews of the *German Dictionary* in *National-Zeitung* (June 12, 1852), *Westminster Review* (January 1, 1855), and *Der österreichische Schulbote* (July 31, 1852), reproduced in Kirkness, *Das Grimmsche "Deutsche Wörterbuch" in der öffentlichen Diskussion,* 169–73, 363–64, 194–200; "An Jakob und Wilhelm mit 'n kleenen grimm" [*sic*], *Kladderadatsch*, June 13, 1852, and "deutsches woerterbuch als supplement zu dem deutschen woerterbuch der gebrueder jacob und wilhelm grimm, herausgegeben von einem verein deutscher gelehrter des kladderadatsch" [*sic*], *Kladderadatsch*, October 24, 1852, reproduced in Kirkness, *Das Grimmsche "Deutsche Wörterbuch" in der öffentlichen Diskussion,* 110–11; Haß-Zumkehr, *"Deutsche Wörterbücher,"* 144–45; Fowkes, "Linguistic Modernity of Jakob Grimm," 57; Kistner, "Dictionary without Definitions," 695.

10. Letter from Jacob to Karl Weigand, November 1859, *BGHF* 366.

11. Letter from Jacob to Luise Dahlmann, March 18, 1854, *BGDG* 1:529.

12. Letter from Jacob to Weigand, November 1859, 366, letter from Jacob to August Friedrich Christian Vilmar, February 28, 1859, 314, and letter from Jacob to Weigand, December 10, 1858, 352, all in *BGHF*.

13. Letter from Jacob to Dahlmann, April 14, 1858, *BGDG* 1:538.

14. Wilhelm Hansen, "Die Brüder Grimm in Berlin," 227–307 (243–56), and Ludwig Denecke, "Blätter und Blüten aus Kassel," 97–113 (97), both in Denecke and Greverus,

Brüder Grimm Gedenken 1963; Adolf Stoll, introduction to Grimm, *Erinnerungen aus meinem Leben*, 10. The Grimms' desks and many of the objects that adorned them are today in the Germanisches Nationalmuseum in Nuremberg.

15. Letter from Jacob to Luise Dahlmann, December 28, 1855, *BGDG* 1:534.

16. Letter from Jacob to Wigand, September 1858, *BGPW* 317; Georg Waitz, "Zum Gedächtnis von Jacob Grimm," *Abhandlungen der Königlichen Gesellschaft der Wissenschaften zu Göttingen* 11 (1864), 3–33 (23–24).

17. KHM7 2:149; letter from Wilhelm to Anna von Arnswaldt (née Haxthausen), March 2, 1859, *BJWG* 189–90.

18. While presenting 155 numbered tales, the first edition occasionally grouped several stories within a single entry. For example, tale 85 in volume 1 of the first edition comprises four different tale fragments. Similarly, the number of tales in the seventh edition is often listed as 211 instead of 210, since two tales there are numbered 151. A total of around 240 different tales, collected from some forty contributors and thirty written sources, appeared in the seven large and ten small editions published during the Grimms' lifetimes; Rölleke, "New Results of Research," 101; Rölleke, *Die Märchen der Brüder Grimm*, 37.

19. Vinzenz Hoppe and Kaspar Renner, "XY (ungelöst)," in *Die Grimmwelt: Von Ärschlein bis Zettel*, issued by the City of Kassel in collaboration with Annemarie Hürlimann and Nicola Lepp (Munich: Sieveking Verlag, 2015), 238–45.

20. KHM7 3:379. See also Schmiesing, "Blackness in the Grimms' Fairy Tales," 213.

21. Schoof, *Die Brüder Grimm in Berlin*, 101; "Rede auf Wilhelm Grimm," JGKS 1:163–79.

22. Jacob Grimm, preface to vol. 2 of *Deutsches Wörterbuch*, JGKS 8:381–82.

23. Berthold Auerbach, *Deutsche Abende* (Stuttgart: J. G. Cotta'schen Buchhandlung, 1867), 198–99.

24. "Rede über das Alter," JGKS 1:188–210 (198); Schmiesing, *Disability, Deformity, and Disease in the Grimms' Fairy Tales*, 30–31.

25. Kistner, "Dictionary without Definitions," 684; letter from Jacob to S. Hirzel, February 18, 1863, in "Zur Geschichte des deutschen Wörterbuches," 259–60.

26. Letter from Jacob to Kemble, December 1, 1838, Wiley, *John Mitchell Kemble*, 169.

27. Schoof, *Die Brüder Grimm in Berlin*, 107–9.

Conclusion

1. Letter from Wilhelm to Karl Weigand, November 6, 1859, *BGHF* 364.

2. Bottigheimer, "Publishing History of Grimms' Tales," 88.

3. Bottigheimer, 86–92.

4. For other examples, see Donald Haase, "'We Are What We Are Supposed to Be': The Brothers Grimm as Fictional Representations," *Narrative Culture* 1, no. 2 (2014): 191–215.

5. Wisława Szymborska, "Possibilities," in *Poems: New and Collected, 1957–1997*, trans. Clare Cavanagh (New York: Harcourt Brace & Company, 1998), 214. Eminent fairy-tale scholar Jack Zipes refers to the anecdote about Albert Einstein both in his book *Breaking the Magic Spell: Radical Theories of Folk and Fairy Tales* (Austin: University

of Texas Press, 1979), where the conversation occurs between Einstein and an uniden-
tified woman concerned about her son; and more recently in *Buried Treasures: The
Power of Political Fairy Tales* (Princeton, NJ: Princeton University Press, 2023), where
Zipes presents the anecdote as a "'true' tall tale" in which his grandmother, walking
with Zipes when he was around six years old, confronts Einstein (2). See also Stephen
Winick, "Einstein's Folklore," *Folklife Today* (Library of Congress blog), December 18,
2013, https://blogs.loc.gov/folklife/2013/12/einsteins-folklore/.

6. Bruno Bettelheim, *The Uses of Enchantment: The Meaning and Importance of Fairy Tales*
(New York: Knopf, 1977), 160–61, 204; Alan Dundes, "The Psychoanalytic Study of
the Grimms' Tales with Special Reference to 'The Maiden without Hands' (AT 706),"
Germanic Review 42 (1987): 50–65; see also Maria Tatar, *Off with Their Heads! Fairy
Tales and the Culture of Childhood* (Princeton, NJ: Princeton University Press, 1992),
xvii–xxvi.

7. Dundes, "Psychoanalytic Study of the Grimms' Tales," 55.

8. Max Höfler, *Deutsches Krankheitsnamen-Buch* (Munich: Piloty and Loehle, 1899),
532; Marianne Rumpf, "Spinnerinnen und Spinnen: Märchendeutungen aus kul-
turhistorischer Sicht," in *Die Frau im Märchen*, ed. Sigrid Früh and Rainer Wehse
(Kassel: Röth, 1985), 59–72 (70); Alan Dundes, *The Meaning of Folklore: The Analyti-
cal Essays of Alan Dundes*, ed. Simon J. Bonner (Logan: Utah State University Press,
2007), 294; Schmiesing, *Disability, Deformity, and Disease in the Grimms' Fairy Tales*,
125. See also Andrea Meyertholen, "Rumpelstiltskin's (Queer) Secret: Nonbinary
Bodies Buried between the Lines of the Brothers Grimm," *Marvels and Tales* 35, no.
1 (2021): 36–61 (51).

9. See, for example, Vanessa Joosen and Gillian Lathey, eds., *Grimms' Tales around the
Globe: The Dynamics of Their International Reception* (Detroit: Wayne State University Press, 2014); Donald Haase, ed., *Fairy Tales and Feminism: New Approaches* (Detroit: Wayne State University Press, 2004); Kay Turner and Pauline Greenhill, eds.,
Transgressive Tales: Queering the Grimms (Detroit: Wayne State University Press, 2012);
Claudia Brinker-von der Heyde, Holger Ehrhardt, Hans-Heino Ewers, and Anneka-
trin Inder, eds., *Märchen, Mythen und Moderne: 200 Jahre "Kinder- und Hausmärchen"
der Brüder Grimm*, 2 vols. (Frankfurt: Peter Lang, 2015); Bottigheimer, *Grimms' Bad
Girls and Bold Boys*; Tatar, *Hard Facts of the Grimms' Fairy Tales*; Schmiesing, *Disability,
Deformity, and Disease in the Grimms' Fairy Tales*.

10. See https://www.unesco.org/xtrans/bsstatexp.aspx?crit1L=5&nTyp=min&topN=50.

11. Qtd. in Haß-Zumkehr, *"Deutsche Wörterbücher,"* 119.

12. Kistner, "Dictionary without Definitions," 684.

13. Kirkness, *Geschichte des deutschen Wörterbuchs*, 2–3.

14. Manuela Böhm, "'Ein Pyrrhussieg der Germanistik': Walter Boehlichs Kritik an der
Grimmschen Philologie," in *Walter Boehlich: Kritiker*, ed. Helmut Peitsch and Helen
Thein-Peitsch (Berlin: Akademie Verlag, 2011), 127–28.

15. Böhm, "'Ein Pyrrhussieg der Germanistik,'" 115–32; Hans Neumann and Theodor
Kochs, "Religion—ja, Manöver—nicht: Das Deutsche Wörterbuch und seine Kriti-
kaster," *Der Monat* 14, no. 158 (1961): 54–61 (55).

16. Detering, "Günter Grass und *Grimms Wörter*," 18, 25.

17. Susanne Völker, "Vom Text zum Raum: Das *Deutsche Wörterbuch* in der Grimmwelt Kassel," in *Historische Lexikographie des Deutschen*, ed. Gerhard Diehl and Volker Harm (Berlin: De Gruyter, 2022), 29–35. Not all scholars have found Grimmwelt's alphabetical organizing principle successful; see, for example, Kraut, *Die Arbeitsweise der Brüder Grimm*, 37n125.

18. Kistner, "Dictionary without Definitions," 692.

19. Kistner, 686.

20. See, for example, Jakob Norberg's recent book *The Brothers Grimm and the Making of German Nationalism*. With respect to the national cultural impacts and premises of the Grimms' scholarship on legends, see Terry Gunnell, ed., *Grimm Ripples: The Legacy of the Grimms'* Deutsche Sagen *on Northern Europe* (Leiden: Brill, 2022).

21. Böhm, "'Ein Pyrrhussieg der Germanistik,'" 129; Wyss, *Die wilde Philologie*, 176.

22. Kraut, *Die Arbeitsweise der Brüder Grimm*, 251.

23. "Über die Alterthümer des deutschen Rechts," JGKS 8:545–51 (547, 551).

Note on Orthography and Translations

1. "Nekrolog: Dr. Ludwig Völkel," JGKS 6:405–9 (405).

2. Letter from Jacob to Dorothee Dahlmann, [183?], *BGHF* 22.

Acknowledgments

Many individuals and institutions have helped me with this book. I am grateful to the librarians and curators at archives and museums in Berlin, Hanau, Kassel, Steinau, and elsewhere who kindly assisted me with accessing materials needed for my research. Ralf Breslau, Birgit Bucher, and their colleagues at the Staatsbibliothek zu Berlin welcomed me during research trips to the Grimm Archives. At the Germanisches Nationalmuseum in Nuremberg, Karin Rhein and Annika Dix generously allowed me to view physical objects from the Grimms' workspaces. My ability to efficiently decipher handwritten German documents across several centuries was greatly aided by a paleography course expertly taught by Dorothea McEwan and Claudia Wedepohl at the Institute of English Studies, School of Advanced Study, University of London. During times when the Covid-19 pandemic made travel to Germany impossible, the rich holdings of the Newberry Library and the University of Chicago Library enabled me to make continued research progress.

For assistance with illustrations, I am grateful to Thomas Aufleger at the Staatliche Schlösser und Gärten Hessen; Claudia Dorn of the city government of Steinau an der Strasse; Kai Jakob at Städtische Museen Hanau; Kelly Sandefer of Beehive Mapping; Bianca Slowik at the Germanisches Nationalmuseum; the Newberry Library; Princeton University Library Special Collections; the University of Illinois Library Digitization Services and Special Collections; and the Julian Edison Department of Special Collections, Washington University

Libraries. As indicated in endnotes, some passages are adapted from my 2014 book *Disability, Deformity, and Disease in the Grimms' Fairy Tales*. I thank Wayne State University Press for permission to adapt this content.

Within the fields of eighteenth- and nineteenth-century studies and fairy-tale studies, I wish to express deep gratitude to John A. McCarthy, who passed away before the publication of this book, and Donald Haase. For their support throughout this project, I also thank University of Colorado colleagues Helmut Müller-Sievers, Katherine Eggert, Michele Moses, Russ Moore, Mark Kavanaugh, Bronson Hilliard, and Janet Braccio as well as the Special Collections Department and the Interlibrary Loan Department. My gratitude extends to my students, whose lively interest in the Brothers Grimm has invigorated my research over many years.

This book could not have reached fruition without Yale University Press editor Jennifer Banks's enthusiasm and guidance. Eva Skewes and Ann-Marie Imbornoni of Yale University Press provided timely and expert assistance. I am also immensely grateful to Nicholas Taylor and my anonymous readers, whose careful reading and helpful suggestions have made this a better book.

Finally, I express thanks to my family. Stephanie, Elizabeth, and Axel were stalwart companions and occasional on-the-spot research assistants during several research trips to Germany and Chicago, and they offered unwavering support through the years I worked on this book. I express further gratitude to my parents and to Heinke and Dieter Reitzig for their encouragement. To my brother Dan and sister Laura: this biography of two siblings is dedicated to you.

Index

Main entries give titles of works in English translation. For German titles of the Grimms' works, see subentries under Brothers Grimm, works of; Children's and Household Tales, individual tales; German Legends; Grimm, Jacob, works of; Grimm, Wilhelm, works of.

Addresses to the German Nation (Fichte), 59

Adelung, Johann Christoph: *Grammatical and Critical Dictionary of the High German Language,* 211

Adolphus, Duke of Cambridge, 184, 197–98

Afanasyev, Aleksandr, 229

Aix-la-Chapelle, Congress of, 110

Albert of Saxe-Coburg and Gotha (Prince Albert), 205, 235

Albrecht, Wilhelm Eduard, 199, 200, 222, 232

Alexander I, Czar of Russia, 109

"All Fur," 73, 147, 172

Altdänische Heldenlieder, Balladen und Märchen. See *Old Danish Heroic Songs, Ballads, and Tales*

Altdeutsche Wälder. See *Old German Forests*

"Alte Marie" (Old Marie), xv, 80

Andersen, Hans Christian, 229–30, 258

anti-Semitism, 15, 61, 69, 138, 259

Apuleius (Lucius Apuleius Madaurensis): *Metamorphoses* (*The Golden Ass*), 89

Arnim, Achim von, 34–36, 54, 65, 76, 91, 105, 120, 174; and anti-Semitism, 69; children of, 86; on *Children's and Household Tales,* 82, 85, 93–95, 112, 145, 149; collaborations with Brentano, 34–36, 48, 66–68, 270; death of, 185, 217, 267, 272; Grimms' sharing of folk songs with, 54; *Halle and Jerusalem,* 16; in Heidelberg, 51; illness of, 134; on Jacob and Wilhelm, xvi, 49–50; *Journal for Hermits,* 52, 114; marriage to Bettina Brentano, 35, 217; on natural poetry, 83–84; portrait of, 49; in support of Ludwig Grimm,